Military Flight Aptitude Tests

FOR DUMMIES®

A Wiley Brand

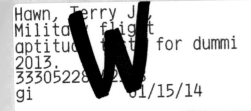

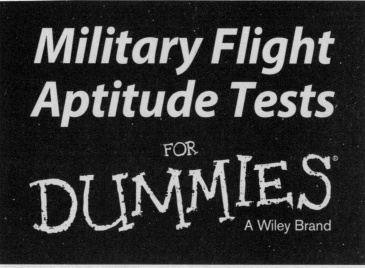

Military Flight Aptitude Tests

FOR DUMMIES®

A Wiley Brand

by Terry J. Hawn and Peter Economy

Military Flight Aptitude Tests For Dummies®

Published by
John Wiley & Sons, Inc.
111 River St.
Hoboken, NJ 07030-5774
www.wiley.com

Copyright © 2013 by John Wiley & Sons, Inc., Hoboken, New Jersey

Published simultaneously in Canada

For general information on our other products and services, please contact our Customer Care Department within the U.S. at 877-762-2974, outside the U.S. at 317-572-3993, or fax 317-572-4002.

For technical support, please visit www.wiley.com/techsupport.

Wiley publishes in a variety of print and electronic formats and by print-on-demand. Some material included with standard print versions of this book may not be included in e-books or in print-on-demand. If this book refers to media such as a CD or DVD that is not included in the version you purchased, you may download this material at http://booksupport.wiley.com. For more information about Wiley products, visit www.wiley.com.

Library of Congress Control Number: 2012939590

ISBN 978-0-470-60032-0 (pbk); ISBN 978-1-118-25893-4 (ebk); ISBN 978-1-118-22062-7 (ebk); ISBN 978-1-118-23421-1 (ebk)

Manufactured in the United States of America

10 9 8 7 6 5 4 3 2 1

About the Authors

Terry Hawn has been in love with flying since childhood, when his dad took him on a flight. After riding his bicycle down to the local airport at age 12, Terry started to work part-time washing dishes to pay for flight lessons. He missed his first day of driver's education in order to solo an airplane on his 16th birthday and received his private pilot's license by the time he was 17. Terry enlisted in the Army, went to college, and graduated from the U.S. Army's Rotary Wing flight training program in 1985. He has flown on active duty, with the National Guard, and with the Army Reserves as an assault, medivac, and attack pilot in addition to serving as an aviation commander. Today, Terry is an Army Senior Aviator qualified in the AH-64 Apache helicopter and holds a civilian flight instructor license for both airplanes and helicopters. During the summer months, he spends his time exploring the lakes of the northern Ontario wilderness in his 108-3 Stinson floatplane.

Peter Economy is a best-selling author with numerous *For Dummies* titles under his belt. Peter is coauthor of *Writing Fiction For Dummies, Home-Based Business For Dummies, Consulting For Dummies,* and *The Management Bible* (all from Wiley), as well as *Creating an Orange Utopia: Eliza Lovell Tibbets and the Birth of California's Citrus Industry* (Swedenborg Foundation Publishers) and many more books. Peter also serves as Associate Editor of *Leader to Leader,* the Apex Award-winning journal of the Leader to Leader Institute, and he's a lecturer at San Diego State University, most recently teaching the course Creativity and Innovation. Peter has had a lifelong fascination with military aviation — particularly reconnaissance aircraft such as the U-2 and SR-71, for which his father, Colonel Peter Economy, served as Air Force project manager for many years. Check out Peter's website at www.petereconomy.com.

Dedication

To all young Americans who have yearned to slip the surly bonds of earth while serving their country and putting their lives on the line. We salute you. To those who paid the ultimate sacrifice, we honor you.

Authors' Acknowledgments

We'd like to thank the many people who took time to provide their advice and input to us as we created the book you're now reading. Specifically, we'd like to thank the folks at Wiley who cared enough to make this book the best it could be, including Erin Calligan Mooney, Tim Gallan, Elizabeth Rea, and Megan Knoll.

Terry would like to thank his coauthor and mentor Peter Economy for his words of encouragement, guidance, and his steadfast commitment to excellence. Thanks, Peter.

Peter would like to thank his coauthor Terry Hawn for his hard work and dedication to this project and for giving him a unique, behind-the-scenes tour of the world of military aviation. He would also like to thank his wife, Jan, and kids, Peter, Skylar, and Jackson, for their ongoing love and support.

Publisher's Acknowledgments

We're proud of this book; please send us your comments at http://dummies.custhelp.com. For other comments, please contact our Customer Care Department within the U.S. at 877-762-2974, outside the U.S. at 317-572-3993, or fax 317-572-4002.

Some of the people who helped bring this book to market include the following:

Acquisitions, Editorial, and Vertical Websites

Senior Project Editor: Tim Gallan

Project Editor: Elizabeth Rea

Acquisitions Editor: Erin Calligan Mooney

Copy Editor: Megan Knoll

Assistant Editor: David Lutton

Editorial Program Coordinator: Joe Niesen

Technical Editors: Doug Dodson, Douglas Smith

Editorial Manager: Michelle Hacker

Editorial Assistants: Rachelle S. Amick, Alexa Koschier

Art Coordinator: Alicia B. South

Cover Photos: © iStockphoto.com/ayzek, © iStockphoto.com/Tim Ashton

Cartoons: Rich Tennant (www.the5thwave.com)

Composition Services

Project Coordinator: Katherine Crocker

Layout and Graphics: Carrie A. Cesavice

Proofreaders: Melissa D. Buddendeck, Jessica Kramer

Indexer: Potomac Indexing, LLC

Illustrator: Precision Graphics

Publishing and Editorial for Consumer Dummies

    Kathleen Nebenhaus, Vice President and Executive Publisher

    David Palmer, Associate Publisher

    Kristin Ferguson-Wagstaffe, Product Development Director

Publishing for Technology Dummies

    Andy Cummings, Vice President and Publisher

Composition Services

    Debbie Stailey, Director of Composition Services

Contents at a Glance

Table of Contents

Introduction

. . . .

Although suggesting that buying this copy of *Military Flight Aptitude Tests For Dummies* will change your life may sound trite, we believe it's true. Your decision to become a military aviator is clear evidence that your life has the potential to take flight in ways that few other people will ever experience. You're joining an exclusive group of remarkably courageous, talented, and patriotic men and women.

You can find other test study guides for potential military aviators, but we're convinced that *Military Flight Aptitude Tests For Dummies* is different. First, this book is as engaging as we could possibly make it. Our approach reflects our strong belief and experience that studying for tests can be interesting and perhaps even entertaining. We even help you maintain a sense of humor in the face of the seemingly insurmountable challenges that all test-takers have to deal with from time to time. On some days, your schedule will be so jammed up with competing demands that you won't have even a minute to set aside for studying. That's okay; the idea is to be consistent and remember that slow and steady is the rule. You have to spend a lot of overall time studying to get the best possible score here, but the method has to be one of consistency and determination.

Second, this book reflects the unique experience and perspective of a veteran military aviator: coauthor Lieutenant Colonel Terry Hawn, U.S. Army. Terry enlisted in the Army, went to college, and graduated from the U.S. Army's Rotary Wing flight training program. He has flown on active duty, with the National Guard, and with the Army Reserves in various capacities in addition to serving as an aviation commander. Today, he's qualified as a military and civilian flight instructor for both airplanes and helicopters. The material in this book has been prepared and vetted by a seasoned military aviator whose experience runs the full gamut of airframes and wing types — both fixed and rotary.

We have worked hard to ensure that *Military Flight Aptitude Tests For Dummies* is the very best, most up-to-date study guide on the topic available anywhere, at any price. It provides a comprehensive overview of the topics covered by all the different military flight aptitude tests, presented in a fun and interesting format. We know from personal experience that taking tests can be an intimidating job. Don't worry. Relax. Help is at your fingertips.

About This Book

Military Flight Aptitude Tests For Dummies is perfect for all levels of prospective military aviators. It covers all the different kinds of test questions you encounter on the military flight aptitude test. It also provides sample tests for each of the three major services — Army, Air Force, and Navy (prospective Marine Corps and Coast Guard aviators take the Navy test). If it's on a military flight aptitude test, even the Army's Selection Instrument for Flight Training (SIFT) test, you'll find the topic covered within the pages of this comprehensive book. In addition to study material and sample questions, you can also find a variety of material to help you wade through the important decision of which aircraft you may want to fly, the pluses and minuses of the military lifestyle, and inside tips and strategies for deciding which test(s) to take and how to prepare yourself.

Despite the obvious resemblance of this book to a big, yellow telephone directory, the proper way to use it isn't as a doorstop or a makeshift paperweight. You can use this book in one of two ways:

- If you want to find out about a specific topic, such as the basics of military rank structure or Air Force flight training programs, you can flip to that section and get your answers quickly.

- If you want a crash course in taking all the military flight aptitude tests, read this book from cover to cover. You'll be as prepared as you can possibly be for any test-taking eventuality. The sample tests in Part IV include not only the answers but also explanations of those answers.

This book is unique because you can read each chapter without having to read what comes before or after. You can read the book backward or forward (or, you know, just carry it around with you to impress your friends).

Conventions Used in This Book

When writing this book, we included some general conventions that all *For Dummies* books use. We use the following:

- We *italicize* any words you may not be familiar with and provide definitions.

- We **bold** all keywords in bulleted lists and the actual steps in numbered lists.

- All web addresses appear in `monofont`.

What You're Not to Read

It's probably no surprise to you that we think every word in this book is worth your time. We know, however, that you may not want or have time to read it all. With that understanding in mind, we help you identify skippable material by placing it into sidebars or flagging it with a Technical Stuff icon. *Sidebars* are shaded boxes that contain information that is interesting and related to the topic at hand but not absolutely essential for your test-taking success. Technical Stuff paragraphs contain more detail than what you need for a basic understanding of the subject.

Foolish Assumptions

As we wrote this book, we made a few assumptions about you, our readers. For example, we assume that you're seriously thinking about choosing a career as a military aviator and that you're truly motivated to do your very best on the military flight aptitude test. We also assume that you're ready, willing, and able to commit yourself to a career in military aviation.

How This Book Is Organized

We've divided *Military Flight Aptitude Tests For Dummies* into five parts. Each part covers a major area of military aviation or the military flight aptitude tests. The chapters within each part cover specific topics in detail. Following is a summary of what you'll find in each part.

Part I: So You Want to Be a Military Aviator

Becoming a successful military aviator means understanding the various pathways available to reaching your goal, so this part begins with a discussion of the different military aircraft you may fly and what being a military aviator is like. It then moves to the different training programs offered by the various services, a look at the tests themselves, and finally some specific test-taking strategies and tips.

Part II: Sharpening Your Language and Math Skills

Your ability to demonstrate a basic command of language and mathematical skills is an important part of doing well on the military flight aptitude test. In this part, we review both language and math skills and provide you with a representative set of sample questions to test your knowledge.

Part III: Honing Your Science, Aeronautical, and Mental Skills

A successful military aviator needs very sharp science, aeronautical, and mental skills. Just as military aircraft continue their rapid technological advancement, the men and women who fly them must also keep up with this change. In this part, we conduct an in-depth review of the necessary science, aeronautical, and mental skills you'll need for the flight aptitude test, and we follow each of these chapters with plenty of sample questions for you to gauge your understanding.

Part IV: Practice Military Flight Aptitude Tests

No book on preparing for military flight aptitude tests would be complete without a sample of each of the three tests, and this one is no different. In this part, you have the opportunity to take a sample Air Force Officer Qualifying Test (AFOQT), Army Selection Instrument for Flight Training (SIFT), and Navy/Marine Corps/Coast Guard Aviation Selection Test Battery (ASTB). Each test has a corresponding answer chapter with both an answer key and explanations.

Part V: The Part of Tens

Finally, we include The Part of Tens: a quick-and-dirty collection of chapters that give you ten (or so) pieces of information that every prospective aptitude test-taker needs to know, including things to do before you take the test and ways to maximize your score. Look to these chapters when you need a quick refresher on test-taking strategies and techniques.

Icons Used in This Book

To guide you along the way, we've included some icons. You see the following icons in this book:

This icon points to tips and tricks that make taking the military flight aptitude test easier.

If you don't heed the advice next to these icons, the situation may blow up in your face. Watch out!

Remember these important points of information, and you'll be a much better test-taker.

This icon points out detailed information that you don't need to worry about if all you're after is a general understanding of the topic at hand.

When we include practice questions in explanatory chapters, we use this icon to single them out.

Where to Go from Here

If you're just thinking about a career as a military aviator, you may want to start at the beginning of the book and work your way through to the end. Simply turn the page and take your first step into the world of military aviation.

If you're already serious about your military aviation career path and are short on time (who isn't short on time?), you may want to turn to a particular topic to address a specific need or question. The table of contents gives a chapter-by-chapter description of the topics in this book. You can also find specific topics in the index.

We wish you well on your journey, wherever it takes you!

Part I
So You Want to Be a Military Aviator

The 5th Wave   By Rich Tennant

"I'm studying for the MFAT, so if you don't mind, I'd like to preview, annotate, outline, and summarize this ticket before signing it."

In this part . . .

We know you're excited to start flying, but before you earn your wings, you need to know more about military aviation. In this part, we explore the different aircraft you may fly as a military aviator and investigate the pay, benefits, and opportunities you can expect. We review the training programs offered by the various military services, and we take a close look at the tests and the different kinds of questions you encounter in each. Finally, we delve deeply into the important subject of test-taking strategies and tips.

Chapter 1

Not Just a Job, an Adventure

In This Chapter
▶ Examining different fixed- and rotary-wing military aircraft
▶ Considering rank, pay, and benefits
▶ Enjoying the military life
▶ Discovering a life after the military

Although military aviation is a key component of the U.S. armed forces — projecting military might and conducting far-reaching operations to protect the interests of the United States of America and its allies — it's also a career, and a very exciting and fulfilling one at that. You're in command of a remarkably effective weapon on the modern battlefield.

Many times in the span of an average military career, the President of the United States requires the use of U.S. military force to disable an enemy's combat capability, to protect vital U.S. interests abroad, and to honor treaties established with allies in the pursuit of the common good of the world. As a military aviator, you can expect that you'll be the tip of the spear — the first strike — in these situations. During the past few conflicts the United States has been part of, military aviators have been the ones to lead the way, and that role will continue into the future.

Military aviators must be intelligent, quick to grasp an unfolding situation, and loyal to both their country and their fellow service members on the ground. Above all, they must be self-sacrificing team players whose love for country and fellow humans will be tested time and time again.

Exploring the Types of Aircraft and Their Roles

The various U.S. military branches use many different aircraft for many different missions. Fighter/attack aircraft conduct multifaceted operations to gain air superiority and to destroy crucial opposing targets; bomber aircraft deliver munitions over a great distance with minimal *collateral damage* (civilian casualties). Cargo aircraft perform long-range airlift and humanitarian efforts. Helicopters support ground offensive operations.

The overall category of military aircraft breaks into two major types: fixed-wing and rotary-wing. Each military branch differs somewhat in its mix and usage of each type and in the way it uses pilots; here's a quick rundown:

- ✔ The Air Force typically uses fixed-wing aircraft to project military might; it calls on helicopter assets in resupply or rescue operations.

- ✔ The Navy also looks to fixed-wing aircraft to project military might while utilizing helicopter assets in resupply or rescue operations.

- The Marine Corps utilizes fixed-wing, rotary-wing, and tilt-rotor in a variety of combat and combat support operations.

- The Army primarily utilizes rotary-wing assets to support ground maneuver operations and relies on a small number of fixed-wing aircraft for logistical support.

- The Coast Guard uses fixed-wing aircraft for long-range search-and-rescue or anti-drug operations and primarily utilizes helicopters for more-localized search-and-rescue efforts.

Fixed-wing (airplanes)

Fixed-wing aircraft consist of airplanes ranging from super-large, heavy-lift cargo planes to the relatively small fighter and attack aircraft. The history of modern fixed-wing aircraft can be traced back to the Wright brothers' famous flight at Kitty Hawk, North Carolina, on December 17, 1903.

Fixed-wing aircraft are distinguished by a fixed or attached lifting device (wing) that allows the aircraft to fly in a forward motion at relatively great speed. The typical fixed-wing aircraft travels down a runway to achieve the velocity required to develop a lifting force that enables it to overcome the earth's gravitational pull. Most military aircraft in today's fleet are powered by turbine engines, which either directly convert the energy to thrust (as in a turbojet) or convert the energy to shaft horsepower to turn a propeller (as in a turboprop).

Rotary-wing (helicopters)

The category of *rotary-wing aircraft* consists of helicopters and tilt-rotor aircraft. The German Focke-Wulf Fw61 — which made its inaugural flight on June 26, 1936 — is generally considered to be the first operational helicopter.

Rotary-wing aircraft have a rotating lifting wing (rotor blade), which develops lift and thrust to overcome the force of gravity. This system allows the helicopter to take off and land in a vertical or near-vertical fashion, a capability that lets the helicopter utilize unimproved areas and greatly enhances its ability to provide ground force protection. Helicopters typically have a much slower forward airspeed than fixed-wing aircraft do but make up for that lack of speed in versatility and the capability to be *forward-placed* in a battlefield environment. That is, helicopters can be placed right up to the front lines and operate from that vantage, as well as hide in a selected spot and wait for a target to appear, providing the element of surprise.

A hybrid aircraft exists today that's hard to place in a particular category, but we include it here because it has some similarities to rotary-wing. This aircraft is the *tilt-rotor aircraft* currently utilized by the U.S. Marine Corps. The V-22 Osprey (which you can see in Figure 1-1) can take off and land vertically and then tilt its rotors to act as a forward-thrusting propeller, giving it excellent midrange lift and the capability to land in unimproved areas.

A little bit of military aviation history

The birth of military aviation in the United States can be traced to the U.S. Civil War; in 1861, the Union Army Balloon Corps was established by Thaddeus S.C. Lowe, who was appointed chief aeronaut of the Union Army. The mission of the Balloon Corps was to perform aerial reconnaissance against the Confederate Army, and the organization participated in a number of major Civil War battles, including Antietam, Yorktown, Seven Pines, and others. In the many decades since then, aviation has become an important and integral part of the U.S. military, and every service has an aviation component.

Figure 1-1:
V-22 Osprey
(U.S. Marine
Corps).

Another past variant on the tilt hybrid model is the *tilt-wing aircraft*. With this type of aircraft, the entire *wing* tilts, not just the engine *nacelles* (cover housings) and rotors. Historically, the military has tested several tilt-wing prototype aircraft — including the Vertol VZ-2, the Hiller X-18 (see Figure 1-2), and the LTV XC-142 — but none was ever put into operational service.

Figure 1-2:
Hiller X-18.

Trainer, experimental, and orbital aircraft

Training aircraft for the armed services are smaller aircraft that can economically train and refresh the training of military aviators. These aircraft can range from small turboprop fixed-wing aircraft to small turbine engine training helicopters.

Experimental aircraft (designated by the *X* identifier, such as the X-15) are test aircraft, and they're truly the cutting edge of new aircraft design technology. This category is where science and flying skills meet for the first time.

Finally, spaceflight relies heavily on the skill and experience of military aviators as both astronaut pilots and mission specialists. All early astronauts were direct recruits from the armed forces, and most space shuttle crewmembers were members of the military. Figure 1-3 gives you a glimpse of a space shuttle.

Why I fly

Here's coauthor Terry's story:

"I have often been asked why I decided to become a pilot, and more specifically, a military aviator. When I was about 5 years old and on vacation with my family, my father paid to take all of us on a scenic flight over Nova Scotia. From that moment on, I knew I was meant to be a pilot. It wasn't that I just wanted to fly — I had to fly.

"It's really hard to explain why I felt that way so strongly, but I'm sure most people reading this story understand completely. I started hanging around the airport and began taking flying lessons at age 12. I washed dishes to pay for my flight training, soloed on my 16th birthday (and missed my first day of driver's education to do so), and finally got my private pilot license at age 17. The small grass strip in rural Indiana where I flew was visited by an Army UH-1 Huey one day, and I remember saying, 'I sure wish I could fly that beast.' I assumed that any sort of military aviation program was out of the question for me because I wore corrective lenses, and I distinctly remember the day that I discovered that the Army gave waivers for corrective lenses to commissioned officers. From that day forward, my entire goal in life was to get my college education and my commission as a Second Lieutenant and gain entry into the Army's helicopter flight training school. I didn't take no for an answer, and I succeeded!

"During my military career, I have served as an assault pilot, a medical evacuation pilot, and finally as an attack pilot flying the AH-64 Apache. As a civilian, I have enjoyed teaching flying for many years now and am a certified flight instructor in single- and multi-engine land/sea airplanes, as well as an instructor in helicopters and instrument flying. I own a classic 1948 Stinson 108-3 that I keep on floats in the summer in Northern Michigan and still, after 40 years of flying, enjoy my love of the air."

Photograph courtesy of Terry J. Hawn

Figure 1-3:
Space shut-
tle (NASA).

Photograph courtesy of www.nasa.gov

Fixating on Fixed-Wing Aircraft

When many people think about flying a military aircraft, they're thinking about flying a fixed-wing airplane. Although you can find many different kinds of fixed-wing aircraft, the following sections cover the major types that you encounter as a military aviator.

Fighter aircraft

Fighter aircraft are designed to gain air superiority over the battlefield and to ensure the safety of U.S. service members from enemy air counterstrikes. Later, fighter aircraft deliver ground munitions. The Air Force F-16 Fighting Falcon, a proven performer in the U.S. arsenal, is a typical modern example of a fighter aircraft (see Figure 1-4).

Figure 1-4:
F-16 Fighting
Falcon (U.S.
Air Force).

Photograph courtesy of www.af.mil

The F-22 Raptor, a much more modern fighter aircraft, was designed to counter an increased air-to-air threat. Although the production is currently limited to fewer than 200 airframes, this aircraft is an example of a technologically superior airframe that the United States can rely on to project might well into the 21st century. You can see this aircraft in Figure 1-5.

Figure 1-5:
F-22 Raptor
(U.S. Air
Force).

Photograph courtesy of www.af.mil

Attack aircraft

Attack aircraft don't have a primary air-to-air mission but rather serve as effective weapons in air-to-ground (on land) or air-to-surface attack operations (on sea). The A-10 Thunderbolt II — also affectionately known as the "Warthog" — gained notoriety during the Gulf War for its successful use as a ground attack aircraft. Check it out in Figure 1-6.

Figure 1-6:
A-10
Thunderbolt
II (U.S. Air
Force).

Photograph courtesy of www.af.mil

Multirole fighter/attack aircraft

Today's military has developed and widely deployed multifaceted fighter/attack aircraft capable of both air-to-air operations and precision ground attack and bombing operations. The Naval F/A-18 Hornet and the F-35 Lightning II Joint Strike Fighter are examples of this type of aircraft. This multirole aircraft is replacing the former attack- or fighter-specific aircraft with one aircraft fully capable of performing both missions and therefore increasing battlefield flexibility for military commanders. Figures 1-7 and 1-8 give you a look at these aircraft.

Figure 1-7:
F/A 18
Hornet (U.S.
Navy).

Photograph courtesy of www.navy.mil

Figure 1-8:
F-35
Lightning II.

Photograph courtesy of www.edwards.af.mil

Bomber aircraft

Bombing enemies' production assets on a mass scale is one of the major factors in past U.S. military victories. Today, the carpet-bombing strategies of past wars are long gone; they've been replaced by sophisticated, electronically shadowed aircraft capable of surprising enemies by delivering lots of precision-guided weapons, all while avoiding electronic detection. The B-2 Spirit bomber (more commonly known as the *stealth* bomber) is a long-range, first-strike aircraft with these capabilities (see Figure 1-9).

Figure 1-9:
B-2 Spirit
(U.S. Air
Force).

Photograph courtesy of www.af.mil

Cargo aircraft

The *cargo mission* consists of operations to resupply troops, troop movement, aero medical operations (similar to medivac), airborne operations (such as parachuting soldiers who drop behind enemy lines), and humanitarian assistance. When the job requires rapidly transporting personnel or goods far and quickly, the cargo pilot and flight crew are the ones that get the job done.

One cargo aircraft is the C-130 Hercules, which can operate in remote and underdeveloped locations because of its capability to land on unimproved roads and fields. The Air Force, Navy, and Coast Guard rely heavily on this workhorse, shown in Figure 1-10, to achieve their missions.

Figure 1-10:
C-130
Hercules
(various
branches).

Photograph courtesy of http://cgvi.uscg.mil

Another, longer-range cargo aircraft capable of delivering combat military troops and equipment to distant lands is the C-17 Globemaster III. The C-17 (see Figure 1-11) is one of the newer aircraft in today's military air inventory; it enables rapid ground force employment worldwide and has been used with great success in Iraq and Afghanistan.

Figure 1-11: C-17 Globemaster III (U.S. Air Force).

Photograph courtesy of www.af.mil

Reconnaissance/surveillance aircraft

Reconnaissance and surveillance aircraft gain critical, time-sensitive intelligence information. The mission can range from standard intelligence-gathering and battlefield surveillance to electronic countermeasures. Airborne Early Warning and Control (AEW&C; some earlier systems are also known as Airborne Warning and Controls System or AWACS) aircraft provide radar coverage on the battlefield, direct targets, and distinguish between enemy and friendly aircraft.

AEW&C works for both defensive and offensive operations and directs fighter aircraft to targets as directed by higher headquarters. An example of an AEW&C aircraft is the E-2 Hawkeye aircraft, shown in Figure 1-12, which is capable of being launched from an aircraft carrier. The Air Force utilizes a larger AWACS aircraft, the E-3 Sentry (see Figure 1-13), for electronic countermeasures and battlefield control functions.

Figure 1-12: E-2 Hawkeye (U.S. Navy).

Photograph courtesy of www.navy.mil

Figure 1-13:
E-3 Sentry
(U.S. Air
Force).

Photograph courtesy of www.af.mil

Rounding Up Rotary-Wing Aircraft

Not all helicopters are created equal, especially in the military. Certain abbreviations let you know the particular role of rotary-wing aircraft: UH for utility helicopter, AH for attack helicopter, CH for cargo helicopter, and OH for observation helicopter. The following sections break down these categories in more detail.

Utility helicopters

From air assault operations to the command and control mission to the life-saving flying medical and rescue crews, *utility helicopters* serve as one of the primary contingents of military rotary-wing aviation. Examples of this type of aircraft range from the UH-60 Blackhawk (see Figure 1-14) to the HH-65 Dauphin (see Figure 1-15).

Figure 1-14:
UH-60
Blackhawk
(U.S. Army).

Photograph courtesy of www.army.mil

Figure 1-15:
HH-65
Dauphin
(U.S. Coast
Guard).

Photograph courtesy of http://cgvi.uscg.mil

Attack helicopters

Attack helicopters primarily function as anti-tank weapons platforms and support infantry forces on the ground. The mission of the attack helicopter is multifaceted; one of its main jobs is as a first-strike weapon, crossing deep into enemy territory to destroy air defense assets prior to fixed-wing bombing campaigns. The two primary services that use this type of aircraft are the U.S. Army and U.S. Marine Corps, which both commonly have troops engaged in close combat. The U.S. Army utilizes the AH-64 Apache (see Figure 1-16), and the U.S. Marine Corps utilizes the modernized AH-1 Cobra (see Figure 1-17).

Figure 1-16:
AH-64
Apache
(U.S. Army).

Photograph courtesy of www.army.mil

Figure 1-17:
AH-1 Cobra
(U.S. Marine
Corps).

Cargo helicopters

Cargo helicopters provide short-distance combat air assaults and cargo operational support very close to or behind the front lines. Additionally, these types of helicopters regularly transport troops to different operating outposts and perform special-use missions. Examples of cargo helicopters are the CH-47 Chinook and the CH-46 Sea Knight, shown in Figures 1-18 and 1-19, respectively.

Figure 1-18:
CH-47
Chinook
(U.S. Army).

Figure 1-19:
CH-46 Sea
Knight (U.S.
Navy).

Photograph courtesy of www.navy.mil

Observation helicopters

Observation helicopters are smaller aircraft primarily utilized to make a light attack and to give the ground commander a real-time operational look at the battlefield. The OH-58D Kiowa Warrior in Figure 1-20 is an example of an observation helicopter that has been enabled with light armament.

Figure 1-20:
OH-58D
Kiowa
Warrior
(U.S. Army).

Photograph courtesy of www.army.mil

Brushing Up on Basic Military Rank Structure

As a pilot in today's military, you're either a commissioned officer or a warrant officer. If you don't know a commissioned officer from a hole in the ground, never fear. The following sections break down each type of rank classification and give you some insight into the duties you encounter.

Enlisted personnel

Typically, when young men or women enter military service after high school without a college degree, they do so in the ranks of the *enlisted personnel.* You can enter the enlisted ranks with a college education, and most enlisted personnel attain some sort of advanced degree while in the service (many use service as a way to pay for college); as a whole, though, enlisted ranks are where you find most service members.

When you enter or *enlist* in the military, you enter into a contract with a specific branch of the military for a given period of time and a given duty or position. Pre-enlistment tests determine whether you can hold the specialty position you want. Enlisted roles may include a Marine assault squad, an Army tank crew, Navy ship personnel, and an Air Force aircraft crew chief, just to name a few. Enlisted personnel are ranks E-1 through E-9.

Many enlisted personnel decide to make the military a career; some later become officers, but many decide to advance up the enlisted ranks and become what are known as *noncommissioned officers* — leaders and senior leaders who don't hold a commission or appointment by Congress. These noncommissioned officers remain in the trenches, so to speak, and are the backbone of the various military branches. Table 1-1 summarizes the different enlisted ranks for the various service branches.

Table 1-1		Enlisted Ranks for All Branches of Service		
Grade	*Army*	*Navy/Coast Guard*	*Air Force*	*Marine Corps*
E-1	Private (PV1)	Seaman Recruit (SR)	Airman Basic (AB)	Private (PVT)
E-2	Private (PV2)	Seaman Apprentice (SA)	Airman (Amn)	Private First Class (PFC)
E-3	Private First Class (PFC)	Seaman (SN)	Airman First Class (A1C)	Lance Corporal (LCpl)
E-4	Corporal (CPL)l	Petty Officer Third Class (PO3)	Senior Airman (SrA)	Corporal (Cpl)
E-4	Specialist (SPC)	Petty Officer Third Class (PO3)	Senior Airman (SrA)	Corporal (Cpl)
E-5	Sergeant (SGT)	Petty Officer Second Class (PO2)	Staff Sergeant (SSgt)	Sergeant (Sgt)
E-6	Staff Sergeant (SSG)	Petty Officer First Class (PO1)	Technical Sergeant (TSgt)	Staff Sergeant (SSgt)
E-7	Sergeant First Class (SFC)	Chief Petty Officer (CPO)	Master Sergeant, First Sergeant	Gunnery Sergeant (GySgt)
E-7			First Sergeant	
E-8	Master Sergeant (MSG)	Senior Chief Petty Officer (SCPO)	Senior Master Sergeant (SMSgt)	Master Sergeant (MSgt)
E-8	First Sergeant (1SG)		First Sergeant (Senior Master Sergeant)	First Sergeant (1stSgt)
E-9	Sergeant Major (SGM)	Master Chief Petty Officer (MCPO)	Chief Master Sergeant (CMSgt)	Master Gunnery Sergeant (MGySgt)
E-9	Command Sergeant Major (CSM)		First Sergeant (Chief Master Sergeant)	Sergeant Major (SgtMaj)
E-9			Command Chief Master Sergeant	

Warrant officers

A *warrant officer* is a specialty rank that falls between the enlisted ranks and the commissioned ranks. The warrant officer concept evolved out of a need to recruit, promote, and retain professional technical support at a higher level than could be found in the noncommissioned ranks (see the preceding section for more on noncommissioned officers). As a warrant officer, you get higher pay and the normal privileges of an officer, but you typically aren't considered a supervisor. (As this rank has evolved, ranks above warrant officer one — abbreviated WO1 — have come to be considered commissioned officers and can technically command a unit if no commissioned officers are available.) The rank structure of warrant officers begins at WO1 and goes all the way up to CW5 (chief warrant officer five). At various points in their careers, many warrant officers decide to become supervisors and opt to become commissioned officers. (Head to the following section for information on commissioned officers.)

Various branches utilize the warrant officer in technical specialties, but the U.S. Army boasts the most warrant officers by far, typically in maintenance and aviation technical positions (Army aviators). Check out Table 1-2 to see the warrant officer ranks for each service branch.

Table 1-2	Warrant Officer Ranks for All Branches of Service			
Grade	**Army**	**Navy/Coast Guard**	**Air Force**	**Marine Corps**
W-1	Warrant Officer 1 (WO1)	Warrant Officer 1 (WO1)	No Warrant	Warrant Officer 1 (WO)
W-2	Chief Warrant Officer 2 (CW2)	Chief Warrant Officer 2 (CWO2)	No Warrant	Chief Warrant Officer 2 (CWO2)
W-3	Chief Warrant Officer 3 (CW3)	Chief Warrant Officer 3 (CWO3)	No Warrant	Chief Warrant Officer 3 (CWO3)
W-4	Chief Warrant Officer 4 (CW4)	Chief Warrant Officer 4 (CWO4)	No Warrant	Chief Warrant Officer 4 (CWO4)
W-5	Chief Warrant Officer (CW5)	Chief Warrant Officer (CWO5)	No Warrant	Chief Warrant Officer 5 (CWO5)

Commissioned officers

Commissioned officers have official leadership responsibilities. Beginning at the rank of Second Lieutenant (Ensign for the Navy and Coast Guard), commissioned officers advance in positions of authority, command various military units, and are responsible for both the function of the units and the health and welfare of those service members under their command. Most branches of the military commission their aviators and allow those most talented in leadership and flying skills to advance to positions of senior authority. (The U.S. Army calls on warrant officers for the bulk of its aviators while relying on a smaller contingent of commissioned officers as leaders of those aviation units.)

The paths to a commissioned rank are quite varied and can range from the different service academies (such as the U.S. Air Force Academy) to the Reserve Officers Training Corps (ROTC) at many different universities to different types of officer candidate schools within each military branch. Chapter 2 gives you the lowdown on finding your own best path for becoming an officer. Table 1-3 presents the commissioned officer ranks for all service branches.

What time is it?

The military uses a 24-hour clock, which at first can seem somewhat strange but really is easy and makes great sense. From midnight until noon, you count the hours just like you would under the 12-hour clock; instead of adding "o'clock" after the number, however, you say "hundred hours" or just "hundred" (so "10 o'clock" is "10 hundred hours" or "10 hundred.")

At noon — or 12 hundred hours — the game changes; you keep counting from 12 rather than starting over at 1. To determine the time based on a 24-hour clock, just add the current 12-hour-system time to 12. If the current time is 1:00 p.m., for example, you add that to 12 to get 13 hundred hours. 2:15 p.m. is 1415 hours (12 + 2:15 = 1415; the military system gets rid of the colon), and so on. Simple, right?

Table 1-3   Commissioned Officer Ranks for All Branches of Service

Grade	Army/Air Force/Marine Corps	Navy/Coast Guard
O-1	Second Lieutenant (Army: 2LT) (Air Force: 2d Lt) (USMC: 2dLt)	Ensign (ENS)
O-2	First Lieutenant (Army: 1LT) (Air Force: 1st Lt) (USMC: 1Lt)	Lieutenant Junior Grade (LTJG)
O-3	Captain (Army: CPT) (Air Force: Capt) (USMC: Capt)	Lieutenant (LT)
O-4	Major (Army: MAJ) (Air Force: Maj) (USMC: Maj)	Lieutenant Commander (LCDR)
O-5	Lieutenant Colonel (Army: LTC) (Air Force: Lt Col) (USMJ: LtCol)	Commander (CDR)
O-6	Colonel (Army: COL) (Air Force: Col) (USMC: Col)	Captain (CAPT)
O-7	Brigadier General (Army: BG) (Air Force: Brig Gen) (USMC: BGen)	Rear Admiral (lower half) (RDML)
O-8	Major General (Army: MG) (Air Force Maj Gen) (USMC: MGen)	Rear Admiral (upper half) (RADM)

Grade	Army/Air Force/Marine Corps	Navy/Coast Guard
O-9	Lieutenant General (Army: LTG) (Air Force: Lt Gen) (USMC: LtGen)	Vice Admiral (VADM)
O-10	General (Army: GEN) (Air Force: Gen) (USMC: Gen)	Admiral (ADM)

Perusing Pay and Benefits

The common misconception that today's service members are poorly compensated couldn't be farther from the truth. The actual pay is quite adequate to raise a family on; add the benefits and the fact that certain portions of your pay have tax advantages, and you end up having a fairly substantial financial compensation package, as we outline in the following sections.

Military pay

Military pay is a complex array of both taxable and non-taxable income sources. Figures 1-21 and 1-22 are pay charts for the year 2013; you can expect an average increase in pay, authorized by Congress, of between 2.5 and 3 percent each year. Here are some of the income sources you encounter as an aviation officer:

✔ **Base pay:** *Base pay* is essentially your flat salary; your rank and years of service determine the rate. In most cases, base pay is taxable, although pay earned in combat gets a special break that we discuss later in this section.

✔ **Basic allowance for subsistence (BAS):** *BAS* is a predetermined stipend for groceries. The breakdown is based on rank and marital status. BAS is tax-exempt.

✔ **Basic allowance for housing (BAH):** *BAH* is a predetermined amount to provide off-base housing for service members and their families; this nontaxable rate is also determined using rank and marital status. If you decide to live on post or on base at your duty location, you forfeit your BAH. You can read a bit about on-base housing in the later section "Medical and housing benefits."

✔ **Specialty pay:** Depending on the conditions you serve in, you may be eligible for additional, tax-exempt monetary compensation, or *specialty pay*. The most common type of specialty pay is imminent danger, hazardous duty, or hostile fire pay.

✔ **Incentive pay:** Military career fields that are highly competitive and have a high turnover rate offer extra financial compensation to keep qualified candidates in their positions. Examples of this *incentive pay* include special pay for medical/dental officers and aviation career incentive pay (flight pay). This pay is taxable unless earned in a combat zone.

Figure 1-21: 2013 pay scale along with BAS, BAH, and aviation career incentive pay for years of service 2 or less up to over 18.

Grade	Cumulative Years of Service										
	2 or less	Over 2	Over 3	Over 4	Over 6	Over 8	Over 10	Over 12	Over 14	Over 16	Over 18
O-10[1]											
O-9[1]											
O-8[1]	9847.8	10170.3	10384.5	10444.2	10711.5	11157.6	11261.4	11685	11806.5	12171.6	12700.2
O-7[1]	8182.5	8562.9	8738.7	8878.5	9131.7	9381.9	9671.1	9959.4	10248.6	11157.6	11924.7
O-6[2]	6064.8	6663	7100.1	7100.1	7127.1	7432.8	7473	7473	7897.8	8648.7	9089.4
O-5	5055.9	5695.5	6089.7	6164.1	6410.1	6557.1	6880.8	7118.4	7425.3	7895.1	8118
O-4	4362.3	5049.9	5386.8	5461.8	5774.7	6109.8	6527.7	6852.9	7078.8	7208.7	7283.7
O-3	3835.5	4347.9	4692.9	5116.5	5361.6	5630.7	5804.7	6090.6	6240	6240	6240
O-2	3314.1	3774.3	4347	4493.7	4586.4	4586.4	4586.4	4586.4	4586.4	4586.4	4586.4
O-1	2876.4	2994	3619.2	3619.2	3619.2	3619.2	3619.2	3619.2	3619.2	3619.2	3619.2
O-3[3]				5116.5	5361.6	5630.7	5804.7	6090.6	6332.1	6470.7	6659.4
O-2[3]				4493.7	4586.4	4732.5	4978.8	5169.3	5311.2	5311.2	5311.2
O-1[3]				3619.2	3864.6	4007.7	4153.8	4297.2	4493.7	4493.7	4493.7

Grade	Cumulative Years of Service										
	2 or less	Over 2	Over 3	Over 4	Over 6	Over 8	Over 10	Over 12	Over 14	Over 16	Over 18
W-5											
W-4	3963.9	4263.9	4386	4506.6	4713.9	4919.1	5126.7	5439.6	5713.5	5974.2	6187.5
W-3	3619.5	3770.4	3924.2	3975.9	4137.2	4457.1	4789.2	4945.5	5126.4	5313	5648.1
W-2	3202.8	3505.8	3599.4	3663.3	3871.2	4194	4353.9	4511.4	4704	4854.3	4990.8
W-1	2811.6	3114	3195.3	3367.5	3570.9	3870.6	4010.4	4205.7	4398.3	4549.8	4689

Grade	Cumulative Years of Service										
	2 or less	Over 2	Over 3	Over 4	Over 6	Over 8	Over 10	Over 12	Over 14	Over 16	Over 18
E-9[4]							4788.9	4897.5	5034.3	5194.8	5357.4
E-8						3920.1	4093.5	4200.9	4329.6	4469.1	4720.5
E-7	2725.2	2974.5	3088.2	3239.1	3357	3559.2	3673.2	3875.7	4043.7	4158.6	4281
E-6	2357.1	2593.8	2708.1	2819.4	2935.5	3196.5	3298.5	3495.3	3555.6	3599.7	3650.7
E-5	2159.4	2304.3	2415.9	2529.9	2707.5	2893.5	3045.6	3064.2	3064.2	3064.2	3064.2
E-4	1979.7	2081.1	2193.9	2304.9	2403.3	2403.3	2403.3	2403.3	2403.3	2403.3	2403.3
E-3	1787.4	1899.9	2014.8	2014.8	2014.8	2014.8	2014.8	2014.8	2014.8	2014.8	2014.8
E-2	1699.8	1699.8	1699.8	1699.8	1699.8	1699.8	1699.8	1699.8	1699.8	1699.8	1699.8
E-1	1516.2	1516.2	1516.2	1516.2	1516.2	1516.2	1516.2	1516.2	1516.2	1516.2	1516.2

Source: www.militaryfactory.com

Figure 1-22: 2013 pay scale along with BAS, BAH, and aviation career incentive pay for years of service over 20 to over 40.

Grade	Cumulative Years of Service										
	Over 20	Over 22	Over 24	Over 26	Over 28	Over 30	Over 32	Over 34	Over 36	Over 38	Over 40
O-10[1]	15913.2	15990.6	16323.6	16902.6	16902.6	17747.7	17747.7	18634.8	18634.8	19566.9	19566.9
O-9[1]	13917.6	14118.6	14408.1	14913.3	14913.3	15659.4	15659.4	16442.4	16442.4	17264.4	17264.4
O-8[1]	13187.1	13512.3	13512.3	13512.3	13512.3	13850.4	13850.4	14196.6	14196.6	14196.6	14196.6
O-7[1]	11924.7	11924.7	11924.7	11985.6	11985.6	12225.3	12225.3	12225.3	12225.3	12225.3	12225.3
O-6[2]	9529.8	9780.6	10034.4	10526.7	10526.7	10736.7	10736.7	10736.7	10736.7	10736.7	10736.7
O-5	8338.8	8589.9	8589.9	8589.9	8589.9	8589.9	8589.9	8589.9	8589.9	8589.9	8589.9
O-4	7283.7	7283.7	7283.7	7283.7	7283.7	7283.7	7283.7	7283.7	7283.7	7283.7	7283.7
O-3	6240	6240	6240	6240	6240	6240	6240	6240	6240	6240	6240
O-2	4586.4	4586.4	4586.4	4586.4	4586.4	4586.4	4586.4	4586.4	4586.4	4586.4	4586.4
O-1	3619.2	3619.2	3619.2	3619.2	3619.2	3619.2	3619.2	3619.2	3619.2	3619.2	3619.2
O-3[3]	6659.4	6659.4	6659.4	6659.4	6659.4	6659.4	6659.4	6659.4	6659.4	6659.4	6659.4
O-2[3]	5311.2	5311.2	5311.2	5311.2	5311.2	5311.2	5311.2	5311.2	5311.2	5311.2	5311.2
O-1[3]	4493.7	4493.7	4493.7	4493.7	4493.7	4493.7	4493.7	4493.7	4493.7	4493.7	4493.7

Grade	Cumulative Years of Service										
	Over 20	Over 22	Over 24	Over 26	Over 28	Over 30	Over 32	Over 34	Over 36	Over 38	Over 40
W-5	7047.9	7405.5	7671.6	7966.5	7966.5	8365.2	8365.2	8783.1	8783.1	9222.9	9222.9
W-4	6395.4	6701.1	6952.2	7238.7	7238.7	7383.3	7383.3	7383.3	7383.3	7383.3	7383.3
W-3	5874.46	6009.92	6153.75	6349.35	6349.35	6349.35	6349.35	6349.35	6349.35	6349.35	6349.35
W-2	5153.7	5261.1	5346.3	5346.3	5346.3	5346.3	5346.3	5346.3	5346.3	5346.3	5346.3
W-1	4858.2	4858.2	4858.2	4858.2	4858.2	4858.2	4858.2	4858.2	4858.2	4858.2	4858.2

Grade	Cumulative Years of Service										
	Over 20	Over 22	Over 24	Over 26	Over 28	Over 30	Over 32	Over 34	Over 36	Over 38	Over 40
E-9[4]	5617.49	5837.26	6068.82	6422.51	6422.51	6743.34	6743.34	7080.91	7080.91	7435.22	7435.22
E-8	4847.8	5064.79	5184.75	5481.09	5481.09	5591.14	5591.14	5591.14	5591.14	5591.14	5591.14
E-7	4328.58	4487.29	4572.85	4897.71	4897.71	4897.71	4897.71	4897.71	4897.71	4897.71	4897.71
E-6	3650.96	3650.96	3650.96	3650.96	3650.96	3650.96	3650.96	3650.96	3650.96	3650.96	3650.96
E-5	3064.2	3064.2	3064.2	3064.2	3064.2	3064.2	3064.2	3064.2	3064.2	3064.2	3064.2
E-4	2403.3	2403.3	2403.3	2403.3	2403.3	2403.3	2403.3	2403.3	2403.3	2403.3	2403.3
E-3	2014.8	2014.8	2014.8	2014.8	2014.8	2014.8	2014.8	2014.8	2014.8	2014.8	2014.8
E-2	1699.8	1699.8	1699.8	1699.8	1699.8	1699.8	1699.8	1699.8	1699.8	1699.8	1699.8
E-1	1516.2	1516.2	1516.2	1516.2	1516.2	1516.2	1516.2	1516.2	1516.2	1516.2	1516.2

Source: www.militaryfactory.com

Some examples of military pay

An E-9 enlisted member with 26 years of federal service earns $6,422 per month, so that's how much normally taxable pay is exempt for other members. A First Lieutenant (or Lieutenant, junior grade in the Navy) just out of flight school with two years of service earns $3,774 per month for base pay and another $156 for flight pay (though that amount increases with experience). The net taxable pay comes to $3,930, which is below the E-9 rate. The entire amount is therefore tax-free.

A Major or Lieutenant Commander with more than 14 years served earns $7,079 for base pay and another $840 for flight pay, for a total of $7,919. If you deduct the tax-free cap of $6,215, you see that the Major owes taxes on $7,919 – $6,215 or $1,704 per month. Even though the Major's pay isn't entirely tax-exempt, she still gets an extremely big tax benefit and ultimately a much larger equivalent pay rate.

When you're serving overseas in a combat zone, your taxable pay receives an additional tax break: All your income is tax-exempt up to the level that the highest enlisted members receive (that would be an E-9 pay rate). This exemption means that roughly the first $92,866 of your normally taxable pay is tax-exempt.

In addition to a large portion of your income being tax-exempt, you have some other important tax incentives to consider while looking at military aviation as a career. For example, many states don't tax your military income, and you can maintain your tax residency in one of those states relatively easily, regardless of where you're stationed.

Educational benefits

All branches of the armed forces value and encourage education. Starting at the junior enlisted ranks and continuing to top-level military management, they urge and expect you to continue your education to progress in rank. The military backs up this expectation with tremendous education benefits that range from 75-percent to 100-percent tuition reimbursement for completing an advanced degree. As a career military aviator, you have the opportunity to achieve advanced degrees; in some cases, you can reasonably expect an assignment of two years to pursue an advanced degree full time if you so choose (that is, going to school will be your assigned duty). Many officers elect this competitive option, while others pursue their educations online while deployed.

The Post 9/11 GI Bill is a valuable asset to both you and your family. This bill can provide you financial support as you pursue educational opportunities, and it also has the key feature of allowing you to transfer your educational benefits to your dependents in some cases. This bill has a sliding scale based on deployment experience, but it's a great tool for families looking to pay for education.

Medical and housing benefits

Medical and on-base housing options are important considerations for many service members, especially those with families. As a uniformed service member on active duty, you receive all medical care free of charge at military medical treatment centers throughout the world. Your family can be enrolled in the TRICARE provider network and receive a very good insurance plan regardless of where you're stationed.

You say "brat," we say "well traveled"

Contrary to common stereotypes in the civilian sector, the military can serve as an excellent environment to raise a family in. Excellent base schools, copious family recreation activities, and wonderful opportunities to live in countries throughout the world afford military children — or military brats, as they're affectionately known — a great environment to grow up in. Granted, this kind of military life means lots of moves, but military children learn to be outgoing and make close friends easily. And you'll find that wherever you go in the military, you always encounter friends from locations past. Coauthor Peter was an Air Force "brat," and his positive experience reflects the typical attitude of most military children.

Housing on military bases typically includes very nice three- to four-bedroom homes in well-maintained areas with exceptional schools. Single officers are usually placed in an apartment-type dwelling that's convenient to different duty locations and recreation facilities.

Retirement benefits

Young aviators have a hard time thinking of retirement, especially when all they can think of is flying. Trust us, the retirement years come faster than you'd expect, but by following the path of military aviation (whether as a full-time or reserve aviator), you can develop a very nice retirement at a relatively young age.

Active duty retirement

If you decide to remain in the military after your initial obligation (approximately six years following flight school), you can receive a generous retirement. After 20 years of active federal service, you'll be entitled to 50 percent of your base pay for the rest of your life if you retire then. Each year that you stay beyond 20 years gets you an approximately 3-percent increase in the base pay percentage (so if you retire after 21 years, you'll get 53 percent of your base pay, and so on). Keep in mind that this retirement is a percentage of your base pay only; it doesn't include any of the entitlements (such as BAS) that we discuss in the earlier section "Military pay" (a lot of people are surprised by this fact).

Reserve duty retirement

After completing their service obligations following flight school, many aviators leave the military to pursue career opportunities in the civilian sector. The various state National Guard, Naval, Air Force, and Army Reserve corps have aviation units where you can continue to fly and serve. The advantage of this path, besides the ability to fly high-performance aircraft, is the possibility of excellent retirement benefits.

Basically, reserve duty retirement is based on a points system where you receive one point for each *duty day*. (A four-hour flying period or additional flight training period counts as one day, and one weekend counts as four days.) You need to earn 50 points a year to qualify for a "good" year (but you get 15 points per year for being a member). After you reach the qualifying level of 20 "good" years, you'll be eligible for retirement based on your total number of points and retirement rank. Typically, you don't begin to receive a retirement paycheck in reserve retirement until age 60, but a 2009 law reduces the retirement age by 90 days for every 90 days served in a combat theater.

Enjoying the military life

Another benefit to consider — one that is less tangible but no less important — is the military life. When the Navy's ads say "It's not just a job, it's an adventure," they aren't joking. If you decide to make military aviation your career, you are pretty much guaranteed to enjoy a career that lets you do things your civilian friends can only dream of. Not only can you enjoy the pride that comes from putting your life on the line for your country, but you can also fly some of the most-advanced aircraft in the world. And you can develop a deep and lasting camaraderie with your fellow service members that is unequalled in any other profession. These bonds will last you a lifetime.

You really do have the chance to see the world, and your family will enjoy the benefits of living the military lifestyle along with you. Although the military life can be a hard one — combat is no picnic, and constant rotations can wear on you — in our experience the pluses far outweigh the minuses.

Embracing a World of Opportunities after You Leave Active Duty

As you progress in your military career, you reach a point where you need to decide whether to exit the military after completing your initial obligation or remain on active duty. A multitude of opportunities awaits you in the civilian world. Here are just a few of the most popular examples:

- **Commercial airlines:** When you receive your flight training, you have the opportunity to receive an FAA commercial pilot's license based on your military training, so many aviators who leave the military pursue a career in commercial airline aviation. As an airline pilot, you can live anywhere and commute to work via regularly scheduled flights approximately ten days per month. The typical airline pilot bids on trip assignments and, based on seniority, may fly a domestic or international schedule.

- **Corporate travel:** Many former military aviators have ventured into the world of corporate aviation travel, working either for companies that maintain their own executive transport fleets or for charter flight companies that hire the aircraft and flight crew for special trips and events. Corporate travel is ever-changing; one day you may fly to the heartland of the United States, and the next you may be off to South America. This unpredictability is an exciting and challenging aspect to those attracted to that lifestyle.

- **Management:** If you'd rather pursue flying strictly for pleasure after you leave the military, you may be right at home in the business sector. As a military aviator (and particularly as a commissioned officer), you'll be a sought-after commodity in the civilian business market, where military skills and management styles are an attractive feature. Many former aviators have gone on to be CEOs or COOs for Fortune 500 companies.

Chapter 2

Taking a Look at Training Programs

....

In This Chapter

▶ Breaking down each branch's training and requirements

▶ Checking out paths to becoming an officer

....

Today's military offers you the chance to get flight training that is second to none. Not only can you make a decent salary, but you also have the opportunity to operate some of the most advanced aviation equipment in the world.

In this chapter, we discuss the various military training programs, examine the paths to becoming an officer for the different branches, and present the selection criteria that are important to each military service (each branch has subtle variations in what it deems important).

Exploring the Different Military Training Opportunities

Deciding that you want to be a military aviator is only the first step in choosing your career path. Each branch of the armed services is different, and each has its own set of priorities and selection processes. If you think you may not meet the requirements for one branch, talk directly with an aviation flight recruiter from that branch (be sure it's a flight recruiter) to see whether your status or condition is waiverable. For example, gone are the days when strict eyesight standards sidelined many potentially great aviators. The following sections break down the different services, what each branch looks for, and what you can expect as an aviation candidate in each.

Most criteria for all the branches have waivers that you can apply for on a case-by-case basis. Check with your flight recruiter for details.

Addressing Army aviation flight training programs

Army aviation can trace its roots to the balloon observers in the Civil War. Steeped in history and tradition, being an Army aviator means you can look forward to a challenging career flying difficult airframes.

The Army mission and aircraft

The mission of Army aviation is to conduct prompt and sustained combat operations. To accomplish this mission, aviation units are generally organized into combat, combat support, and combat service support units.

The Army uses aircraft to provide another prong to the attack in an air-land battle. Aviators in the Army fly differing missions, ranging from attack to medical evacuation. The Army primarily utilizes helicopters, so it conducts all initial flight training in rotary-wing rather than fixed-wing aircraft (see Chapter 11 for details on these types of aircraft). The other military branches conduct primary flight training in fixed-wing aircraft.

Army selection criteria/requirements for pilots and demographics

The U.S. Army has developed its selection criteria based on the experiences and traits that past successful warrant and commissioned officer flight candidates have shown. The Army actively recruits and trains previous enlisted personnel from the other branches of the military who want to fly but may not have the civilian educational requirements that the other military services require for flying assignments. Because so many aviation officers come from an enlisted background, aviation warrant officers understand the needs of (and have an affinity toward) the soldiers on the ground. Demographically, approximately 80 percent of new Army aviation warrant officers come from the enlisted ranks of all the different service branches.

Selection is based on academic qualification, previous flight experience, demonstrated performance and potential, and the following criteria:

- U.S. citizenship.

- Age: 18 to 32.

- Minimum score of 40 on the Selection Instrument for Flight Training (SIFT). This requirement may change over time as this new test is validated.

- Education: High school graduate (most do have a college degree, but it's not required).

- Medical: Ability to meet the standards of a Class 1A flight physical (Army Regulation 40-501).

- Vision: 20/50 uncorrected and correctable to 20/20 with normal color and depth perception. Photorefractive keratectomy (PRK) is waiverable, but the Lasik eye procedure is not.

- Standard height/weight per Army Regulation 600-9.

- Eligibility for security clearance.

Army flight training programs

The U.S. Army currently conducts all primary and most advanced training at Fort Rucker, Alabama. (*Note:* Flight training is the same for warrant and commissioned officers; head to Chapter 1 for more on these designations.) Not counting the specific warrant officer candidate training or commissioned officer initial branch training, Army flight school involves approximately 34 to 43 weeks of training, depending on the aircraft you'll be flying.

Eyeing Air Force flight training programs

The Air Force — the nation's youngest branch of service — originated with the Army Air Corps; during WWII, the military realized the value and importance of a strong aviation component on the modern battlefield and gave it its own branch.

The Air Force mission and aircraft

The mission of the U.S. Air Force is to fly, fight, and win in air, space, and cyberspace. The Air Force supports the joint mission first and foremost and provides compelling air, space, and cyber capabilities for the combat commander. The Air Force has six distinctive capabilities: air and space superiority, global attack, rapid global mobility, precision engagement, information superiority, and agile combat support.

The Air Force uses many different types of aircraft to provide it with these capabilities. These aircraft — from smaller, agile fighter aircraft to large transport vehicles — allow the Air Force and its sister services to project military might worldwide. As an Air Force aviator, you can expect to fly one of a wide range of aircraft on a specific mission format.

Air Force selection criteria/requirements and demographics

The U.S. Air Force has developed selection criteria based on success established since before the branch's founding shortly after World War II. The Air Force utilizes only commissioned officers in its aviation programs, and although waivers do exist, the branch tends to have tight standards because of its operating environment.

Typically, an Air Force applicant comes from one of three sources, all of which require a bachelor's degree prior to flight training:

- The Air Force Academy
- Air Force ROTC
- Officer Training School

If you want to fly in the Air Force and you have at least two years of college remaining, we highly recommend you enter either a service academy or ROTC. The simple fact is that your odds of getting into an Air Force flight training program are greater if you choose these paths. We're not saying that entry into flight training after OTS is impossible, but it's a very competitive field for few potential slots. If you've already graduated from college with at least a bachelor's degree, you can still achieve your goal. You've already shown your commitment to excellence by purchasing this book. Study hard and affect any other selection criteria you have control over.

The Air Force utilizes a pilot candidate selection method (PCSM) to determine who enters into flight training. If you're coming into flight training as a member of the National Guard or Reserves, you fly the aircraft that is assigned to that unit. All other candidates get aircraft choice based on their standing during flight school.

The PCSM uses different determining factors but primarily focuses on three main categories:

- **Air Force Officer Qualifying Test:** This test is scored and broken down into the following six categories (with minimum scores required to qualify as a pilot):

  - **Academic aptitude (no minimum score required).**
  - **Verbal (15).**
  - **Quantitative (10).**
  - **Pilot (25).**
  - **Navigator (10).**
  - **Combined pilot and navigator (50).** You may notice that this threshold is actually higher than the combined minimum scores for the pilot and navigator sections; to excel in this category, you have to score better than the bare minimum on these sections.

- **Your test of basic aviation skills (TBAS):** The Air Force uses this format to assess your skill level and assigns a numerical value for evaluation purposes.

- **Any pre-test flight time:** The Air Force actually gives you bonus points for up to 200 hours of flight time you already have. (Flip to Chapter 11 for more on the benefits of taking flying lessons before your aptitude test.)

Other qualifying factors for entry into the Air Force flight training program are

- U.S. citizenship.

- Age: Under 29.1 years old at date of application. If you're close to this age, you face special requirements to ensure you're able to begin flight training before you reach the age cutoff. See an Air Force aviation recruiter for the latest regulation changes.

- Education: Bachelor's degree from an accredited university (can be waived under certain circumstances in the Reserve). No minimum GPA is necessary.

- Medical: Ability to pass a pre-commissioning physical and to pass a class 1 physical upon selection into flight training (an exception is age-critical candidates, who must pass the class 1 physical before their applications are processed to make the age cutoff).

- Vision: 20/70 uncorrected and correctable to 20/20 with normal depth and color perception. You can get a waiver for PRK but not for the Lasik eye procedure.

- Height: 64 to 77 inches standing and 34 to 40 inches sitting.

- Eligibility for security clearance.

Typically, if you attend the Air Force Academy and are medically qualified, you're offered a *flying quota* upon graduation. ROTC fills a majority of the total 1,000 to 1,500 available quotas for initial flight training; OTS candidates fill 10 to 13 percent of the positions each year.

Air Force flight training programs

After you're selected into the Air Force flight training program, you enroll in a commissioning program to earn the rank of Second Lieutenant (unless you've already been commissioned through another source). After you receive your commission, you first report to Pueblo, Colorado, for a six-week initial flight screening program. This training — given by civilian instructors under contract from the Air Force — provides you with an initial 25 hours of flight training and 58 hours of ground training before you advance to the next phase of training (undergraduate flying training program).

Undergraduate pilot training is a three-phase, 58-week program taught in Mississippi, Texas, or Oklahoma. In the first phase, you take academic classes and preflight training. Phase two includes 90 hours of primary flight training, where you're ranked every day. When you complete the second phase, you get to pick an aircraft track for phase three based on your order of merit and the Air Force's specific needs.

You choose from four potential tracks, each of which consists of follow-on training at various locations:

- **Helicopter:** The helicopter track is conducted by the U.S. Army and consists of 115 flight hours over a 28-week period.

- **Multi-engine turboprop:** The multi-engine turboprop track consists of 115 hours of flight training over a 26-week period.

- **Airlift/tanker:** The airlift/tanker track consists of 90 hours of instruction and is 28 weeks long.

- **Fighter/bomber:** The fighter/bomber track is 100 hours of flight training lasting 27 weeks.

After you complete phase three, you select an aircraft based on your order of merit and begin graduate pilot training in that aircraft before getting an operational assignment.

Noting Navy and Marine Corps flight training programs

The U.S. Navy and U.S. Marine Corps maintain separate aviation entities but combine much of their mutual training throughout the entire aviation training process under the umbrella of the U.S. Navy.

Navy aviation mission and aircraft

The naval aviation mission is to protect and support U.S. naval forces and provide a rapid-strike capability worldwide. Naval aviators range from anti-submarine patrols to joint-strike fighters to helicopter search and rescue; their aircraft include fighters, turboprop cargo aircraft capable of carrier based landings, and a large fleet of helicopters (which the Navy calls "helos" rather than "rotary-wing aircraft").

Marine Corps aviation mission and aircraft

The Marine Corps operates both fixed-wing and rotary-wing assets to provide close air support and transport to its ground forces. The six main functions of Marine aviation are anti-aircraft warfare, offensive air support, assault support, electronic warfare, control of aircraft and missiles, and aerial reconnaissance. Corps aircraft range from transport and attack helicopters to joint-strike fighters.

Navy and Marine Corps selection criteria/requirements and demographics

Naval aviation officer candidates come from a variety of commissioning sources: the U.S. Naval Academy, Naval ROTC, and the Naval Officer Candidate School (formerly geared to naval aviators but now organized to train applicants for the entire Navy). As with the Air Force (which we cover earlier in the chapter), a large percentage of aviation slots go to both Naval Academy graduates and ROTC cadets/midshipmen. The approximate percentage of officer candidate school slots for naval aviation runs around 10 to 15 percent a year. Other qualifications to become a naval aviator are

- ✔ U.S. citizenship.

- ✔ Age: 28 upon commissioning.

- ✔ Education: Bachelor's degree from an accredited university.

- ✔ Medical: Ability to pass Class 1 flight physical.

- ✔ Vision: 20/40 uncorrected and correctable to 20/20 with normal depth and color perception. Waivers are available for PRK but not for the Lasik eye procedure.

- ✔ Swimming ability.

- ✔ Eligibility for security clearance.

Naval/Marine flight training programs

After you're accepted into a naval aviation program, the first step is to earn your commission (if you're not already commissioned through another source). This process means officer candidate school — a 12-week program taught by both Marine and Navy instructors at Newport, Rhode Island.

When you receive your commission, you begin your first phase in the path toward becoming a naval aviator: Introductory Flight Screening (IFS). IFS consists of 15 hours of flight training and is taught by contracted civilian instructors at three different locations throughout the country. Next, you attend *aviation preflight indoctrination,* a six-week introductory phase taught at Pensacola, Florida. This program consists of four weeks of academic instruction and two weeks of survival and psychological warfare training.

Finally, you go to one of two locations (Florida or Texas) to begin a six-month primary flight training program. At the end of primary flight training, you're assigned to one of four intermediate flight training paths based on the Navy's needs and your performance and preference. Each path has its continuing training program:

- ✔ **Tailhook:** Aviators selected for *tailhook* training (aircraft equipped to land on an aircraft carrier) report for an additional 27 weeks of training. Of those, approximately 80 percent are selected for advance strike aircraft and spend an additional 23 weeks in flight training before transitioning to specific aircraft.

- ✔ **E2/C2 pipeline:** Those selected for the E2/C2 pipeline receive an additional 8 weeks of training for other carrier-based aircraft and then report for a 16-week multi-engine training program.

- ✔ **Helos:** Those selected for helos report to Naval Air Station (NAS) Whiting in Florida for primary and advanced training in the fundamentals of rotary-wing flight.

- ✔ **Maritime:** Those selected for this path receive initial multi-engine training with the E2/C2 group and then separate for specific training to operate larger, non-carrier-based, multi-engine aircraft.

Upon graduation, the three respective services (the Navy, the Marine Corps, and the Coast Guard, which utilizes naval training facilities) separate for advanced training in both the mission and specific aircraft of their individual branches.

Considering Coast Guard flight training programs

The Coast Guard is the oldest continuous seagoing service in the United States. Aligned under the Department of Homeland Security (rather than the Department of Defense), this branch of the military aviation is a welcome sight to vessels in distress and also serves as a larger shield in the fight against global terrorism. As an old saying goes, when the weather gets too bad for others to fly, that's when the Coast Guard goes out.

Coast Guard aviation mission and aircraft

The U.S. Coast Guard has the mission to protect the public, the environment, and U.S. economic and national interests in the nation's ports and waterways, along the coast, in international waters, and in any maritime region required. The Coast Guard has a fleet of both helicopters and fixed-wing aircraft that it uses to conduct rescue and anti-drug missions.

Coast Guard selection criteria and demographics

The U.S. Coast Guard utilizes naval aviation training facilities to train unrated prospective pilots. Even though the Navy does a majority of the Coast Guard's aviation training, we've placed the Coast Guard in its own separate category simply because of the way it acquires aviators. All Coast Guard aviators are commissioned officers. Flip to the later section "Choosing Your Path to Becoming an Officer" for more on becoming an officer.

A large portion of the Coast Guard's aviators (approximately 60 percent) are actually direct transfers and direct commissions from the other branches of the military, specifically the Army. The Coast Guard doesn't accept pilot applicants for OCS. To transfer to the Coast Guard, you must be 21 to 32 years old, be a rated military aviator with at least 500 hours of military flight time, and have had full-time flying experience within the previous two years. Because of these requirements, many prospective Coast Guard pilots either attend the U.S. Coast Guard Academy or first begin their careers as Army aviators. Many Army aviators who want to become commissioned aviators but don't like the fact Army commissioned officer aviators primarily serve as leaders first and pilots second choose this aviation path.

Coast Guard flight training programs

Aircraft transition and indoctrination into the Coast Guard way of life takes place in Mobile, Alabama, where the Coast Guard aviation center is located. Coast Guard aviators focus much more heavily on instrument flying than Army aviators do, so a specific amount of transition time is spent on this task. All Coast Guard aviators return to this station one week each year to maintain training in their selected aircraft.

Meeting the Other Basic Requirements

The preceding sections cover some of the specific requirements (age, education, and so on) for each branch of the military, but those aren't the only categories the service branches look at. Here are some basic guidelines for military aviation service as a whole.

If you don't meet the requirements (and can't get a waiver) for one branch, make sure you look at the others, which may have completely different sets of requirements.

- **Aptitude:** As the title of this book suggests, all branches give you a flight aptitude test to predict how successful you'll be as an aviator. This aptitude is one of the single most important selection criteria that you can affect, so read on!

- **Moral character:** *Moral character* is basically your legal record; that is, have you broken laws or been arrested for or convicted of a crime? Don't automatically panic if you're remembering a couple of youthful indiscretions; you can get waivers for certain minor infractions (check with your flight recruiter for details).

- **Psychological makeup:** The military is looking for competent, confident team players who can handle the pressures of aviation service under duress, so you take a series of tests and screenings to predict your ability to successfully fulfill the role of a military aviator. Individual military services do give medical waivers for specific minor behavioral health issues.

- **Marital status and dependents:** Although certain commissioning programs have restrictions on marital status, flight training has no such constraints. Certain phases of candidate programs are considered to be *unaccompanied,* so the branch doesn't provide you with accompanied housing, but during the majority of your flight training, you can live with your family.

Choosing Your Path to Becoming an Officer

You may decide that you want your military career path to include becoming an officer. If you come to that conclusion, do some soul searching to determine whether you want to be a pilot first or an officer first. We know that the standard interview answer is to say that you want to be an officer first, but be honest with yourself; some branches' officers don't put in a lot of time in the sky, so if you truly want to be a pilot first, those paths/branches may not be for you. Based on your answer, look at how the different branches utilize both commissioned and warrant officers and what the various mission profiles are to help you make your decision. The best way to discover this information is to get insight from current and former pilots from all branches of the military.

A well-kept secret: National Guard and Reserve aviation opportunities

One of the lesser-known secrets of flying for the military is that you can get started with the National Guard or Reserve. Although getting accepted into one of these units can be a much tougher road, it can be a great opportunity to fly as a military aviator while maintaining your civilian life. You also have the benefit of knowing ahead of time which aircraft you'll be flying.

Coauthor Terry took this route and began his career flying for a National Guard unit. He went first to an Officer Basic course and then to flight school. The day he graduated, he was both working as a civilian commercial pilot and flying as a National Guard aviator during evenings and weekends. Terry was able to get more flight time than his active-duty fellow classmates during the first five years of his flying career. As both a National Guard and Reserve aviator, Terry flew air assault, medical evacuation, and finally attack missions in various rotary-wing aircraft.

Although the structure of the Guard/Reserve program is different from the regular armed services, you can earn a healthy retirement by being a Reserve or National Guard aviator. Each state has at least one Air Force and one Army National Guard aviation facility with the most-modern aircraft in the inventory. Your role as a Reserve or National Guard aviator is to be trained and ready to defend the nation when you're needed. Quite a few pilots serving in the overseas theater are Reserve or National Guard aviators.

If you do decide that life as an officer is for you, officer training is in your future. Here's an overview of each branch's training program, as well as some of the various paths to becoming an officer:

- **Warrant officer training (Army):** Upon selection as an Army Warrant Officer Candidate (WOC), you report to Fort Rucker, Alabama, for a rigorous six-week course.

- **Officer Training School (Air Force):** The Air Force Officer Training School consists of a 12-week indoctrination and training program at Maxwell Air Force Base in Montgomery, Alabama.

- **Officer Candidate School (Navy):** The Navy operates its Officer Candidate School in Newport, Rhode Island. The program consists of a 12-week course that fully integrates future leaders into the lifestyle and responsibilities of a Navy commissioned officer.

- **Officer Candidate School and Platoon Leaders Class (Marine Corps):** Marine officer candidates go through either a ten-week initial officer candidate training program or two separate six-week training sessions over two different summers in Quantico, Virginia. After this training, Marines are commissioned as Second Lieutenants and then attend a six-month *basic school* to expand on their leadership skills before aviation training.

- **Coast Guard paths:** You can follow multiple paths to become a commissioned officer within the U.S. Coast Guard, ranging from the U.S. Coast Guard Academy to Coast Guard Officer Candidate school to direct appointments as a commissioned officer.

- **Military service academies:** The United States has four military service academies in various locations throughout the country. (Why only four? Future Marines attend the U.S. Naval Academy because the Marine Corps is a department of the Navy.) Graduates of the academies receive both a four-year degree and a commission.

- **Direct appointments:** A relatively smaller and lesser-known program is a direct appointment utilized in the Reserve and Coast Guard. This rarely used, needs-directed program fills personnel shortfalls with otherwise-qualified applicants.

Chapter 3

Understanding the Tests at a Glance

In This Chapter
▶ Approaching subject matter on the tests
▶ Digging into the details of branch-specific flight aptitude tests

*T*he various military flight aptitude tests are designed to measure your ability to success-fully understand and complete a military flight training program. Because of the specific needs and priorities of the various military services, the test formats and priorities differ slightly among the branches. In this chapter, we take a look at the various types of questions you can expect to encounter on each of the different flight aptitude tests. We cover language skills and vocabulary, mathematic problems, reading comprehension, science problem solving, and of course aviation-specific test questions. We also provide you with a brief description and breakdown of the various branch-specific flight aptitude tests.

Making Sense of the Major Question Types

All the different types of test questions are really interrelated, so understanding each category can help you master the others. In this section, we cover all the types of questions you can expect on each branch's test.

Verbal, word knowledge, and reading

The verbal, word knowledge, and reading comprehension sections on the flight aptitude tests evaluate your overall mastery of vocabulary and of the basics of the English language, plus your ability to read, analyze, and draw rational conclusions from given materials. The question types vary from test to test, but you can expect word definitions, analogies, and short essays to appear on whichever test you take.

Math and arithmetic reasoning

The mathematical portions of the flight aptitude tests evaluate your ability to analyze and solve problems involving quadratic formulas, geometry, trigonometry, ratios, and algebra. In addition, these questions require you to apply conversion formulas to known values to solve for any unknown values, as well as to calculate area and volume.

Some of the problems can seem daunting, but with practice, mastering the required skills to solve the problems is possible. You can't use a calculator on the actual tests. You may find that some of the practice problems in this book are difficult and are designed to strengthen your understanding of a mathematical or scientific concept; if you need a calculator to solve the practice problem, go ahead and use one. After you understand the problem, immediately go back and try to solve the same problem without a calculator.

General science

Each flight aptitude test expects you to have a basic grasp of biology, chemistry, and physics (covered under the mechanical function section). In addition, you encounter questions on earth sciences, geography, and a variety of other scientific subjects.

Mechanical function and comprehension

This section evaluates your ability to apply basic physics formulas and principles to a variety of problems involving mechanical, waveform, and electrical functions. In addition to forces and mechanical advantage devices, you find questions about the concepts of electrical power, wavelength, and acceleration/velocity.

Aviation and nautical information

What would a flight aptitude test be without a check of your aviation knowledge? This test section covers basic aerodynamics (with a fixed- or rotary-wing focus, depending on the branch) and aviation fundamentals, including any atmospheric properties or conditions that directly affect an aircraft and military aviation in high-speed/high-altitude profiles. These questions test both your knowledge of the basic scientific principles of flight as well as the fundamentals of flying from an aviator's perspective. In addition, the Aviation Selection Test Battery (ASTB) used by the Navy, Marine Corps, and Coast Guard, contains a section on nautical information and seamanship.

To gain a better understanding of basic fixed-wing aerodynamics, we highly recommend *Aerodynamics for Naval Aviators* by Hugh H. Hurt (Skyhorse Publishing), which is available at most pilot supply companies and Amazon.com. For basic rotary-wing aerodynamics, we recommend Army Field Manual FM 3-04.203, *Fundamentals of Flight,* which you can also order from most pilot supply companies.

Instrument comprehension

This portion of the test assesses your ability to infer the aircraft's orientation superimposed on the horizon. This section provides you with graphical representations of two basic aeronautical instruments (a compass and an artificial horizon) that are designed to give you a perceptual view of an aircraft and asks you to identify the correct silhouette of the airframe.

Mental skills

This section of the test includes block counting, rotated blocks, hidden figures, and spatial apperception. All are designed to evaluate your ability to conceptualize complex mental problems and to problem-solve in a 3-D perspective.

Singling Out the Different Service Tests

As we note earlier in the chapter, various branches of the military administer various flight aptitude tests. The Air Force and Army each have their own unique tests, while the Navy, Marine Corps, and Coast Guard all share the same test (and sometimes testing centers). You'll be happy to know that there's no fee to take any of the tests.

Each of these tests is slightly different; some tests focus more in one area than others do. (Check out the earlier section "Making Sense of the Major Question Types" for a look at the kinds of knowledge tested.) We strongly suggest that you familiarize yourself with all the tests and take each one, starting with the branch you're least interested in joining. We discuss this approach in more detail in Chapter 4.

The following sections break down the various branch flight aptitude tests.

The Air Force Officer Qualifying Test (AFOQT)

Today's Air Force has a single test — the Officer Qualifying Test — that covers all officer candidates, regardless of whether they plan to be aviators. The Air Force believes that this one test is the single best predictor of overall success within the various fields of this service branch.

The AFOQT takes about three and a half hours to complete, which accounts for pre-test instruction and a break. Calculators aren't permitted. Here's a breakdown of the testing time:

Subtest	# of items	Time
1. Verbal Analogies (VA)	25	8 minutes
2. Arithmetic Reasoning (AR)	25	29 minutes
3. Word Knowledge (WK)	25	5 minutes
4. Math Knowledge (MK)	25	22 minutes
10-minute break		
5. Instrument Comprehension (IC)	20	6 minutes
6. Block Counting (BC)	20	3 minutes
7. Table Reading (TR)	40	7 minutes
8. Aviation Information (AI)	20	8 minutes
9. General Science (GS)	20	10 minutes
10. Rotated Blocks (RB)	15	13 minutes
11. Hidden Figures (HF)	15	8 minutes
12. Self-Description Inventory (SDI)	220	40 minutes

The following categories show how the Air Force combines your scores into five specific composite scores. (**Note:** Various sections are weighted differently according to a secret formula, so you can't find your composite score by just adding up the number of correct answers for each section.)

- **Pilot (AR + MK + IC + TR + AI):** This score predicts your success in the aviation field by measuring how your knowledge and abilities stack up to those the Air Force feels you need for successful pilot training. The components of this score measure mathematical ability, aeronautical knowledge, spatial relation of the aircraft to its systems and instruments, and perceptual speed. Pilot candidates must score at least 25 for this composite; if you're a navigator candidate, you need to score at least 10.

- **Navigator-technical (VA + AR + MK + BC + TR + GS):** This grouping measures the abilities that Air Force navigator training requires. This score doesn't focus on aeronautical knowledge and spatial orientation. Pilot candidates need a minimum score of 10 for this composite; navigator candidates need a minimum score of 25.

✔ **Academic aptitude (VA + AR + WK + MK):** This score looks at verbal and quantitative knowledge — important aspects of your military officer career. Good news: You don't need a particular minimum score for this composite.

✔ **Verbal (VA + WK):** This composite measures verbal knowledge and abilities. The combined subtest determines your ability to reason, understand synonyms, and recognize relationships between words. All candidates must have a minimum score of 15.

✔ **Quantitative (AR + MK):** This grouping measures your math-related abilities and knowledge. All candidates must achieve a minimum score of 10.

You receive a score for each of these five areas, but you don't get a total combined score. For pilot and navigator candidates, just reaching the minimum composite scores isn't enough; they also need a combined pilot and navigator-technical score of at least 50. However, you can perform marginally on one section (as long as you don't go below the minimum) and make up the points in another, higher-scoring section. All commissioning sources determine how high these scores must be for the test-taker to be selected.

Selection Instrument for Flight Training (SIFT)

This new test, developed by the U.S. Army and implemented in 2013, was designed to predict whether you can successfully complete the Army's Initial Entry Rotary Wing Aviator course and become an Army Aviator. The SIFT test doesn't allow you to use a calculator. The test includes seven sections with varying numbers of questions — the first section has 100 questions, but others have fewer and two don't have a fixed number. (This setup is possible because the test is computer based.) These seven sections take a total of two to three hours to complete. The seven sections — with the individual breakdown of their allotted times — are listed here:

Subtest	*# of items*	*Time*
1. Simple Drawings (SD)	100	2 minutes
2. Hidden Figures (HF)	50	5 minutes
3. Army Aviation Information Test (AAIT)	40	30 minutes
4. Spatial Apperception Test (SAT)	25	10 minutes
5. Reading Comprehension Test (RCT)	20	30 minutes
6. Math Skills Test (MST)	varies	40 minutes
7. Mechanical Comprehension Test (MCT)	varies	15 minutes

Here are a few important points to keep in mind about the subtests:

✔ The first section, Simple Drawings, is designed to be virtually impossible to complete in the allotted time, so don't get discouraged if you can't complete all the questions. The simple drawings are very basic, and developing speed is the important thing here. This speed is facilitated by the computer-based nature of the test; when you select an answer, you're automatically and quickly advanced to the next question.

✔ The second subtest, Hidden Figures, challenges you by giving you drawings in which you must find hidden figures. Finding these figures can be an acquired skill, so use the practice test in Chapter 18 to build your skills.

✔ The third section, Army Aviation Information Test, covers your knowledge of Army-specific aspects of aviation, such as helicopter knowledge. Read and have an understanding of basic helicopter principles as outlined in the Army Field Manual (FM)

3-04.203 *(Fundamentals of Flight).* If you have a chance, we highly recommend that you speak to someone who can at least show you how helicopter controls work while on the ground (either at your local airport or at a National Guard unit). If you explain that you're taking the test for Army flight school, most helicopter aviators will be happy to assist you.

✔ The fourth subtest, Spatial Apperception Test, evaluates your conceptual ability to think about and project aircraft movements in a three-dimensional space. Some answers may look slightly off based on your assumption of what the aircraft profile should be, so select your best guess or the answer that best matches what's in your head.

✔ The fifth section tests your reading comprehension. Divide the time allotted for this test by the number of sections and then try to allocate that amount of time to each section. *Tip:* Briefly read the questions in each section first and then read the passage; that way, you know what information to focus on as you read.

✔ The sixth section, Math Skills Test, evaluates your ability to solve basic math and algebra-type problems without a calculator. Some questions may seem hard, but if you relax, remember some basic conversions and formulas, and apply proper problem-solving techniques, you can solve these problems. The number of questions varies in this and the next section, so go as quickly as you can while taking care not to make careless errors.

✔ The seventh section, Mechanical Comprehension Test, deals with mechanical functions. These questions let you apply your basic physics and mechanical understanding, your conceptual knowledge, and your ability to solve problems by applying scientific formulas. As with the previous subtest, the actual number of questions varies with each test. Be aware of your time allowed for completion and go as quickly as you can without making careless errors.

After you pass the SIFT, you can't take it again to improve your score, so do your best the first time around. If you don't pass it on your first attempt, you can retake the exam once, no earlier than the 181st day following the first attempt. For example, if you fail your first attempt on January 1, you can't retake the test until July 1. If you fail a second time, that's it; you can't retake the test again.

Aviation Selection Test Battery (ASTB)

The current ASTB (formally known as the Navy/Marine Corps/Coast Guard Aviation Selection Test Battery) comes in three versions. Each test contains different questions but has the same six-subtest format and takes approximately two and a half hours (including administrative time) to complete. Calculators aren't permitted. The six subtests are as follows:

Subtest	*# of items*	*Time*
1. Math Skills Test (MST)	30	25 minutes
2. Reading Skills Test (RST)	27	25 minutes
3. Mechanical Comprehension Test (MCT)	30	15 minutes
4. Spatial Apperception Test (SAT)	25	10 minutes
5. Aviation and Nautical Information Test (ANIT)	30	15 minutes
6. Aviation Supplemental Test (AST)	34	25 minutes

The Aviation Selection Test Battery is generally administered in a standard paper format; however, a limited number of testing locations offer a web-based test called APEX (short for *Automated Pilot Examination*). Depending on where you take the ASTB, you may or may not take the APEX version of the test.

You can take the ASTB only three times (once on each version). In order to retake the test, you must wait until the 31st day following your first try; you can take your third and final attempt following the 91st day after the initial test. For example, if you take your first test on June 1, you can try again on July 2. To make a third attempt, you have to wait until August 31. Any test taken outside these restrictions (say you take test three on the 90th day after the first test, or you retake a version you've already taken) is considered an illegal test; an illegal test counts against your three-test lifetime limit but doesn't count as a scorable test.

Chapter 4

Tackling Test Prep and Test-Taking Strategies

In This Chapter

▶ Preparing in the weeks leading up to the test

▶ Getting ready on the day of the test

▶ Conquering multiple-choice tests

*I*n this chapter, we discuss different techniques and strategies you can use to get ready for whichever flight aptitude test(s) you plan to take. The suggestions in this chapter help you slowly but surely work your way up to test day, set yourself up for success on that day, and put your best foot forward on the test itself.

Studying Prior to Test Day

Preparation for and commitment to the task ahead can mean all the difference in your future occupation. When the task is testing into your dream service branch, that means taking a good, objective look at what you know, what you need to brush up on, and how hard you need to work to reach your goal. We can't stress enough that in order to be successful (at the aptitude test and anything else), you must know where you are; know where you want to be; have a plan to get there; and *stick to the plan*. This section gives you some study tips and guidelines to ensure your overall success.

Commit to a study schedule

Getting ready for the military flight aptitude test is a process that requires dedication and determination. You must remain committed to improving the required skills. A proper study schedule is going to eat up a lot, if not most, of your free time; you have to be prepared to resist temptations and distractions as much as possible.

Depending on how far out you are from the planned day of testing, you should commit to test preparation of at least two to three hours per day. If at all possible, start your schedule at least three to six months before your first exam (the more time the better) and plan to schedule at least a month between each branch service test you intend to take. Continue evaluating your progress and adjust your study time as necessary if you aren't improving as quickly as you want/need to.

Focus on your weakest skills

When studying for your flight aptitude test, you must first identify your strengths and weaknesses. Be honest with yourself: What do you need to work on the most to increase your test score? After you identify the weak areas, tailor a long-term study plan or goal that hits those weak areas hard.

You may be tempted to focus mainly on the areas that you enjoy most (which are likely the areas you're best at). But devoting all your time to those fun areas probably isn't going to improve their scores much, and it certainly doesn't do your weak scores any good. Resist this temptation and concentrate on the areas you're weakest in.

Apply the 2/3-to-1/3 rule: Spend two-thirds of your time on weak areas and one-third of your time shoring up strong areas. If you have poor vocabulary skills, read and use flashcards for two-thirds of your work sessions. Struggle with math? Carve out most of your study time for math review.

Practice taking tests

Practice tests are a great way to both improve your knowledge and practice the test-taking strategies we cover later in the chapter. We recommend that you take selected portions of the practice tests in Part IV (everything but the self-description-type sections that have no correct answers) in an informal setting at the beginning of your test preparation to determine your exact strong and weak areas. Approximately two-thirds of the way through your study program, begin taking the practice exams (one per sitting) in a formalized setting. Start with the branch you least want to join and work up to your highest-priority test; doing so helps you work out the kinks in your test-taking experience so that you're as sharp as possible for the most important exam. Pretend you're taking the real test; try to find an unfamiliar setting without the possibility of distractions and use the same mental approach as you would for the real deal.

The tests differ slightly from one another and put different emphasis on different subjects, but they all test concepts you need to be familiar with and are all a great way to practice for the real test.

Score your practice test and then informally review the questions you answered incorrectly, spending time boning up on those topics. A few days later, retake the questions you answered incorrectly to cement this information into your long-term memory. Now you can do additional review and set a time to take the next practice test.

Another great strategy to improve your actual test score is to plan on taking all the branch services tests you can. (Some branches may not let you take the test if you're disqualified — for, say, being too old — from joining that branch.) Start with the branch you're least interested in joining/least likely to join and work your way up to your preferred branch. This approach has two advantages:

✓ **Combating test jitters:** Taking the less-desired tests first gives you real-world experience and a sense of the level of anxiety you'll encounter when taking the test you most want to do well on. Sitting in a room with other motivated applicants with a proctor watching serves as excellent training and prepares you far more than any test practice session you may do by yourself.

✔ **Setting the stage for Plan B (or C):** If you put all your eggs in one test's basket, you run the risk of delaying your dream if that particular branch doesn't accept you. Taking all the tests as part of your test prep gives you a head start on pursuing secondary options instead of forcing you to gear up for more studying and testing after your initial disappointment. Hope for the best, but plan for the worst!

For example, if you've decided your priorities are Marine Corps/Navy first, Air Force second, and Army/Coast Guard helicopter program third and you know you meet all the eligibility requirements, you'd take the Army's Selection Instrument for Flight Training, the Air Force Officer Qualifying Test, and the Navy/Marine Corps/Coast Guard Aviation Selection Test Battery in that order so that you give yourself a backup for all three branches and use the lower-priority tests as run-throughs for the one that matters most.

Getting Ready for Test Day

Bright eyed and bushy tailed. We don't know where that term comes from (probably something to do with squirrels), but we do know it's how you must arrive at the test site. Be ready!

This section covers proper rest, nutrition, and schedule management in the weeks and days leading up to the test. We really feel that attending to these areas can boost your test score significantly (maybe by 10 percent). That isn't a scientific percentage, just our estimate. By taking care of these variables, you can show up to the test site mentally ready to kick butt!

Arriving well rested

We can't stress enough how important being well rested for your test is. The best technique for preparing yourself to rest up for the test is to start adjusting your body at least two weeks ahead of time to the schedule you'll need to adhere to on test day. If you feel that you must get up at 0500 hours to avoid having to rush to the test site, spend the two weeks leading up to that day getting up at 0500 hours and going to bed no later than 2200 hours. (That's 5 a.m. and 10 p.m., respectively, if you're a little rusty on your military time.) Of course, this schedule is just an arbitrary example, but it's a good one to use. The bottom line is to get the normal amount of sleep your body is used to.

Another component to getting enough rest is considering the effects of late-evening caffeine or alcohol. Both interfere with your sleep patterns (even if you don't notice it), so slowly back off your intake of both during your schedule adjustment period to get your body used to a good night's rest. Finally, keep in mind that the body encounters a natural rhythm in which most people get drowsy at 1400 hours (2 p.m.). If you're taking a test that will last into this time, be aware of that tendency.

Rescheduling if necessary

Make sure you're ready for the exam before you take it. If you aren't feeling up to taking the exam on your scheduled day, don't hesitate to reschedule! You're better off to wait and make sure you're on your game for the exam than to muff it. Be aware, though, that rescheduling more than once reduces the likelihood that the application staff will be willing to accommodate any additional changes in schedule.

If you must reschedule an exam, do it as early as possible. Although not taking the test may be better than taking the test while coping with an unexpected sickness or personal tragedy, you must let your aviation recruiter know so that he or she can reschedule you as soon as possible.

Dressing in layers

Have you ever been too hot or too cold and unable to do anything about it? Both conditions are miserable, and you don't want to be in that state of mind when taking a test that can determine the course of the rest of your life; that's enough pressure as it is. Dress in layers that you can easily remove or add as the test environment changes.

Specifically, bring a sweater or light jacket with you. If you end up not needing it, great; if you find yourself cold, having the extra layer available will be a huge relief.

Fueling up before the test

Although you don't want to go into the exam on an empty stomach, you shouldn't just mindlessly grab whatever's handy while you do some last minute studying. When preparing your test-day breakfast (most if not all tests start in the morning), don't consume tons of carbohydrates, especially the simple carbohydrates found in such foods as sugary cereal, maple syrup, and sweet tea. Simple carbohydrates can cause a mental rush followed by a crash — not exactly helpful in inspiring your best performance on the test. Enjoy a balanced meal with an emphasis on proteins (eggs, sausage, bacon, and so on) to maximize your mental alertness.

As unsavory as mentioning this info in a section on eating may seem, we'd be remiss if we didn't remind you to monitor your bowel patterns and habits. To minimize your chances of intestinal distress, don't eat foods that you know you're sensitive to within three days of your test date. Keep your bowel patterns as regular as possible on the day of the test.

Go easy on the caffeine

Although we recommend watching your caffeine intake to help your sleep patterns in the weeks before your exam (see "Arriving well rested" earlier in the chapter), go ahead and drink caffeine on the day of the test if you like. A small-to-moderate amount of caffeine will increase your alertness and perhaps even your performance on the test. And if you typically have a cup or two of coffee or a soda with breakfast, continuing this routine will help calm your nerves. But moderation is the key here (isn't it always?). If you usually drink no caffeine or a lot of caffeine, changing that tendency on test day may lead you to become agitated and lose the ability to focus. Caffeine junkies who stop just for the test may actually experience a withdrawal-type headache. Our recommendation is that you stick with what your body is used to. Just don't overdo it!

Hydrate, but don't overhydrate

Staying hydrated enables you to process mental information quickly and correctly. Of course, drinking large amounts of fluids can result in an excessive number of trips to the restroom, and you can't exactly escape whenever nature calls during the test; bathroom breaks are scheduled. Few things are worse than looking at the clock, fidgeting in anticipation of using the bathroom when you should be focusing on the test.

Arriving early

A common mistake that a lot of people make is planning on arriving at the test site as they would any event, where being fashionably late if they're running behind is often no big deal. But showing up right at the wire or even late for your aptitude test is a bad idea, so plan accordingly. One of the worst things you can do is cut your schedule close and then end up stuck in traffic. That move can make the difference between a nice, leisurely drive where you arrive fresh and ready to go and a frustrating drive where you arrive frazzled and mentally incapacitated.

Map out the route to the test site and make a practice run (preferably at the same time of day) to get a feel for the route, the traffic, and the time required to get there. One option to help ensure you get there in plenty of time on test day is to have a light-to-medium-sized breakfast at a restaurant close to the test site. (Just be sure to follow our pre-test meal guidelines in the earlier section "Fueling up before the test.")

Packing for test day

What do you bring with you? Although some locations don't allow you to carry a bag with you, we suggest you plan to pack a light duffel or book bag with a sweater/jacket, some light snacks full of complex carbohydrates (such as an energy bar or fruit), a bottle of water, and if you're a coffee drinker, perhaps a small thermos of coffee. In winter, you may want to consider bringing a change of shoes so you don't have to take the test in soggy snow boots.

Mastering Multiple-Choice Questions

Being successful in multiple-choice tests requires a combination of core knowledge on the subject, confidence, and mastery of the various tricks of the multiple-choice trade. Just knowing how to think when it comes to multiple-choice questions can vastly improve your test scores. Now, we aren't saying that you don't have to know your material. You do! What we *are* saying is that by knowing your material and applying a few simple strategies we show you here, you'll improve your chances at a higher score. ***Note:*** A lot of these tips apply to any test you take in any format. More for your money!

Reading (and understanding) the directions

Most people are both apprehensive and excited when they get in front of the actual test. These emotions, and the chemical responses that result, often cause them to misread or misunderstand the test's directions. For example, some vocabulary questions ask you to choose the one word in a group that doesn't fit with the others. A common mistake many quick-acting test-takers make is to mark an answer choice with the nearly identical meaning.

To combat this effect, sit down, take a deep breath, and make sure that you clearly understand what the test is asking you to understand and to do. If you have a question about the directions, ask the proctor (although the proctors have specific guidelines about what information they can give you that may or may not allow them to answer your question).

A few more important points to note about the directions:

- **The time limit:** You don't want to be a constant clock-watcher, but you do want to stay on top of how much time you have so that you manage your time accordingly.

- **The number of questions:** Divide the allotted time by the number of questions to give yourself a rough idea of how long you can devote to each question. Of course, this number is an average; some questions are more difficult than others and will take longer to solve. One trick for managing your time well is to do spot checks at each quarter of the test to determine how you're tracking; if you've answered approximately the right number of questions for that time period, you're on pace. If you haven't, adjust your time spent on each question accordingly.

- **The extra materials allowed/required:** Some tests let you use scratch paper, so make sure you have some handy if necessary. *Tip:* Use said scratch paper to write down hard-to-remember formulas at the beginning of the test. That way, they're at your fingertips and less likely to slip through the cracks if you get jittery.

Start with the easier questions

Because all questions in each test section count the same, you don't want to spend so much time on one difficult question that you miss the opportunity to answer five other questions. (Time management strikes again!) When you encounter a difficult or time-consuming question, set that question aside and answer questions that are easier or that require less time to complete. You can then go back and tackle the hardest ones and allocate your time accordingly.

Coauthor Terry recalls skipping an easy problem on a physics midterm because he knew he had it in the bag and focusing on the remaining problems first. Well, time flew by, and the next thing Terry knew, the proctor was saying, "ten minutes." Suddenly, Terry had to scramble to complete the "surefire" problem as much as possible. Don't make the same mistake!

Maximize guesses with the process of elimination

Invariably, you're going to come across a question that you just don't know the answer to, regardless of how hard you've studied. What do you do in this situation: Throw a dart? Punt?

The answer (no pun intended) is to first eliminate those answers you know for a fact can't be correct. Decide how likely you think each remaining answer is to be correct, and then pick the one you feel most strongly about. If you're left with two answers that you're evenly split between, consider choosing the longest answer and/or eliminating an answer that includes the term *always* or *never.* These last two criteria aren't hard and fast rules; they're just suggestions for helping you pull the trigger on a final educated guess. These simple techniques can reasonably increase your chances of guessing the right answer from 20 or 25 percent (if you guess without narrowing down the choices at all) to 60 percent (if you can eliminate one or two choices). We like those odds.

Even a 20-percent chance is better than no chance at all, so be sure to mark some answer for every question, even if you can't make an educated guess. The flight aptitude tests don't penalize you for guessing incorrectly, so filling in something always gives you a better chance at earning more points than leaving the question blank does.

Computerized testing: Coming soon to an aptitude test near you?

As of this writing, many branches' flight aptitude tests hadn't changed over to any sort of computerized style of testing. That's right: You still sit in a room with a bunch of other candidates and work on a test booklet, with just two pencils, some scrap paper, a calculator, and an answer sheet. As we note in Chapter 3, however, the new Army SIFT is computer-based, and some sites now offer a computerized Navy Aviation Selection Test Battery through a web-based program called the Automated Pilot Examination, or APEX.

Mark answers carefully

Make sure you mark the correct answer, on the correct section, on the correct form, and that it indeed correlates to the question you're answering on the test. Putting Answer 22 on the spot for Question 23 is an easy mistake, so be sure to double-check your work periodically.

After you find the correct spot for your answer, don't sabotage your correct answer by filling in the oval sloppily. You need to completely fill in the oval ("make your mark heavy and dark," as the test instructions always seem to say) without running outside the lines. The answer sheets are scanned by computers, so a faint mark or one that runs into another answer's oval may register as an incorrect response even if you knew the right answer. These computerized answer scanners usually require the infamous number 2 pencil, which will be provided for you at the test site.

Part II
Sharpening Your Language and Math Skills

The 5th Wave   By Rich Tennant

"Those of you who did well in the math portion of the MFAT, line up in multiples of 3 to form columns which, when divided by 5, would give you a composite number."

In this part . . .

If you want to do well on your military flight aptitude test (and we're sure you do), you need to make sure your language and math skills are up to snuff. In this part, we begin by reviewing and then testing your language skills. And if that wasn't already enough, we review your mathematics skills — and test them, too.

Chapter 5

Brushing Up on Language Skills

- -

In This Chapter

▶ Improving your vocabulary

▶ Getting to the root of prefixes and suffixes

▶ Understanding synonyms and antonyms and working with analogies

▶ Reviewing noun and verb basics

▶ Reading passages with an eye toward the test

- -

In this chapter, we discuss ways to improve your word knowledge and vocabulary. We've broken down this chapter in such a way to help you understand the basic concepts and help you form the building blocks you need to be successful on any of the military flight aptitude tests. After you have tackled this chapter, you'll be able to navigate the various language sections of any of the tests and improve your overall score in reading comprehension, vocabulary, and word analogies.

Beefing Up Your Vocabulary

The thought of improving your vocabulary may bring to mind the workbooks and quizzes of your school years, but building an extensive vocabulary doesn't have to be a test. Everyday activities such as reading and playing games can go a long way toward giving you the word bank you need to succeed on the aptitude test. The following sections give you tons of suggestions for taking the sting out of studying for the vocab sections on the test.

Read widely

If you're not much of a reader, start by finding any subject you want to learn more about. People tend to read more when they're reading things they find interesting, so starting with a fun topic makes the process less of a chore.

When looking for reading material on subjects that interest you, choose materials that push the limits of your word knowledge. Try to cover a multitude of topics and materials related to the subject you find most interesting.

For example, if you're interested in flight, read aviation scientific manuals, aviation-based suspense novels, biographical novels about past aviators, physics books dealing with flight, and books on the general history of flight. If you like comedy, start reading some of the ancient comedies, Shakespeare's comedies (you may have to adjust to the antiquated language a bit), and early American folk humor. Reading your way to a better vocabulary isn't an overnight proposition, but if you read a decent amount every day, you'll soon notice an expansion of your knowledge. (Bonus: Developing a love for reading can help you deal with the stresses — and often the boredom — of your chosen occupation.)

If you can't stomach the thought of sitting down for structured "reading time," you can still improve your vocab simply by indulging in your curiosity. Spend half an hour or so every day exploring new subjects or mysteries that you have wondered about. Or just jump on the Internet and start letting your mind and mouse wander.

Look for contextual clues

Contextual clues are a great way to decipher the meanings of words you run across by looking for indicators in the rest of the passage. Consider the following example:

> So you've committed to the onerous task of improving your vocabulary. It's a difficult process, but you can find many clues to help you understand the meanings of unfamiliar words.

Did you know what *onerous* meant when you first read it? If not, did you figure out what it meant while reading the rest of the paragraph? The second sentence gives you a pretty good contextual clue when it also calls improving your vocabulary "difficult."

Look it up

As you read, or even as you're just going about your day-to-day activities, make a point to look up any unknown words you encounter. This step is critical to achieving a great score on vocabulary test. Don't accept not knowing the meaning of certain words. Hopefully, you'll set a high goal; depending on your current vocabulary, a reasonable goal may be to look up at least 50 words per day. We particularly recommend adding at least ten Latin-based words to the list each day. Trust us; if you know Latin, you *will* have a good vocabulary.

Keep a running list of the words you need to look up for the day. Whenever you see a word you don't understand, copy it down in a notebook, on your phone or computer, or whatever else is handy. Then, before you go to bed each night, make it your last task to look up all those unknown words. The next morning, reread your word list from the previous day and add any words you still can't easily identify to that day's list.

Check out vocabulary builders and word games

You can find many computer aids specifically designed to increase your vocabulary and word knowledge. Use them! They're a remarkably effective and entertaining way to increase your skills and improve your score on the vocabulary section of whatever branch test you take.

Another fun way to improve your skill level is to play word games such as Scrabble, Hangman, or Words With Friends. These games give you the opportunity to develop new words and actually help you transfer knowledge from short-term to long-term memory, which ultimately is what you're striving for.

Listen for unfamiliar words, too

Meeting new people and listening to what they say is a great way to improve your skills and your conceptual understanding of unfamiliar subjects. Seek out people who have the knowledge you want, or do a search for university or other lectures online. We highly recommend the TED videos (www.ted.com), which cover a wide variety of different topics and often use lots of words that *we* aren't familiar with. Listen closely and then follow up on what you didn't quite grasp by looking up more information.

Study! Study! Study!

As we note in Chapter 4, studying for the aptitude test means making and sticking to a plan. That chapter discusses preparing for the test as a whole, but the vocabulary portions in particular require some dedicated studying. The following sections provide some tried-and-true tricks of the trade when it comes to studying and improving your vocabulary.

Make and use flashcards

Flashcards are a great way to test and improve your vocabulary skills, whether you buy them off the shelf or make your own. The added benefit of homemade flashcards is that the act of writing the information down tends to help cement the knowledge in your long-term memory. Follow these steps to create and use your own flashcards:

1. **Place the word(s) on the front with definitions on the back.**

2. **Review all the cards, both front and back, and go through the set several times.**

3. **Test yourself, sorting the cards into piles based on whether you answered correctly or incorrectly.**

4. **Review the "incorrect" pile and retest.**

5. **Repeat Steps 3 and 4 until you have all cards in the "correct" pile.**

Follow the 45-minutes-a-day plan

At a minimum, plan to spend 45 minutes a day on your vocabulary skills. We recommend this time include reading from a variety of materials (and recording words to look up later) and working with flashcards or some other vocabulary helper.

Use it or lose it

The title of this section says it all. Looking up a word once and then forgetting about it isn't helpful in the long term. Repeat the words and meanings you've looked up until you fully understand and have transferred the specific knowledge to your long-term memory. (Flashcards can help with this task; we cover those earlier in the chapter.) Try to work your new words into conversation so that you become familiar with them in context. Coauthor Terry still spends approximately 15 minutes a day increasing his vocabulary. He found it that useful in preparing to become a military aviator — and in navigating life.

Stick to the program

Okay, you have a good plan; now you just have to stick to it! Don't be distracted or let anything keep you from your goal. Think of vocabulary building as a ten-mile race; you're at the eight-mile mark. You may be exhausted, but dig in and keep up a steady pace, and you'll be at the finish line in no time. If you trip and fall, so to speak, just pick yourself up, dust yourself off, and continue with the plan. Going off the plan for one or two days won't hurt you, but one or two days can easily turn into one or two weeks. Don't let that happen to you. Stick to the program, and don't give up!

Inferring Meaning from Roots, Prefixes, and Suffixes

The *root* of a word is the stem or basic meaning of the word. Prefixes and suffixes added to the beginning or end of the word (respectively) further shape the root's meaning. Understanding various roots, prefixes, and suffixes gives you a unique and helpful insight into the meanings of unfamiliar words.

Consider the word *illegal*. The prefix *il-* means "not"; therefore, *illegal* means "not legal." The following list provides some common examples of roots, prefixes, and suffixes. The prefixes are followed by hyphens; the suffixes start with hyphens. If you don't see a hyphen, the entry is a root. This list isn't all-inclusive, so continue to search out different lists and examples to improve your vocabulary.

ab-: away from	brevi-: short	deca-: ten
-able: capable	bronchi-: windpipe	deci-: tenth
acro-: height, top, beginning	cap-: take, seize	demi-: half
ad-: toward	capi-, capit-: hair, head	demo-: people
albu-: white	cardi-: heart	derm, dermat-: skin
alveol-: cavity	carn-: flesh	di-, diplo-, dicho-: double, two
angio-: vessel, case, closed	cata-: down	dia-: through
anthro-, anthropo-: human	-centesis: puncture, tap	dic-: speak, say
anti-: against	cereb-, cerebro-: brain	dis-: apart, bad
aqua: water	chemo-: by chemicals	dys-: bad, painful
arthro-: joint	circum-: around	e-: out of
-ary: relating to	com-: with, together	eco-, oeco-: house
audi-, audio-: hear	con-: with, together	encephalo-: brain
auto-: self	contra-: against, opposite	endo-: within
bene-: good	corpor-, corpus: body	epi-: upon, beside
bi-, bis-: double, twice, two	crypto-: hidden	equ, equi-: equal
bio-: life	cysto-, cyst-: bag	ex-: out of
brachi-: arm	cyt-, cyto-, -cyte: cell	-fer: bring, carry, bear
brady-: slow	de-: down, away	flex-: bend
		flu-, flux: flow

foli-: plant

for-: before

-form-: shaped like

-fuge-: expelling

ganglio-: knot

gastro-: stomach

geo-: earth

gen-, -gen, -genesis: to produce; born

germ: seed

graph: writing, printing

gyn-: female

helic-: a spiral

hem-, hemat-: blood

hemi-: half

hepat-: liver

histo-: tissue

homo-: similar, man

hydro-: water, hydrogen

hyper-: above, excessive

hypo-: under, below

-ian-: belonging to

il-: not

im-, in-, into: inside

immuno-: safe

infra-: below

intra-: within

inter-: between

-ion-: action or condition

-ism: condition, doctrine

iso-: equal

-ite-: like, similar to

-itis-: inflamed condition

-ity-: state of being

-ize-: combine with

junct-: near

kilo-: 1,000

later-: side

liga-: bind

loco-, loca-: place

-logy: study of

macro-: big, large

magna-: large

mal-: bad, evil

-mania: madness

mega-: large

-ment: action

meso-: middle

meta-: beyond

micro-: small

mono-: one

morph: form

mort-: death

myo-: muscle

narco-: stupor, numbness

naso-: nose

neo-: new

neph-, nephro-: kidney

neuro-: nerve

neutro-: neither

nitro-: nitrogen

nocti-: night

nomo-, -nomy: name

non-: not

noto-: back

ob-: against

oculo-: eye

-oid, -ous, -ode: like, resembling

oligo-: few

olfact-: smell

omni-: all

ortho-: straight

-osis: disease, condition

os-, osteo-: bone

-ostomy, -otomy: to make an opening into

-ous: full of; similar to

ovi-, ova-: egg

paleo-: ancient

palpit-: flutter

pan-: all

para-: beside, beyond, against

par-, paro, -parous: to bear, to bring forth

-path, patho-: disease, suffer

ped-: foot, child

per-: by, with

perfora-: bore through

peri-: around

phago-, -phage: eat

-phas: speak

pheno-: appear

-phil: attraction to, love

phleb, phlebo-: vein

-phobia: fear

phone: sound

-phore: carry, bearer

photo-: light

phre-: diaphragm or mind

plas-, -plasia, plasm: form, grow

-plasty: repair, reconstruction

pluri-: many

pne-, pneu-: breath

pneumo-: lung, air

pod-, podi-: foot

poly-: many

-pore, poro-: passage

post-: after, behind

potent: powerful

pre-, pro-: before, in front of, forward

proto-: first

pseudo-: false

psych-: mind

-pter, pter-: wing

-ptosis: fall, drop

pulmo-: lung

pyo-: pus

pyro-: fire

quad-, quadri-: four

radio-: wheel, ray

re-: back, again

ren-: kidneys

retro-: backward, located behind

-rhea: discharge

rhin-, rhino-: nose

rhizo-: root

sacchar-: sugar

salta-: leap

sapiens: thinking

schiz-: split

sclero-: hard

scolio-: twisted

-scope: to examine; to show

sect-: cut

semen, semin: seed

semi-: half

-simi-: an ape

soma-, somato-, -some: body

soph: wisdom, knowledge

-spasm: to cramp, to convulse

speci-: type

sperm, spermato-: seed

spiro-, spira-: breathe

spleno-: spleen

-stasis, -stat, stato-: standing, stoppage, balance

steno-: narrow

stimul: tease, touch

-stom-: mouth

sub-: less than, below

super-, supra-: above or excessive

sym-, syn-: similar, with

taxo-: arrangement

tele-, telo-: end

ten: to hold fast

tetra-: four

therap-: treatment

-therm, thermo-: heat

thorac-: chest

thrombo-: a clot

-tion: process of

-tom, -tomy: cutting

topo-: place

toxi: poison

trans-: across, through, beyond

tri-: three

tropo-, -trope, -trophy: nutrition, growth, turning

tympan: drum

ultra-: beyond, excess

un-: not, back

uni-: one

ur-: earliest

vacu-: empty

vario: change

vas, vaso-: vessel, duct, vein

ven-: vein

ventr-: stomach

vermi: worm

vert-: to change or turn

vestigi-: trace

viru: slime, ooze

virul-: poisonous

vis-, vid-: see

viv, vivi-: living

-vore, -vorous: eat

vort-, -volv: to change or turn

xantho-: yellow

xero-: dry

zoo-: animal

zygo-: united or yolk

zyme: ferment, leaven

Searching for Synonyms, Antonyms, and Homonyms

This section will most likely be one of the most helpful language aids in this chapter. By improving your ability to recognize words with similar or opposite meanings, you gain skill and confidence in an important area of the exam.

Differentiating between synonyms and antonyms is important because the aptitude test often uses antonyms as incorrect answer choices on word knowledge questions that ask for synonyms, and vice versa.

Synonyms and antonyms

A *synonym* is a word that has the same meaning (or almost the same) as another word. The test you're studying for is difficult, hard, herculean, and arduous. All these words indicate that the task is challenging; they're all synonyms.

Here's an example of what you may see on the test:

Fear most nearly means

(A) Happiness

(B) Excitement

(C) Bravery

(D) Dread

The correct answer here is Choice (D), Dread. Choices (A) and (B) are antonyms of *fear* (see the following section), and Choice (C) doesn't fit either.

An *antonym* is a word that means the opposite (or nearly the opposite) of a word. For example, antonyms of *difficult* may be *simplified, easy, effortless,* and *cushy.* If you know various antonyms, or can recognize what isn't a synonym, you can excel, surpass, exceed, and not falter.

An example of an antonym question you see on the test may be like the following:

Which of the following words does not mean the same as happy?

(A) Blissful

(B) Bright

(C) Wretched

(D) Laughing

The correct answer here is Choice (C), Wretched; all the other choices mean or imply happiness.

If you aren't sure about an answer, rule out what you can and then take your best guess from the remaining choices. Think carefully about the words and look for subtle clues based on roots, prefixes, and suffixes. (Check out the earlier section "Inferring Meaning from Roots, Prefixes, and Suffixes" for more on breaking down word parts.)

Homonyms

A *homonym* is a word that can sound like another word but has a completely different meaning, even though they may be spelled similarly. An example of homonyms includes the words *pear, pair,* and *pare.* All sound alike but have differing meanings. Another example is the word *fair.* This word can mean "free from bias," "a pleasing complexion," or "a carnival or event." Spelled *fare,* it can refer to the amount of money you pay to ride a bus, train, or other form of transportation.

Developing Meaningful Relationships with Analogies

Analogies deal with forming relationships and comparisons between words or groups of words. Analogy questions appear on the military flight aptitude test to assess both your word knowledge and your ability to reason and decipher relationships between words and what their meanings are. If the phrase "_____ is to _____ as . . ." gives you hives, never fear. The following sections show you the two types of analogy questions you can expect on the tests. Practice these types of questions by using the language review test in Chapter 6, the formal practice tests in Part IV, and the many examples you can find online, and you'll be well on your way to success.

Although we use the common "_____ is to _____ as" phrasing in this section, some aptitude tests use colons to separate the analogous items ("_____:_____::"). One colon represents the phrase *is to,* and two colons replace *as.*

Tackling the two types of analogy questions

Analogy questions come in two main flavors:

✔ Three words, you choose one

✔ Two words, you choose the right pair

The following sections explain each type and work you through an example.

Three words, you choose one

In the three-words version, you get the first pair of words and the first word of the second pair. You then select the word from the answer choices that best completes the second pair so that it mirrors the relationship of the first pair. Here's an example:

Flight is to sky as sail is to

(A) Earth

(B) Water

(C) Wave

(D) Wind

The correct answer is Choice (B), Water.

Why not Choice (D), Wind? First, look at the relationship between the first pair: The sky is the substance or thing through which flight takes place. Wind indicates a force causing motion; it relates to sailing, but it doesn't match the relationship closely enough. Water is the substance you sail on. *Note:* This example is simplistic; some of the test questions are quite challenging. Remember to look for clues and choose the one best answer.

Two words, you choose the right pair

In the two-words analogy question, you get the first relationship and have to select the answer that best correlates to that relationship. Here's an example:

Pilot is to aircraft as

(A) Captain is to boat

(B) Engineer is to railroad

(C) Driver is to gas

(D) Priest is to cross

The correct answer is Choice (A), Captain is to boat.

As you can see, the first pairing of words gives you a pilot and the vehicle he or she flies, an aircraft. Choice (A) gives you a similar pair — a captain steers a boat — so that's the correct answer. Choice (B) doesn't work because the engineer rides on the railroad but doesn't actually drive it. Choices (C) and (D) present people and items they use but not items they operate.

Table 5-1 lists common analogy relationships you may see in the language section of the flight aptitude test.

Table 5-1	Common Analogies in the MFAT
Relationship	*Example*
Synonyms	Soft; Fluffy
Antonyms	Soft; Hard
Homonyms	Ball; Bawl
Cause and effect	Shoot; Kill
Early stage and later stage	Bloom; Flower
Raw material versus finished product	Iron; Steel
Beginning versus end	Birth; Death
Larger versus smaller	Teenager; Infant
More versus less	Mega; Micro
Comparative versus superlative	Faster; Fastest
Object versus user	Scalpel; Surgeon
Object versus function	Television; Entertainment
Measurement	Centimeter; Foot
Location	Bagdad; Iraq
Whole versus part	Book; Chapter

Using familiar relationships to your advantage

When trying to figure out analogies, you must draw on your past relationships or experiences to help you sort through the weeds. If you don't recognize a word, try to sort out a part of the word that matches up with part of a word you do know. Often, this critical thinking leads you on the right path and at least helps you eliminate some incorrect answers.

Minding Your Nouns and Verbs

This section touches on a couple of the most basic parts of speech that you need to understand to be successful on this portion of the military flight aptitude tests. We don't intend this section to be a comprehensive review of English. Rather, its goal is to give you a refresher on the ins and outs of nouns and verbs.

Nouns

A *noun* is a word that indicates a person, a place, a thing, an abstract idea, or an animal. A noun in a sentence can function as the subject, a *direct object* or *indirect object* (what the subject is acting on or on behalf of), an appositive (don't worry about what that is), adjective, or adverb. In the following sentence (and all the examples), the bold words are all nouns we're highlighting.

The **inspector** searched the **luggage** for **explosives**.

Nouns are either proper or common. A *proper noun* details a specific person, place, or thing (such as Texas) and always starts with a capital letter. A few examples of proper nouns are organizations, days of the week, months, and institutions:

The scheduled election is **Tuesday** morning.

A *common noun* is a noun referring to a person, place, or thing in a general sense; it starts with a lowercase letter unless some other grammatical rule (such as capitalizing at the beginning of a sentence) indicates otherwise. Here's an example that includes some common nouns:

The **garden** showed many signs that **animals** had been eating the **vegetables.**

The preceding example features the plural nouns *animals* and *vegetables. Plural nouns* adapt to indicate increased numbers. Some nouns become plural by adding *s* or *es* to the end of the word:

I yelled in the valley and listened as the **echoes** carried on.

The **tests** were administered to all **students.**

Other nouns form a plural by changing the last letter of the word and adding *s.* For example, some words ending in *f* delete the *f* and add *ves.* Words ending in *y* drop the *y* and add *ies*:

Leaf. I raked up all the **leaves.**

Pony. They rode their **ponies** in the parade.

A *possessive noun* changes form in such a way to show that the noun owns something else. In most cases, a noun shows a possessive nature by adding an apostrophe and the letter *s.* Singular nouns that already end in *s* still take an apostrophe and another *s.* Here are some examples:

Terry. Aircraft number 364 is **Terry's** Apache.

Simmons. **Simmons's** aircraft is tail number 368.

Verbs

A *verb* asserts something about the subject of the sentence and expresses an action, state of being, or event. Here are some examples with the verbs highlighted in bold:

A rabid dog **bites** the little girl.

I **am** a pilot.

The pilots **completed** their mission.

Some verbs require a direct or indirect object to complete their meaning; these verbs are called *transitive verbs. Intransitive verbs* don't require objects.

Verbs can also be expressed as finite or non-finite. A *finite verb* expresses a state of being or makes an assertion; these verbs can stand alone and serve as the main verb of a sentence.

The bomb **destroyed** the target.

The refugees **were** hungry.

Think of *non-finite verbs* as verbs that can't stand alone as the main verb in a sentence by themselves.

> The **frightened** refugee . . .

> The **deposed** dictator . . .

Non-finite verbs often function as another part of speech; for example, *frightened* in the earlier example acts as an adjective modifying *refugee*. These verbs are often known as *verbal adjectives, verbal nouns,* and so on depending how they're used.

Cruising through Reading Comprehension

Some parts of the flight aptitude test ask you to read a passage and answer questions based on what you read. To do well in this area, you must be able to correctly identify the main points and concepts of a passage and remember details so that you can answer questions and make inferences about the reading.

To help find the main idea of a passage, ask yourself the following questions:

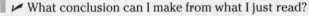

- ✔ What is the paragraph or section about?
- ✔ What specific point is the writer trying to make?
- ✔ What conclusion can I make from what I just read?

Asking these questions before and as you read can help you anticipate what questions the test may ask about the passage.

Look for the key details — such as examples, descriptions, and comparisons — in the reading. These items indicate what the writer felt was important to share with readers.

Chapter 6

Language Skills Practice Test

This chapter tests you on the three basic word knowledge portions you can expect to see on the various military flight aptitude tests. This test is designed to give you both the flavor of what questions you can expect on the different branch tests and the format they appear in.

Use the strategies in Chapter 5 to maximize your score and achieve your full potential.

Analogies

This part of the exam measures your ability to reason and see relationships between words. Choose the answer that best completes the analogy developed at the beginning of each question.

1. SQUARE is to ROUND as

    (A) CAVITY is to MOUND

    (B) HILL is to HOLE

    (C) RECTANGLE is to OBLONG

    (D) ROUND is to POINTED

    (E) HILL is to CONVEX

2. TRESPASS is to ENTER as

    (A) ABANDON is to EXIT

    (B) CONCENTRATE is to FOCUS

    (C) MARVEL is to WONDER

    (D) ROB is to STEAL

    (E) SMELL is to ODOR

3. TREE is to LEAF as

    (A) ROSE is to THORN

    (B) BOOK is to CHAPTER

    (C) PLANT is to FLOWER

    (D) ROOT is to STEM

    (E) SEWER is to LAKE

4. PUPPY is to DOG as

    (A) RODENT is to SKUNK

    (B) BIRD is to BAT

    (C) HAWK is to DOVE

    (D) KITTEN is to CAT

    (E) GOAT is to COW

5. WINCE is to JOY as

    (A) EXPORT is to IMPORT

    (B) MINIMIZE is to SHRINK

    (C) PROLIFERATE is to EXPAND

    (D) SMILE is to SAD

    (E) AIRPORT is to CAB

6. EXPOSURE is to INFECTION as

    (A) SNEEZE is to COUGH

    (B) COUGH is to COLD

    (C) CUT is to BLEED

    (D) FOOD is to EAT

    (E) SKY is to BLUE

7. LORD is to NOBILITY as
   (A) RETIREMENT is to INJURE
   (B) QUEEN is to ROYALTY
   (C) SOUSA is to MUSIC
   (D) BEAT is to DRUM
   (E) UP is to SKY

8. HAND is to FINGER as
   (A) BREAK is to SHATTER
   (B) STRONG is to RAPID
   (C) FOOT is to TOE
   (D) SMELL is to ODOR
   (E) EASE is to DUTY

9. HELIUM is to BALLOON as
   (A) OXYGEN is to AIR
   (B) TRANSPORT is to AIRPLANE
   (C) WING is to AIRPLANE
   (D) GAS is to ENGINE
   (E) SUFFER is to WINTER

10. IMPRISONMENT is to PUNISHMENT as
    (A) TRIAL is to LESSON
    (B) CONFINED is to EDUCATION
    (C) BRIDGE is to ROAD
    (D) FALTER is to GLORY
    (E) HOLD is to CAPTURE

11. SADNESS is to BLUE as
    (A) BANJO is to COUNTRY
    (B) SANCTUARY is to REFUGE
    (C) MUSIC is to HEAR
    (D) GIFT is to REGISTER
    (E) HAPPY is to WARM

12. LOYALTY is to DUTY as
    (A) SACRIFICE is to COUNTRY
    (B) HONOR is to HOPE
    (C) POSSIBLE is to RESULT
    (D) ATTAIN is to HONEST
    (E) FAITHFUL is to COMMITMENT

13. UTENSIL is to CHEF as
    (A) BOOK is to LIBRARY
    (B) WOOD is to AXE
    (C) LIQUID is to SHIP
    (D) WRENCH is to MECHANIC
    (E) SOUP is to BROTH

14. SEW is to CLOTHING as
    (A) SCHOOLING is to RESULT
    (B) READ is to EDUCATION
    (C) MEDICINE is to HARM
    (D) PRISON is to GUARD
    (E) DINOSAUR is to BONE

15. SPITE is to KINDNESS as
    (A) CLAP is to HANDS
    (B) CAVE is to SHIELD
    (C) HURT is to FRIENDLINESS
    (D) AUTHOR is to WRITING
    (E) BOSS is to EMPLOYMENT

16. PLANET is to UNIVERSE as
    (A) PLANT is to FOOD
    (B) RIBOSOME is to CELL
    (C) PACK is to SUITCASE
    (D) IGNORE is to OVERLOOK
    (E) CLIMB is to WALK

17. DOCTOR is to HEALING as
    (A) GUARD is to PRISON
    (B) COACH is to VICTORY
    (C) OFFICER is to TICKET
    (D) COW is to GOAT
    (E) LEARN is to REMEMBER

18. AGREE is to CONSENT as
    (A) GAMUT is to PROVINCIAL
    (B) SOLDIER is to ARMY
    (C) LIBEL is to PRAISE
    (D) REFUSE is to RESIST
    (E) OBLIVIOUS is to KEEN

19. PROMOTION is to ADVANCEMENT as
    (A) MONOTONY is to HOMOGENOUS
    (B) RECOGNITION is to RESULT
    (C) QUIET is to TACIT
    (D) DULL is to SHARPEN
    (E) ATTACH is to SEPARATE

20. TEACHER is to CLASSROOM as
    (A) COOK is to FOOD
    (B) RUSTIC is to CITY
    (C) ISOLATION is to LONELINESS
    (D) SHORTEN is to NIP
    (E) ACTOR is to STAGE

21. NOMADIC is to WANDERING as
    (A) HALLOWED is to SACRED
    (B) PATIENT is to DOCTOR
    (C) GARAGE is to CAR
    (D) SEDENTARY is to IMMOBILE
    (E) METER is to ELECTRIC

22. PUDDLE is to OCEAN as
    (A) CRACK is to DESTROY
    (B) PRIDE is to FALL
    (C) SOUND is to MICROPHONE
    (D) OUTSIDE is to BENCH
    (E) CRUMB is to LOAF

23. PACIFIST is to PEACE as
    (A) CONSTELLATION is to STARS
    (B) AGGRESSIVE is to ANGRY
    (C) MONTH is to YEAR
    (D) INSOMNIAC is to SLEEPLESSNESS
    (E) ANARCHIST is to DISORDER

24. YAWN is to BOREDOM as
    (A) SMILE is to HAPPY
    (B) GOOD is to BEST
    (C) ACCEDE is to RESPECT
    (D) SLOTH is to LAZINESS
    (E) FEATHER is to QUILL

25. BOW is to ARROW as
    (A) CRYPT is to TOMB
    (B) SHEEP is to LAMB
    (C) PIG is to BACON
    (D) CANNON is to BALL
    (E) DOGWOOD is to OAK

26. DOCTOR is to PATIENT as LAWYER is to
    (A) JUDGE
    (B) CLIENT
    (C) COURTROOM
    (D) DISPOSITION
    (E) LAWSUIT

27. FISH is to HOOK as BUTTERFLY is to
    (A) COCCOON
    (B) FLOAT
    (C) FLUTTER
    (D) INSECT
    (E) NET

28. FLY is to FAST as ROWBOAT is to
    (A) SLOW
    (B) WATER
    (C) OAR
    (D) RHYTHM
    (E) MOTOR

29. LION is to TIGER as HUMAN is to
    (A) MAN
    (B) WOMAN
    (C) CIVILIZATION
    (D) APE
    (E) WORK

30. DEER is to FAWN as SHEEP is to
    (A) RAM
    (B) LAMB
    (C) MUTTON
    (D) LAWN
    (E) GOAT

31. KNIT is to SWEATER as RIVET is to
    - (A) FLAME
    - (B) AIRFRAME
    - (C) PILE
    - (D) STEEL
    - (E) GAS

32. FIRE is to HEAT as ICE is to
    - (A) WARM
    - (B) TEPID
    - (C) COOL
    - (D) MILD
    - (E) COLD

33. TYPEWRITER is to LETTER as COMPUTER is to
    - (A) PAPER
    - (B) DOCUMENT
    - (C) NEWS
    - (D) E-MAIL
    - (E) FILE

34. BACKPACK is to TENT as SHOPPING BAG is to
    - (A) SIGHT
    - (B) FEAR
    - (C) DRINK
    - (D) SACK
    - (E) GROCERIES

35. SPEED is to ACCELERATION as BRAKE is to
    - (A) DECELERATION
    - (B) DISTANCE
    - (C) URGENCY
    - (D) THRUST
    - (E) STOP

36. HORSE is to CAVALRY as TANK is to
    - (A) ARMY
    - (B) ARMOR
    - (C) FISH
    - (D) FUEL
    - (E) WATER

37. PAGE is to BOOK as OFFICE is to
    - (A) STORY
    - (B) ROOF
    - (C) BUILDING
    - (D) WING
    - (E) LOBBY

38. DRESS is to GOWN as SUIT is to
    - (A) TUX
    - (B) PANTS
    - (C) SHORTS
    - (D) SHIRT
    - (E) SWEATER

39. WALK is to RUN as SIT is to
    - (A) STAND UP
    - (B) SLEEP
    - (C) GALLOP
    - (D) FALL
    - (E) LAY

40. PARACHUTE is to DESCEND as ROCKET is to
    - (A) LAND
    - (B) ASCEND
    - (C) FALL
    - (D) TRAVEL
    - (E) SPACE

41. WALK is to RUN as DRIVE is to
    - (A) SPEED
    - (B) BRAKE
    - (C) GO
    - (D) STEER
    - (E) GAS

42. BABY is to TODDLER as CHILD is to
    - (A) MONKEY
    - (B) BABY
    - (C) TEEN
    - (D) ADULT
    - (E) LITTLE

43. ORDER is to MAYHEM as NEAT is to
    (A) CLEAN
    (B) STRAIGHTENED
    (C) OBSERVED
    (D) UNTIDY
    (E) FAST

44. ORDER is to DIRECT as INSTRUCT is to
    (A) DUPLICATE
    (B) EDUCATE
    (C) TRANSFER
    (D) LEARN
    (E) KNOWLEDGE

45. SLOTH is to LAZINESS as FAST is to
    (A) SPEED
    (B) ENERGETIC
    (C) SLOPPINESS
    (D) CAREFUL
    (E) UNCARING

46. STUMBLE is to FALL as SKIP is to
    (A) LEAP
    (B) STOMP
    (C) SING
    (D) STOP
    (E) MOVE

47. ROUGH is to TEXTURE as SMOOTH is to
    (A) RANDOM
    (B) GRAB
    (C) HOLD
    (D) SOFT
    (E) FEEL

48. SIGNAL is to STOPLIGHT as RADIO is to
    (A) STRENGTH
    (B) FREQUENCY
    (C) AIRPORT CONTROL TOWER
    (D) WAVE
    (E) TRANSMIT

49. KNIFE is to BLADE as FISHING ROD is to
    (A) FISH
    (B) HOOK
    (C) WATER
    (D) BOAT
    (E) FLEX

50. COMMAND is to OBEY as DIRECTIVE is to
    (A) COMPLY
    (B) ANSWER
    (C) CHALLENGE
    (D) INFORM
    (E) DICTATE

Word Definitions

This section tests your conceptual knowledge and understanding of the use of words in the English language. Select the best answer that means the same as the word given.

51. Challenging
    (A) Demanding
    (B) Dull
    (C) Marked
    (D) Simple
    (E) Surprising

52. Accentuate
    (A) Acquire
    (B) Climb
    (C) Consent
    (D) Emphasize
    (E) Participate

53. Apparent
    (A) Complicated
    (B) Inferior
    (C) Superior
    (D) Evident
    (E) Equal

54. Tepid
    (A) Mental communication
    (B) Marketing goods or services by telephone
    (C) Lukewarm
    (D) Study of climactic variations
    (E) Rashness

55. Adjuvant
    (A) Concise
    (B) Helpful
    (C) Important
    (D) Misleading
    (E) Sweet

56. Proximal
    (A) Away from a center or axis
    (B) Relating to the feet
    (C) Having more than 100 petals
    (D) Toward a center or midline
    (E) Circular

57. Dilapidate
    (A) Criticize
    (B) Conserve
    (C) Erode
    (D) Neutralize
    (E) Retreat

58. Repetitive
    (A) Brilliant
    (B) Held back
    (C) Redundant
    (D) Unruly
    (E) Isolated

59. Affright
    (A) Alarm
    (B) Confirm
    (C) Explain
    (D) Guarantee
    (E) Question

60. Gratify
    (A) Silent
    (B) Sour
    (C) Ornament
    (D) Talkative
    (E) Pleasing

61. Temporary
    (A) Migrant
    (B) Not permanent
    (C) Cure-all
    (D) Schedule
    (E) Character

62. Retrieve
    (A) Forget
    (B) Ignore
    (C) Recover
    (D) Polish
    (E) Snub

63. Egotistical
    (A) Hopeless
    (B) Lazy
    (C) Lenient
    (D) Rude
    (E) Selfish

64. Pity
    (A) Have compassion
    (B) Specious
    (C) Unpredictably changeable
    (D) Metallic
    (E) Contain mercury

65. Malleable

    (A) Flammable

    (B) Fragile

    (C) Pliable

    (D) Rigid

    (E) Separable

66. Irritate

    (A) Predict the outcome

    (B) Cut in two

    (C) Identify a situation

    (D) Antagonize

    (E) Speak about

67. Veto

    (A) Controversy

    (B) Defeat

    (C) Irritation

    (D) Substitution

    (E) Vexation

68. Mayhem

    (A) Dealing with the digestive system

    (B) Havoc

    (C) Get back

    (D) Correct

    (E) Give fresh life to

69. Vex

    (A) Put chronologically out of place

    (B) Curse

    (C) Hit repeatedly

    (D) Attribute conscious thoughts to inanimate objects or animals

    (E) Disturb

70. Discombobulate

    (A) Confuse

    (B) Cooperative

    (C) Energetic

    (D) Helpful

    (E) Respectful

71. Protracted

    (A) Faulty

    (B) Lengthy

    (C) Oral

    (D) Pointed

    (E) Written

72. Elaborate

    (A) Cleared

    (B) Clouded

    (C) Decrease

    (D) Enlarge

    (E) Tightened

73. Calamitous

    (A) Unnoticed

    (B) Insignificant

    (C) Intense

    (D) Hot

    (E) Unfortunate

74. Alacritous

    (A) Relating to the motion of material bodies

    (B) Referring to motion pictures

    (C) Quick and eager

    (D) Relating to a sensory experience

    (E) Referring to a relative

75. Frock

    (A) Angrily silent

    (B) Grayish yellow

    (C) Mildly nauseated

    (D) Soaking wet

    (E) Apparel

Reading Comprehension

This section of the test checks your ability to fully grasp what message written documents are attempting to convey. Read each passage and answer the questions. Remember that incorrect response options may still appear to be true; however, only one answer to each item can be derived solely from the information in the passage.

Raoul Wallenberg

Many people have never heard of Raoul Wallenberg, one of the bravest and noblest people to ever walk the Earth.

Wallenberg was born in Lidingo, Sweden, in 1912 and received his degree from the University of Michigan in 1935. He was a businessman and later became a Swedish diplomat assigned as the special envoy to Hungary during the German invasion of that country in World War II. In March of 1944, the Nazi regime initiated a massive effort to deport the Hungarian Jews to the concentration camp Auschwitz-Birkenau. Wallenberg decided to take a personal stand by aiding any Jews he could through various means. As a senior diplomat, he began to issue provisional passes for Jews and convinced the Germans those with passes were considered Swedish citizens and exempt from deportation. Wallenberg's office often resorted to bribery and extortion threats, and his unusual efforts saved an estimated 30,000 Jews.

On January 17, 1945, the Soviet army entered the city of Budapest. They found Wallenberg and, despite his assertion that he was under protection of the Swedish flag, took him prisoner. He was never seen in public again; it was later reported that he died of a heart attack in the Lubyanka prison in Moscow, but sightings of him were reported for many years after. Today, Raoul Wallenberg has been honored many times; the nation of Israel designated him as one of the Righteous among the Nations.

76. What nation did Raoul Wallenberg represent?

(A) The United States of America

(B) Sweden

(C) Hungary

(D) Italy

77. Raoul Wallenberg was educated in America and received his degree from

(A) Bregetta College

(B) Georgetown University

(C) The University of Michigan

(D) The Ohio State University

78. Raoul Wallenberg saved an estimated _____ Jews

(A) 30,000

(B) 10,000

(C) 20,000

(D) 8,000

79. Raoul Wallenberg saved Jewish lives by issuing people

(A) Diplomatic passports

(B) Housing and sanctuary

(C) Swedish driver's licenses

(D) Provisional passes considering them citizens of Sweden

80. Raoul Wallenberg

(A) Continued on as a Swedish diplomat after World War II

(B) Was captured by the Soviets during the siege of Budapest in 1945

(C) Became a successful businessman following the war

(D) Was released from prison in 1947

Early Female Aviators

Early aviators were mostly male, but a few brave female aviators were destined to break into flying history. Balloon flights in the late 1700s and early 1800s featured an estimated 20 female aeronauts, the first of whom was Elisabeth Thible, who flew over the French countryside. In the early 1900s, another French aviator, Elise Deroche, became the world's first licensed female aviator. The first American woman to fly solo was Blanche Scott, who was hired by the Curtis Aircraft Company in order to demonstrate the safety of its aircraft from 1910 to 1916. Another female aviator, Bessie Coleman, was denied entry into a U.S. flight school because of her race, so she received her license from a French flying school and then returned to the United States to open a flight school in 1921. Other notable early aviators were Harriet Quimby (who was ejected from her aircraft and killed before the days of safety belts), Ruth Law (who tried to gain entry into combat aviation in World War I), and Amelia Earhart. During World War II, the Soviet Union employed many female aviators, with Lydia Litvyak scoring 12 aerial victories before being shot down and killed.

81. How many female aeronauts were there in the early 1800s?

   (A) Approximately 10

   (B) Approximately 20

   (C) Approximately 30

   (D) Approximately 40

82. Who was the first American woman to fly solo?

   (A) Harriet Quimby

   (B) Ruth Law

   (C) Amelia Earhart

   (D) Blanche Scott

83. In what year did Bessie Coleman return to the United States to begin a flight school?

   (A) 1919

   (B) 1920

   (C) 1921

   (D) 1922

84. Which female aviator attempted to gain a combat flying role in World War I?

   (A) Bessie Coleman

   (B) Harriet Quimby

   (C) Ruth Law

   (D) Amelia Earhart

85. How many air victories did the highest-ranking female ace have in World War II?

   (A) 12

   (B) 14

   (C) 15

   (D) 18

Mackinac Island

Mackinac Island is an island in Lake Huron between Michigan's Upper and Lower Peninsulas. The island was a Native American settlement first visited by French Canadians in 1634, with a mission established in 1670. Because of the mission in the Straits of Mackinac and the value of fur trading, the location's importance grew, and the British built Fort Mackinac on the bluffs overlooking Lake Huron shortly after the French and Indian War.

The fort, important in protecting the area from hostile native tribes, didn't see any military action during the American Revolution, and the fledging United States acquired the entire area through the treaty of Paris in 1783. During the War of 1812, the British launched a surprise attack from St. Joseph Island in Ontario (with help from Canada) and captured the unsuspecting fort; the Americans weren't aware that war had been declared at the time. In a second battle, the Americans failed to recapture the island, and they didn't regain possession of it until 1815.

Mackinac Island is currently a popular tourist resort, with a majority of the island belonging to the Michigan state park system. The island is 3.8 miles long and has approximately 500 year-round residents. During the summer, ferries, along with an active port, bring as many as 15,000 tourists a day. The fort overlooking the straits still exists and, along with the Grand Hotel, serves to capture an era gone by. With the exception of emergency vehicles, no motorized vehicles are allowed on the island; travel is by foot, bicycle, or horse-drawn carriage. An eight-mile road follows the perimeter and is the only U.S. highway that does not allow motorized vehicles.

86. How many battles did the fort on Mackinac Island participate in during the American Revolution?

    (A) 0

    (B) 1

    (C) 2

    (D) 3

87. Where did the group who launched a surprise attack on Fort Mackinac depart from?

    (A) The Upper Peninsula of Michigan

    (B) The Lower Peninsula of Michigan

    (C) St. Joseph Island in Ontario

    (D) Fort George in Niagara, Ontario

88. Which of the following isn't a method of transportation on the island?

    (A) Automobile

    (B) Bicycle

    (C) Walking

    (D) Horse-drawn carriage

89. Who first built the fort on the island?

    (A) The French

    (B) Native Americans

    (C) American colonists

    (D) The British

90. Which of the following isn't a true statement?

    (A) The fort was built after the French and Indian War.

    (B) The Americans recaptured the fort during a battle in the War of 1812.

    (C) The island was the location for two battles during the War of 1812.

    (D) Except for emergency vehicles, no motorized form of transport is allowed on the island.

The Legend of Sleeping Bear

The Ojibwa tribe has a tale about a mother's love and the formation of the Sleeping Bear dunes along the western shore of Michigan and two Manitou islands. As the story goes, a mother bear and her two cubs lived on the shores of Wisconsin. Wisconsin suffered from a great famine, and the bear and her cubs looked longingly over Lake Michigan toward the western Michigan shoreline. Eventually, their fear of the long swim was overcome by hunger and the prospect of living in the land of plenty. The bears swam and swam, the mother followed by her two cubs. As they neared the western Michigan shoreline, a forest fire obscured the shoreline, and the cubs lost their way. Twelve miles from shore, the mother turned around to see that one cub had dropped out of sight; just two miles closer to shore, she lost sight of the second cub. The exhausted mother bear made it to the shore alone and mourned for her lost cubs, lying on the sandy shore and looking over the water for the cubs she knew had perished. The great god Manitou took pity on the mother bear; while she was watching over the waters of Lake Michigan, two islands slowly arose, marking the spots where each of her cubs disappeared. Manitou then marked the spot to honor the faithful mother by forming a solitary dune along the shoreline where she waited for the cubs that would never join her.

91. Why did the bear and her two cubs leave Wisconsin?

(A) Adventure

(B) Forest fire

(C) Famine

(D) To escape hunters

92. This legend is from which Native American tribe?

(A) Huron

(B) Chippewa

(C) Ottawa

(D) Ojibwa

93. Where were the mother bear and cubs attempting to go?

(A) Gitchegumee

(B) Wisconsin

(C) Michigan

(D) Canada

94. How far from shore did the first cub vanish?

(A) 2 miles

(B) 12 miles

(C) 10 miles

(D) 12 kilometers

95. Which god, seeing the mother's love, raised two islands and then created sand dunes to honor the bears?

(A) Manitou

(B) Ypsilanti

(C) Potawatomi

(D) Hiawatha

The Wreck of the Edmund Fitzgerald

One of the most famous of all Great Lakes shipwrecks is the *Edmund Fitzgerald*. Many legends and one famous song have commemorated the demise of the ship and the entire 29-man crew one stormy November night in 1975.

The *Edmund Fitzgerald*, 729 feet long, departed the port of Superior, Wisconsin, with approximately 26,000 tons of iron ore bound for Detroit, Michigan, on November 9, 1975. At 7:00 p.m. that same day, the National Weather Service issued a gale warning for Lake Superior; that forecast was later upgraded to a storm warning. The captain of the *Fitzgerald* consulted with the captain of a ship traveling the same route; they decided to change the route by hugging north, closer to the coast of Canada, to protect them from large waves formed along the open body of water. On the afternoon of the 10th, the *Fitzgerald* contacted the *Anderson* and reported "a fence rail down, two vents lost, and a list." The *Anderson* reported that waves were 12 to 16 feet high and the winds were steady at 43 knots.

Later in the afternoon, the *Fitzgerald* made contact with another ship, the *Avafor*, and reported that the *Fitzgerald* had a bad list, had lost both radars, and was taking heavy seas over the deck in one of the worst seas the captain had ever been in. At 7:10 p.m., the *Anderson* made contact with the *Fitzgerald* and had her on its radar. The *Fitzgerald* was 17 miles from Whitefish Point when the captain replied, "We are holding our own." The *Fitzgerald* disappeared from radar contact shortly afterward and was lost at sea with all souls on-board. Shipwreck expeditions in 1989, 1994, and 1995 showed evidence that no attempts were made to abandon the ship and that the sinking must have come suddenly, with no distress signals issued. On July 4, 1995, the ship's bell was removed from the *Edmund Fitzgerald;* it's now on display at the Great Lakes Shipwreck Museum on Whitefish Point, Michigan.

96. How many men were lost at sea on the *Edmund Fitzgerald?*

    (A) 24

    (B) 31

    (C) 27

    (D) 29

97. Which port did the *Edmund Fitzgerald* depart from on November 9, 1975?

    (A) Thunder Bay, Ontario

    (B) Superior, Wisconsin

    (C) Milwaukee, Wisconsin

    (D) Sault Sainte Marie, Ontario

98. The last statement from the *Edmund Fitzgerald* was

    (A) "We are holding our own."

    (B) "We are listing to the port side."

    (C) "How long till the Coast Guard arrives?"

    (D) "Mayday!"

99. The ship disappeared how far from Whitefish Point?

    (A) 13 miles

    (B) 17 miles

    (C) 17 kilometers

    (D) 13 kilometers

100. The ship's brass bell now sits at the

    (A) Coast Guard Academy

    (B) *Edmund Fitzgerald* museum

    (C) Great Lakes Shipwreck Museum

    (D) Home of the late captain's family members

Answer Key

1. C	26. B	51. A	76. B
2. A	27. E	52. D	77. C
3. D	28. A	53. D	78. A
4. D	29. D	54. C	79. D
5. D	30. B	55. B	80. B
6. B	31. B	56. D	81. B
7. B	32. C	57. C	82. D
8. C	33. D	58. C	83. C
9. C	34. E	59. A	84. C
10. B	35. A	60. E	85. A
11. E	36. B	61. B	86. A
12. E	37. C	62. C	87. C
13. D	38. A	63. E	88. A
14. B	39. E	64. A	89. D
15. C	40. B	65. C	90. B
16. B	41. A	66. D	91. C
17. B	42. C	67. B	92. D
18. D	43. D	68. B	93. C
19. B	44. B	69. E	94. B
20. E	45. B	70. A	95. A
21. D	46. A	71. B	96. D
22. E	47. E	72. D	97. B
23. E	48. C	73. E	98. A
24. A	49. B	74. C	99. B
25. D	50. A	75. E	100. C

Chapter 7

Getting a Handle on Mathematics Review

• •

In This Chapter

▶ Reviewing your mathematical skills

▶ Reacquainting yourself with algebra and geometry

▶ Remembering basic statistics principles

• •

All branches place a high emphasis on a potential aviator's mathematical abilities. From making ballistic calculations to figuring out weapons loading and configurations to knowing how much fuel you need to safely complete the mission, math skills and knowledge are key to helping you perform in a synchronized, effective fashion with your aviation cohorts.

In this chapter, we provide you with an in-depth review and summary of the mathematical knowledge you need to be able to successfully navigate the mathematical portion of all the military flight aptitude tests. We cover math operations; conversions; and basic algebra, geometry, and statistics. You don't have to worry about calculus, differential equations, or any other headache-inducing math. This stuff is the easy math, and you'll do fine.

Brushing Up on the Basics

First things first: a quick trip though the most-basic math concepts. If you've got fond memories of your high school math classes, you should be fine here. (And if your memories aren't so warm and fuzzy, we guarantee this round-up will be less traumatic.)

You want to work from a good foundation, and what's more foundational to math than numbers? An *integer* is any positive whole number (such as 16), negative whole number (such as –4), or zero (no example necessary). A *whole number* doesn't include any fractional part. Whole numbers are either prime or composite. A *prime* number is one that can be divided evenly by only itself and by the number 1. Examples of prime numbers include 1, 2, 3, 5, 7, 11, and 13. A *composite* number is one that can be divided evenly by itself, by 1, and by at least one other whole number. Examples of composite numbers are 4, 6, 8, 9, 10, and 12.

The following sections give you the lowdown on ways math utilizes numbers and some considerations you should keep in mind as you tackle the math questions your flight aptitude test throws your way.

Maintaining order in your operations

When you add, subtract, multiply, or divide numbers, you are performing a basic *mathematical operation*. What's more, each of these operations has an opposite operation called an *inverse operation*. The inverse operation of addition is subtraction; the inverse of multiplication is division; and so on.

However, when it comes to numbers, inverse doesn't mean opposite. The *opposite* of a positive number is a negative number, but the inverse is its reciprocal. A *reciprocal* is the number that a given number must be multiplied by to get the answer of 1. So the opposite of 4 is –4, but the inverse of 4 is 1/4.

To get the correct answer (a good thing to do, in our humble opinion), you have to perform mathematical operations in a specific order:

1. **Do any calculations in parentheses.**

2. **Calculate any terms with exponents.**

   An *exponent* is a space-saving way to express repeat factors in multiplication. The smaller number written above and to the right of the main number (known as the *base*) is called the *exponent,* and this number indicates the number of times you must multiply the base number times itself. For example, instead of writing 6×6, you write 6^2 (known as "six squared"). This notation comes in handy when a factor repeats several times, such as $6 \times 6 \times 6$ (6^3 or six cubed), $6 \times 6 \times 6 \times 6$ (6^4, six to the fourth [power], or six to the power of four), and so on.

3. **Do any multiplication and division.**

4. **Do any addition and subtraction.**

To help you remember the order of operations, use a handy sentence such as "**P**lease **E**xcuse **M**y **D**ear **A**unt **S**ally" (**p**arentheses, **e**xponents, **m**ultiplication, **d**ivision, **a**ddition, **s**ubtraction).

Now put the order of operations into action with the expression $4 \times (10 + 2) + 2 \times (4 - 6)$. First, do the operations in parentheses to simplify the expression to $4 \times 12 + 2 \times -2$; this expression doesn't contain any exponents, so you can skip that step. Multiply to get $48 - 4$. Finally, a quick subtraction gives you a final answer of 44.

Reinforcing fractions

A *fraction* is a part or portion of a whole number. The fraction 3/4 means that something has been divided into four parts and that you're working with three of those four parts. The top number of the fraction is called the *numerator,* and the bottom number is called the *denominator.* A fraction is an expression of division; therefore, 3/4 is the same as 3 ÷ 4. A fraction is also an expression of a ratio, so 3/4 is the same as the ratio 3 to 4 or 3:4. The following sections show you how to do basic fractional math.

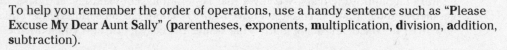

In any operation you do with fractions, you have to make sure your final answer is as simplified as possible — that is, that the numerator and denominator can't both be divided by some *common factor*. For example, both parts of the fraction 6/18 can be divided by 6, so you have to take that step to reduce your answer to 1/3.

Adding and subtracting fractions

To add and subtract fractions, you first have to convert one or more of the fractions so that all the fractions have a *common denominator* — that is, that the denominators are identical. Depending on the fractions, this task may be relatively easy; one of the fractions may have a denominator that can serve as the common factor. Here's how to use that method:

1. **Divide the larger denominator by the smaller denominator.**

   Say you want to add 3/4 and 1/8. Divide 8 by 4 to get 2. *Remember:* You must be able to divide the numbers without any number or portion left over. If the numbers don't divide completely, you can't use this method.

2. **Multiply the fraction with the smaller denominator by the number you got in Step 1.**

   You have to multiply both the numerator and the denominator. In this example, you have 2 × 3/4 = 6/8.

3. **Substitute the new fraction for the initial fraction with the smaller denominator and complete the addition or subtraction.**

   You now have 6/8 + 1/8. Now you just add the numerators and use the same denominators to get 7/8.

But suppose you have to add the fractions 3/4 and 2/3. This situation is a little more challenging because you don't have a readily available common denominator; you have to do a little extra math to find it:

1. **Multiply the two denominators.**

   In this example, it's 4 × 3 = 12.

2. **Convert the fractions to reflect the new denominator.**

   For 3/4, you multiply both the numerator and denominator by 3 (because 4 goes into 12 three times) to get 9/12. For 2/3, you multiply both the numerator and denominator by 4 (because 3 goes into 12 four times) to get 8/12.

3. **Add or subtract the converted fractions.**

   9/12 + 8/12 = 17/12.

   This result is an *improper fraction* (the numerator is bigger than the denominator), so you have to convert that to a *mixed number* by subtracting 12/12 (which equals 1) from the total to get the number 1 5/12.

If you have three or more fractions with different denominators, you have to find a common denominator for all the fractions. The easiest and quickest route in most cases is to multiply the largest denominator by whole numbers until you find a number that the remaining denominators can be divided into.

For example, if you're adding 1/3 + 1/7 + 1/9, you start multiplying the largest denominator (9) by whole numbers. 9 × 2 = 18 . . . nope (the 7 doesn't go into that). 9 × 3 = 27 . . . nope. You have to go all the way to 9 × 7 = 63 to find a number that all three denominators can work with. When you have that number, follow Steps 2 and 3 of the process for adding unlike denominators to find your answer. Converting this example gives you 21/63 + 9/63 + 7/63 = 37/63.

Multiplying and dividing fractions

Multiplying fractions is simply multiplying the numerators and then multiplying the denominators. Multiplying $3/4 \times 2/3$ is simply $(3 \times 2) \div (4 \times 3)$ or $6/12$. Note that 12 isn't the lowest denominator possible, so you have to reduce it to express the fraction in its lowest possible state by dividing by a common factor. In this case, you have a common factor of 6, so you can divide both the numerator and denominator by 6 to get the end product of $1/2$.

Large numbers and lots of steps can take valuable test-taking time; you can make your work a lot easier by cancelling out common factors before multiplying. In the example of $15/32 \times 4/5$, the numerator of the first fraction (15) and the denominator of the second fraction (5) are both divisible by 5. Additionally, the denominator of the first fraction (32) and the numerator of the second fraction (4) are both divisible by 4. You can divide by these common factors to simplify your expression to $3/8 \times 1/1$ to quickly get the final answer of $3/8$ instead of multiplying and then trying to simplify $60/160$. Calculating is a lot simpler when you take this cancelling-out step.

Dividing fractions is really a simple process. With the exception of zero, dividing a fraction is the same as multiplying times the *inverse* or *reciprocal* of that number. To find the inverse of a fraction, simply swap its numerator and denominator. If you want to divide $2/3$ by $3/4$, all you have to do is multiply $2/3$ by the inverse of $3/4$, or $4/3$. $2/3 \div 3/4 = 2/3 \times 4/3$. The answer is $(2 \times 4) \div (3 \times 3) = 8/9$.

Dealing with decimals

You can express a fraction as either a percentage or a decimal. To convert a fraction into a decimal, just divide the numerator by the denominator. For example, $1/4$ is $1 \div 4$ or $.25$. (See the earlier section "Reinforcing fractions" for info on working with fractions.)

Rounding up or down

Sometimes your decimals don't come out as cleanly as $.25$; you may have a decimal that has more decimal places than your calculator can register. In these instances, you round the number to cut off the run of decimal places.

To *round* a decimal, decide which decimal place you want to round to. (The first place to the right of the decimal point is the tenths place; the second is the hundredths; the third is the thousandths; and so on.) Look one place to the right of your desired rounding place; if the number there is lower than five, the number in your rounding place stays the same. If the number to the right of the rounding place is five or higher, the number in your rounding place bumps up to the next higher number.

For the purposes of a military flight aptitude test, you can round extended decimals to the nearest hundredth. For example, $5/9$ is 5 divided by 9 or $0.\overline{5}$. (The bar over the 5 means that number repeats to infinity.) To round it to the hundredths place, you check the third number to the right of the decimal place (thousandths); that number is 5, so you round up to the next number to get 0.56.

Adding and subtracting decimals

Addition and subtraction are easy with decimals. You just have to remember to line up the columns correctly before you start. Align the terms so that the decimal points match up, and you'll be fine.

Multiplying decimals

When multiplying decimals, you multiply as if you're multiplying whole numbers and then adjust the placement of the decimal point based on the total number of decimal places in the factors. For example, to multiply 1.111×1.03, you treat the problem as $1111 \times 103 = 114433$. Next, you add up the number of decimal places in the problem: 1.111 has three decimal places, and 1.03 has two, for a total of five places. Starting at the farthest right decimal place in the answer, you move five places to the left and drop in the decimal point to get 1.14433, which you can round off to 1.14. (See the earlier section "Rounding up or down" for instructions on rounding.)

Dividing decimals

When dividing a decimal by a whole number, you first move the decimal point in the *dividend* (the number you're dividing into) to the right until you have a whole number; perform the division with the whole numbers and then move the decimal place back to the left the same number of spaces you moved it to the right. For example, to divide 0.3 by 2, you move the decimal point in 0.3 one space to the right so that the equation is $3 \div 2 = 1.5$. Then you move the decimal point back the same amount, or one space, to the left to get your final answer of 0.15.

If the decimal is divided by another decimal, you move the decimal point in the *divisor* (the number that is going into the other number) just enough to make it a whole number. Move the decimal point in the dividend the same number of spaces (even if the dividend won't be a whole number) and divide as you normally would. For example, take $.002 \div .08$. First, you move the point out by two decimal places to get $0.2 \div 8$, which is the same as $0.200 \div 8$, or 0.025. (You can add zeros to the right of a decimal point without changing the value of the number.) In this case, you don't have to move the decimal point in the final answer.

Calculating percentages

Percentages are parts of 100, so to make a decimal a percentage, simply multiply the decimal by 100, moving the decimal point two places to the right, and then add a percentage sign. If you need to convert 0.56 to a percentage, you multiply by 100 to get 56 and then add a percentage sign to get 56%.

To add, subtract, multiply, or divide using percentages, convert them to decimals first. Move the decimal point two places to the left, do the assigned calculation, and then move the point back the same number of spaces.

Digging Up Roots and Radicals

As we note earlier in the chapter, a number multiplied by itself results in a number called a *square* (but not because it's unhip). For example, the square of 5, (5×5), is 25. But you can reverse that process to find the *square root*, or the number being squared. The sign for a square root is called the *radical sign* and looks like $\sqrt{}$. For example, $\sqrt{16} = 4$.

Perfect squares are numbers, such as 16, whose square roots are whole numbers. Most square roots are *irrational numbers,* or numbers with decimals that continue on indefinitely. An example of a number with an irrational root is 17, whose square root is 4.123105 . . . . For your aptitude test, round irrational roots to the nearest hundredth.

You can find roots other than the square root — really, the root function can go on and on — but the only other root you should really concern yourself with for a military flight aptitude test is the *cube root,* which is a number multiplied by itself three times to get a cubed number. For example, $\sqrt[3]{27} = 3$ because $3 \times 3 \times 3 = 27$.

Converting Measurements

You should be able to recognize and use scales to convert from miles to kilometers, miles per hour to knots, pounds to kilograms, inches to centimeters, and so on. Here is a basic list of key conversions; you'll use them throughout your career and certainly on your aptitude test.

Distance:

> 1 kilometer = .62 miles
>
> 1 mile = 1.61 kilometer
>
> 1 mile = 0.869 nautical miles
>
> 1 nautical mile = 1.151 miles
>
> 1 inch = 2.54 centimeters
>
> 1 meter = 3.281 feet

Weight:

> 1 kilogram = 2.205 pounds
>
> 1 metric ton = 2,205 pounds
>
> 1 short ton = 2,000 pounds

Volume:

> 1 cubic foot = 7.481 gallons
>
> 1 cubic centimeter = 0.061 cubic inches
>
> 1 cubic meter = 1.308 cubic yards
>
> 1 liter = 1.057 liquid quarts

Getting Up to Speed with Basic Algebra

Algebra is a fun subject in which letters represent variables, and your role is to find out exactly what that variable stands for. The most common algebraic variable is x, which is why you often hear the phrase "solve for x" in reference to unknown quantities. But you can use any variable you like as long as the same variable represents only one quantity throughout a given problem.

Algebra deals in *equations,* or statements that two given quantities are equal. 16 + 17 = 33 is an equation. In algebra, equations include variables that you have to solve for. Here's an example problem: Three fuel tankers, each carrying 2,000 gallons of jet fuel, completely empty their loads to fill up an empty tank. How much fuel total is in the tank?

Let T stand for the fuel in the tank and F stand for the fuel in one tanker. You can use these variables to create an algebra formula of $T = 3F$ for this problem. You know that $F = 2{,}000$ gallons, so you can substitute that into the equation to get $T = 3 \times 2{,}000$ gallons, or $T = 6{,}000$ gallons.

The four arithmetic operations (addition, subtraction, multiplication, and division) are all possible in algebra. You can express each operation through algebra equations as follows:

- ✔ The sum (addition) of two numbers x and y is written as $x + y$.

- ✔ The difference (subtraction) between two numbers x and y is written as $x - y$.

- ✔ The product (multiplication) of two numbers x and y is written as xy or $x \times y$.

- ✔ The quotient (division) of two numbers x and y is written as x/y or $x \div y$.

You can perform any calculation on either side of an equation as long as you do it to both sides of the equation. The following sections show you how to use these operations with algebraic expressions, as well as tackle a few more-complicated topics that may pop up.

Using mathematical operations to solve for x

An *algebraic expression* is a collection of numbers and variables. You can solve simple algebraic expressions by using the basic mathematical operations to isolate the variable. To add or subtract algebraic expressions for this purpose, start by arranging like terms and combining or subtracting them. For example, to solve $x + 27 = 23$, you can simply subtract 27 from both sides to get $x = 23 - 27$ or $x = -4$.

You can add and subtract like terms only. For instance, you can subtract $2x$ from $10x$ to get $8x$, but you can't subtract $2x^2$ from $10x$ because x and x^2 aren't the same term.

When you have a simple formula such as $10x = 50$, you can solve for x by isolating it with division. To do so, you must divide each side by 10 to get $x = 5$. The same goes for multiplication; you can solve $x \div 2 = 8$ by multiplying both sides by 2. Remember that multiplying two positive or two negative numbers creates a positive answer; multiplying one positive and one negative number results in a negative answer.

With any operation, you should always double-check your answer by plugging it in for the variable to ensure that the equation works. If not, check your math.

Examining algebra and exponents

As we note in the earlier section "Maintaining order in your operations," exponents are a way to show that the number is multiplied by itself a certain number of times. The following is a list of rules for working with exponents in algebra:

- ✔ Any base raised to the power of zero (except 0) equals 1: $x^0 = 1$.

- ✔ Any base raised to the power of one equals itself: $x^1 = x$.

- ✔ To multiply items with the same base, add the exponents: $x^2 \times x^3 = x^{2+3} = x^5$.

- ✔ To divide items with the same base, subtract the exponents: $x^6 \div x^2 = x^{6-2} = x^4$.

- ✔ A base raised to a negative exponent is equal to the base's reciprocal (inverse) raised to a positive exponent: $x^{-3} = 1/x^3$.

- ✔ When a product has an exponent, each factor is raised to that power: $(xy)^4 = x^4 \times y^4$.

Queuing up quadratic equations

A *quadratic equation* is an equation that includes the square of a variable. An example of a quadratic equation is $x^2 - x - 6 = 0$. In a quadratic equation, the exponent is never higher than 2 (x^2). You can solve a simple quadratic equation (one that contains just one squared term and a number) by using the *square root rule,* which states that if $x^2 = z$, $x = \pm\sqrt{z}$, as long as z isn't a negative number. To solve a quadratic equation, follow these steps.

1. **Get all the terms onto one side of the equal sign so that the equation is equal to zero.**

   To solve for the example of $x^2 - x = 6$, you subtract 6 from each side of the equation to get $x^2 - x - 6 = 0$. ***Note:*** Make sure you're performing operations (such as subtracting 6 in this example) to switch terms from one side to the other and not just moving them over. Otherwise, you run the risk of forgetting any appropriate sign changes (for example, the fact that the 6 here becomes –6 when you subtract it).

2. ***Factor*** **the equation (break it down into multiplied factors).**

   The key to factoring an equation is to find two factors that provide the equation desired, which sometimes involves some trial and error. In this example, you find that the factors $(x + 2)$ and $(x - 3)$ multiplied together give you $x^2 - x - 6 = 0$.

3. **Set each factor equal to 0 and then solve the resulting equations.**

   For this example, you get $x + 2 = 0$ and $x - 3 = 0$. Therefore, x can equal –2 or 3.

4. **Check the accuracy of your answers by putting the two resulting numbers back into the original equation.**

   First, plug –2 into the equation to get $-2^2 - (-2) - 6 = 0$, or $6 - 6 = 0$. Congratulations; that answer is correct! Next, plug in 3 to get $3^2 - 3 - 6 = 0$, or $9 - 9 = 0$ — another correct answer. You now know both your answers are correct.

Shaping Up with Geometry

Geometry is the area of mathematics concerned with defining the properties of and relationships among shapes, lines, points, angles, and other such objects. A military flight aptitude test may require you to make some kind of geometrical measurement or infer a measurement from other information. The following sections break down the components of geometry and show you how to calculate a few common geometrical quantities.

Looking at lines

A *line* is the distance between two points and can have a definite or indefinite length. In all your test questions, you can assume that the line doesn't have a calculated width. *Perpendicular* lines intersect at a *right angle* (90-degree angle) as shown in Figure 7-1.

Parallel lines (see Figure 7-2) are lines that run along the same plane and always remain the exact same distance from each other; they never cross.

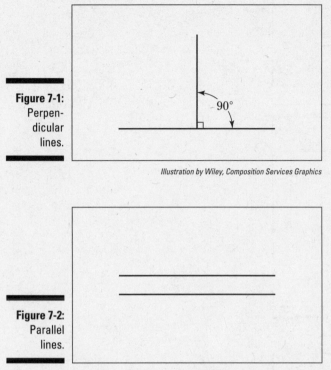

Figure 7-1:
Perpen-
dicular
lines.

90°

Illustration by Wiley, Composition Services Graphics

Figure 7-2:
Parallel
lines.

Illustration by Wiley, Composition Services Graphics

Addressing angles

When two lines converge and meet at a point, they form some sort of *angle.* The point at which the lines meet is called the angle's *vertex.* Angles are measured in degrees; the more degrees, the wider the angle. A few key points to remember about angles include the following:

- A straight line is 180 degrees.
- A right angle is 90 degrees.
- An *acute angle* is more than 0 degrees but less than 90 degrees.
- An *obtuse angle* is more than 90 degrees but less than 180 degrees.
- *Complementary angles* are two angles that equal 90 degrees when added together.
- *Supplementary angles* are two angles that equal 180 degrees when added together.

You can see examples of these angles in Figures 7-3 through 7-8.

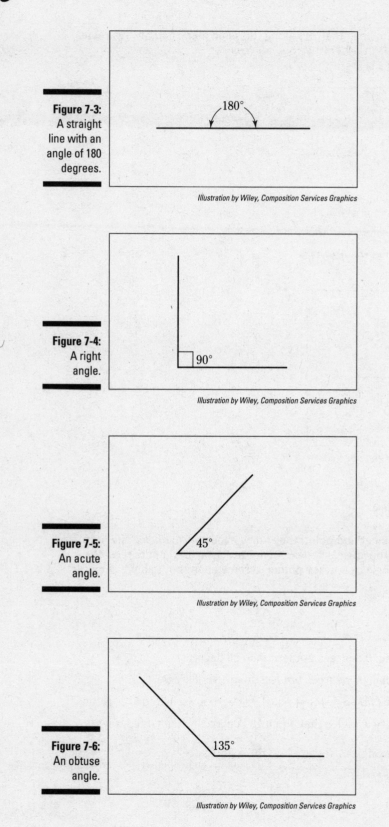

Figure 7-3:
A straight line with an angle of 180 degrees.

Illustration by Wiley, Composition Services Graphics

Figure 7-4:
A right angle.

Illustration by Wiley, Composition Services Graphics

Figure 7-5:
An acute angle.

Illustration by Wiley, Composition Services Graphics

Figure 7-6:
An obtuse angle.

Illustration by Wiley, Composition Services Graphics

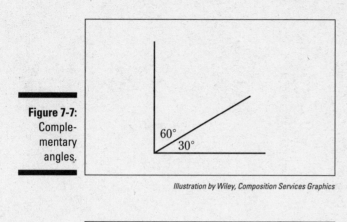

Figure 7-7:
Comple-
mentary
angles.

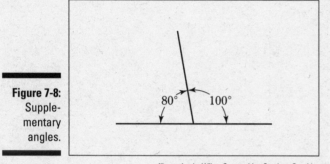

Figure 7-8:
Supple-
mentary
angles.

Exploring the many sides of polygons

A *polygon* is a shape made up three or more lines that are connected to form an enclosed area. A polygon's internal angles add up to 180 degrees. Polygons come in many shapes, but here are some of the most common ones; check them out in Figures 7-9 through 7-14:

- Triangle: Three sides
- Quadrilateral: Four sides
- Pentagon: Five sides
- Hexagon: Six sides
- Octagon: Eight sides
- Decagon: Ten sides

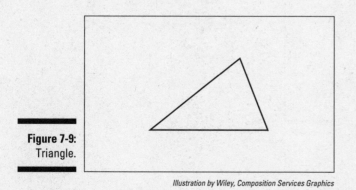

Figure 7-9:
Triangle.

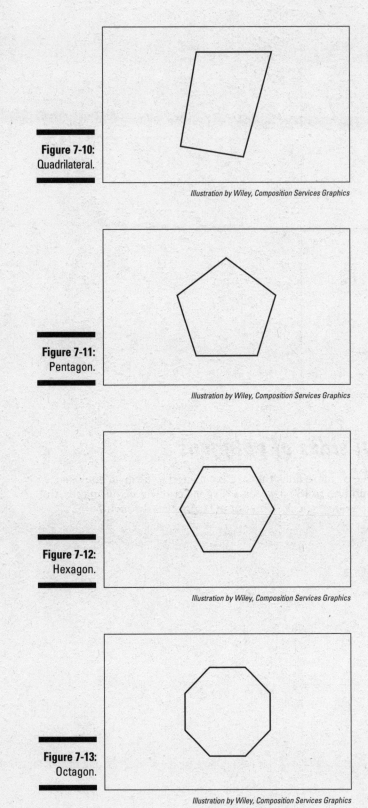

Figure 7-10:
Quadrilateral.

Illustration by Wiley, Composition Services Graphics

Figure 7-11:
Pentagon.

Illustration by Wiley, Composition Services Graphics

Figure 7-12:
Hexagon.

Illustration by Wiley, Composition Services Graphics

Figure 7-13:
Octagon.

Illustration by Wiley, Composition Services Graphics

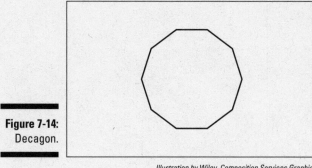

Figure 7-14:
Decagon.

Illustration by Wiley, Composition Services Graphics

Finding your way around triangles

A *triangle* is simply a polygon with only three sides. The total of all the angles of a triangle must add up to 180 degrees. Triangles are the polygon that you most often work with on the flight aptitude test, so get familiar with the various kinds, which you can see in Figures 7-15 through 7-20:

- ✔ **Right triangle:** A *right triangle* has one 90-degree angle; the other two angles are complementary angles.

- ✔ **Isosceles triangle:** An *isosceles triangle* has two equal sides, and the angles opposite the equal sides are equal.

- ✔ **Equilateral triangle:** An *equilateral triangle* has three equal sides, and each angle measures 60 degrees (all add up to 180 degrees).

- ✔ **Obtuse triangle:** An *obtuse triangle* has one angle that measures more than 90 degrees.

- ✔ **Acute triangle:** An *acute triangle* is a triangle where all three angles are less than 90 degrees.

- ✔ **Scalene triangle:** A *scalene triangle* is one in which all three sides and all three angles are unequal.

Note: Some triangles fall into more than one category. For example, the isosceles triangle in Figure 7-16 is also a right triangle.

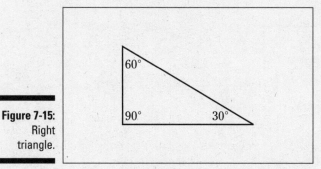

Figure 7-15:
Right
triangle.

Illustration by Wiley, Composition Services Graphics

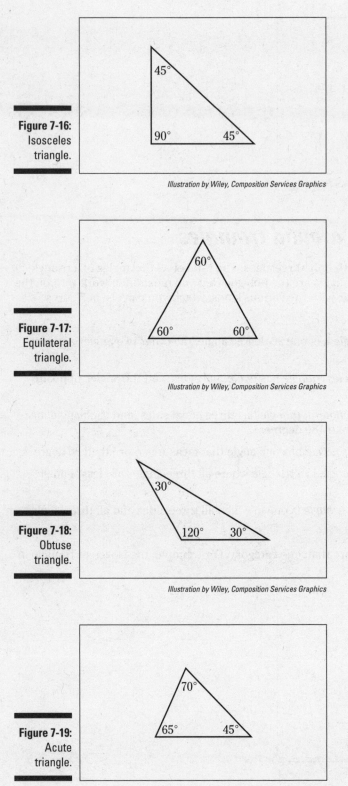

Figure 7-16:
Isosceles
triangle.

Illustration by Wiley, Composition Services Graphics

Figure 7-17:
Equilateral
triangle.

Illustration by Wiley, Composition Services Graphics

Figure 7-18:
Obtuse
triangle.

Illustration by Wiley, Composition Services Graphics

Figure 7-19:
Acute
triangle.

Illustration by Wiley, Composition Services Graphics

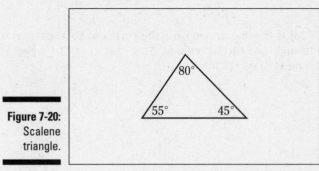

Figure 7-20:
Scalene
triangle.

Considering special triangle relationships

Sometimes, you can find commonalities among triangles. For example, *congruent triangles* (see Figure 7-21) are identical in every way; their sides and angles are identical to each other. *Similar triangles* (shown in Figure 7-22) are triangles with the same shape but different sizes. The angle measurements are the same; the sides are proportional but not the same lengths.

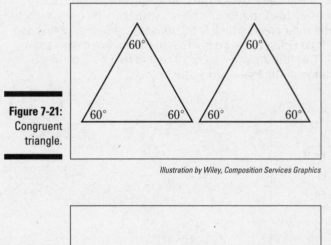

Figure 7-21:
Congruent
triangle.

Figure 7-22:
Similar
triangles.

Making room for medians

The *median* of a triangle (see Figure 7-23) is the line drawn from the vertex of an angle to the midpoint of the opposite side. Every triangle has three medians. Note that in any triangle, the three lines containing the medians meet in one point.

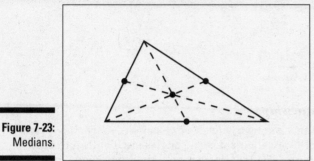

Figure 7-23:
Medians.

Illustration by Wiley, Composition Services Graphics

Grasping the basics of the Pythagorean theorem

The *Pythagorean theorem* states that if you know two of the side lengths of a right triangle, you can figure out the third side by using the formula $a^2 + b^2 = c^2$, with the side c always being the *hypotenuse* (the side opposite the right angle, which is the longest side). If $a = 2$ feet and $b = 3$ feet, $a^2 = 4$ feet and $b^2 = 9$ feet. If you plug those numbers into the theorem, you know that 4 feet plus 9 feet = c^2, or $c^2 = 13$. Take the square root of 13 to find that $c = 3.61$ feet. Figure 7-24 gives you a basic illustration of the Pythagorean theorem.

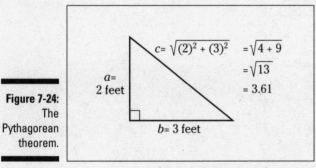

Figure 7-24:
The
Pythagorean
theorem.

Illustration by Wiley, Composition Services Graphics

Getting around to circles

A *circle* is an enclosed line curving in such a fashion that all the points are equidistant from the center. Circles are divided into 360 degrees. Remember these basic aspects of circles:

- ✔ **Diameter:** The *diameter* of the circle is a line from one point on the outer circumference passing through the center point of the circle to the opposite end of the circumference. The diameter is represented by line AB in Figure 7-25.

- ✔ **Radius:** The *radius* is a line that extends from the center point in a circle to the outside circumference. The radius is exactly one-half the distance of the diameter. The radius is represented by the line OC in Figure 7-25.

- ✔ **Circumference:** The *circumference* of a circle is the distance around the outside of the circle. It's roughly the circular equivalent of the perimeter of a polygon. (Head to the following section for more info on perimeters and circumferences.)

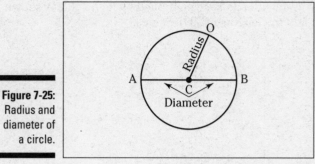

Figure 7-25:
Radius and
diameter of
a circle.

Illustration by Wiley, Composition Services Graphics

Calculating perimeter and area of geometrical shapes

All geometric shapes have a perimeter and an area. The *perimeter* is the sum of the lengths of all the shape's sides, and the *area* is the size of the region the shape encloses. The following sections show you how to figure out these measurements for common shapes.

Squares, rectangles, parallelograms, and triangles

For squares and rectangles, you calculate the area by multiplying length × height ($L \times H$), as shown in Figure 7-26. You get the perimeter by using the formula $2 \times (L + H)$.

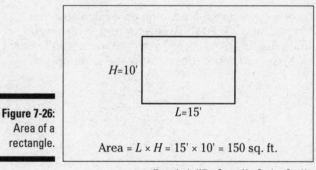

Figure 7-26:
Area of a
rectangle.

Area = $L \times H$ = 15' × 10' = 150 sq. ft.

Illustration by Wiley, Composition Services Graphics

For a parallelogram, you determine the area by multiplying the base by the height, as shown in Figure 7-27. The perimeter calculation is the same as for the square or rectangle.

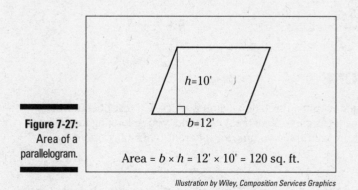

Figure 7-27:
Area of a
parallelogram.

Area = $b \times h$ = 12' × 10' = 120 sq. ft.

Illustration by Wiley, Composition Services Graphics

The area of a triangle is half the measurement of its base multiplied by its height, as shown in Figure 7-28. To find the perimeter, add the lengths of all the sides.

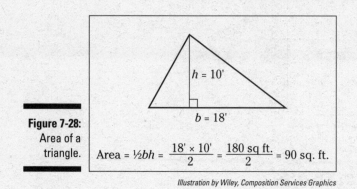

Figure 7-28: Area of a triangle.

Easy as pi: Circles

To find the circumference of a circle, you use the mathematical constant π (the Greek letter pi), which is commonly expressed as 3.14 or simply 22/7. In geometry, π represents the unchanging relationship between the circumference of a circle and its diameter; on most test problems, you can decide which form, the fraction or the decimal, is easier for you to use.

The formula for circumference is $C = \pi d$ or $C = 2\pi r$ (because the diameter is twice the radius). The area of a circle has a relationship to π as well. The area of a circle is the square of the radius, or r^2 times π: $A = \pi r^2$. In Figure 7-29, you can see calculations of both circumference and area of a circle.

Note: Figure 7-29 uses the 22/7 version of π. If you use the π button on a calculator, this answer rounds to 50.27 feet (circumference) and 204.20 square feet (area). Whichever π number you use, be aware of this subtle rounding difference; if your answer doesn't quite match any of the choices on the test, be ready to double check using the other option.

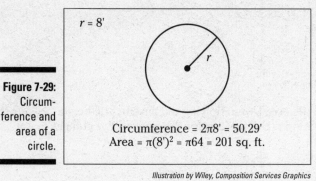

Figure 7-29: Circumference and area of a circle.

Working with volume

Volume is basically what's contained within a three-dimensional space. If a test question asks you how much a container (such as a gas can or fuel tank) can hold, you're looking for volume. The following sections show you how to find the volume for different types of containers.

Cubes and rectangular solids

For any rectangular solid, you find the volume by multiplying length $\times$ width $\times$ height:

$V = lwh$

A *cube* is a rectangle whose length, width, and height are all the same. To find the volume of a cube, you can just take any one of the side measurements to the third power:

$$V = l^3$$

Figures 7-30 and 7-31 show you these formulas in action.

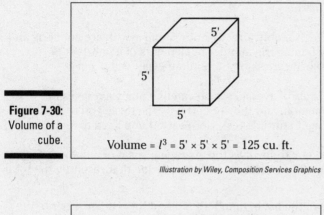

Figure 7-30:
Volume of a cube.

Volume = l^3 = 5' × 5' × 5' = 125 cu. ft.

Illustration by Wiley, Composition Services Graphics

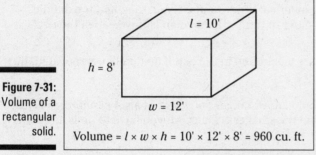

Figure 7-31:
Volume of a rectangular solid.

Volume = $l \times w \times h$ = 10' × 12' × 8' = 960 cu. ft.

Illustration by Wiley, Composition Services Graphics

Cylinders

A *cylinder* is a solid where both the upper and lower bases are circles that lie in parallel planes. All you have to do to find a cylinder's volume is figure the area at the base (see the earlier section "Easy as pi: Circles" for this calculation) and multiply times the base area times the height (see Figure 7-32), which also uses 22/7 for π:

$$V = \pi r^2 h$$

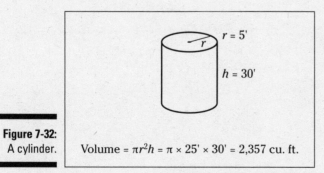

Figure 7-32:
A cylinder.

Volume = $\pi r^2 h$ = π × 25' × 30' = 2,357 cu. ft.

Illustration by Wiley, Composition Services Graphics

Statistics: Focusing on Math That Counts

We've all stood outside the classroom looking at the midterm grades posted on the wall and asking, "What's my score? Did the teacher curve the grades? Did I beat the average?" (If you're anything like the aviation candidates we know, you're highly competitive, so that last one is probably especially true.) These questions are really all about *statistics* (where you draw conclusions based on collected data), and in this section we show you some of the key principles of this branch of math.

A couple of statistics concepts you're probably already quite familiar with are counting and probability. *Counting* is the action of finding the number of elements of a finite set of objects. *Probability* is a measure of the likeliness that a random event will occur.

Mean, median, and mode are three kinds of averages. You can find many averages in statistics, but these three are the most common, and they're certainly the three you're most likely to encounter on any military flight aptitude test. Here's what you need to know:

- The *mean* is what people commonly think of as the average of a set of numbers. To calculate mean, you simply add up all the numbers and then divide that result by the total number of numbers.

- The *median* is the middle value in the list of numbers. To find the median, rewrite the list so that the numbers are in numerical order (a must) and then find the middle number. If you have an even number of terms, the median is the mean of the two middle numbers.

- The *mode* is the value that occurs most often in the list. If no number is repeated, the list has no mode.

One more statistics concept you should know: range. The *range* of a set of numbers is just the difference between the largest and the smallest values. All you have to do is subtract. Pretty easy, right?

Chapter 8

Mathematics Practice Test

*T*his mathematics practice test is pretty straightforward. It covers those math skills you need to successfully navigate this particular subject on the various flight aptitude tests. The mathematics test is a very important section because all military services place a high degree of importance on a potential aviator's math skills.

Choose the most correct answer to each question.

Subtest 1: Whole Numbers and Integers

1. If x is an even integer, which of the following results in an odd integer?

   (A) $2x + 2$

   (B) $2x - 1$

   (C) $x + 2$

   (D) $3 + x + 1$

   (E) None of the above

2. Which of the following is an integer?

   (A) 0.1

   (B) 0.4

   (C) 0

   (D) 2.1

   (E) 2.2

3. An integer is

   (A) Any positive number

   (B) Any negative number

   (C) A fraction

   (D) A positive or negative whole number or zero

   (E) None of the above

Subtest 2: Mathematical Operations

4. An athlete jogs 10 laps around a circular track. If the total distance jogged is 6.2 kilometers, what is the distance around the track?

   (A) 0.25 meters

   (B) 62 meters

   (C) 6.2 meters

   (D) 620 meters

   (E) 0.62 meters

5. $3 + 4 + 2 - 16 =$

   (A) −7

   (B) 7

   (C) 4

   (D) 6.8

   (E) −6

6. 8 − 4 + 6 =
    (A) 5
    (B) −5
    (C) −6
    (D) 7
    (E) 10

7. A gasoline generator has a 5-gallon tank and burns 4 gallons per hour. About how many times must the fuel tank be filled to run the generator from 6:30 p.m. to 7:00 a.m.?
    (A) 10
    (B) 11
    (C) 5
    (D) 6.2
    (E) 12.0

8. 63 maintenance personnel require three meals per day for a training operation overseas expected to last 28 days. An MRE (meal, ready to eat) costs $4.20 per person, and a hot ration costs $6.40 per person. If one meal per day is an MRE, how much must be allocated to fund the food expense?
    (A) $23,428
    (B) $22,564
    (C) $29,988
    (D) $865
    (E) None of the above

9. Suppose the unit in Question 8 deployed with an extra ten personnel with the same meal requirements. How long can they now conduct training with the same amount of meal funding?
    (A) 16 days
    (B) 24 days
    (C) 18 days
    (D) 22 days
    (E) None of the above

10. $2 \times 8 \div 12 =$
    (A) 1.7
    (B) 2.1
    (C) 3
    (D) 1.3
    (E) 4

Subtest 3: Maintaining Order

11. $4(a + b) − 4(a + 3b) =$
    (A) $6a − 10b$
    (B) $6a + 2b$
    (C) $−8b$
    (D) $6a − 8b$
    (E) $6a + 10b$

12. $5(4 − 1) + 2(3 + 2) \div 4 =$
    (A) 17.5
    (B) 17
    (C) 1.75
    (D) 62.5
    (E) 6.25

13. $2(a+b)^2 + 16(2+b)^2 =$
    (A) $2ab + 4ab + 64b + 18b + 64$
    (B) $2a^2 + 4ab^2 + 64 + 18b^2$
    (C) $4ab^2 + 4ab + 64b + 18b + 64$
    (D) $4ab + 2ab + 64 + 16b^2 + 64$
    (E) None of the above

14. $(1+5) \div 4 + 2(2+3)^3 \div 7 =$
    (A) 10
    (B) 12
    (C) 9.8
    (D) 37.21
    (E) 12.3

15. $2(a+b)^2 + 2(a+b)^3 + 2(a+b) =$
    (A) $2a^2 + 4ab + 2b + 2a^2 + 6ab^2 + 2b^2 + 2a$
    (B) $2a^2 + 4ab + 2b^2 + 2a^2 + 6a^2b + 6ab + 2a + 2b$
    (C) $4a^2 + 2ab + 2b^3 + 2a^2 + 6ab^2 + 2b^3 + 2a + 2b$
    (D) $2a + 4ab + 2b + 2a^2 + 6a^2b + 6ab + 2b$
    (E) None of the above

16. $3^2 + 3(2-3)^2 - 12 \div 5^2 =$
    (A) 12.48
    (B) 0.75
    (C) 23/24
    (D) 22/24
    (E) 1.12

Subtest 4: Prime and Composite Numbers

17. Which of the following is the smallest prime number greater than 100?
    (A) 101.5
    (B) 102
    (C) 101
    (D) 104
    (E) 105

18. Which of the following is a composite number?
    (A) 1
    (B) 2
    (C) 3
    (D) 4
    (E) 5

19. Which of the following is a prime number?
    (A) 6
    (B) 7
    (C) 8
    (D) 9
    (E) 10

20. Which of the following is a composite number?
    (A) 5
    (B) 7
    (C) 11
    (D) 13
    (E) 15

21. Which of the following is a prime number?
    (A) 9
    (B) 10
    (C) 12
    (D) 13
    (E) 15

Subtest 5: Exponents

22. If $4^n = 9$, what is the value of 4^{n+1}?

    (A) 27

    (B) 144

    (C) 45

    (D) 36

    (E) None of the above

23. 100,000 may be represented as

    (A) 10^4

    (B) 10^5

    (C) 10^6

    (D) 10^7

    (E) 10^8

24. $10^x \div 10^y =$

    (A) $10^{\frac{x}{y}}$

    (B) 10^{xy}

    (C) 10^{x+y}

    (D) 10^{x-y}

    (E) None of the above

25. $10^x \times 10^y =$

    (A) $10^{\frac{x}{y}}$

    (B) 10^{xy}

    (C) 10^{x+y}

    (D) 10^{x-y}

    (E) None of the above

26. $4x^6y^3z^2 \div 2x^4y^3z =$

    (A) $2x^2z$

    (B) $4xyz$

    (C) $4x^4y^2z$

    (D) $2x^2y^2z$

    (E) None of the above

Subtest 6: Fractions

27. Sarah donates 4/15 of her paycheck to her favorite charity. If she donates $32.90, what is the amount of her paycheck?

    (A) $125.80

    (B) $123.38

    (C) $187.10

    (D) $131.50

    (E) $198.40

28. A pound of margarine contains four equal sticks of margarine. The wrapper of each stick has markings that indicate how to divide the stick into eight 1-tablespoon sections. If a recipe calls for eight tablespoons of margarine, the amount to use is

    (A) 1/16 pound

    (B) 1/8 pound

    (C) 1/4 pound

    (D) 1/2 pound

    (E) 3/4 pound

29. Fred earns $12.50 an hour plus an overtime rate equal to 1½ times his regular pay for each hour worked above 40 hours per week. What are his total gross earnings for a 50-hour workweek?

    (A) $636.00

    (B) $710.25

    (C) $499.50

    (D) $687.50

    (E) $599.90

30. When you add 200 gallons of oil to an oil tank that is 1/4 full, the tank becomes 1/3 full. The capacity of the oil tank is

    (A) 2,400 gallons

    (B) 2,390 gallons

    (C) 2,430 gallons

    (D) 2,470 gallons

    (E) 1,510 gallons

31. The reciprocal of 9, rounded to the nearest thousandth, is

    (A) 0.143

    (B) 1.428

    (C) 0.111

    (D) 0.112

    (E) 0.11

32. The reciprocal of 7, rounded to the nearest thousandth, is

    (A) 14.28

    (B) 1.428

    (C) 14

    (D) 0.143

    (E) 49

33. The reciprocal of 4 is

    (A) 1/4

    (B) 1/8

    (C) 1/6

    (D) 1/2

    (E) −4

Subtest 7: Dealing with Decimals

34. $0.0024 \times 0.073 =$

    (A) 0.1752

    (B) 0.0001752

    (C) 0.001752

    (D) 0.0021

    (E) None of the above

35. $1.24 \times 0.03 =$

    (A) 0.372

    (B) 3.72

    (C) 3.72×10^{-2}

    (D) 3.72×10^{-3}

    (E) None of the above

36. $0.04 \div 0.035 =$

    (A) 1.14

    (B) 1.28

    (C) 1.33

    (D) 0.875

    (E) None of the above

37. $0.12 \div 0.0003 =$

    (A) 187

    (B) 40.0

    (C) 0.0400

    (D) 400

    (E) None of the above

Subtest 8: Preparing Proportions

38. The ratio of 3x to 5y is 1:2; what is the ratio of x to y?

    (A) 1:2

    (B) 2:3

    (C) 3:4

    (D) 4:5

    (E) 5:6

39. The ratio of 2x to 3y is 2:3; what is the ratio of x to y?

    (A) 2:1

    (B) 1:1

    (C) 3:2

    (D) 4:5

    (E) 2:5

40. The ratio of 4x to 2y is 1:2; what is the ratio of x to y?

    (A) 2:2

    (B) 3:7

    (C) 4:2

    (D) 4:1

    (E) 5:7

Subtest 9: Calculating Percentages

41. During a season, a basketball player attempted 67 shots and completed 57 of them. What is his completion percentage?

    (A) 70.4 percent

    (B) 85.1 percent

    (C) 88.8 percent

    (D) 87.7 percent

    (E) 73.9 percent

42. Jan found a boat for $22,400. However, because the model had been discontinued, the dealer discounted the price to $21,150. What was the percentage of the reduction?

    (A) 6.7 percent

    (B) 6.0 percent

    (C) 5.0 percent

    (D) 6.9 percent

    (E) 5.6 percent

43. After passports were required for travel to Canada, the traffic on the International Bridge declined from 14,680 cars per day to 9,480 cars per day. What was the percentage of the decline in traffic?

    (A) 35.4 percent

    (B) 22.5 percent

    (C) 31.1 percent

    (D) 28.9 percent

    (E) 39.3 percent

44. Thomas earns an average of $24 an hour in tips as a parking lot attendant. If his hourly wage is $3.45 and he has to pay a 25-percent share of his tips to the doorman, how much does he take home at the end of a day when he has worked from 6:30 a.m. to 5:30 p.m.?

    (A) $332.90

    (B) $222.60

    (C) $235.95

    (D) $256.70

    (E) $271.00

45. A jar contains red, green, and yellow marbles. 20 percent of those marbles are either red or green. What are the chances of blindly picking a yellow marble out of the jar?

    (A) 1 out of 3
    (B) 1 out of 5
    (C) 2 out of 3
    (D) 2 out of 5
    (E) 4 out of 5

46. Deck cleaner contains approximately 10 percent bleach and 90 percent water in each gallon (128 ounces). Someone further dilutes the mixture by adding 32 additional ounces of water. What percent of the new solution is bleach?

    (A) 4 percent
    (B) 8 percent
    (C) 9 percent
    (D) 11 percent
    (E) 12 percent

Subtest 10: Roots and Radicals

47. The expression $\sqrt{35} - \sqrt{9}$ reduces to

    (A) 2.92
    (B) 2.76
    (C) 2.88
    (D) 3.14
    (E) 3.08

48. Find the square root of 105 to the nearest tenth.

    (A) 10.1
    (B) 10.2
    (C) 10.3
    (D) 10.4
    (E) 10.5

49. The cube root of 4,096 is equal to the square of

    (A) 16
    (B) 8
    (C) 5
    (D) 4
    (E) 3

50. $\sqrt{8} - \sqrt[3]{8} =$

    (A) 1
    (B) 2
    (C) 0.83
    (D) 0.67
    (E) 80

Subtest 11: Converting Measurements

51. An Army infantry platoon did a 12-mile road march. How many kilometers did it march?

    (A) 23 kilometers
    (B) 18.2 kilometers
    (C) 19.6 kilometers
    (D) 24.7 kilometers
    (E) 19.3 kilometers

52. A small, light-training aircraft flies at 122 miles per hour. How fast does it fly in knots?

    (A) 106 knots
    (B) 110 knots
    (C) 140 knots
    (D) 128 knots
    (E) None of the above

53. A 122 millimeter insurgent rocket is used to attack your forward operating base. What is the diameter of the rocket in inches?

    (A) 4.5 inches

    (B) 4.8 inches

    (C) 5.2 inches

    (D) 4.2 inches

    (E) None of the above

54. A patient is airlifted to the nearest medical center. His wife states that he weighs 180 pounds. The flight medic is giving a drug that calls for a dose of 0.1 milligrams per kilogram. How much of the drug should the medic give the patient?

    (A) 82 milligrams

    (B) 16.4 milligrams

    (C) 8.2 milligrams

    (D) 0.82 milligrams

    (E) None of the above

55. A 450-gallon fuel tank contains how many cubic feet?

    (A) 45 cubic feet

    (B) 50 cubic feet

    (C) 55 cubic feet

    (D) 60 cubic feet

    (E) 65 cubic feet

Subtest 12: Basic Algebra

56. One phone plan charges a $15 monthly fee and $0.07 per minute on every phone call made. Another phone plan charges an $11 monthly fee and $0.12 per minute for every call. At how many minutes will the charge be the same for each phone plan?

    (A) 60 minutes

    (B) 80 minutes

    (C) 75 minutes

    (D) 95 minutes

    (E) 25 minutes

57. An older, "deuce and a half" vehicle can carry 2.5 tons of cargo, while an over-the-road hauler can carry 6 tons of cargo. If an equal number of both vehicles is used to ship 221 tons of cargo and each truck carries its maximum cargo load, how many tons of cargo are shipped on the 2.5-ton trucks?

    (A) 65 tons

    (B) 60 tons

    (C) 75 tons

    (D) 100 tons

    (E) 120 tons

58. A large auditorium for a USO show contains x rows with y seats in each row. 50 seats are reserved for officers of the division staff. How many total seats are left for all the other service members who want to see the show?

    (A) $(x + y) - 50$

    (B) $x - y$

    (C) $(xy) - 50$

    (D) $y - x$

    (E) $2x + y + 50$

59. Solve for z: $4z - 4 + 3z = 22 - 6z$

    (A) $z = 1$

    (B) $z = 3$

    (C) $z = -3$

    (D) $z = 0$

    (E) $z = 2$

60. If $8x + 4y = 40$ and $x - y = 2$, then $y =$

    (A) 1

    (B) 2

    (C) 3

    (D) 4

    (E) 5

61. For the quadratic equation, $2x^2 + 3x + 20 = x^2 + 2x + 40$, solve for x.

    (A) 4; –5

    (B) –4; –5

    (C) 0; –4

    (D) 3; –3

    (E) None of the above

Subtest 13: Geometry

62. The sum of the angle measures of a triangle is

    (A) 360 degrees

    (B) 540 degrees

    (C) 180 degrees

    (D) 90 degrees

    (E) 120 degrees

63. If one angle of a triangle measures 80 degrees, the sum of the other two angles is

    (A) 110 degrees

    (B) 100 degrees

    (C) 280 degrees

    (D) 65 degrees

    (E) None of the above

64. An obtuse angle is

    (A) Less than 90 degrees or more than 180 degrees

    (B) Less than 90 degrees

    (C) More than 180 degrees

    (D) More than 90 degrees but less than 180 degrees

    (E) None of the above

65. If one of the angles of a right triangle is 45 degrees, what are the degree measurements of the other two angles?

    (A) 30 degrees; 120 degrees

    (B) 60 degrees; 45 degrees

    (C) 45 degrees; 90 degrees

    (D) 40 degrees; 95 degrees

    (E) 45 degrees; 120 degrees

66. A decagon is a polygon with how many sides?

    (A) 2

    (B) 4

    (C) 6

    (D) 8

    (E) 10

67. Using the Pythagorean theorem, figure out the length of the hypotenuse if the lengths of the other two sides are 10 meters and 16 meters.

    (A) 21.06 meters

    (B) 18.87 meters

    (C) 19.00 meters

    (D) 19.45 meters

    (E) None of the above

Subtest 14: Calculating Perimeter and Area

68. The area of one circle is six times as large as a smaller circle with a radius of 3 inches. The radius of the larger circle is

    (A) 7.34 inches

    (B) 9.1 inches

    (C) 8.65 inches

    (D) 6.27 inches

    (E) None of the above

69. How many meters does a point on the rim of a wheel travel if the wheel has a radius of 2 meters and makes 40 rotations?

    (A) 340 meters

    (B) 503 meters

    (C) 410 meters

    (D) 336 meters

    (E) 240 meters

70. The forward operating base you're assigned to is arranged in a perfect circle, with the headquarters exactly in the center. The headquarters is 1.2 kilometers to the perimeter road. How far must you travel to drive around the base one time on the perimeter road?

    (A) 10.1 kilometers

    (B) 6.89 kilometers

    (C) 8.21 kilometers

    (D) 7.54 kilometers

    (E) 5.75 kilometers

71. The secure area of your airfield is 2 miles by 1 mile. The area of the secured area is

    (A) 4 square miles

    (B) 6 square miles

    (C) 2 square miles

    (D) 1 square mile

    (E) None of the above

72. What's the perimeter of the secured airfield in Question 71?

    (A) 4 miles

    (B) 6 miles

    (C) 2 miles

    (D) 1 mile

    (E) None of the above

73. Two circles have the same center. If their radii are 5 centimeters and 15 centimeters, find the area that is part of the larger circle but not part of the smaller one.

    (A) 300 square centimeters

    (B) 200π square centimeters

    (C) 51π square centimeters

    (D) 71π square centimeters

    (E) 91π square centimeters

74. The area of a right triangle that has a height of 10 centimeters and a base of 20 centimeters is

    (A) 314 square centimeters

    (B) 400 square centimeters

    (C) 200 square centimeters

    (D) 66 square centimeters

    (E) 100 square centimeters

Subtest 15: Calculating Volume

75. If the weight of water is 52.4 pounds per cubic foot, the weight of the water that fills a cube with 2-foot sides is

    (A) 395 pounds

    (B) 257 pounds

    (C) 419 pounds

    (D) 344 pounds

    (E) 624 pounds

76. What is the volume of a container that is 12 feet long, 14 feet wide, and 8 feet high?

    (A) 1,344 cubic feet

    (B) 1,450 cubic feet

    (C) 1,795 square feet

    (D) 1,795 cubic feet

    (E) 1,280 cubic feet

77. The volume of a cylinder with a radius of 2 inches and a height of 6 inches is

    (A) 75.4 cubic inches

    (B) 67.2 cubic centimeters

    (C) 67.2 cubic inches

    (D) 75.4 cubic centimeters

    (E) None of the above

78. A gallon contains 231 cubic inches. If a cylindrical container has a radius of 10 inches and a height of 20 inches, how many gallons of hydraulic fluid can it hold?

    (A) 25.1 gallons

    (B) 14.8 gallons

    (C) 27.2 gallons

    (D) 21.4 gallons

    (E) 23.1 gallons

Subtest 16: Statistics

79. The following test scores were posted: 92, 91, 89, 87, 83, 83, 72. What is the mean score?

    (A) 89

    (B) 85.3

    (C) 86.1

    (D) 87

    (E) 83

80. The following test scores were posted: 92, 91, 89, 87, 83, 83, 72. What is the median score?

    (A) 89

    (B) 85.3

    (C) 86.1

    (D) 87

    (E) 83

Answer Key

1. B	21. D	41. B	61. A
2. C	22. C	42. E	62. C
3. D	23. B	43. A	63. B
4. D	24. D	44. C	64. D
5. A	25. C	45. E	65. C
6. E	26. A	46. B	66. E
7. A	27. B	47. A	67. B
8. C	28. C	48. B	68. A
9. B	29. D	49. D	69. B
10. D	30. A	50. C	70. D
11. C	31. C	51. E	71. C
12. A	32. D	52. A	72. B
13. E	33. A	53. B	73. B
14. D	34. B	54. C	74. E
15. E	35. C	55. D	75. C
16. A	36. A	56. B	76. A
17. C	37. D	57. A	77. A
18. D	38. E	58. C	78. C
19. B	39. B	59. E	79. B
20. E	40. D	60. B	80. D

Part III

Honing Your Science, Aeronautical, and Mental Skills

The 5th Wave   By Rich Tennant

"Physics explains motion. Like the acceleration of this glass moving backward creating a velocity that results in a displacement. Any weenie knows that.

In this part . . .

Doing well on the military flight aptitude tests requires more than just good language and math skills. You must also have solid skills in the science, aeronautical, and mental departments. That's why, in this part, we brush up and then test your science skills, your aeronautical skills, and your mental skills.

Chapter 9

Tackling Technical Information and Science Review

*B*elieve it or not, the military flight aptitude tests require you to have knowledge in a wide range of technical and scientific topics, so you need to *cover down on* those subjects (that's a military term for getting a grasp of something) to ensure your exam success. In this chapter, we review all the scientific subject matters that you need to know to perform well on your test. We cover the basic fundamentals of biology, physics, anatomy, chemistry, and the earth sciences.

This review chapter and the accompanying practice test in Chapter 10 won't make you an expert scientist, but they should serve as a good review for most of the courses you may have already taken. If you haven't previously studied the subjects, use this text to gain a basic understanding and identify your weaknesses, and then dig deeper into the material by using various other subject matter materials found in any library. Who knows? You may actually enjoy this review; it's all really fun and interesting stuff.

Brushing Up on the Metric System

So, what's so great about the metric system? The answer is simple, just like the metric system itself. In the metric system, everything operates on a scale of ten, unlike the *U.S. customary* system — the system you're probably used to — which is based on a scale of . . . well, who knows. The simple fact is that most folks in the United States know little about the metric system. You were probably exposed to it during your high-school and college math and science classes, but if not, the following sections have you covered.

Reviewing units and abbreviations

Forget about feet, pounds, and Fahrenheit. The metric system uses a different system of units than you may be used to. The following list showcases some common metric units:

- **Seconds (s):** The *second* is the main metric unit of time.

- **Meters (m):** *Meters* are the main metric unit of distance.

- **Degrees Celsius or centigrade (°C):** These degrees are the metric unit of temperature in everyday use; check out the later section "Taking the temperature: Going from Fahrenheit to Celsius and back" for help converting Fahrenheit temperatures to Celsius and vice versa. **Note:** We say "in everyday use" because temperature in the metric system is officially measured in Kelvin (K). You find the temperature in Kelvin by adding 273 to the temperature in degrees Celsius. Temperature in Kelvin is useful when describing things in term of *absolute zero* (0 degrees Kelvin is the coldest temperature possible).

- **Kilograms (kg):** *Kilograms* are the metric unit of mass. The first time you order something from a deli that uses the metric system, be careful!

- **Hertz (Hz):** The metric unit of frequency is *hertz*. If something happens once per second, it happens with a frequency of 1 hertz.

- **Joule (J):** The *Joule* is the metric unit of work/energy.

- **Pascal (Pa):** *Pascals* are the metric units of pressure. There are 101,325 pascals (101.325 kPa) in 1 atmosphere (1 atm). Regardless, inches of mercury is the standard measure of barometric pressure throughout the world aviation community. One inch of mercury is equal to 3,386.389 pascals at 0 degrees Celsius.

Preparing for prefixes

The metric system uses prefixes to indicate how a particular quantity relates to its base unit (see the preceding section). Table 9-1 lists some of the more common metric prefixes:

Table 9-1	Prefixes Used in the Metric System	
Prefix (Symbol)	**Numeric Equivalent**	**Example**
nano (n)	10^{-9}	0.000000001 meters = 1 nanometer (nm)
micro (μ)	10^{-6}	0.000001 meters = 1 micrometer (μm)
milli (m)	10^{-3}	0.001 meter = 1 millimeter (mm)
centi (c)	10^{-2}	0.01 meter = 1 centimeter (cm)
deci (d)	10^{-1}	0.1 meter = 1 decimeter (dm)
kilo (k)	10^{3}	1,000 meters = 1 kilometer (km)
mega (M)	10^{6}	1 million meters = 1 megameter (Mm)
giga (G)	10^{9}	1 billion meters = 1 gigameter (Gm)

Covering conversions and equivalents

Need to quickly convert a metric unit to a U.S. customary one? No problem. Here are some fast conversion formulas for your viewing pleasure:

- Seconds to minutes: Number of seconds ÷ 60 = number of minutes
- Meters to inches: Number of meters ÷ 0.0254 = number of inches
- Centimeters to inches: Number of centimeters ÷ 2.54 = number of inches
- Kilograms to pounds: Number of kilograms ÷ 0.45 = number of pounds
- Pascals to atmospheres: Number of pascals ÷ 101.325 = number of atmospheres
- Joules to calories: Number of joules ÷ 4.184 = number of calories

Tables 9-2 through 9-4 provide a handy list of metric equivalents that you can use to get the hang of the various metric measurements.

Table 9-2	Length Metric Equivalents		
Unit	**Abbreviation**	**Number of Meters**	**Approximate U.S. Customary Equivalent**
kilometer	km	1,000	0.62 miles
hectometer	hm	100	328.08 feet
dekameter	dam	10	32.81 feet
meter	m	1	39.37 inches
decimeter	dm	0.1	3.94 inches
centimeter	cm	0.01	0.39 inches
millimeter	mm	0.001	0.039 inches
micrometer	μ	0.000001	0.000039 inches

Table 9-3	Area Metric Equivalents		
Unit	**Abbreviation**	**Number of Square Meters**	**Approximate U.S. Customary Equivalent**
square kilometer	sq km or km^2	1,000,000	0.3861 square miles
hectare	ha	10,000	2.47 acres
acre	a	100	119.60 square yards
square centimeter	sq cm or cm^2	0.0001	0.155 square inches

Table 9-4	Volume Metric Equivalents		
Unit	**Abbreviation**	**Number of Cubic Meters**	**Approximate U.S. Customary Equivalent**
cubic meter	m^3	1	1.307 cubic yards
cubic decimeter	dm^3	0.001	61.023 cubic inches
cubic centimeter	cu cm, cm^3, or cc	0.000001	0.061 cubic inches

Taking the temperature: Going from Fahrenheit to Celsius and back

The *degree Fahrenheit* (°F) is the U.S. customary scale of temperature measurement; the freezing point of water is 32 degrees, and the boiling point is 212 degrees. The formula for converting Fahrenheit to Celsius is

$$°F = °C \times 9/5 + 32$$

The degree Celsius (which we introduce in the earlier section "Reviewing units and abbreviations") is an easy system of measurement with the freezing point of water at 0 degrees and the boiling point at 100 degrees. (Of course, pressure has some impact on these figures, but these base figures are for standard pressure.) The formula for converting Celsius to Fahrenheit is

$$°C = (°F - 32) \times 5/9$$

Wrapping Your Brain around the Scientific Method and Scientific Notation

The *scientific method* is a formalized method for objectively observing, experimenting with, developing, and further modifying a given scientific idea, or *hypothesis*. The scientific method is how companies test new drugs and how astronomers figure out whether a new planetary theory is correct. It's the basis of all experimentation.

You have probably used the scientific method in your lab classes, where you performed a series of experiments to confirm your (or the class's) idea. Of course, your instructor already knew the outcome in these experiments, but the tests gave you an understanding of the systematic and objective process necessary to understand and develop scientific principles. Newton didn't just come up with his laws; he developed them through the scientific method.

Scientific notation is a way to express very large or very small numbers in a more concise way without diminishing the accuracy. Writing that something weighs 3.4×10^{-6} grams is much easier than writing 0.0000034 grams. The scientific world uses scientific notation in most content.

To convert a number less than one or greater than ten to scientific notation, follow these steps:

1. **Convert the number you're working with into a number between 1 and 10 by moving the decimal to the left or right.**

   For example, you convert 35,000 to 3.5 by moving the decimal four spaces to the left. To convert 0.00035 to 3.5, you move the decimal four spaces to the right. *Remember:* Keep track of how many places you move the decimal point.

2. **Write the number that you came up with in Step 1, followed by $\times$ *10*.**

3. **Add the appropriate exponent based on the number of spaces you moved the decimal.**

   If the original number was greater than 10 (that is, you moved the decimal point to the left in Step 1), write the number of moved decimal places as a positive exponent attached to the 10. In the 35,000 example from Step 1, you move the decimal point four places to the left, so your final result would be 3.5×10^4. If the original number was less than 1 (you moved the decimal to the right), attach the number of places you moved as a negative exponent. For the 0.00035 example, your final result would be 3.5×10^{-4}.

Getting Physical with the Natural Sciences

Ah, the natural sciences. *Natural sciences* is really just an encompassing term for all subjects that try to explain life as we know it. From how much force is required to lift a bag of cement to how a plant makes energy, the natural sciences cover a wide range of disciplines. The following sections introduce you to some of the main branches of natural science.

Living it up with life sciences

Life science is just the study of living organisms. Some life sciences you may be familiar with include *biology* (the basic science concerned with life and living organisms), *anatomy* (the study of a living thing's structure), and *physiology* (the study of living systems' functions); we cover these topics in more detail later in this chapter. Here are a few other life sciences to be aware of:

- **Botany:** *Botany* is the part of biology that concerns itself with the study of plants and their mechanisms: plant structure, growth, reproduction, energy production, and nutrition; plant diseases; the chemical properties of plants; and plant classification relationships. Botany is one of the oldest known sciences; after all, primitive peoples had to learn what was safe to eat. More than 550,000 known species of living plants exist today.

- **Ecology:** *Ecology* is the study of the hierarchical relationships living organisms have with their natural environments (*ecosystems*) and with other species. Ecology spans natural environments from the microscopic to the planetary level.

- **Zoology:** *Zoology* is the study of the classification, habits, evolution, health, and social patterns of all species in the animal kingdom, and it deals with both current and extinct animals.

Digging into the earth sciences

Another division of natural science is *earth science,* which focuses on the makeup and function of our planet. The earth sciences use tools from all the other sciences (such as studying the composition of particular rocks through chemistry), but earth science is primarily geared toward understanding this and other planets. The following sections cover a few important earth science fields.

Geography

Geography is the science that studies land masses, their structures, and their movement patterns over the ages, as well as the people who inhabit the areas of interest. You can break geographical studies down into two basic subcategories: human geography and physical geography. *Human geography* looks at the cultures, people, and communities in various regions of the earth and considers their interactions with their environments. *Physical geography* deals with the structures or functions of the different sections of the earth and its atmosphere.

Geology

Geology is the branch of science that deals with the study of the earth, its structure, and its past and continuing evolution. In modern times, you may find geologists working for energy companies by helping to discover new sources for oil or working to understand the possible impact of underground earthquake faults.

Hydrology

Hydrology focuses on the study of water movement, sources of distribution, and quality on earth and other planets, including the water cycle, water resources, and environmental watershed sustainability. Some projects for hydrologists may include working on planetary water research for NASA or working on a watershed initiative at a local environmental group.

Meteorology

Meteorology deals with the scientific study of the atmosphere and assists in the forecasting of weather patterns. *Meteorological phenomena* are observable weather events, which are then interpreted by scientists who are experts in meteorology. Natural variables, such as temperature, pressure changes, and humidity, can severely impact the weather of the earth, and the meteorologist's job is to interpret the phenomena and give predictions based on past observations and computer models. Meteorology impacts everyday life, from planning a social outing outside to hurricane tracking and level prediction to monitoring windspeed at upper altitudes for flying conditions. Meteorological training is a huge part of flight school, and throughout your career, you'll regularly seek the advice of meteorological experts; flying in a thunderstorm is no fun. As the old aviation saying goes, "It's better to be down here wishing you were up there than to be up there wishing you were down here!"

Astronomy

Astronomy is the science that studies the celestial sky, including stars, planets, comets, nebulae, different star clusters, and galaxies. Astronomy is one of the oldest sciences; early man used astronomy as both a supernatural predictor of events and as a way to navigate the exploration of the earth. Today, astronomy breaks down into various subcategories. *Observational astronomy* deals with gathering hard data from observations and using basic laws of physics to clarify those findings. *Theoretical astronomy* is the section of astronomy that deals with developing computer models to predict and describe astronomical locations and events. Flip to the later section "Exploring Your Solar System" for information on the sun and planets.

Cramming Life Science Essentials

In the earlier section "Living it up with life sciences," we introduce you to some of the many branches of life science. One we don't cover in detail there is *biology,* the basic science concerned with life and living organisms and their structures, origins, classification, functions, and growth. Biologists have agreed to five basic fundamentals:

- Cells, from plants to bacteria to humans, are the foundation of life as we know it.
- Evolution results in new species and new traits.
- All organisms use and transmit some form of energy.
- Genes form the basis for heredity.
- An organism attempts to control its environment to maintain function and stability.

Biology breaks down into smaller disciplines, such as biochemistry, physiology, and cellular biology. The following sections look at some of the biology basics you should be familiar with for your flight aptitude test.

Classifying all living things

Taxonomy is the classification of organisms in a way that corresponds with their relationships to each other. Here's the standard classification system for bringing together various species into progressively larger levels:

- ✓ **Species:** A category of organisms that has the capability to interbreed and produce fertile offspring

- ✓ **Genus:** One or more related species

- ✓ **Family:** Similar subfamily

- ✓ **Order:** Families with similar characteristics

- ✓ **Class:** Orders with similar characteristics

- ✓ **Phylum:** Related species

- ✓ **Kingdom:** Related divisions of phyla

- ✓ **Domain:** Broadest level of classification

The most widely accepted classification scheme currently recognizes three domains: Archaea, Eubacteria, and Eukarya. Domain Eukarya (the one humans are part of) is subdivided into four kingdoms: Protista, Fungi, Plantae, and Animalia. All living organisms are given a two-part name; the first name reflects the organism's genus, and the second name is the species. For example, humans are called *Homo sapiens*.

All you wanted to know about cells

Cells are the basic structural unit in any living organism; they're the building blocks of animal, bacteria, fungi, and human life. The following sections highlight important cell considerations to know for your flight aptitude test.

Cell theory

Cell theory puts forth the idea that new cells are created from other cells that already exist. The tenets of modern cell theory include the following:

- ✓ Every known living thing is comprised of one or more cells. *Unicellular organisms* are comprised of just one cell, while *multicellular organisms* are comprised of more than one cell.

- ✓ In every living organism, the cell is the fundamental unit of structure and function.

- ✓ New cells are created by the division of pre-existing cells.

- ✓ Metabolism and biochemical energy development occurs within cells.

- ✓ DNA (genetic information) is contained in the cells and is passed to new cells during cell division.

- ✓ Similar species' cells have the same basic chemical makeup.

- ✓ The total activity of independent cells makes up the net activity of an organism.

Cell parts

Cells — both plant and animal — have specific parts that serve particular functions, from cell energy production to genetic reproduction and beyond.

In the following sections, we break down the important cell components.

Membrane

The *cell membrane* (also known as the *plasma membrane*) is the structure that separates the inside of a cell from the outside of a cell. The cell membrane is selectively permeable to certain items (specifically, ions and organic molecules) and it can control what substances are able to move in and out of a cell. Cell membranes play a vital role in many different processes, including ion conductivity, cell signaling, and cell adhesion.

Cytoplasm and endoplasmic reticulum

Cytoplasm is the material that resides within the cell membrane. It's a liquid, gel-like substance that contains the cell's internal structures except the nucleus.

The *endoplasmic reticulum* (ER) is a eukaryotic organelle within cells comprising an interconnected network of complex structures. (A *eukaryotic* organism's cells contain complex structures enclosed within membranes.) The ER is made up of two parts. The *rough endoplasmic reticula* make proteins. The *smooth endoplasmic reticula* metabolize carbohydrates and steroids, regulate the concentration of calcium, make *lipids* (fatty substances) and steroids, and assist in attaching receptors on cell membrane proteins.

Golgi body

The *Golgi body* (also called the *Golgi apparatus*) is found in most eukaryotic cells. After proteins are synthesized, the Golgi body processes them as they make their way to their destinations. The Golgi body plays a crucial role in preparing proteins for movement within and out of the cell. Part of the cellular endomembrane system is formed by the Golgi body.

Mitochondrion and nucleus

A *mitochondrion* (the plural is *mitochondria*) is an organelle found in most eukaryotic cells. An *organelle* is a structure within a cell that performs a role in helping the cell function properly. Mitochondria act as the cell's power plant because they create most of the cell's chemical energy source, adenosine triphosphate (ATP). Mitochondria are involved in a range of other processes, including chemical signaling and controlling the cell's growth and eventual death. A number of human diseases, such as cardiac dysfunction and mitochondrial disorders, have potential mitochondria sources. Studies suggest mitochondria play a role in the aging process as well.

Another membrane-enclosed organelle found in eukaryotic cells is the *nucleus,* where most of the cell's genetic material appears. This material is mostly comprised of DNA molecules that are organized into *chromosomes.* The *genes* (units of heredity, comprised of specific DNA sequences) in these chromosomes create the cell's genome and an organism's specific characteristics. For all practical purposes, the nucleus is a cell's control center, kind of like the bridge of the ship.

Ribosome

Within plant and animal cells, DNA produces RNA, which in turn produces proteins. Genes contain a DNA sequence that is copied into a messenger RNA (mRNA). After this step, the *ribosomes* read the information in this mRNA, arrange the required amino acid out of the 20 specific ones, and use it to create proteins in a sequence for genetic transfer. This process is known as *translation.*

How cells survive and thrive

Ever wonder how the foods you eat give you the eventual energy you need to run five miles? Where does the waste that you eliminate (through defecation and urination) come from? This section gives you the basic knowledge you need on these and related topics for the flight aptitude test.

Metabolism

Metabolism is the process by which cells convert nutrient molecules into energy, and it is further divided into two distinctly different processes. *Catabolism* is the process through which cells derive their energy by breaking down complex molecules, and *anabolism* is the process by which cells use catabolic energy to build complex molecules and carry out other cellular tasks.

Osmosis

Osmosis is the tendency of fluids (most often water, in the case of cells) to pass through a semipermeable membrane into a solution where the solvent concentration is higher. This movement of fluids ultimately equalizes the concentration of dissolved materials (*solutes*) on both sides of the membrane. Osmosis is the primary route for transport of water in and out of cells, and is therefore essential for life.

Phagocytosis

Cells have the capability to engulf or eat substances or particles — kind of like a football player with a pizza — by way of a process called *phagocytosis.* The result of phagocytosis (found only among eukaryotic cells) is a food vacuole, where the engulfed substances or particles are digested by *lysosomes.* The engulfed substances or particles enter cells through a cell opening called a *cytostome.* Some cells use phagocytosis to consume pathogens; other cells use it to generate energy (known as *phagotrophic energy,* which is different from *absorption* — a kind of *osmotrophic* nutrition.

Photosynthesis

Plants, algae, and some types of bacteria use the process of *photosynthesis* to convert light into chemical energy. The actual process uses sunlight and *chlorophyll* (the green pigment in plants) to transform water and carbon dioxide gas into glucose (which is used for food) and oxygen — a waste product expelled into the earth's atmosphere (and gladly breathed by humans and other animals).

The chemical reaction of photosynthesis is represented by this formula:

$$6H_2O + 6CO_2 + light \rightarrow C_6H_{12}O_6 \text{ (glucose)} + 6O_2$$

Cellular respiration

The conversion of energy-laden molecules (for example, molecules of glucose) into energy by breaking down their chemical bonds is known as *cellular respiration.* With the exception of viruses, all life forms on earth use cellular respiration to create the energy they need to function.

The chemical reaction for the oxidation of glucose is represented by this formula:

$$C_6H_{12}O_6 + 6O_2 \rightarrow 6CO_2 + 6H_2O + energy$$

There are two categories of cellular respiration: anaerobic and aerobic. *Anaerobic* respiration, the more primitive of the two, takes place without oxygen and results in less energy than aerobic respiration does. *Aerobic* respiration is a more recent innovation in the history of life on earth, and it requires oxygen.

Cellular respiration occurs in three steps:

1. Glycolysis
2. Krebs cycle
3. Electron transport chain

A systemic approach to human anatomy and physiology

You may have taken an anatomy and physiology class in your undergraduate training. Basically, *human anatomy* is the study of the structures or systems of the human body, and physiology studies the function of these living systems; anatomy discusses what you have, and physiology discusses how it works. In the following sections, we highlight the important concepts of each field in enough detail to prepare you for the exam.

No bones about it: The skeletal system

The skeleton serves an essential function: providing the structure (comprised of both fused and individual bones) that supports the human body with the help of ligaments, tendons, muscles, and cartilage. The six main functions of the skeletal system include the following:

- Supporting the body and maintaining its shape
- Permitting movement at the joints between the bones
- Protecting vital organs
- Serving as the site for *hematopoiesis* (blood cell formation)
- Storing calcium and metabolizing calcium
- Regulating blood sugar by releasing a hormone called *osteocalcin*

Bones within the skeletal system range in size from the tiny stapes bone in the middle ear to the femur, which is the largest bone in the body. In a normal adult, the skeleton comprises about 30 to 40 percent of total body weight, and half of the weight of the skeleton is water.

Putting some muscle on them bones

The *muscular system* enables humans to move and carry out a variety of other functions by way of the coordinated contraction of muscle tissue. For the most part, muscles don't function on their own; their action is largely controlled and coordinated through the nervous system. The exception to this rule is certain autonomous muscles (such as the heart) that act independently of this control. (See the later section "Nervous? That's your nervous system talking" for more on the nervous system.)

The muscular system consists of three types of muscles: *skeletal muscles, cardiac muscles,* and *smooth (non-striated) muscles.* In total, more than 600 different muscles make up the human body, ranging in size from the tiny inner-ear muscle that controls the movement of the stapes bone to the large gluteus maximus muscle in the buttock. Now coauthor Terry knows why he was so sore after walking for a year in Iraq.

The cardiovascular and respiratory systems

The *cardiovascular system* is made up of the heart, blood, and blood vessels, which serve to transport blood throughout the body. Blood is a liquid comprised of plasma (mostly water), oxygen-carrying red blood cells, disease-fighting white blood cells, and blood-clotting platelets. The typical adult body contains an average of five to six quarts of blood (approximately 4.7 to 5.7 liters).

The human cardiovascular system boasts two major kinds of circulation: *pulmonary circulation*, in which the heart's pulmonary artery pumps oxygen-depleted blood through the lungs to be enriched with oxygen, and *systemic circulation*, in which the pulmonary vein moves oxygenated blood from the lungs back to the heart and then on to the rest of the body.

The respiratory system pulls air into the lungs, where the movement of the diaphragm and the contraction of respiration muscles facilitate gas exchange. Molecules of oxygen from the air are taken into the bloodstream, and carbon dioxide is expelled from the bloodstream in the lung *alveoli,* areas rich with very small blood vessels called *capillaries.*

Nervous? That's your nervous system talking

Both the central and the peripheral nervous system play the primary role in the control of behavior and emotions. The *central nervous system* (CNS) processes the information it receives from the environment and then transmits impulses to the *peripheral nervous system* to coordinate movements and actions throughout the body.

The brain is the main organ of the nervous system; it's divided into three parts. First is the *brain stem,* which is an extension of the spinal cord. It controls a lot of automatic responses and muscles. The second part is the *forebrain* (which consists mainly of the cerebrum), and the third is the cerebellum. Down the middle of the cerebrum and the cerebellum is a groove that divides the two hemispheres of the brain, which are further divided into lobes. These hemispheres are linked by a thick band of nerve fibers (the *corpus callosum*) that control electrical impulses back and forth. The brain is connected to various nerves throughout the body via the spinal column; these nerves provide a two-way communication system among the brain; the spinal cord; and parts of the arms, legs, neck, and trunk of the body.

The digestive system

Digestion is the breakdown of large food molecules by both chemical (for example, saliva and stomach acid) and mechanical (for example, chewing) means into smaller particles that can then be absorbed into the bloodstream to be utilized by the cells for energy production and other purposes.

The digestive breakdown starts when you chew the food you eat and is helped along by saliva. This initial process is called *mastication*. Food then moves down the esophagus into the stomach, where hydrochloric acid kills most contaminating microorganisms (though not all) and further breaks down and chemically alters the food. The hydrochloric acid has a low *pH* (a chemical scale that labels acidity), which enables digestive enzymes to work more efficiently. The result of the initial digestion is a thick liquid called *chyme* that goes through the small intestine, where 95 percent of nutrient absorption occurs. (The importance of small intestine absorption is why physicians become so concerned with bowel obstructions.) Finally, after the nutrient-depleted food passes into the large intestine, waste material is collected and water is removed to eventually become fecal matter purged from the body during defecation.

The endocrine system: It's a hormone thing

The *endocrine system* is comprised of hormone-producing glands that — through the hormones they produce — are capable of regulating such things as metabolism, sexual development, growth, and much more. (*Hormones* are powerful chemical messengers that travel in the bloodstream and have an effect on cells, organs, and bodily functions.) Some of the major endocrine glands include the adrenal, pituitary, hypothalamus, thyroid, ovaries, and testes.

The specialized endocrine glands aren't the only organs that have an endocrine function; a variety of other organs, including the heart, liver, and kidneys, also have a secondary endocrine function.

Making babies: The reproductive system

The *reproductive system* or *genital system* is the complex system of specialized sex organs that work together, along with fluids, hormones, and pheromones, for the purpose of reproduction, sustaining life, and evolution. Although males and females of a particular species often have similarities in major systems, their reproductive systems are typically quite different. For example, men and women have more or less the same circulatory system, but their reproductive systems vary greatly. The ultimate goal of the reproductive system is to produce living, viable offspring, and it accomplishes this goal by uniting one male sperm with one or more female eggs — combining genetic material and producing an individual who shares characteristics of both the father and the mother.

Traditional human reproduction begins through sexual intercourse and leads to internal fertilization. During this process, the male ejaculates *semen*, a liquid that contains *sperm* (the male reproductive cells); the sperm then makes its way through the *vagina* to the *uterus* and then on to the *fallopian tubes* where fertilization of the *ovum* — the female reproductive cells, or *eggs* — takes place. The successfully fertilized ovum implants itself on the inner wall of the uterus, where the resulting *fetus* matures for approximately nine months in a process called *gestation*. The natural process of childbirth is achieved through contractions of the uterus, dilation of the *cervix*, and the baby's exit through the vagina. Unlike many other mammals, a human infant is nearly helpless and requires a high level of protection and parental support for years.

Flushing the system: The urinary system

The *urinary system* has the task of producing, storing, and excreting urine, the liquid waste product produced by your kidneys. In most people, the urinary system is composed of a pair of *kidneys* (though humans can survive with just a part of one kidney), *ureters* (which direct urine from the kidneys to the *bladder*, where urine is stored), and the *urethra* (which provides a pathway for the urine out of the body). Kidneys are complex organs that perform a variety of tasks, such as regulating *electrolytes* (such as sodium, potassium, and calcium) and blood pressure, concentrating urine, and maintaining equilibrium.

The lymphatic system

The *lymphatic system* is a network of vessels (separate from the blood vessels), nodes, and organs that transport lymph throughout the body. *Lymph* is a clear liquid comprised of *interstitial fluid* (the fluid surrounding cells in the body), white blood cells, proteins, and fats. The adenoids, spleen, tonsils, and thymus are all a part of the lymphatic system. The system is part of the immune system; it filters cancer cells and bacteria and produces white blood cells and other immune cells that fight disease.

Cracking Open the Chemistry Kit

Oh, chemistry — one of the subjects that tends to make people cringe. *Chemistry* is the science that deals with substance and matter, the distinct properties of certain types of matter, and how those kinds of matter interact with other types of matter. It also serves as a foundation or building block for other scientific studies, such as physics or biology.

Chemistry breaks down into two basic studies: inorganic and organic. *Inorganic chemistry* is the division of chemistry that deals with *inorganic,* or non-carbon compounds. It's the basic branch of chemistry — the one you probably studied in your basic high-school or college chemistry course.

Organic chemistry is the division of chemistry involving carbon-based compounds, hydrocarbons, and their derivatives. *Organic compounds* form many everyday products, and *organic reactions* are chemical reactions involving those organic compounds. These organic reactions are the basis of virtually all biological mechanisms. (Don't worry; you won't encounter any complex organic chemistry equations on your flight aptitude test. However, you must be familiar with what organic chemistry is and some of its principal concepts.)

What stuff's made of

Time to get down to the basic elements of what "stuff" is. The following sections go down to the smallest level so you can grasp the concept of how stuff is combined and how properties of certain elements function.

Matter

Matter is anything that has a definite mass and takes up volume. Three states of matter exist: solid, liquid, and gas. *Solids* have a defined shape, mass, and volume. *Liquids* have a defined mass and volume, but not a defined shape. *Gases* have a mass and no defined shape; they expand to fill any volume and take any shape. Usually, matter transforms in sequence from a solid to a liquid to a gas (for example, think of a solid ice cube that melts into liquid water and then evaporates into water vapor).

Matter can go directly from a solid to a gas, or vice versa, without passing through the liquid phase. This process is called *sublimation*.

Elements

The 118 existing chemical elements make up the billions of different objects in the world. Most materials aren't made up of just one type of element but rather of a combination of elements called *compounds* that are joined through chemical reactions (see the later section "The different types of chemical reactions").

Atoms

The *atom* is a basic unit of matter. An atom has a compacted central nucleus surrounded by orbitals of negatively charged electrons. Inside the atomic nucleus, you find a mix of positively charged protons as well as neutrons with zero electronic charge. An atom's electrons are attracted to the nucleus by *electromagnetic force*. (Head to the following section for details on these particles.) A group of atoms can remain bound to each other and form a molecule.

An atom with equal numbers of protons and electrons is electrically neutral. If the atom has fewer electrons than protons, it has a positive charge; more electrons than protons means a negative charge. An atom with a positive or negative charge is known as an *ion*. A positively charged ion is a *cation,* and a negatively charged ion is called an *anion*.

Subatomic particles

The atom is comprised of three major *subatomic particles:* protons, neutrons, and electrons. The protons and neutrons in an atom make up the small atomic nucleus (together, they're called *nucleons*). All atoms of a particular element always have the same number of protons (referred to as the *atomic number*); however, atoms of a single element can have different numbers of neutrons. Such atoms are *isotopes* of that element; flip to the later section "The periodic table" for more details.

Here's the lowdown on what you need to know about the subatomic particles:

- **Electrons:** The negatively charged *electron* has a mass of 9.11×10^{-31} kilograms; that's the lowest mass of the three major subatomic particles. The electron's size is too small to be measured; rather, its size has been determined through scientific experimentation and calculation.

  Electrons circle the nucleus in defined orbits. These electrons are transferred to and received from other elements during chemical reactions to form a bond (the strength varies). This exchange of electrons is the basis for millions of chemical reactions. Therefore, the number of electrons in an atom determines that atom's chemical properties.

- **Protons:** The positively charged *proton* has a mass of 1.6726×10^{-27} kilograms (more than 1,800 times larger than the electron's mass) and is about the same size as a neutron. As we note earlier in the section, the number of protons in an atom determines the element — period! Say you have an atom with six protons. Every atom that has six protons is a carbon atom, so you know your atom is carbon regardless of how many neutrons it has.

- **Neutrons:** The neutrally charged *neutron* has a mass of 1.6929×10^{-27} kilograms (approximately the same as the proton). Elements are typically in their normal state when the number of protons and neutrons are equal (for your test purposes, you don't need to worry about the exceptions).

Orbital shells and valence electrons

An *electron shell* is basically an orbit or electronic cloud circling an atom's nucleus. The fundamental principle of chemistry is the sharing of electrons from the outermost, or *valence*, shell between elements. The *valence electrons* are those electrons circling in the outermost shell of an atom that can give or capture valence electrons to or from another element. A single *covalent bond* occurs when both atoms contribute one valence electron to form a shared pair, thus making the molecule inherently more stable. For the main group elements (see the later section "The periodic table"), only the outer electrons are valence electrons. However, keep in mind that in the transition metals, some inner-shell electrons are also valence electrons capable of being shared.

Valence electrons are a crucial concept because they give you a clue for predicting chemical behavior. Atoms tend to have a set number of *orbital shells*. When an atom contains a complete (*closed*) outer shell, its bonding electrons are all accounted for. Such atoms are considered *stable*. Because stable atoms' electrons don't easily interact with one another, these atoms aren't very reactive with other atoms. However, an atom with one or two more or fewer valence electrons in the outside orbital than what's required for a closed shell can easily give those electrons or receive more electrons to equalize the shell and become stable. This kind of atom is highly reactive, or *unstable*.

Each shell is composed of one or more sub-shells, which are themselves composed of *atomic orbitals*. You don't need to worry about a lot of detail here; just be aware that suborbitals exist.

The periodic table

The *periodic table* (or, more officially, the *periodic table of elements*) is a display of the 118 known chemical elements arranged according to particular properties of their atomic structures. Specifically, it orders elements by increasing atomic number in *periods* (rows) and *groups* (columns). Check out the periodic table online at www.dummies.com/how-to/content/periodic-table-of-elements0.navId-403202.html; as you can see, the rectangular table includes gaps in the periods to group together elements with similar properties. For example, the table contains groups for alkali metals and halogens.

This table may seem confusing at first, but it's very useful after you understand how it works. When you read from left to right across the table, the elements are arranged in order of the number of protons in the nucleus. Hydrogen (H) is first because it has one proton; helium (He), the next element to the right (despite the gap), has two protons; and so on.

On some periodic tables, you also see an *atomic mass* number, which is the sum of the numbers of protons and neutrons, under the symbol; atomic masses correspondingly increase as you go across and down the table.

Lanthanoids and actinoids (the f-block) are separated from other elements within the standard periodic table.

Basically, the elements within each group react similarly because they all have the same number of valence electrons in the outer shell or orbit (we discuss these concepts in the earlier section "Orbital shells and valence electrons"). An example is the column group 1A, which contains H, Li, Na, K, Rb, Cs, and Fr. These elements all have one electron in the outer shell. All elements in group 2A have two electrons in the outer shell. Group 6A's elements contain six electrons in the outer orbit, and the elements in group 8A contain eight valence electrons. All the elements in a group either freely accept or give off an electron based on what will make the shell fuller and therefore more stable.

As we mention earlier in the chapter, an atom with a different number of neutrons than its element usually is an isotope of that element. For example, a copper atom has 29 protons; anything with 29 protons is a copper atom. But these 29-proton atoms don't always have the same number of neutrons; some have 34 neutrons, and some have 36 neutrons. These different varieties are two different isotopes. Elemental isotopes, because they have a differing number of neutrons, have a different mass than the "regular" form of the element. The atomic mass listed on a periodic table is the average of the atomic masses for naturally occurring isotopes.

The different types of chemical reactions

A *chemical reaction* is the process that transforms one set of chemical substances called *reactants* or *reagents* into another substance or substances known as the *product*. For example, the reactants hydrogen and oxygen can chemically react to form the product water. The process of chemical reaction is responsible for life itself. Chemical reactions typically (but not always) require some form of energy input such as heat, light, or electricity to induce the reaction. Reactions can be *exothermic*, where energy is released (that is, the reaction gives off heat), or *endothermic*, where heat is absorbed.

How chemical reactions are written

Generally speaking, a chemical reaction is written to show the reactants' transformation to the product. As an example, take one of the most basic fuels for equation purposes, propane. Propane (C_3H_8) is combined with oxygen (O_2) to get carbon dioxide (CO_2) plus water (H_2O). You first write this reaction as (a) C_3H_8 + (b) O_2 → (c) H_2O, where a, b, and c are the numbers required to balance the equation to follow the law of conservation of mass. Your final equation is (1) C_3H_8 + (5) O_2 → (3) CO_2 + (4) H_2O or $C_3H_8 + 5O_2 → 3CO_2 + 4H_2O$.

According to the *law of conservation of mass,* a reaction can't create or destroy matter. The number of atoms in the reactant(s) must be the same as the number of atoms in the product.

It's basic, or acidic

Acid-base reactions involve transferring protons from one molecule (an *acid*) to another (a *base*). Acids act as proton donors and bases as proton acceptors. The following equation represents an acid-base reaction, where HA is acid, B is base, A⁻ is conjugated base, and HB⁺ is conjugated acid. (A *conjugated* acid or base is just one that loses or gains a proton.)

$$HA + B \rightleftharpoons A^- + HB^+$$

The *pH scale* measures how much acid is in a solution. A low pH level (0 to 7) is considered an acid, while a high pH level (above 7) is considered a base. Pure or distilled water is *neutral*.

Picking up a Brief Course in Physics

The term *physics* can intimidate a lot of students; coauthor Terry recalls dreading the subject until his instructor told him one day that physics is simply a course on the application of math and science to everyday life. Hearing that put Terry more at ease; in fact, physics became his favorite subject. This section aims to follow that lead by reviewing how to apply math and science to everyday problems. Thank you, Mr. Schembeckler.

Mass (and weight)

Mass and weight are two different animals. *Mass* is the amount of matter contained within an object, while *weight* is the force exerted by gravity on the object's mass. This force acts on an object whether the object is falling, resting, or being elevated and results in a downward acceleration of 9.81 meters per second squared. The formula for calculating weight is

$$W = mg$$

where W is weight, m is the mass of an object, and g is the acceleration that results from gravity.

Motion and Newton's laws

Motion occurs when an object is moved from one point to another. Three types of motion exist: *translational* (linear or moving in a straight line), *rotational* (motion occurring about an axis), and *vibrational* (motion around a fixed point).

All motion is governed by Sir Isaac Newton's three laws of motion. These laws are important to know for your aptitude test because every aviation achievement begins with these fundamental concepts; they're the scientific building blocks enabling modern military aviation. Drumroll, please:

- **Newton's First Law of Motion:** A body at rest tends to remain at rest, and a body in motion tends to remain in motion unless acted upon by an outside force.

- **Newton's Second Law of Motion:** An object will change velocity if it is pushed or pulled on. When an object is acted upon by an outside force, the acceleration is directly proportional to the applied force and inversely proportional to the mass of the object. This law derives the formula of $F = ma$, where F is the force acting on an object, m stands for the object's mass, and a is the object's acceleration.

- **Newton's Third Law of Motion:** For every action, there is an equal and opposite reaction.

The second law deals with acceleration. To understand acceleration, you must first look at velocity. *Velocity* is a descriptor of how fast an object is moving.

Many people use *speed* and *velocity* interchangeably, but the terms aren't quite the same. The difference between speed and velocity is that velocity specifies the direction of motion. You can calculate velocity with the following equation:

Velocity = Displacement ÷ time

(For comparison, the formula for speed is Speed = Distance traveled ÷ time.)

In general, the increase in velocity over time is called *acceleration,* and the decrease in velocity over time is called *deceleration.* You can calculate acceleration with the following formula:

Acceleration = Change in velocity ÷ time

Motion in a plane (not in an airplane)

The preceding section gives you some conceptual ideas on motion; here you can look at how motion is applied. Motion can occur in one dimension, such as a car moving along a road or a ball thrown upward into the air. The big difference between these examples is the effect of gravity on the objects.

Kinematics equations involve five variables and can be used to mathematically solve for velocity and acceleration. (*Kinematics* is the study of the motion of a body.) If you know any three of the variables, you can easily find the rest. The five variables are

- D = displacement
- a = acceleration
- V_i = initial velocity
- V_f = final velocity
- T = time

Given a constant acceleration, the equations that you use to find whichever variables you're missing are

- $V_f = V_i + aT$
- $D = V_i T + 1/2 aT^2$
- $D = 1/2(V_i + V_f) \times T$
- $V_f^2 = V_i^2 + 2aD$

Force

Force is any kind of input that causes an object to experience a change in direction, speed, or shape. Force has both magnitude and direction, which makes it a vector quantity. The formula for force (measured in *newtons*) is as follows:

$F = ma$

where F is the force, m is the mass, and a is the acceleration.

Force can be *frictional, electromagnetic,* or *gravitational. Static frictional force* is the force that opposes any movement of an object when the object is at rest, and *kinetic frictional force* is created by the opposing forces between the surfaces of objects that are in relative motion. *Gravitational force* is the effect of gravity on an object. You don't need to worry about electromagnetic force for the flight aptitude test. (***Note:*** Other forces exist, but you don't need those for the test either.)

Energy and work

Energy is defined as the potential to do work. The energy of an object can be divided into two types: potential and kinetic. *Potential energy* is the energy that an object has because of its position (for example, the bowling ball sitting in the upper shelf of your closet). *Kinetic energy* is energy that results from motion. Both potential and kinetic energy change when work is done by or on an object. *Work* is the transfer of energy to an object when the object, because of the application of a force, moves. You can calculate the work done on an object by using the following formula:

$$W = F \times d$$

where W is work in joules, F is the force in newtons, and d is the distance in meters.

The work you do against gravity is *gravitational potential energy,* and you can calculate it by using the following formula:

$$PE = mgh$$

where PE is the potential energy in joules, m is the mass, g is the acceleration because of gravity (9.8 meters/second squared), and h is the height above ground in meters.

Pulleys

A *pulley* is a device used to exert rotational motion, alter an applied force's direction, or gain mechanical advantage. Pulleys usually take the form of a belt, rope, cable, or chain that runs over a grooved wheel on a shaft. The *mechanical advantage* derived from the pulley or combination of pulleys is calculated by dividing the weight lifted by the lifting force.

Although a pulley system makes lifting a heavy object easier, it doesn't actually have any impact on the amount of work done to lift the object. In reality, you're trading force for distance; you use less force to lift an object, but you must do so over a longer distance. (See the preceding section for info on calculating work.)

Pulley systems come in three different types (see Figure 9-1):

- ✔ **Fixed:** As the name indicates, a *fixed pulley* is anchored in place. This kind of pulley is also known as a *class 1 pulley.*

- ✔ **Movable:** A *movable pulley* is not anchored in place but rather is able to move. This kind of pulley is also known as a *class 2 pulley.*

- ✔ **Compound:** A *compound pulley* combines fixed and movable pulleys into a single system, gaining the advantages (and disadvantages) of each.

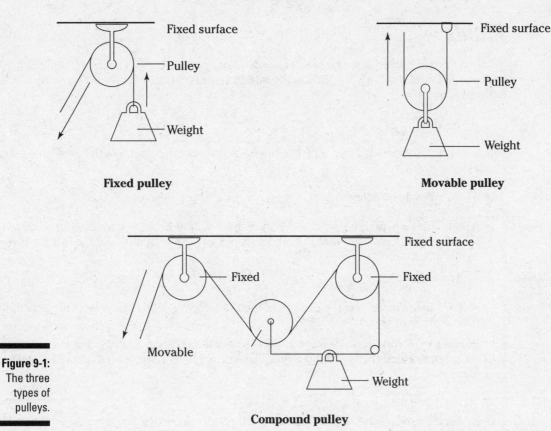

Figure 9-1:
The three
types of
pulleys.

Levers

A *lever* is simply a mechanical device in which rotating around a central point (called the *fulcrum*) allows you to achieve your desired goal by either minimizing your input force or maximizing your output force. In short, a lever reduces the force required to move or lift a weight. Figure 9-2 shows you the two types of levers that you may encounter on the various flight aptitude tests.

- ✔ **A first class lever** (Figure 9-2a) rotates around a fulcrum to achieve a load, or effect, on the opposite side of the fulcrum from the applied force.

- ✔ **A second class lever** (Figure 9-2b) reduces the effort to achieve a lifting result with both forces on the same side of the fulcrum.

Anyone who has ever used pliers or carried a wheelbarrow full of dirt has utilized a lever.

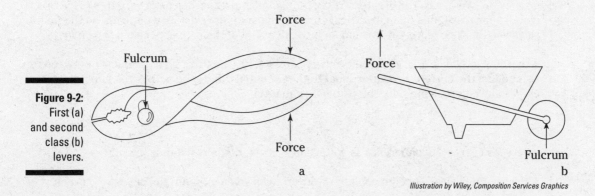

Figure 9-2:
First (a)
and second
class (b)
levers.

Fluids

A *fluid* is any substance that changes its shape under pressure; both gases and liquids are considered fluids. *Pressure* in a fluid is the force exerted on the area and is shown by the following equation:

$$P = F \div A$$

where P is the pressure (in pascals), F is the force (in newtons) and A is the area (in square meters).

Three principles govern fluids: Archimedes's, Pascal's, and Bernoulli's.

- ✓ **Archimedes's principle:** An object immersed in a fluid is buoyed up by a force equal to the weight of the fluid that the object displaces. The magnitude of the force is given by the equation

$$F = \rho V g$$

  where F is the force, ρ is the density of the fluid, V is the volume, and g is the acceleration because of gravity.

- ✓ **Pascal's principle:** Any pressure applied to a confined fluid, at any point, is transmitted undiminished throughout the fluid. This principle is represented by the following equation:

$$P = \rho g(h)$$

- ✓ **Bernoulli's principle:** As the velocity of a fluid increases, the pressure exerted by that fluid decreases. This principle makes your future in aviation possible because the low area of pressure creates a lifting force that allows planes to fly.

  The following equation shows Bernoulli's principle:

$$P(\text{static pressure}) + P(\text{dynamic pressure}) = P(\text{total pressure})$$

  Dynamic pressure is the velocity pressure (or kinetic energy) for the fluid at a certain point. You can find dynamic pressure by using the following formula:

$$P(\text{dynamic pressure}) = (\rho \times \text{velocity}^2) \div 2$$

Electricity

Electricity involves the flow of an *electrical current* (energy) from a *source* (battery or electrical outlet) to a load (light or motor). A *load* is a device that transforms electrical energy into other forms of energy. The electrical energy transported via electrical current consists of a flow of electrons. For an electrical current to flow in a conductor (such as an extension cord), a potential difference or voltage must exist between the conductor's ends. The greater the voltage is, the greater the current is. All substances, from a wire to a piece of wood, offer resistance to an electrical current; the amount resistance depends on the material's length, area, temperature, and an intrinsic value of the property called *resistivity*.

According to *Ohm's law,* when an electrical current passes through a conductor between two points, the current is proportional to the potential difference across the two points. Ohm's law is represented by the following equation:

$$I = V \div R$$

where I is current in amperes, V is voltage in volts, and R is resistance in ohms.

The chart in Figure 9-3 helps you take any variables given and find the answer you seek.

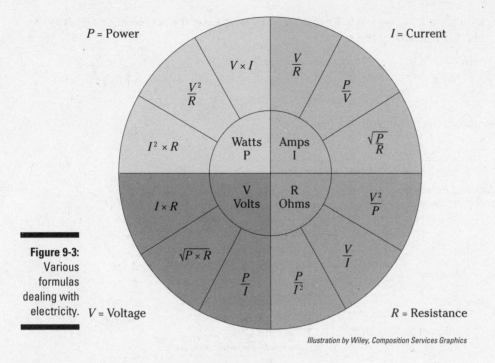

Figure 9-3: Various formulas dealing with electricity.

Sound and light waves

Two common physics principles are sound and light waves. *Sound waves* are pressure variations that are transmitted through matter. The speed at which sound travels depends on temperature and the medium (air) in which the sound waves travel. Here are a few sound wave highlights:

✔ When sound waves hit a hard surface, they reflect off it, causing an *echo*.

✔ The number of compressions by sound waves that occur in one second is called the *frequency* or *pitch* of the sound.

✔ If the source of the sound is in motion (such as a car coming down the street), you hear or perceive sound of higher or lower frequencies. This sensation is because of the *Doppler effect*.

Light waves can be visible or nonvisible. A light wave is measured in terms of its *wavelength*, or how far it travels before the wave's shape repeats itself. If you know the distance between repeating corresponding points of the same phase of the wave, you can figure out wavelength.

The wavelength λ of a *sinusoidal* waveform (a smooth succession of curves) traveling at the speed of light v (about 3×10^8 meters per second) is given by

$$\lambda = \frac{v}{f}$$

where *f* is the wave's frequency.

Pendulums

For any pendulum problem, remember that given a small initial swing, the pendulum's weight has no impact on the *frequency* (the number of *periods* — back-and-forth swings — the pendulum makes per second). Rather, the frequency (*f*) is affected by the length of the attachment string and the acceleration caused by gravity. Frequency is measured in hertz;

you can calculate it by using the following formula, where g is the acceleration becasue of gravity and L is the length of the string:

$$f = \left(\sqrt{\frac{g}{L}} \right) \div 2\pi$$

Figure 9-4 shows the movement of a pendulum.

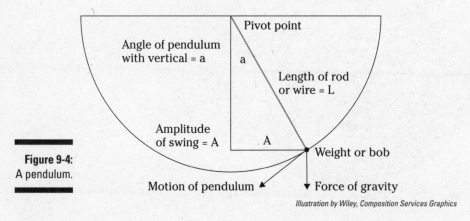

Figure 9-4:
A pendulum.

Illustration by Wiley, Composition Services Graphics

Getting down to Earth Science

Earth science is the study of the world we live in and even other planets. Everything from the internal core of the earth to the upper atmosphere is covered in this branch of science. The following sections cover some important earth science topics.

Earth trivia

Here are some interesting facts about the earth to give you a better insight to the planet:

- **Age:** 4.5 to 4.6 billion years

- **Atmospheric content:** 77 percent nitrogen; 21 percent oxygen; and traces of argon, carbon dioxide, and water

- **Chemical composition:** 34.6 percent iron, 29.5 percent oxygen, 15.2 percent silicon, 12.7 percent magnesium, 2.4 percent nickel, 1.9 percent sulfur, and 0.05 percent titanium

- **Ratio of water to land:** 70.8 percent to 29.2 percent

- **Highest elevation:** Mt. Everest, 29,035 feet (8,850 meters)

- **Tallest mountain from base to peak:** Mauna Kea, Hawaii, 33,480 feet (10,204 meters)

- **Lowest elevation:** Dead Sea, 1,369 feet (417.27 meters) below sea level

- **Deepest ocean depth:** Challenger Deep, Mariana Trench (in the western Pacific Ocean), 35,840 feet (10,924 meters)

- **Point at greatest distance from center of the earth:** Peak of volcano Chimborazo, Ecuador, 20,561 feet (6,267 meters)

- **Highest recorded temperature:** Al Aziziyah, Libya, September 13, 1922, 135.8 degrees Fahrenheit (57.7 degrees Celsius)

- **Lowest recorded temperature:** Vostok, Antarctica, July 21, 1983, –128.5 degrees Fahrenheit (–89.2 degrees Celsius)

- **Diameter at the equator:** 7,926.28 miles (12,756.1 kilometers)

- **Diameter at the North and South Poles:** 7,899.80 miles (12,713.5 kilometers)

- **Circumference at the equator:** 24,901.55 miles (40,075.16 kilometers)

- **Circumference between the North and South Poles:** 24,859.82 miles (40,008 kilometers)

- **Rotation rate on axis:** 23 hours, 56 minutes, and 4.09053 seconds

- **Revolution rate around the sun:** 365.2425 days

- **Distance from the sun:** 93,020,000 miles (149,669,180 kilometers) on average

- **Distance from the moon:** 238,857 miles (384,403.1 km) on average

Standard temperature and pressure use for aviation planning purposes is 59 degrees Fahrenheit (15 degrees Celsius) and 29.92 inches of mercury of pressure. These figures are a standard or average to base aircraft performance on. You calculate the actual performance based on flight performance charts and *density altitude* (the pressure altitude adjusted for non-standard temperature). Standard altitude temperature lapse rate is 2 degrees Celsius or 3 degrees Fahrenheit for every thousand feet of elevation climbed above the surface.

The earth in layers

Our planet is a fascinating example of planetary structure, evolution, and ecosystems. The following sections look at some of the structures that make this planet unique and capable of supporting life.

Layers of the planet

The interior structure of the earth is layered. You don't need to get into too much depth here (no pun intended); just know that the earth has an outer crust, a mantle, a liquid outer core, and a solid inner core.

Atmospheric layers

Onward and upward. Most people who are reading this text have probably been fascinated with the sky and flying for as long as they can remember. The sky, or atmosphere, is really a sea of gas with varying levels of concentration and life-sustaining capabilities. Here's a breakdown of your future office space:

- **Troposphere:** This layer begins at the earth's surface and goes 4 to 12 miles (6 to 20 kilometers). You'll do most of your flying in this layer. The transition boundary between the troposphere and the stratosphere is called the *tropopause.*

    In general, you have to start worrying about oxygen when you fly for a given time at 10,000 feet above sea level (well within the troposphere). Don't worry; though; flight training will give you experience with oxygen depletion.

- **Stratosphere:** The *stratosphere* extends from the top of the troposphere to around 31 miles (50 kilometers). This layer contains very little water vapor, but 19 percent of the atmosphere's gases occur here. The boundary that separates the stratosphere from the mesosphere is called the *stratopause.* The troposphere and stratosphere together are known as the *lower atmosphere.*

- **Mesosphere:** This atmospheric layer extends from the top of the stratosphere to about 56 miles (90 kilometers). Gases here continue to become thinner and thinner the higher you go. The boundary separating the mesosphere from the thermosphere is called the *mesopause.*

- **Thermosphere:** Above the mesosphere, the *thermosphere* or *upper atmosphere* reaches to almost 375 miles (600 kilometers).

✔ **Exosphere:** The *exosphere* is the outermost layer of the atmosphere. It goes from the top of the thermosphere to 6,200 miles (10,000 kilometers) above the earth.

Exploring Your Solar System

From *Star Trek* to *Star Wars* to Facebook pages demanding Pluto be reinstated as a planet, humans are fascinated with space and the distant planets. In the following sections, you can find some good information to know about our solar system for your aptitude test.

Sun facts and figures

The *sun* is a medium-sized, spherical star that just happens to be located at the center of our solar system. (Of course, medium is relative; the sun's diameter is about 1.392 million kilometers, and its mass is approximately 2×10^{30} kilograms, nearly 99 percent of the total mass of the solar system.) It's comprised of 71 percent hydrogen, 27.1 percent helium, and less than 2 percent of assorted other elements. The sun's surface temperature is in the neighborhood of 5,780 degrees Kelvin. It's a very hot place.

Closer to the sun: The inner planets

Astronomers decided somewhere along the line that dividing up the planets into two groups was a good idea. No, we're not talking about lists of naughty and nice planets or anything like that. The divisions in question deal with the planets' proximity to the sun. The *inner* planets include some of our personal favorites: Mercury, Venus, Earth, and Mars, which are also known as the *terrestrial* planets:

✔ **Mercury:** *Mercury* is the planet closest to the sun, and because it has just a smidgen of atmosphere, its surface is pocked with meteor craters. Mercury is the smallest of all the planets in the solar system, and it has no moons. Although it's no sun, it can be a hot place, with high temperatures of up to about 800 degrees Fahrenheit. But it knows extreme cold, too; temperatures on the side away from the sun dip to about –280 degrees Fahrenheit.

✔ **Venus:** The second planet from the sun is *Venus* — a planet that shares much in common with Earth, including (approximately) size, mass, density, and elemental composition. However, the similarities with Earth pretty much end there. Venus's thick, cloudy atmosphere (which makes it the brightest object in the night sky after Earth's moon) would be toxic to humans — it's comprised mostly of carbon dioxide gas with a fine mist of sulfuric acid droplets. (Sounds lovely, doesn't it?) Surface temperatures on Venus run to about 880 degrees Fahrenheit, but scientists believe that the planet once had extensive oceans. Any oceans are long gone today, though, replaced by large fields of hardened basaltic lava.

✔ **Earth:** The third planet from the sun is our home sweet home planet *Earth*. Check out the earlier section "Getting down to Earth Science" for the nitty-gritty on the earth.

✔ **Mars:** The fourth planet from the sun — and the last of the inner planets — is *Mars*. It's also known as the *Red Planet* because of the iron oxide content of its surface, which gives it a red appearance when viewed from telescopes. Mars has a thin atmosphere with surface features that are similar to the craters of Earth's moon, volcanoes, and ice caps. Mars has two moons, Phobos and Deimos, and surface temperatures that range from about –125 degrees Fahrenheit to about 23 degrees Fahrenheit.

Planets on the fringe: The outer planets

The planets beyond Mars are known as the *outer planets* or *Jovian gas giant planets.* These planets are primarily made up of the same stuff as the sun: helium and hydrogen. Here are some other facts about these far-out neighbors:

- **Jupiter:** The fifth planet from the sun is *Jupiter,* by far the largest planet in our solar system. Hydrogen makes up about 75 percent of Jupiter's total mass, and helium accounts for the other 25 percent. In fact, if Jupiter's mass were just 80 times greater than it is, the planet would have ignited and become a second sun within our solar system. Jupiter's upper atmosphere is quite turbulent, with strong winds that push the planet's ammonia clouds into long stripes. Jupiter's Great Red Spot is the result of a huge storm that has raged for centuries, and the planet's magnetic field is 20,000 times stronger than the Earth's. Jupiter's average temperature is –234 degrees Fahrenheit.

- **Saturn:** The sixth planet from the sun is *Saturn.* The planet has 52 known moons and is notable for its complex system of rings, comprised of nine continuous and three discontinuous main rings. The rings are primarily made up of ice crystals, dust, and rocky debris. Although Saturn's mass is more than 95 times that of Earth's, its average density is just one-eighth that of our own planet. The average temperature on Saturn is a frosty –288 degrees Fahrenheit.

- **Uranus:** The seventh planet from the Sun is *Uranus,* which has 11 known rings and 27 known moons. Uranus is larger than all the other planets except for Jupiter and Saturn, and its average temperature is –357 degrees Fahrenheit.

- **Neptune:** The planet farthest from the sun is *Neptune,* which is slightly smaller than Uranus; its mass is 17 times that of Earth. Neptune's temperature averages –353 degrees Fahrenheit.

Not quite a planet: Pluto

As you've probably heard by now, Pluto was categorized as a planet for decades. However, the International Astronomical Union stripped this designation from Pluto in 2006 and reclassified it as a *dwarf planet.* We're including it in the discussion here anyway because it's still an important entity. *Pluto* is the second-most-massive known dwarf planet and the tenth-most-massive body that directly orbits the sun. It has three known moons and is composed primarily of rock and ice, with a total mass approximately one-fifth the mass of Earth's moon. It's quite cold at a temperature of about –356 degrees F.

Putting Science to Good Use: Applied Sciences

The meaning of *applied science* is spelled out in its name; this branch applies concepts from other sciences toward your environment.

Digging agriculture: A major growth industry

Agriculture (also known as *farming*) is the backbone of most countries, and it deals with all the processes that get food on the table, including feed production, fertilizers, land management, and food growth. *Subsistence agriculture,* where a farmer produces enough food to meet his family's needs, was the primary type of farming in the United States until the turn of the 20th century, and it's still the principal type of farming in many undeveloped nations.

The change from subsistence to *commercial agriculture,* where growers produce crops in large quantities specifically to sell as a commercial product, was largely responsible for the migration of people in the rural United States to cities. Agriculture also produces consumption goods such as nursery plants, animal hides, industrial chemicals, fibers (such as cotton or wool), and now even fuel through the use of corn ethanol. A subsection of agriculture is *animal husbandry,* which concerns breeding and raising animals for meat and products (such as milk, eggs, or wool) on a continual basis.

One goal of farmers worldwide is to make farming more efficient in order to feed more people with the same amount of land and natural resources. In the United States, for example, improved science and farming practices, soil conservation, pesticides, genetic engineering, and modern machinery have greatly increased yields per acre. One of the key components of modern warfare is teaching unimproved nations how to implement subsistence farming and thereby win the hearts and minds of that country's people. While serving in Iraq, coauthor Terry was fortunate enough to witness troops teaching the local populations drip irrigation, sugar refining, and catfish farming.

Planting your roots in forestry

Forestry is the practice of growing, managing, harvesting, and conserving forests and their associated resources for the use of mankind. The nature of forestry (no pun intended) is to continue a system that allows for a renewable resource that's both very forward-thinking toward sustainability and able to meet the current needs of a growing economy. Forestry has come a long way from the past practices of clear-cutting entire forests and not worrying about future growth. The challenge of the forestry industry is to balance maintaining company profitability, meeting the resource needs of a growing population, and managing assets in a way that is acceptable to environmental groups.

Keeping others healthy with the health sciences

From medicine to dentistry, the health sciences are an all-encompassing field geared toward maintaining a healthy life, preventing of diseases, and repairing injuries. Two important fields in this category are medicine and nutrition, which you can read about in the following sections.

Medicine

Medicine is the science that deals with the health and well being of the population. Medicine includes current treatment, scientific research, and preventative practices, all in a variety of specialties. Many advances in the modern medical world have been developed by the different branches of the military services.

The medical field works as an interdisciplinary team and includes many highly trained health professionals; coauthor Terry is proud to now be a member of this community. In the lead are medical providers such as physicians, dentists, physician assistants, and nurse practitioners; these folks are assisted by nurses, emergency medical responders, pharmacists, X-ray and laboratory technicians, and many others, with behind-the-scenes research by scientists and research doctors. And of course, don't forget the medical evacuation pilots and flight crews who transport the critically ill both from the front-line battlefield and to and from hospitals throughout the world.

Nutrition

Nutrition is providing, at a cellular level, the substances necessary to support life. A proper diet can prevent or alleviate many common health problems (such as cardiovascular disease, diabetes, and obesity). On the flip side, poor dietary practices can negatively impact health; they've been estimated to lead to approximately 30 to 50 percent of annual U.S. health care expenditures.

Chapter 10

Technical Information and Science Practice Test

• •

*T*his technical information and science practice test is quite comprehensive and detailed, exploring the key information you need to successfully navigate this particular subject on the various flight aptitude tests. These topics are very important because every military service stresses the need for technical and science skills for potential aviators.

Choose the most correct answer for each question.

Subtest 1: The Natural and Applied Sciences

1. Anatomy is the branch of science that considers

   (A) The structure of human beings

   (B) The structure of a living thing

   (C) The cell parts

   (D) The structure of plants

2. Biology is the science concerned with

   (A) The study of only the cellular level

   (B) The study of only new species and traits

   (C) The study of structure, origin, classification, function, and growth

   (D) The study of only evolution

3. Botany studies

   (A) Plant life and its mechanisms

   (B) Floral arrangements

   (C) Ecological interactions

   (D) All mechanisms of plant and animal life

4. The study of interactions between organisms and their physical environments is known as

   (A) Biology

   (B) Embryology

   (C) Ecology

   (D) Cytology

5. Physiology is the study of

   (A) The psycho-social aspects of living systems

   (B) Detailed anatomical systems

   (C) Cell biology

   (D) The function of living systems and how they work

6. The study of classifications, habits, evolution, health, and social patterns of all species in the animal kingdom is

   (A) Pathology

   (B) Zoology

   (C) Classology

   (D) Morton-heights functional studies

7. The science that looks at land masses, their structures, and the movement patterns of people who inhabit the areas of interest is

   (A) Geography

   (B) Geology

   (C) Histology

   (D) Morphology

8. The study of the earth and its structure is

   (A) Ecology

   (B) Meteorology

   (C) Geology

   (D) Functional capacity studies

9. The study of water movement, sources of distribution, and quality on Earth and other planets is

   (A) Planetary water studies

   (B) Geography

   (C) Ecology

   (D) Hydrology

10. Meteorology deals with

    (A) The impact of space objects entering Earth's atmosphere

    (B) The study of the atmosphere and the forecasting of weather patterns

    (C) The formation of geological deposits

    (D) Crater impacts on Earth and terrestrial planets

11. The study of the celestial sky is

    (A) Astronomy

    (B) Astrology

    (C) Meteorology

    (D) Cosmetology

12. Agriculture involves

    (A) Lawn management

    (B) Feed production, fertilizers, land use, food growth, and animal husbandry

    (C) Watershed management

    (D) Forest management

13. The practice of growing, managing, harvesting, and conserving forests is

    (A) Agriculture

    (B) A department of the Bureau of Land Affairs

    (C) Land management

    (D) Forestry

14. Lack of vitamin C, or ascorbic acid, causes which disease(s)?

    (A) Goiter

    (B) Rickets and osteoporosis

    (C) Scurvy

    (D) Alzheimer's

15. Lack of vitamin D causes which disease(s)?

    (A) Goiter

    (B) Rickets and osteoporosis

    (C) Scurvy

    (D) Alzheimer's

16. Lack of iodine causes which disease(s)?

    (A) Goiter

    (B) Rickets and osteoporosis

    (C) Scurvy

    (D) Alzheimer's

Subtest 2: The Metric System

17. The International System (SI) standard uses what unit of measurement for mass?

    (A) Pound

    (B) Ton

    (C) Joule

    (D) Gram

    (E) Kilogram

18. What is the SI unit for work?

    (A) Pascal

    (B) Joule

    (C) Hertz

    (D) Hercules

19. A nanosecond equals

    (A) 0.000000001 seconds

    (B) 0.00000001 seconds

    (C) 0.0000001 seconds

    (D) 0.000001 seconds

20. A kilogram equals

    (A) 10 grams

    (B) 100 grams

    (C) 1,000 grams

    (D) 10,000 grams

21. A 165-pound man weighs how many kilograms?

    (A) 72.5 kilograms

    (B) 75 kilograms

    (C) 77.5 kilograms

    (D) 80 kilograms

22. Six inches equals how many centimeters?

    (A) 12.1 centimeters

    (B) 30.48 centimeters

    (C) 7.5 centimeters

    (D) 15.24 centimeters

23. 638 kilometers equals how many miles?

    (A) 382.8 miles

    (B) 395.6 miles

    (C) 403.7 miles

    (D) 412.1 miles

24. A container has a volume of 310 cubic centimeters. What is the volume in cubic inches?

    (A) 18.91 cubic inches

    (B) 19.48 cubic inches

    (C) 21.48 cubic inches

    (D) 25.79 cubic inches

25. You're traveling and hear that the temperature is 16.4 degrees Celsius. Convert that temperature to degrees Fahrenheit.

    (A) 76 degrees

    (B) 84 degrees

    (C) 62 degrees

    (D) 45 degrees

26. Convert 78 degrees Fahrenheit to degrees Celsius.

    (A) 24 degrees

    (B) 25.2 degrees

    (C) 26 degrees

    (D) 22.5 degrees

Subtest 3: The Scientific Method and Scientific Notation

27. A formalized method for the observation, experimentation, development, and further modification of a scientific idea is called the

    (A) Product development

    (B) Unit experimentation

    (C) Procedural sampling

    (D) Scientific method

28. The measurement 0.000000000000025 grams can be written as

    (A) 2.5×10^{-12} grams

    (B) 2.5×10^{-14} grams

    (C) 2.5×10^{-16} grams

    (D) 2.5×10^{-18} grams

Subtest 4: Life Science Essentials

29. The classification of organisms in a way that corresponds with their relationships among each other is

    (A) Taxonomy

    (B) Taxidermy

    (C) Genetic design

    (D) Evolution

30. The three domains that are most commonly recognized in classification are

    (A) Amoeba, Eubacteria, Eukarya

    (B) Archaea, Eubacteria, Eukarya

    (C) Amoeba, Bacteria, Animalia

    (D) Archaea, Eubacteria, Animalia

31. Domain Eukarya is subdivided into four kingdoms, which are

    (A) Protista, Rotistae, Plantae, and Animalia

    (B) Amoeba, Protista, Plantae, and Animalia

    (C) Protista, Fungi, Plantae, and Animalia

    (D) Amoeba, Fungi, Plantae, and Animalia

32. Humans are part of domain

    (A) Amoeba

    (B) Protista

    (C) Eubacteria

    (D) Eukarya

33. The fundamental unit of structure, function, and organization in all living organisms is

    (A) The cell

    (B) The nucleus

    (C) The atom

    (D) Muscle tissue

34. Which of the following statements is false?

    (A) Metabolism and biochemistry energy development occur within cells.

    (B) Some living organisms have no cells.

    (C) Cells arise from pre-existing cells by division.

    (D) DNA is contained in the cells and is passed to new cells during cell division.

35. An organism whose cells contain complex structures enclosed within membranes is

    (A) Eukaryotic

    (B) Prokaryotic

    (C) Membaryotic

    (D) Mesoaryotic

36. The gel-like substance containing all the cell's internal structures except the nucleus is the

    (A) Cytoplasm

    (B) Golgi apparatus

    (C) Organelle

    (D) Endoplasmic reticulum

37. What structure is responsible for protein synthesis?

    (A) Nucleus

    (B) Smooth endoplasmic reticulum

    (C) Rough endoplasmic reticulum

    (D) Ribosome

38. What structure is responsible for metabolizing carbohydrates/steroids, regulating calcium concentration, making lipids, and assisting in attaching receptors on cell membrane proteins?

    (A) Nucleus

    (B) Smooth endoplasmic reticulum

    (C) Rough endoplasmic reticulum

    (D) Ribosome

39. Following synthesis, what structure is responsible for the processing of proteins for secretion?

    (A) Membrane

    (B) Endoplasmic reticulum

    (C) Ribosome

    (D) Golgi apparatus

40. What separates the exterior of a cell from the interior?

    (A) Golgi body

    (B) Cell membrane

    (C) Organelles

    (D) Cytoplasm

41. Also known as the cell's power plant, what structure generates ATP, used as a source of chemical energy?

    (A) Nucleus

    (B) Mitochondrion

    (C) Golgi body

    (D) Endoplasmic reticulum

42. What structure is responsible for maintaining cell heredity and functional integrity?

    (A) Nucleus

    (B) Mitochondrion

    (C) Golgi body

    (D) Endoplasmic reticulum

43. The process of dividing one cell nucleus into two nuclei is called

    (A) Division

    (B) Subtraction

    (C) Mitosis

    (D) Cell division

44. What structure assists in the genetic transfer of information in a process known as translation?

    (A) Nucleus

    (B) Golgi body

    (C) Mitochondrion

    (D) Ribosome

45. The biological process in which cells process nutrient molecules through catabolism and anabolism is called

    (A) Nutrition

    (B) Metabolism

    (C) Phagocytosis

    (D) Photosynthesis

46. The function of an enzyme is to

    (A) Speed up a chemical reaction with less heat required

    (B) Slow down a chemical reaction

    (C) Absorb energy during a chemical reaction

    (D) Transfer energy during a chemical reaction

47. The diffusion of a solvent through a semi-permeable membrane from a region of low solute concentration to a region of high solute concentration is known as

    (A) Lipid bypass transfer

    (B) Active transfer

    (C) Proton pump

    (D) Osmosis

48. When a biological cell engulfs a substance or particle to form a food vacuole, that process is called

    (A) Golgi gorging

    (B) Photosynthesis

    (C) Phagocytosis

    (D) Osmosis

49. The process where energy is converted from light to chemical energy in plants is called

    (A) Golgi gorging

    (B) Photosynthesis

    (C) Phagocytosis

    (D) Osmosis

50. What broad term indicates the process where chemical bonds of energy rich molecules are converted into energy that is useable for all life processes and functions?

    (A) Glucose transfer

    (B) Metabolism

    (C) Nutrition

    (D) Cellular respiration

51. Which system serves as support, allows for movement at the joints, and protects vital organs?

    (A) The skeletal system

    (B) The muscular system

    (C) The digestive system

    (D) The nervous system

52. Which of the following isn't a function of the skeletal system?

    (A) Serves as the site for hematopoiesis

    (B) Stores and metabolizes calcium

    (C) Regulates metabolism by releasing a hormone called osteonutricin

    (D) Regulates blood sugar by releasing a hormone called osteocalcin

53. Which of the following isn't a type of muscle tissue?

    (A) Connective muscle tissue

    (B) Skeletal muscle tissue

    (C) Cardiac muscle tissue

    (D) Smooth muscle tissue

54. Which system allows movement through a coordinated contraction of its tissue and is controlled primarily through the nervous system?

    (A) The skeletal system

    (B) The muscular system

    (C) The digestive system

    (D) The nervous system

55. The _____ transports _____ blood from the heart to the lungs.

    (A) Pulmonary vein; deoxygenated

    (B) Pulmonary artery; deoxygenated

    (C) Pulmonary vein; oxygenated

    (D) Pulmonary artery; oxygenated

56. Which of the following isn't a component of the cardiovascular and respiratory systems?

    (A) Heart

    (B) Lungs

    (C) Blood

    (D) Liver

57. Gas exchange takes place

    (A) In the lungs at the alveoli

    (B) At the junction of the pulmonary artery and the lungs

    (C) At the junction of the pulmonary vein and the lungs

    (D) In the pancreas

58. The brain stem controls

    (A) Kidney function

    (B) Automatic-type responses and muscles

    (C) Cardiac output

    (D) Smooth muscle tissue

59. Which system is responsible for transporting oxygen-rich blood to the various parts of the body?

    (A) Capillary circulatory system

    (B) Alveoli gas exchange system

    (C) Pulmonary circulatory system

    (D) Systemic circulatory system

60. The brain and spinal cord make up the central nervous system. What makes up the peripheral nervous system?

    (A) Respirations and the automatic response

    (B) Nerves on the hands and feet

    (C) Motor and sensory nerves outside the brain and spinal column

    (D) Cardiac muscle

61. The initial substance formed in your stomach by a combination of mastication, hydrochloric acid, and enzymes is called

    (A) Chyme

    (B) Campascil

    (C) Bolus

    (D) Nutrient sub pack

62. Where are most nutrients absorbed?

    (A) Stomach

    (B) Small intestine

    (C) Large intestine

    (D) Rectum

63. Sugars that are found in foods are called

    (A) Carbohydrates

    (B) Lipids

    (C) Amino acids

    (D) Proteins

64. Which system serves as a chemical information signal system to the nervous system?

    (A) The lymphatic system

    (B) The digestive system

    (C) The endocrine system

    (D) The urinary system

65. Which of the following isn't one of the functions of the endocrine system?

    (A) Growth and development

    (B) Metabolism

    (C) Sense of smell

    (D) Mood

66. Which system is responsible for the combining of genetic material for evolutional survival of a species?

    (A) The urinary system

    (B) The lymphatic system

    (C) The nervous system

    (D) The reproductive system

67. Upon normal fertilization, a normal human egg attaches to the _____ and has a gestation period of approximately _____ months.

    (A) Fallopian tubes; nine

    (B) Uterus; nine

    (C) Fallopian tubes; eight

    (D) Uterus; eight

68. If one parent has a dominant trait gene (Dd) and the other parent doesn't have the trait (dd), what is the chance that their offspring will have the dominant trait?

    (A) 25 percent

    (B) 50 percent

    (C) 75 percent

    (D) 100 percent

69. Women are more susceptible to urinary and bladder infections, primarily because of the fact that

    (A) Men have a shorter urethra.

    (B) Men have a larger urethra.

    (C) Women have a shorter urethra.

    (D) Women have a larger urethra.

70. Which of the following isn't a function of the kidneys?

    (A) Regulating blood pressure

    (B) Regulating electrolytes

    (C) Maintaining acid-base equilibrium

    (D) Ejecting urine from the body

71. Which system moves a clear liquid toward the heart and deals with the immunity of the body?

    (A) The lymphatic system

    (B) The urinary system

    (C) The nervous system

    (D) The digestive system

72. The lymphatic system doesn't include

    (A) Bone marrow

    (B) Gonads

    (C) Spleen

    (D) Thymus

Subtest 5: Chemistry

73. Which branch of chemistry deals with carbon-based compounds?

    (A) Physical chemistry

    (B) Microscopic chemistry

    (C) Organic chemistry

    (D) Inorganic chemistry

74. Which branch of chemistry deals with non-carbon-based compounds?

    (A) Physical chemistry

    (B) Microscopic chemistry

    (C) Organic chemistry

    (D) Inorganic chemistry

75. What type of matter has a defined shape, mass, and volume?

    (A) Solid

    (B) Liquid

    (C) Gas

    (D) Semisolid

76. When a substance transfers directly from a solid to a gas, the process is called

    (A) Condensation

    (B) Reduction

    (C) Boyle's melting

    (D) Sublimation

77. A pure chemical substance containing one type of atom is called a

    (A) Compound

    (B) Element

    (C) Substance

    (D) Solvent

78. The basic unit of matter is the

    (A) Block

    (B) Unit

    (C) Atom

    (D) Neutron

79. Electrons are bound to the nucleus of an atom by

    (A) Carbon bonds

    (B) Electromagnetic force

    (C) Acid-base balance

    (D) Opposite attraction

80. The acceptance, sharing, and giving of electrons form the basis for all

    (A) Chemical reactions

    (B) Photosynthesis

    (C) Cellular respiration

    (D) Mitosis

81. The number of _____ in an atom determines what type of element that atom is.

    (A) Neutrons

    (B) Electrons

    (C) Protons

    (D) Isotopes

82. Inside the nucleus of an element, you find both neutrons and

    (A) Brentons

    (B) Electrons

    (C) Protons

    (D) Isotopes

83. Which of the following statements is true?

    (A) A proton has a larger mass than an electron does.

    (B) An electron has a larger mass than a proton does.

    (C) The masses of protons and electrons are equal.

    (D) The difference between the masses of protons and electrons varies such that one isn't always larger than the other.

84. Neutrons carry what type of charge?

    (A) Positive charge

    (B) Negative charge

    (C) Alternating positive and negative charge depending on orbital

    (D) Neither positive nor negative charge

85. An element that has its usual number of protons but a different number of neutrons is called a(n)

    (A) Neutron

    (B) Electron

    (C) Gamma differential

    (D) Isotope

86. Which electrons of an atom can participate in the formation of chemical bonds?

    (A) Electrons in the p orbital only

    (B) Valence electrons

    (C) Free radical electrons

    (D) Isotope electrons

87. Atoms with a complete, or closed, shell of valence electrons tend to be

    (A) Chemically inert

    (B) Chemically unstable

    (C) Explosive

    (D) Reactive

88. An orbital or electron cloud of electrons orbiting the nucleus of an atom is called the

    (A) Cloud orbital

    (B) Electron puff

    (C) Electron shell

    (D) Electron cloud region

89. What determines an element's atomic number?

    (A) The weight of the atom

    (B) The number of neutrons in the atom

    (C) The number of electrons in the atom

    (D) The number of protons in the atom

90. The atomic mass listed with an element on the periodic table is the average of

    (A) All elements listed in order

    (B) The number of electrons surrounding the element

    (C) The naturally occurring isotopes of that element

    (D) The average of the number of protons in an element

91. Elements listed in any particular column (group) on the periodic table share the same characteristics for chemical bonding because

    (A) They have the same number of valence electrons.

    (B) They have differing numbers of valence electrons.

    (C) They're subject to the order of metal sublimation.

    (D) They're in the same row.

92. When heat is given off during a chemical reaction, the reaction is called

    (A) Hot

    (B) Thermal

    (C) Endothermic

    (D) Exothermic

93. When heat is consumed during a chemical reaction, the reaction is called

    (A) Hot

    (B) Thermal

    (C) Endothermic

    (D) Exothermic

94. The law of _____ states that a chemical reaction can't create or destroy matter.

    (A) Classification of substances

    (B) Conservation of mass

    (C) Matter effectiveness

    (D) Newton's mass equity

95. When something has a pH below 7, that thing is considered a(n)

    (A) Acid

    (B) Base

    (C) Electrolyte imbalance

    (D) Balanced electrolyte

96. Acids act as

    (A) Proton receptors

    (B) Proton donors

    (C) Electron receptors

    (D) Electron donors

97. Acid-base reactions involve the transfer of _____ from one molecule (acid) to another (base).

    (A) Electrons

    (B) Neutrons

    (C) Valence electrons

    (D) Protons

Subtest 6: Physics

98. What effect does a low-gravity environment, such as spaceflight, have on weight and mass?

    (A) Both mass and weight increase.

    (B) Both mass and weight decrease.

    (C) Mass increases, and weight decreases.

    (D) Mass remains the same, and weight decreases.

99. Which of the following isn't a type of motion?

    (A) Translational

    (B) Rotational

    (C) Vertical

    (D) Vibrational

100. An 80-kilogram man jumps off a raft that weighs 100 kilograms. His initial velocity from jumping is 7 meters per second. Assuming that the friction resistance of the water is zero, the velocity of the raft after the man jumps will be

    (A) 3.33 meters per second

    (B) 5.6 meters per second

    (C) –3.33 meters per second

    (D) –2.7 meters per second

101. Which of the following isn't one of Newton's three laws of motion?

    (A) For every action, there is an equal and opposite reaction

    (B) For every reaction, there is an inversely opposed force to resist acceleration because of the gravitational force.

    (C) When an object is acted upon by an outside force, the acceleration is directly proportional to the applied force and inversely proportional to the mass of the object.

    (D) A body at rest tends to remain at rest and a body in motion tends to remain in motion unless acted upon by an outside force.

102. Two objects collide with one another from opposite directions. Object A weighs 7 kilograms and is traveling at 10 meters per second, and object B weighs 7 kilograms and is traveling at 5 meters per second. If the two objects remain attached following the collision, what is their combined speed?

    (A) 2 meters per second

    (B) 0 meters per second

    (C) 2.5 meters per second

    (D) 3 meters per second

103. The speed of the projectile with a momentum of 13.7 kilograms meters per second and a mass of 0.005 kilograms is

    (A) 2,740 meters per second

    (B) 1,908 meters per second

    (C) 5.2 meters per second

    (D) 0.275 meters per second

104. If a car drives due east for 20 meters at 20 meters per second and then immediately drives due west for 20 meters at 20 meters per second, what is the car's average velocity after 2 seconds?

    (A) 20 meters per second

    (B) 10 meters per second

    (C) –20 meters per second

    (D) 0 meters per second

105. An object can accelerate by

    (A) Changing speed

    (B) Changing velocity

    (C) Changing the direction of its velocity but not the magnitude

    (D) All of the above

106. The formula for calculating force (F) is

    (A) $F = ma$, with the result measured in newtons

    (B) $F = va$, with the result measured in joules

    (C) $F = ma$, with the result measured in joules

    (D) $F = va$, with the result measured in newtons

107. Which of the following isn't a type of force?

    (A) Frictional

    (B) Physical

    (C) Electromagnetic

    (D) Gravitational

108. An object moves 2 meters after a force of 2 newtons is applied. How much work has occurred?

    (A) 2 newtons

    (B) 2 joules

    (C) 4 newtons

    (D) 4 joules

109. Two items A and B weighing 5 and 10 pounds, respectively, are dropped at the same time from a 200-foot tower (with each having the same wind resistance). Which item will impact the ground first?

    (A) A

    (B) B

    (C) A and B will impact at the same time.

    (D) A and B will randomly impact one before the other.

110. In Question 109, which item will have the greater potential energy (PE)?

    (A) A.

    (B) B.

    (C) A and B have the same PE.

    (D) You can't estimate the PE in the given situation.

111. Not including friction, a single pulley gives a mechanical advantage of

    (A) 2

    (B) 1

    (C) 2.5

    (D) 3

112. The wheelbarrow is an example of

    (A) A second class lever

    (B) A first class lever

    (C) A third class lever

    (D) A fourth class lever

113. A pressure of 23 pascals is applied to an area of 2.2 square meters. What is the force?

    (A) 50.6 pounds

    (B) 46.6 joules

    (C) 50.6 newtons

    (D) 48.7 foot pounds

114. An object immersed in a fluid is buoyed up by a force equal to the weight of the fluid that the object displaces. This result is an example of

    (A) Bernoulli's principle

    (B) Archimedes's principle

    (C) Vermillion's principle

    (D) Pascal's principle

115. Any pressure applied to a confined fluid at any point is transmitted undiminished throughout the fluid. This result is an example of

    (A) Bernoulli's principle

    (B) Archimedes's principle

    (C) Vermillion's principle

    (D) Pascal's principle

116. _____ states that as the velocity of a fluid increases, the pressure exerted by that fluid decreases.

    (A) Bernoulli's principle

    (B) Archimedes's principle

    (C) Vermillion's principle

    (D) Pascal's principle

117. 110 volts is applied to a light that has a resistance of 10 ohms. What is the smallest circuit breaker you can use to handle that current?

    (A) 10-amp breaker

    (B) 12-amp breaker

    (C) 15-amp breaker

    (D) 20-amp breaker

118. A 110-volt power source results in 3 amps to the load. The total power delivered is

    (A) 100 watts

    (B) 330 watts

    (C) 360 watts

    (D) 210 watts

119. The unit of measurement for electrical resistance to oppose the current or flow of electrons is

    (A) Watts

    (B) Amperes (amps)

    (C) Ohms

    (D) Joules

120. In the electromagnetic spectrum, which of the following has the longest wavelength?

    (A) Microwaves

    (B) Visible light

    (C) Ultraviolet light

    (D) Infrared light

121. A pendulum has a frequency of oscillation f. To triple f, the length of the pendulum should be

    (A) Increased by a factor of 3

    (B) Decreased by a factor of 9

    (C) Decreased by a factor of 3

    (D) Changing the length of the pendulum has no impact on f.

Subtest 7: Earth Sciences

122. What percentage of the earth's surface is made up of water?

    (A) 66.2 percent

    (B) 56.9 percent

    (C) 81.0 percent

    (D) 70.8 percent

123. Which of the following is the most accurate description of the earth's atmospheric content?

    (A) 21 percent nitrogen; 77 percent oxygen; and traces of argon, carbon dioxide, and water

    (B) 77 percent nitrogen; 21 percent oxygen; and traces of argon, carbon dioxide, and water

    (C) 52 percent nitrogen, 38 percent oxygen, 5 percent ozone, and traces of argon and carbon dioxide

    (D) 66 percent nitrogen, 18 percent oxygen, 13 percent ozone, and 11 percent carbon dioxide/water mix

124. The troposphere begins at the earth's surface and extends approximately

    (A) 4 to 12 miles

    (B) 3 to 6 miles

    (C) 5 to 7 miles

    (D) 18,000 feet

125. The age of Earth is approximately

    (A) 2.3 to 3.0 billion years

    (B) 4.5 to 4.6 billion years

    (C) 3.1 to 3.6 billion years

    (D) 4.8 to 5.1 billion years

126. Which of the following most accurately describes the chemical content of Earth?

    (A) 34.6 percent iron, 29.5 percent oxygen, 15.2 percent silicon, 12.7 percent magnesium, 2.4 percent nickel, 1.9 percent sulfur, and 0.05 percent titanium

    (B) 28.4 percent iron, 32.1 percent oxygen, 16.4 percent silicon, 12.8 percent magnesium, 6.7 percent nickel, 2.4 percent sulfur, 1.1 percent titanium

    (C) 35.7 percent iron, 33.4 percent oxygen, 15.1 percent silicon, 11.8 percent magnesium, 3.4 percent nickel, 0.3 percent sulfur, 0.1 percent titanium

    (D) 32.4 percent iron, 28.9 percent oxygen, 22.1 percent silicon, 9.7 percent magnesium, 5.6 percent nickel, 1.1 percent sulfur, 0.2 percent titanium

Subtest 8: Solar System

127. Which of the following planets isn't farther from the sun than Earth is?

    (A) Neptune

    (B) Venus

    (C) Saturn

    (D) Uranus

128. Which of the following represents Earth's position from the sun?

    (A) Second planet; beyond Mars and before Venus

    (B) Second planet; beyond Venus and before Mars

    (C) Third planet; beyond Mars and before Venus

    (D) Third planet; beyond Venus and before Mars

129. Our solar system consists of how many planets?

    (A) 6

    (B) 7

    (C) 8

    (D) 9

130. The largest planet in our solar system is

    (A) Venus

    (B) Neptune

    (C) Saturn

    (D) Jupiter

Answer Key

1. B	26. C	51. A	76. D
2. C	27. D	52. C	77. B
3. A	28. B	53. A	78. C
4. C	29. A	54. B	79. B
5. D	30. B	55. B	80. A
6. B	31. C	56. D	81. C
7. A	32. D	57. A	82. C
8. C	33. A	58. B	83. A
9. D	34. B	59. D	84. D
10. B	35. A	60. C	85. D
11. A	36. A	61. A	86. B
12. B	37. C	62. B	87. A
13. D	38. B	63. A	88. C
14. C	39. D	64. C	89. D
15. B	40. B	65. C	90. C
16. A	41. B	66. D	91. A
17. E	42. A	67. B	92. D
18. B	43. C	68. B	93. C
19. A	44. D	69. C	94. B
20. C	45. B	70. D	95. A
21. B	46. A	71. A	96. B
22. D	47. D	72. B	97. D
23. B	48. C	73. C	98. D
24. A	49. B	74. D	99. C
25. C	50. D	75. A	100. B

101. **B**	109. **C**	117. **B**	125. **B**
102. **C**	110. **B**	118. **B**	126. **A**
103. **A**	111. **B**	119. **C**	127. **B**
104. **D**	112. **A**	120. **A**	128. **D**
105. **D**	113. **C**	121. **B**	129. **C**
106. **A**	114. **B**	122. **D**	130. **D**
107. **B**	115. **D**	123. **B**	
108. **D**	116. **A**	124. **A**	

Chapter 11

Basic Aeronautical Knowledge

• •

In This Chapter

▶ Deciding whether to take flying lessons

▶ Getting a handle on the fundamental science of aviation

▶ Exploring fixed-wing and rotary-wing aircraft

▶ Using two sample flight lesson plans

• •

ou can ride a bike without a lot of detailed training, but the same can't be said for flying an aircraft; you have to be familiar with all sorts of aircraft parts and instruments and know how outside conditions and your actions will affect how your craft flies. In this chapter, we look at the basic aeronautical knowledge that you need for the various flight aptitude tests. Note that we cover only the minimum knowledge you need to successfully complete the tests; after you're selected for a military flight training program, that program will instruct you in much greater detail in each of these subjects.

We first consider the advantages and disadvantages of taking flying lessons before you take a military flight aptitude test. We then explore both fixed- and rotary-wing aircraft to give you a conceptual knowledge of each. We cover the correlation between the various flight instruments and end the chapter with two sample flight lesson plans.

Getting a Flying Start: Debating Pre-Test Flying Lessons

The question, "Should I take flying lessons before I take the test?" comes up more often — and sparks a far greater number of differing opinions — than any other subject in this book.

On the pro side of the argument, anything that gives you an edge on the test has to be a good thing, right? Flying lessons not only teach you the basics of such topics as aviation fundamentals (including lift, drag, weight, and power), aircraft parts and control surfaces, and instruments and controls but also give you time in the sky.

On the other hand, many feel that the military is seeking only a potential skill level and that, after you're selected, you'll receive all the required flight training you'll ever need — and perhaps a bit more. After all, the military's goal for the test is to find those who are potentially best suited for a career in military aviation, not those who are already talented aviators. Some observers will even tell you that previous flight training only ensures that you've developed bad habits that a military instructor pilot will have to correct.

Although this last argument has some validity, we strongly believe that a minimal amount of flight training can provide you with enough conceptual knowledge to give you an edge on the flight aptitude test. We're not talking about hours and hours in the cockpit; a minimum of two to three hours of flight experience and the associated ground schooling can give you a leg up (though we recommend getting a private pilot's license if possible). If you're determined to pass the exam (and we can guess you are because you're reading this book), even a slight edge may be well worth the time and the relatively small amount of money you spend for flying lessons at a local airport. In fact, the U.S. Air Force actually increases (on a graduated scale) your chance of being selected for pilot training for up to 200 hours of flight time.

Before you begin your flight training, be sure your instructor knows your goals for taking the flight training (that is, getting a better score on the military flight aptitude test). You may also want to show the instructor the flight training lesson plans we include later in this chapter, which give what we feel is the minimum amount of pre-test flight instruction.

Understanding the Basic Science of Flight

Although people often marvel at airplanes as feats of technology, few have stopped to think about just how the plane gets in the air. But as a military aviator, those scientific concepts are vital parts of your training, and your flight aptitude test is sure to quiz you on them. The following sections give you the skinny on some of the critical scientific principles for flying.

For additional coverage, we recommend *Aerodynamics for Naval Aviators* by H. H. Hurt, Jr. (Skyhorse Publishing) and either *Rotary Wing Flight* by the FAA (Aviation Supplies and Academics, Inc.) or the Army field manual called *Fundamentals of Flight (FM 1-203)*.

Appreciating the atmosphere

The aircraft you pilot someday will penetrate the atmosphere somewhat like a boat paddle going through the water, so you want to know a little more about the makeup of the wild blue yonder than just "It's made of air and stuff." The earth's atmosphere is comprised of various elements (Chapter 9 covers the more-exact composition); as a whole, it affects your aircraft and its performance. But aviators are primarily concerned with the oxygen in the atmosphere and the effect that element has on their bodies, as well as how temperature and humidity affect aircraft performance. Just a little more than 20 percent of the atmosphere is made up of oxygen; this element is relatively heavier than most other gaseous elements in the atmosphere, so you find more of it below 30,000 feet. The higher you fly, the less oxygen pressure you have available, and that's why pilots wear oxygen masks above a certain altitude.

During the test, you can expect questions about the atmosphere and how it relates to the aviation world. Here's an example of an atmosphere-type question you may encounter:

The most accurate description of earth's atmosphere is that it is made up of

(A) 78 percent oxygen, 19 percent nitrogen, and 2 percent carbon dioxide, with trace amounts of water vapor and dust particles.

(B) 3 percent water vapor, 78 percent ozone, and 20 percent nitrogen.

(C) 20 percent oxygen, 77 percent hydrogen, 3 percent carbon dioxide, and some water vapor.

(D) 21 percent oxygen, 78 percent nitrogen, .03 percent carbon dioxide, trace amounts of rare gases, water vapor, and some dust particles.

(E) 77 percent oxygen, 21 percent hydrogen, and 2 percent carbon dioxide, with trace amounts of nitrogen, water vapor, and dust particles.

The correct answer is Choice (D).

Focusing on the four forces acting on an aircraft

Four forces are necessary for an aircraft to fly, and understanding them helps you recognize the limitations you must overcome to successfully challenge the bonds of earth. Here's a basic description of each; you can see the forces in Figure 11-1:

- **Lift:** *Lift* is the upward force vector resulting from air movement along both the upper and lower portions of the wing. (We describe this vector in more detail in the later section "Lifting off with the airfoil.")

- **Drag:** *Drag* is the air resistance that slows down the forward movement of an aircraft. You encounter two types of drag: *induced*, which is the drag that results from the wing's developing lift, and *parasite*, which is the drag associated with the resistance to forward movement.

- **Weight:** *Weight* is the downward force resulting from the gravitational pull of the earth.

- **Power:** *Power,* or *thrust,* is the force that enables an aircraft to move forward though the air.

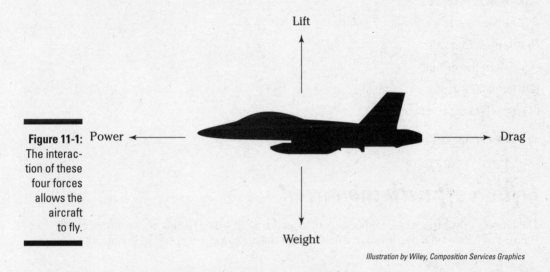

Figure 11-1: The interaction of these four forces allows the aircraft to fly.

Illustration by Wiley, Composition Services Graphics

Your test will feature questions that both directly and indirectly relate to the four forces on an aircraft in a given situation. An example of one such question may include the following:

The four forces that act on an aircraft in flight are

(A) Lift, weight, thrust, and drag

(B) Lift, mass, propulsion, and resistance

(C) Aerodynamics, mass, propulsion, and drag

(D) Lift magnitude, mass, thrust, and drag

(E) Roll, pitch, yaw, and magnitude

The correct answer is Choice (A).

Knowing Newton's three laws of motion

Sir Isaac Newton's laws of motion are basic scientific principles that explain how flight is possible. Without them, no flight.

- ✔ **Newton's First Law of Motion:** Unless acted upon by an outside force, a body at rest tends to remain at rest, and a body in motion tends to remain in motion.

- ✔ **Newton's Second Law of Motion:** An object changes velocity if it's pushed or pulled on. When an outside force acts on an object, the object's acceleration is directly proportional to the applied force and inversely proportional to the mass of the object. This law derives the formula of $F = ma$, where F is the force acting on an object, m is the object's mass, and a is the object's acceleration.

- ✔ **Newton's Third Law of Motion:** For every action, there is an equal and opposite reaction.

The flight aptitude test will test your ability to apply Newton's laws. An example of a type of question on this topic includes the following:

A body at rest tends to

(A) Accelerate at a constant velocity

(B) Remain in motion

(C) Fall to the ground

(D) Remain at rest

(E) Reach escape velocity

The correct answer is Choice (D).

Lifting off with the airfoil

The *airfoil* — the structure commonly known as the *wing* — is what allows an aircraft to fly (see Figure 11-2). Basically, the airfoils travel through the air at a given speed to enable lift to occur.

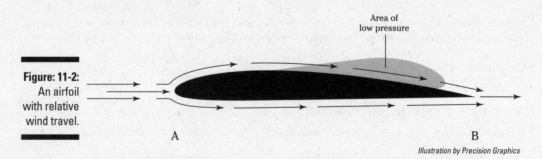

Figure: 11-2: An airfoil with relative wind travel.

Area of low pressure

A   B

Illustration by Precision Graphics

When an airfoil travels through the air, the air separates over and under the wing. Both streams of air must divide at point A and reach point B at the same time. As you can see in Figure 11-2, the upper curvature of the wing is greater than the lower curvature. Therefore, the air traveling over the top of the wing must move at a faster speed than the air traveling under the lower portion to reach point B at the same time.

Bernoulli's principle states that as the velocity of a fluid (in this case, air) increases, the pressure exerted by that fluid decreases. Simply put, the faster air traveling over the top of the airfoil causes a decrease in pressure, which results in a lifting force. That's why a wing needs forward motion to gain lift. Without enough forward motion (airspeed), lift is reduced, and the airplane won't fly.

But speed isn't the only vital component of lift. The *angle of attack* is a reference line that represents the angle of the *chord line* (the line from the leading edge of an airfoil to the trailing edge) in relation to the forward airflow against the wing. As you increase the angle of attack, lift increases to a point (usually around 17 degrees) called the *critical angle of attack;* going past that point disturbs the airflow, and you lose lift (also known as experiencing a *stall* of the wing).

A stall happens when you exceed the critical angle of attack. To recover from a stall and begin allowing the wing to develop lift, you must reduce the angle of attack to below the critical level.

Bernoulli's principle and wing lift are critical in aviation. Here's how the exam may test you on this subject:

Most of the lift on an aircraft's wings is because of

(A) A decrease in pressure on the bottom side of the wing

(B) A decrease in pressure on the upper side of the wing

(C) A vacuum created under the wing

(D) An increase in pressure on the upper side of the wing

(E) None of the above

The correct answer is Choice (B).

Figuring out the Operation of Fixed-Wing Aircraft

A *fixed-wing aircraft* is characterized by rigidly or semirigidly attached wings that gain lift by the forward movement of the aircraft in relation to relative wind (see Figure 11-3). The following sections let you in on some of the important aspects of fixed-wing aircraft that you want to know for the aptitude test.

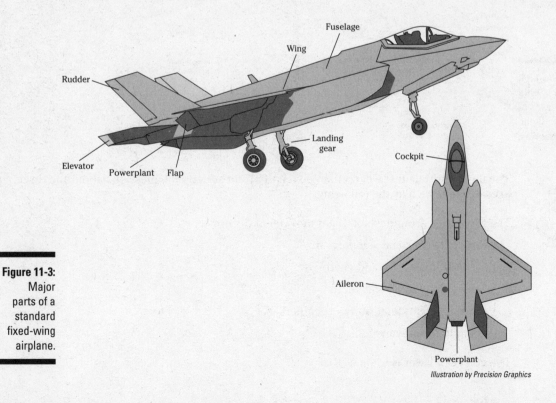

Figure 11-3: Major parts of a standard fixed-wing airplane.

Illustration by Precision Graphics

Addressing aircraft axes of movement

Whenever an aircraft changes its position in flight, *movement* is defined as a rotation around one of three axes of flight. These *axes of movement* are imaginary lines that run through the aircraft's *center of gravity* (a point where the force of gravity is centered on the aircraft):

- ✔ **Longitudinal:** The imaginary line from the front to the rear of the aircraft is the *longitudinal axis,* and it's characterized by a rolling motion (that's why it's sometimes called the *roll axis*).

- ✔ **Lateral:** The imaginary line from the aircraft's center of gravity to the opposite wingtip center point is called the *lateral axis* or the *pitch axis,* and it involves a pitching motion.

- ✔ **Vertical:** The imaginary line that is vertical through the aircraft's center of gravity is the *vertical axis* or *yaw axis,* and movements around it are yawing motions.

All angles intersect at a relative 90-degree angle, and movements along the three axes are controlled by changes in various surface structures (see Figure 11-4).

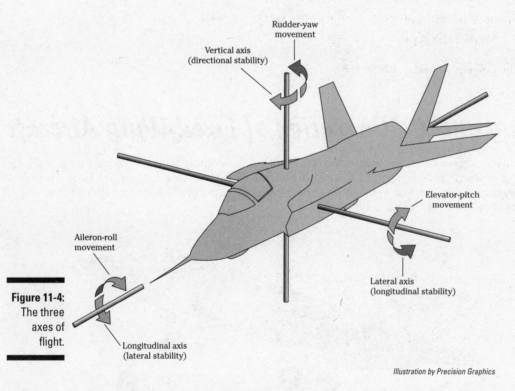

Figure 11-4: The three axes of flight.

Illustration by Precision Graphics

The flight aptitude test will contain conceptual and situational questions about the three axes of flight, such as the following:

The three axes around which flight movement occurs are

(A) Horizontal, vertical, and lateral

(B) Latitude, longitude, and vector

(C) Lateral, longitude, and vector

(D) Lateral, longitudinal, and perpendicular

(E) Roll, pitch, and yaw

The correct answer is Choice (E).

Whizzing through wing types and placement

Although you don't need to worry about the aeronautical design and efficiencies of various wing shapes, you should at least be aware of the different wing shapes and placements, each of which has distinct advantages and disadvantages. (Check out the wing designs in Figure 11-5; you don't need to worry about the specific pros and cons of each for the test.)

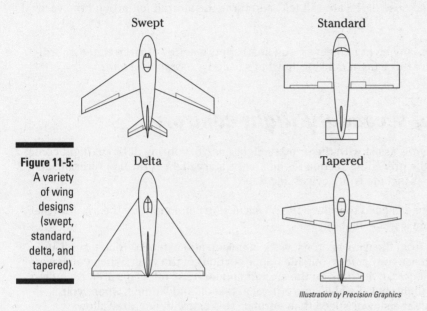

Swept   Standard

Figure 11-5: A variety of wing designs (swept, standard, delta, and tapered).

Delta   Tapered

Illustration by Precision Graphics

Looking at landing gear

Landing gear is the fuselage attachment that allows the aircraft to absorb the impact upon a positive and sometimes abrupt contact with a landing area. Landing gear can be either *fixed* or *retractable* and designed to land on hard or rough surfaces, land, or water. Military aircraft that land on hard surfaces (except helicopters) usually employ retractable landing gear to reduce the negative effects of drag.

Perusing the primary flight controls

Different controls in the crewmember station effectively change the way the different airfoils on an aircraft react with the relative wind. The *primary flight controls* are the stick-and-rudder controls that change the movement of the rudder, ailerons, and elevators. (Don't worry, future rotor-heads: We cover rotary wing controls later in this chapter.)

✔ **Pitch:** *Pitch* is controlled by the elevators and changes as a result of pulling the stick, or yoke, fore and aft. If you pull back the yoke or stick, the aft edges of the elevators move up (each in the same direction), forcing the tail of the aircraft down and the nose up and creating pitching, or a rotation around the lateral axis.

✔ **Roll:** *Roll* is controlled by the wing *ailerons* (small movable sections of the wings, located at the trailing edges, that control roll movements) and changes as a result of pushing the stick, or rotating the yoke, left or right. The ailerons move opposite from one another to gain a rolling motion along the longitudinal axis (as we note earlier, like a paddle in the water). If you turn the stick or yoke left, the aileron on the left wing has its trailing edge pointed upward, pushing the left wing down, and the right wing has its aileron pointed downward, pushing the right wing up. This action results in a left rolling motion.

✔ **Yaw:** Pushing your feet against the rudder pedals establishes a *yaw* motion. If you push the left rudder pedal left, the *aft* (rear) section of the rudder moves left (forcing the tail right and nose of the aircraft left) and turns the aircraft left around the vertical axis.

To perform a turn or any flight maneuver, you must apply a series of interrelated coordinated applications of these flight controls in what's called a *coordinated turn*.

Considering secondary flight controls

Secondary flight controls assist with the primary flight controls during different flight configurations. (Head to the preceding section for info on primary flight controls.) Aircraft secondary flight controls include trim devices and flaps.

✔ *Trim devices* are designed to reduce the physical effort and input by the aviator (that's you) to maintain a stable flight profile.

✔ *Flaps,* inboard from the wing ailerons, work in unison and extend during takeoff and landing to increase the *camber* (outside upper portion) of the wing. When you lower the flaps, you increase the drag on the aircraft and increase lift. Flaps aren't required at level cruise flight, but they become critical at takeoff and landing, where you want greater lift at a slower speed than normal. This extra lift and drag allows your aircraft to land at much slower speeds and clear obstacles on both takeoff and approach.

Firing up for flight instruments

The early aviators didn't have much in the way of flight instruments, but today's pilots have more than a piece of string in the windshield (yes, they actually used that) to give guidance on what their aircraft are doing. The flight instruments tell you how high you are, which way you're heading, how fast you're flying, and if you're in a turn. Trust us, the instruments in the following sections come in handy when you're flying visually at night and punch into the clouds without warning.

Altimeter

You can determine your altitude based on the atmospheric pressure; the greater the altitude, the less the outside pressure. Your aircraft's *altimeter* is an instrument that uses the barometric pressure to accurately tell you your elevation in relation to *mean sea level* (the average surface level of the sea). To do so, it applies a *standard* (a constant for comparison); the standard atmospheric condition is 29.92 Hg (inches of mercury).

The altimeter, shown in Figure 11-6, features an elevation dial and a small pressure window (called the *Kollsman window*) where the barometric pressure is set. Just about every initial aviation communication includes the barometric pressure; by setting this number in the

Kollsman window, you can tell your altitude in relation to sea level. If you know how high the surface elevation you're flying over is, you know your above ground level (AGL) altitude.

Kollsman window
(barometric
pressure
setting)

Ten thousand

Hundred

Thousand

Figure 11-6:
An
altimeter.

Illustration by Precision Graphics

Say you're flying in a relatively high-pressure area; approach control has told you the pressure is 30.22. You set the altimeter to reflect the information given to you by air traffic controllers (along with current safety hazards), and you see that your altimeter reads 1,275 feet. Looking at your approach chart or map, you see that the airfield that you're over has an elevation of 230 feet, so you know you're 1,045 feet above the ground (that's your altimeter reading minus the airfield's elevation).

Density altitude is the correction based on variations from standard temperature and is used in aircraft performance charts to determine things such as distance required to clear a given obstacle.

Attitude indicator

The *attitude indicator* (see Figure 11-7), also known as the *artificial horizon*, gives you an aircraft orientation relative to the horizon of the earth. Before each takeoff, you set the attitude indicator to level flight. This instrument, in conjunction with others, can then tell you whether you're climbing or descending (pitch indication) and whether your wings are in a turning attitude (roll indication). This indicator is one of the primary instruments for nonvisual (inclement weather) flying.

Pointer

Aircraft indicator

Bank scale

Artificial horizon

10° 20° 30°

60°

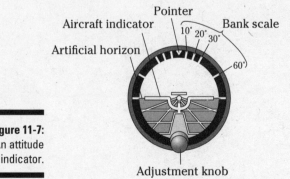

Figure 11-7:
An attitude
indicator.

Adjustment knob

Illustration by Precision Graphics

Turn indicators

Turn indicators serve as backups to the attitude indicator (see the preceding section) and utilize *gyroscopic inertia* (the tendency of a gyroscope wheel to continue rotating in the same plane about the same axis in space). Turn indicators fall into two basic categories, both of which are shown in Figure 11-8.

TECHNICAL STUFF

- ✔ A *turn-and-slip indicator* shows the rate and direction of a turn. The slip portion of the indicator tells you you're performing a coordinated turn and using all the controls efficiently.

  In a standard turn, with all aerodynamic forces being efficient, you will complete 360 degrees in two minutes.

- ✔ A *turn coordinator* shows the rate of turn and the roll rate (how fast you enter into the turn at a specified bank angle).

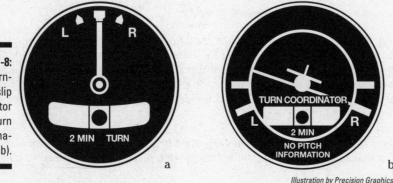

Figure 11-8: A turn-and-slip indicator (a) and turn coordinator (b).

a

b

Illustration by Precision Graphics

Heading indicator

The *heading indicator*, also known by the older term *directional gyro*, is a mechanical instrument that backs up and serves as an aid to the magnetic compass. The heading indicator (shown in Figure 11-9) stabilizes the readings and allows you to navigate without the fluctuation errors found in the magnetic compass.

Figure 11-9: A heading indicator.

Illustration by Wiley, Composition Services Graphics

Airspeed indicator and vertical speed indicator

The *airspeed indicator* (shown in Figure 11-10) detects and displays a differential pressure that adjusts ram airspeed *(pitot pressure)* for static pressure. Basically, that means that the airspeed indicator tells you vital airspeed rates critical to achieving a desired flight profile (such as a climb, descent, or level). If you look closely at the indicator, you see various colored lines. The white arc represents the stall (minimum) and maximum speeds you can operate at with the flaps extended. The green arc shows the normal airspeed operating range of the aircraft. The yellow arc is the caution range in which you can safely operate the aircraft in smooth, non-turbulent air only. The red line at the upper edge of the yellow arc is the velocity at which the aircraft sustains structural damage, so don't cross it.

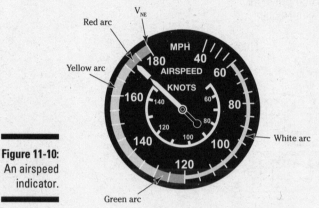

Figure 11-10:
An airspeed indicator.

Illustration by Wiley, Composition Services Graphics

The *vertical speed indicator* (shown in Figure 11-11) tells you whether you're climbing or descending and at what rate of speed by detecting the rate of change in static air pressure.

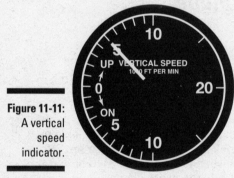

Figure 11-11:
A vertical speed indicator.

Illustration by Precision Graphics

Examining engines (piston and turbine)

The modern military utilizes the turbine engine (also known as a *powerplant*), which is designed to deliver power by exhaust thrust or is geared to a controlled pitch propeller. You can check out a turbine engine in Figure 11-12. Piston engines, like the ones you experience during any pre-test flight training, are commonly used in civilian aviation. (Because you won't use a piston engine in your military flight training, we don't feature a cross section figure of one here. See the earlier section "Getting a Flying Start: Debating Pre-Test Flying Lessons" for info on taking lessons.)

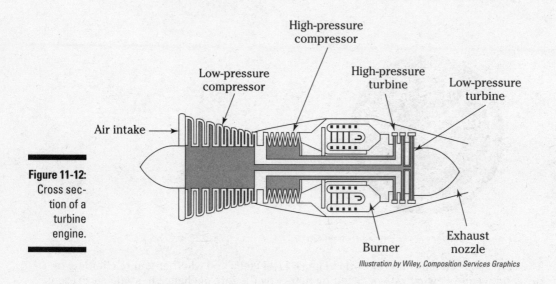

Figure 11-12: Cross section of a turbine engine.

Illustration by Wiley, Composition Services Graphics

Putting the instruments and plane setup concepts together

When taking a military flight aptitude test, you need to understand the correlation between the aircraft flight instruments and the relative position of the airframe in 3-D perspective. You must comprehend how the different flight instruments are connected to give you an overall view of the aircraft at a particular point in space.

The test gives you pictures of a situational view of an aircraft, and you must be able to correctly decide what the cockpit instruments will look like for that particular aircraft attitude. Because the gauges may be difficult to read when they're reduced to fit in the cockpit dashboard in these figures, we also duplicate the gauges in an enlarged view. Following are examples of how the aircraft instruments correlate to the aircraft attitude.

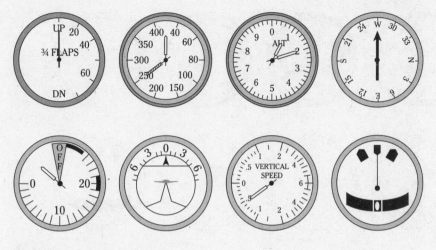

View from Cockpit

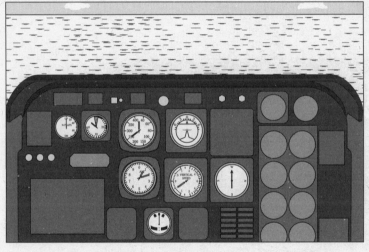

Outside View of
Aircraft Profile

Descent/Dive

Illustration by Wiley, Composition Services Graphics

View from Cockpit

Outside View of
Aircraft Profile

Climb

Illustration by Wiley, Composition Services Graphics

View from Cockpit

Outside View of
Aircraft Profile

Descending
Right Turn

Illustration by Wiley, Composition Services Graphics

View from Cockpit

Outside View of
Aircraft Profile

Climbing
Right Turn

Illustration by Wiley, Composition Services Graphics

In the figure, which of the four aircraft attitudes pictured is the correct aircraft as depicted by the aircraft instruments?

View from Cockpit

Illustration by Wiley, Composition Services Graphics

(A) Aircraft A

(B) Aircraft B

(C) Aircraft C

(D) Aircraft D

The correct answer is (A).

Reviewing the Components of Rotary-Wing Aircraft

A *rotary-wing aircraft,* shown in Figure 11-13, is characterized by airfoils or wings that are attached to a hub and rotate to achieve lift. (Although various types of rotary-wing aircraft exist, the only one you need to concern yourself with for the test is the helicopter; that's the one we discuss here.) Rotary-wing aircraft gain lift and forward momentum by tilting the plane of the rotor disk and changing the direction of lift toward a somewhat forward (or sideways, if desired) direction. This rotating lifting capability allows the aircraft to either hover stationary above a fixed point or to land or take off with minimal forward motion.

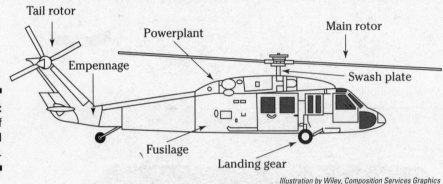

Figure 11-13: Key parts of a standard helicopter.

Illustration by Wiley, Composition Services Graphics

The three vector axes of flight are effectively the same with rotary-wing aircraft as with fixed-wing aircraft. Flip to the earlier section "Addressing the aircraft axes of movement" for the lowdown on these axes, and then take a look at Figure 11-14 to see how they apply to helicopters.

Talking about types of rotor blade systems

Rotor blade systems basically describe the different ways in which the rotor blades are attached to the engine. Three types of rotor blade systems are most commonly in use today:

- ✔ **Fully articulated:** A *fully articulated* rotor blade system typically has three or more rotor blades. Each rotor blade is attached to the rotor hub independently; through a series of hinges, the blades are allowed to flap and lead/lag independently to overcome the effects of *dissymmetry of lift,* or the difference in lift between the advancing main rotor blade and the retreating main rotor blade.

- ✔ **Rigid:** A *rigid* rotor blade system usually refers to a hingeless system with blades that are flexibly attached to the hub.

- ✔ **Semirigid:** A *semirigid* rotor blade system is a two-bladed system that is rigidly attached to the rotor hub and allows for flapping and feathering. The two blades flap rather like a seesaw: As one flaps down, the other flaps up.

Landing gear

Helicopter landing gear consists of either skids or wheels to facilitate movement while taxiing on land. Helicopters are designed to land in *unimproved areas* — that is, areas without paved runways in good condition — so proper landing gear is vital.

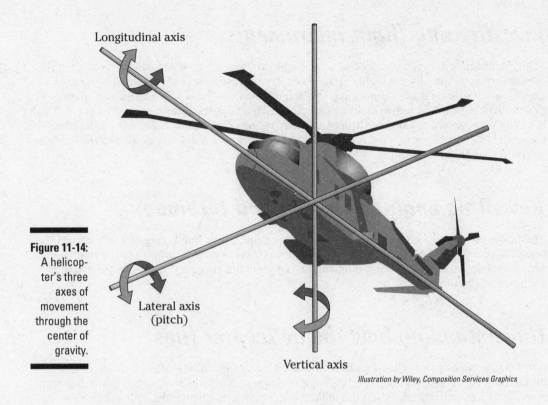

Longitudinal axis

Figure 11-14:
A helicopter's three axes of movement through the center of gravity.

Lateral axis (pitch)

Vertical axis

Illustration by Wiley, Composition Services Graphics

Peeking at primary flight controls

In a helicopter, the primary flight controls consist of the cyclic, the collective, and the anti-torque pedals.

- **Cyclic control:** The *cyclic control*, which looks much like the stick in a fixed-wing aircraft, tilts the entire rotor disc by changing the pitch angle (that is, the angle of attack) of each rotor blade in cycles from a maximum position to a minimum position during each rotation.

- **Collective control:** The *collective control*, located on the left side of the pilot, allows for a simultaneous increase or decrease in pitch of the main rotor blades. This pitch change results in the lifting force of a helicopter. As the pitch increases, you get more lift, but the main rotor system also needs more engine power from the transmission. This increase in power is controlled by a mechanical governor or by a twist-grip throttle control located on the collective handle.

- **Anti-torque control:** *Anti-torque* (or the *counter main rotor torque*) helps prevent the aircraft fuselage from turning as a result of the torque of the overhead spinning main rotor system. Mechanically, the tail rotor is geared to turn faster — usually about three revolutions to each revolution of the main rotor system — and counters this torque to control any yaw movement. By pushing the anti-torque pedals (located where the rudder pedals appear in fixed-wing aircraft), you maintain the ability to move the nose of the aircraft to the left or right as desired.

Note: The discussion of secondary controls for rotary-wing craft is quite murky and complicated, so we don't open that can of worms here. You won't be required to know about those controls for the flight aptitude test anyway.

Investigating flight instruments

The helicopter employs basically the same flight instruments as fixed-wing aircraft (see the earlier section "Firing up for flight instruments"), with just a few exceptions. The most important difference is the *torque gauge,* which informs you how much *torque,* or engine power, is being applied to the main rotor system. This important indicator gives you critical information regarding available thrust to lift any required payload. Torque is the limiting factor in helicopter carrying capability because of either absolute engine power available or transmission limitations.

Revisiting engines (piston and turbine)

The powerplant for a helicopter is essentially the same as for fixed-wing aircraft, except the power is geared through a main transmission and delivers power directly to the main and tail rotor system. Head to "Examining engines (piston and turbine)" earlier in the chapter for more on the aircraft engine.

Understanding how the helicopter flies

A helicopter turns its overhead main rotors until it reaches an operational speed determined by the aircraft manufacturer's design engineers. The tail rotor, which is smaller and sometimes has more blades than the main rotor, rotates more quickly. This tail rotor counters the overhead lateral rotational torque.

You begin to take off by increasing the pitch of the main rotor blade, with the tail rotor automatically increasing its rotational speed. However, you usually have to use the anti-torque pedals to correct a turning tendency as this initial takeoff occurs. At the same time, you have to correct a drifting motion (caused by dissymmetry of lift) by applying a cyclic control movement (left or right, depending on which way the rotor turns). All these corrections require constant power adjustments (unless your aircraft adjusts the power automatically through a governor). Each and every input requires an adjustment to the others; the balancing act of power and inputs is called *hovering,* and it's a challenging task.

Basic flight principles

The helicopter hovers either in *ground effect* (increased lifting efficiency) or out of ground effect depending on power available (which depends on ambient conditions). During a normal takeoff, you apply a forward tilt of the rotor disc to gain forward momentum. At first, the aircraft is in disturbed air and isn't as efficient as it can be. But as the aircraft begins its forward acceleration, it eventually overcomes the downward rotor wash effect and moves into completely undisturbed air. When this shift happens, you'll notice a substantial increase in aircraft efficiency, called *effective translational lift.* If you've ever flown in a helicopter and experienced a vibration at the beginning of takeoff and toward the end of an approach, that was effective translational lift.

Cruise flight, ascents, and descents are connected just like hovering, with varying degrees of rotor disc inputs, collective levels, and counteractive anti-torque movements. Because the instruments in helicopters are largely the same as in fixed-wing aircraft, the instrument usage is basically the same as well, with the exception of the torque indicator.

You will be expected to understand the basic flight principles and differences between fixed- and rotary-wing aircraft for the flight aptitude test. An example of a test question over this knowledge may be the following:

The lift differential that exists between the advancing main rotor blade and the retreating main rotor blade is known as

(A) Coriolis effect

(B) Dissymmetry of lift

(C) Translating tendency

(D) Translational lift

(E) Lift vector

The correct answer is Choice (B).

Helicopter-specific flight principles

Two important, helicopter-specific flight principles are retreating blade stall and autorotation.

✔ *Retreating blade stall* occurs when the retreating blade loses speed and increases its angle of attack. As the helicopter flies forward, the rotor's tip speed approaches the speed of sound. The advancing blade has the forward speed of the aircraft speed plus the rotor turn speed. The retreating blade's overall effective speed decreases as the aircraft speed increases, to the point where the retreating blade actually stalls and suddenly loses its lift, resulting in a very dangerous condition.

✔ *Autorotation* describes the situation where, upon losing engine power, the pilot releases the gear-driven aspect of the rotor blades by immediately reducing the cockpit collective lever and thereby reducing rotor blade pitch. This action allows the blades to freely windmill with the forward upward flow of air through the rotor system. The aircraft begins a (very) rapid rate of descent but builds up or retains inertia in the rotor system to trade off for lift in the final seconds before impact with the ground, as shown in Figure 11-15.

Autorotation is a timed event, and if you trade the inertia for lift too soon, the aircraft will run out of lift too high above the ground. And if you make the trade too late . . . well, that's why autorotation timing will be a primary focus of your helicopter training.

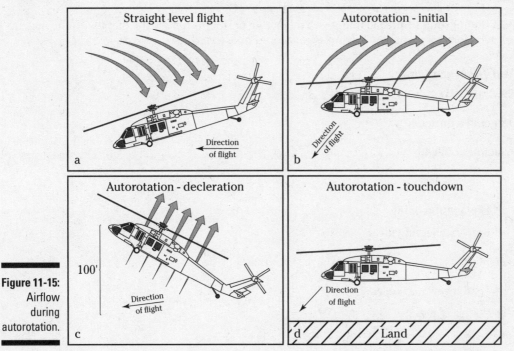

Figure 11-15: Airflow during autorotation.

Illustration by Wiley, Composition Services Graphics

Sample Flight Lesson Plans

If you do decide to take some flying lessons before you take your military flight aptitude test, here are two handy flight lesson plans specifically designed to provide you with the basic information you'll need to get an advantage on the test. We cover the pros and cons of taking flying lessons in the earlier section "Getting a Flying Start: Debating Pre-Test Flying Lessons."

When taking flight training, focus particularly on the artificial horizon and compass (but not at the expense of situational awareness and safety). Be aware of how the aircraft is in all situations and think in a 3-D perspective.

If you have no flight experience and plan to do the minimal amount to gain situational awareness, show your flight instructor these lesson plans and a sample of the test you'll be taking. Get at least two to three hours in the air focusing on the situations that the test will cover. If money is the determining factor, we suggest you take minimal actual flight lessons (in a real airplane), take a formal ground school (you can often find classes at colleges and universities), and use some of the flight simulation software found commercially.

Flight lesson #1

Objectives: To familiarize the potential aviation officer candidate with the basic aerodynamic principles, engine, aircraft systems, and flight instruments. To provide the potential aviation officer candidate with a hands-on knowledge of basic flight maneuvers.

Pre-lesson ground school time: 5 hours. This self-research is designed to give you conceptual knowledge of the aircraft flight principles you'll be covering.

Pre-flight ground time: 45 minutes. You spend this time before the flight period with a flight instructor, who explains in detail the flight objectives and answers any questions you may have.

Flight time: 1.5 hours.

Post-flight ground time: 30 minutes. You us this period to review the flight with the instructor, who follows up on any of your unanswered questions.

Non-flight content

Newton's laws

Bernoulli's principle

Principles of flight

Lift

- ✔ Explanation of lift
- ✔ Factors effecting lift

Weight

- ✔ Load terms and types
- ✔ Center of gravity

Drag

- ✔ Parasite
- ✔ Induced

Thrust

- ✔ Powerplant and propeller
- ✔ Piston versus turbine
- ✔ Propeller thrust development
- ✔ Turbine (jet) thrust development
- ✔ Controllable pitch propellers

Wing design

Aircraft design

Fuselage

Ailerons

Flaps

- ✔ Plain
- ✔ Slotted
- ✔ Split
- ✔ Fowler

Rudder

Elevators

Flight controls

Flight content
Introduction to takeoff

Straight and level flight

Orientation to flight instruments and power settings

Climbs

Descents

Climbing and descending turns

Stalls

Basic navigation reference

Introduction to landings

Flight lesson #2

Objectives: To give the potential aviation officer candidate a continued grasp of aviation fundamentals to further instruct the candidate on the aircraft system and navigation instruments and how they correlate with pilot maneuver inputs.

Pre-lesson ground school time: 5 hours

Pre-flight ground time: 1.5 hours

Flight time: 1.5 hours

Post-flight ground time: 30 minutes

Non-flight content

Review of lesson #1

Aircraft systems and flight instruments

Navigation instruments

Basic flight principles and flight instruments

Examples of flight instrument displays/aircraft attitude

Flight content

Instrument correlation of aircraft

Takeoff

Climbing and descending turns

Steep turns

Slow flight

Stalls

Introductions to landing

Chapter 12

Basic Aeronautical Knowledge Practice Test

● ●

1 n this chapter, we provide some sample test questions to firm up your knowledge of flying and check what you know about the differences between fixed-wing and rotary-wing flying. We focus on some of the instrumentation that both types of pilots use and also cover flight controls of both airplanes and helicopters. (You can find more coverage of certain subjects and test-type questions in the practice tests in Part IV.)

What this chapter doesn't test is your knowledge of the various power plants (turbojet, turboprop, and piston); none of the flight aptitude tests seems to put much focus on that subject. Just know that most pilots start out in small piston engine aircraft because they're relatively inexpensive to fly; if you've already done some flying, that's probably the kind of craft you've flown. Eventually, you'll be flying turbine engine powerplants in the military.

This test doesn't just give you a measuring tool to judge where you stand on this subject; it also helps cement the knowledge in your memory and gives you important test-taking practice.

Choose the most correct answer for each question.

Aeronautical Knowledge Test

1. The most accurate description of earth's atmosphere is that it's made up of

    (A) 24 percent oxygen, 72 percent nitrogen, 3 percent carbon dioxide, and 1 percent water vapor

    (B) 21 percent oxygen, 77 percent nitrogen, 0.03 percent carbon dioxide, and trace amounts of rare gases and water vapor

    (C) 66 percent oxygen, 31 percent nitrogen, 0.09 percent carbon dioxide, and trace amounts of rare gases and water vapor

    (D) 18 percent oxygen, 66 percent nitrogen, 12 percent carbon dioxide, and 4 percent water vapor

2. The four forces acting on an aircraft are

    (A) Lift, air pressure, weight, and velocity

    (B) Gravity, negative pressure, drag, and power

    (C) Lift, drag, weight, and thrust

    (D) Weight, drag, angle of attack, and speed

3. The air resistance that slows down and creates resistance to the forward movement of an aircraft is called

    (A) Lift

    (B) Drag

    (C) Weight

    (D) Thrust

4. The upward force vector resulting from air movement along both the upper and lower portions of the wing is called

   (A) Lift

   (B) Drag

   (C) Weight

   (D) Thrust

5. The downward force that is a result of the gravitational pull of the earth is called

   (A) Lift

   (B) Drag

   (C) Weight

   (D) Thrust

6. The force that enables an aircraft to move forward through the air is called

   (A) Lift

   (B) Drag

   (C) Weight

   (D) Thrust

7. The two types of drag are

   (A) Induced and parasite

   (B) Induced and resistivity

   (C) Parasite and resistivity

   (D) Induced and relative

8. Newton's Third Law of Motion states that

   (A) Opposites attract.

   (B) Resistance to a motion is inversely proportional to the mass.

   (C) For every action, there is an equal and opposite reaction.

   (D) Chemical properties can't be changed.

9. Newton's First Law of Motion states that

   (A) Force equals mass times acceleration.

   (B) For every action, there is an equal and opposite reaction.

   (C) A body at rest tends to remain at rest, and a body in motion tends to remain in motion, unless acted upon by an outside force.

   (D) When an object is acted upon by an outside force, the acceleration is directly proportional to the applied force and inversely proportional to the mass of the object.

10. Bernoulli's principle states that

    (A) As the velocity of a fluid decreases, the pressure exerted by that fluid decreases.

    (B) As the velocity of a fluid increases, the pressure exerted by that fluid decreases.

    (C) The faster the air travels over the wing, the more pressure the wing encounters.

    (D) Wind resistance is inversely proportional to the airspeed.

11. What shape characteristic gives the wing the ability to gain lift?

    (A) The wing's upper curvature is greater than the lower curvature.

    (B) The wing's lower curvature is greater than the upper curvature.

    (C) The wing has the ability to extend flaps.

    (D) The wing has a thin shape.

12. The air traveling along the top of the wing causes a(n) _____ in air pressure, resulting in _____.

    (A) Increase; lift

    (B) Increase; drag

    (C) Decrease; lift

    (D) Decrease; drag

13. The chord line is the line from the

    (A) Leading edge to the trailing edge of the airfoil

    (B) Leading edge along the greater curvature to the trailing edge

    (C) Leading edge along the lesser curvature to the trailing edge

    (D) Direction of airflow to wing placement

14. The angle of attack is

    (A) The angle at which the wing is mounted on the fuselage

    (B) The angle of the chord line in relation to relative wind

    (C) The angle of the forward airflow in relation to the lifting vector

    (D) The aircraft nose pitch angle during initial engagement

15. When you exceed the critical angle of attack, your aircraft wing _____ lift and _____.

    (A) Gains; climbs

    (B) Gains; stalls

    (C) Loses; climbs

    (D) Loses; stalls

16. A _____ aircraft is characterized by a rigidly attached set of wings that gain lift by the forward movement of the aircraft in relation to relative wind.

    (A) Rotary-wing

    (B) Fixed-wing

    (C) Gyrocopter

    (D) Gyroplane

17. Pitch in airplanes is controlled by the _____ and changes as a result of pulling the stick, or yoke, fore and aft.

    (A) Rudder

    (B) Ailerons

    (C) Trim tab

    (D) Elevators

18. Roll is controlled by the _____ and changes as a result of pushing the stick, or rotating the yoke, left or right.

    (A) Rudder

    (B) Ailerons

    (C) Trim tab

    (D) Elevators

19. Yaw is controlled by the _____ and changes as a result of pushing either foot pedal.

    (A) Rudder

    (B) Ailerons

    (C) Trim tab

    (D) Elevators

20. The three axes around which flight movement occurs are

    (A) Roll, angle, and yaw

    (B) Roll, pitch, and pivot

    (C) Roll, pitch, and yaw

    (D) Turn, pitch, and yaw

21. What devices are designed to reduce the physical effort and input required by the aviator to maintain a stable flight platform?

    (A) Friction locks

    (B) Vortex devices

    (C) Auto pilot

    (D) Trim tabs

22. _____ are extended during some take-offs and most landings; they're designed to increase the camber of the wing and result in an increase in both lift and _____.

    (A) Flaps; speed

    (B) Flaps; drag

    (C) Wing slots; speed

    (D) Wing slots; drag

23. Flaps allow your aircraft to land at much _____ airspeeds or take off sooner to gain clearance of _____.

    (A) Slower; obstacles

    (B) Slower; air traffic control

    (C) Faster; obstacles

    (D) Faster; air traffic control

24. How does landing the aircraft into the wind affect the groundspeed upon touchdown?

    (A) The groundspeed is faster.

    (B) The groundspeed is slower.

    (C) The groundspeed is the same regardless of wind condition.

    (D) The effect on groundspeed depends on pressure altitude.

25. What aircraft instrument tells you your altitude when adjusted to barometric pressure in relation to mean seal level?

    (A) Vertical speed indicator

    (B) Airspeed indicator

    (C) Altimeter

    (D) Attitude indicator

26. When you fly from an area of high pressure to an area of low pressure without setting the barometric setting to the correct new pressure, the altimeter reading will falsely be

   (A) Too high.

   (B) Too low.

   (C) The barometric setting has no effect on the altimeter reading in this situation.

   (D) Either high or low depending on winds aloft.

27. Which aircraft instrument gives the pilot an aircraft orientation relative to the horizon of the earth?

   (A) Vertical speed indicator

   (B) Airspeed indicator

   (C) Altimeter

   (D) Attitude indicator

28. The artificial horizon, or attitude indicator, is a _____ instrument.

   (A) Gyroscopic

   (B) Ectopic

   (C) Aerobatic

   (D) Aerobics

29. A _____ and _____ indicator shows the rate and direction of a turn and whether your turn is coordinated.

   (A) Rate; turn

   (B) Turn; table

   (C) Turn; slip

   (D) Rate; rotational

30. The _____ indicator is a mechanical instrument that backs up the magnetic compass and allows the pilot to navigate without the fluctuation errors of a magnetic compass.

   (A) Altimeter

   (B) Heading

   (C) VSI

   (D) Airspeed

31. The _____ indicator detects and displays a differential pressure that adjusts ram airspeed (pitot tube) for static pressure.

   (A) Static

   (B) Altimeter

   (C) Vertical speed

   (D) Airspeed

32. The _____ indicator tells the pilot whether he or she is climbing or descending and at what rate.

   (A) Static

   (B) Altimeter

   (C) Vertical speed

   (D) Airspeed

33. A _____-wing aircraft is characterized by airfoils or wings that are attached to a hub that rotates to achieve lift.

   (A) Tilt

   (B) Rotary

   (C) Fixed

   (D) Delta

34. Helicopters gain lift and forward momentum by tilting the _____ and changing the lift vector toward the direction of intended travel.

   (A) Plane of the rotor disc

   (B) Collective rotational movement

   (C) Cyclic direction of forward movement

   (D) Foot pedals for directional control

35. Helicopters' greatest military asset is their capability to land or take off with _____ forward motion, allowing forward placement on the battlefield.

   (A) Excessive

   (B) Rolling

   (C) Reverse

   (D) Minimal

36. Which of the following isn't a type of helicopter rotor system commonly used today?

   (A) Correlated

   (B) Fully articulated

   (C) Rigid

   (D) Semirigid

37. Which helicopter control adjusts the tilt of the entire rotor disc by changing the pitch angle of each rotor blade in cycles?

    (A) Cyclic

    (B) Collective

    (C) Anti-torque pedals

    (D) Throttle

38. Which control counters any yaw type of movement to counter torque?

    (A) Cyclic

    (B) Collective

    (C) Anti-torque pedals

    (D) Throttle

39. Which control allows for simultaneous increase or decrease in pitch on the main rotor blades?

    (A) Cyclic

    (B) Collective

    (C) Anti-torque

    (D) Throttle

40. Effective translational lift occurs when

    (A) The aircraft lift equals weight.

    (B) The aircraft reaches a maximum effective engine power lifting capacity.

    (C) The aircraft lift capacity reaches the translational torque capacity.

    (D) The aircraft moves into undisturbed air that doesn't suffer from downward rotor wash and substantially improves performance.

41. Why does retreating blade stall limit the forward motion of the aircraft?

    (A) The retreating blade reaches a subsonic speed, which results in vibrational movements.

    (B) As the aircraft approaches certain airspeeds, the retreating rotor blade approaches its own stall speed; when the retreating blade reaches that speed, the aircraft violently pitches upward.

    (C) The forward blade approaches hypersonic speeds.

    (D) The retreating blade falls below the critical angle of attack.

42. Upon losing aircraft power, the pilot will enter into a(n) _____ by immediately lowering the cockpit collective lever, allowing the rotors to freely windmill. At the last moment, the pilot will trade inertia that has been built up for a few seconds of lifting capability just before impacting the ground.

    (A) Autorotation

    (B) Freefall

    (C) Gyro directional descent

    (D) Pancake maneuver

43. Translating tendency is the tendency of the helicopter to

    (A) Drift left or right because of the rotation of the main rotor blades

    (B) Drift up and down because of rotor wash

    (C) Drift in the direction of the tail rotor thrust

    (D) Remain unstable when translating from hover to takeoff

44. Density altitude most adversely affects aircraft performance on a

    (A) Cool day at a sea-level airport

    (B) Hot, humid day at a high-altitude airport

    (C) Hot, humid day at a sea-level airport

    (D) Cool day at a high-altitude airport

45. Relative wind is the

    (A) Windspeed

    (B) Speed of air as it travels over the greater curvature of the wing

    (C) Motion of the air caused by and directly opposite to the motion of an airfoil through the air

    (D) Cross wind adjustment wind factor

Answer Key

1. B	13. A	25. C	37. A
2. C	14. B	26. A	38. C
3. B	15. D	27. D	39. B
4. A	16. B	28. A	40. D
5. C	17. D	29. C	41. B
6. D	18. B	30. B	42. A
7. A	19. A	31. D	43. C
8. C	20. C	32. C	44. B
9. C	21. D	33. B	45. C
10. B	22. B	34. A	
11. A	23. A	35. D	
12. C	24. B	36. A	

Chapter 13

Mastering Mental Skills Questions

· ·

In This Chapter

▶ Understanding the mental skills questions you can expect on all flight aptitude tests

▶ Reviewing tips for performing well on these sections

▶ Getting a feel for examples of the various mental skills problems

· ·

"Mental skills?" you ask. "Don't all exams test mental skills?" Well, yes, but we're talking about a specific kind of mental acuity here. All military flight aptitude tests have at least some portion dedicated to measuring your ability to understand and visualize abstract perceptions and depth dimensions and to make inferences about hidden information based on known details, angles, and distances. Basically, these test sections check your ability to correctly conceptualize and process information from a multidimensional perspective.

In this chapter, we review the skills necessary to maximize your score in the general category called mental skills. Although these spatial relations types of questions may seem very unfamiliar at first, a little practice (such as the examples in this chapter) can help you achieve a much higher score.

Breaking Down Block Counting

The Air Force Officer Qualifying Test (AFOQT) features block-counting questions that test your ability to quickly analyze and understand a three-dimensional stack of blocks and then determine either how many blocks make up the stack or how many blocks touch a given block. The goal is to test your ability to determine spatial relations.

Block counting is a fast-paced test with only 3 minutes to complete 20 questions. The goal is to quickly and accurately determine how many blocks are touching the identified section. Keep in mind that all blocks are assumed to be the same size and shape, and even if just a corner touches the identified block, it counts.

For the following practice questions, determine how many blocks are touching the specified block. Note that on the AFOQT, each diagram is the basis for several questions; we've just simplified the format here to help you get used to it.

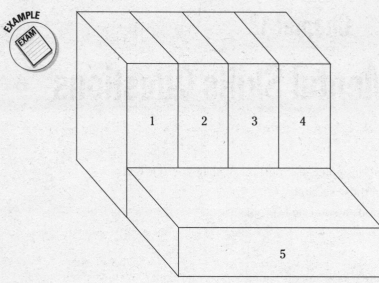

Illustration by Wiley, Composition Services Graphics

Block 2 touches how many other blocks?

(A) 1

(B) 2

(C) 3

(D) 4

(E) 5

The correct answer is Choice (C). Block 2 touches three blocks: Blocks 1, 3, and 5.

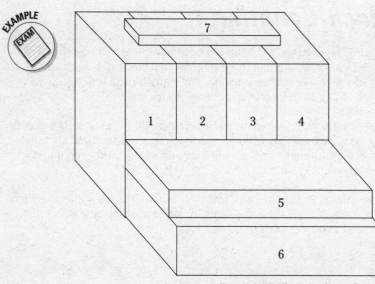

Illustration by Wiley, Composition Services Graphics

Block 3 touches how many other blocks?

(A) 1

(B) 2

(C) 3

(D) 4

(E) 5

The correct answer is Choice (E). Block 3 touches five blocks: Blocks 2, 4, 5, 6, and 7.

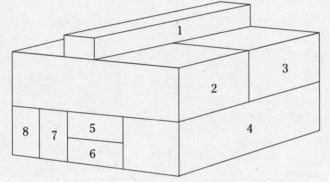

Illustration by Precision Graphics

Block 5 touches how many other blocks?

(A) 1

(B) 2

(C) 3

(D) 4

(E) 5

The correct answer is Choice (E). Block 5 touches five blocks: Blocks 7, 6, 4, 2, and 3.

The following practice questions test your ability to determine how many blocks make up the diagram. Although this kind of question is not a part of the AFOQT as of this writing, our understanding is that this type of question will be included in the near future, so we give you a couple of examples here to help keep you ahead of the curve. The question and answer choices are formatted similarly to the other block-counting questions.

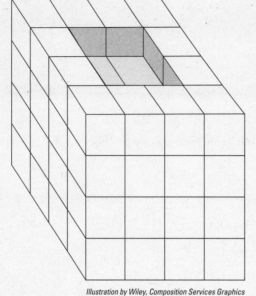

Illustration by Wiley, Composition Services Graphics

How many blocks are in this figure?

(A) 56

(B) 64

(C) 62

(D) 60

(E) 58

The answer is 64 – 4, or 60 blocks, Choice (D). You find the answer by counting the total number of blocks on one side and multiplying that by the number of blocks deep to get a total. Then subtract the number of blocks that are missing (indicated by the shaded portion on top). 16 blocks on one side times 4 blocks deep equals a total of 64 blocks. Four blocks are missing (1 block deep × 4 total blocks = 4 blocks).

Illustration by Wiley, Composition Services Graphics

How many blocks are in this figure?

(A) 16

(B) 14

(C) 15

(D) 20

(E) 88

The answer is 15 blocks, Choice (C). Nine blocks are on the bottom, five blocks are on the second tier, and one block is on top.

One of These Things Is Just Like the Other: Checking out Rotated Blocks

The rotated blocks portion of the AFOQT measures your ability to visualize shapes in differing perspectives in space. The test shows you a block and five choices; you select the choice that represents the exact same block turned some particular way. You must be able to mentally manipulate the objects to select the correct corresponding picture. This section gives you 12 minutes to complete 15 questions; it's not as fast-paced as the block-counting test (see the preceding section), but it's still a skill you'll be better at with some practice. Here are some practice questions:

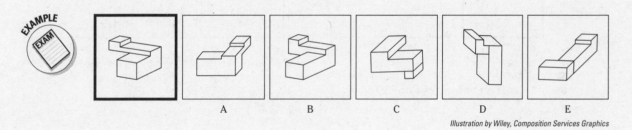

Illustration by Wiley, Composition Services Graphics

The correct answer is Choice (A).

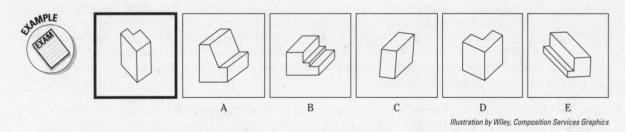

Illustration by Wiley, Composition Services Graphics

The correct answer is Choice (E).

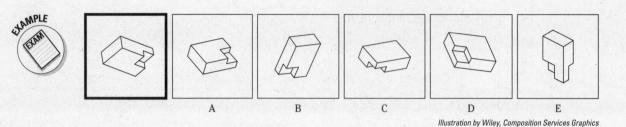

Illustration by Wiley, Composition Services Graphics

The correct answer is Choice (D).

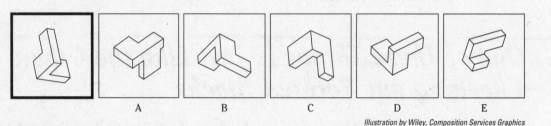

Illustration by Wiley, Composition Services Graphics

The correct answer is Choice (B).

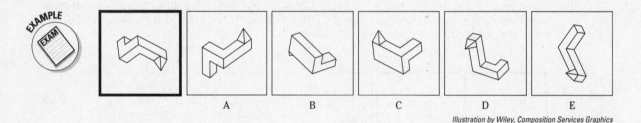

Illustration by Wiley, Composition Services Graphics

The correct answer is Choice (D).

Getting Help with Hidden Figures

Hidden figure questions evaluate your ability to look at a figure and then identify that figure hidden within a complex drawing. In these problems, you see a series of five lettered drawings followed by five numbered complex drawings. Each of these complex drawings contains exactly one of the simple drawings; your challenge is to identify which lettered drawing matches up with which complex drawing. You have 8 minutes to answer 15 questions, so don't spend too much time on any one drawing.

Remember that the simple drawing always appears in the same size and with the same three-dimensional details relative to the position in the complex drawing as it does in the answer choices. To help you see through the clutter in the complex drawings, try focusing on the simple drawing and then immediately transferring your focus onto the complex picture to see whether the image pops out at you.

Check out these examples to help you get the hang of finding hidden figures. First, check out five types of figures you can expect to be asked to find in a collection of lines and angles.

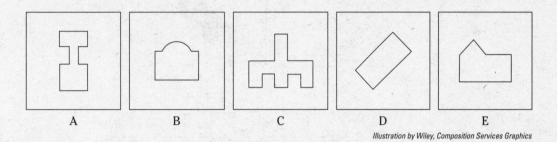

A   B   C   D   E

The following images are examples of all three parts of hidden figure questions: the simple drawing, the complex picture, and the answer revealed.

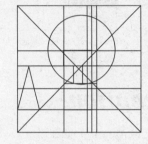

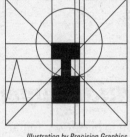

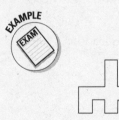

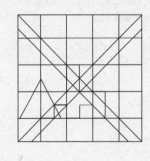

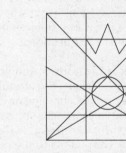
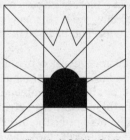
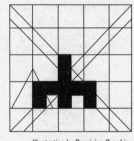

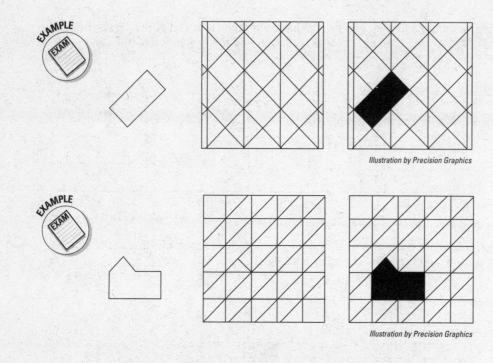

Illustration by Precision Graphics

Illustration by Precision Graphics

Assessing Spatial Apperception

Spatial apperception questions, found on the Aviation Selection Test Battery (ASTB), measure your ability to conceptualize the relative position of an aircraft based on the outside viewpoint or sight picture. (*Apperception* is basically just a fancy word for "observation" here.) You look at a picture or series of pictures and then interpret what position the airframe is in. Typically, the picture includes a ship in the water, but you may also see a coastline or other objects. You have 10 minutes to complete 25 questions.

To solve a spatial apperception problem, first look at the horizon and determine the vertical orientation. If the horizon is at the halfway point in the frame, the aircraft is level. If the horizon is below or above the halfway point, the aircraft is climbing or diving, respectively. Next, decide whether the horizon sight picture is tilted right, left, or neither. Finally, note that if the sea appears above the aircraft in the picture, the aircraft is flying toward the sea. The trick here is to mentally move an airframe with your hands to the position that results in the desired sight picture and then match that image with one of the answer choices. If you have time at the end of the section, go back and double-check your work just to make sure you didn't get something turned around (which is easy to do at first).

The following practice questions give you a taste of spatial apperception questions. Choose the best answer from the choices provided.

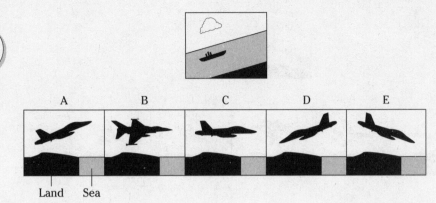

The correct answer is Choice (B).

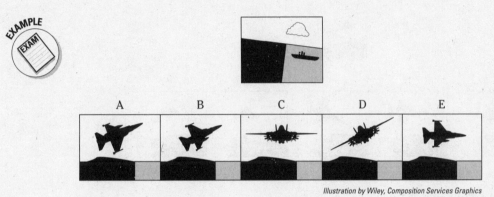

The correct answer is Choice (D).

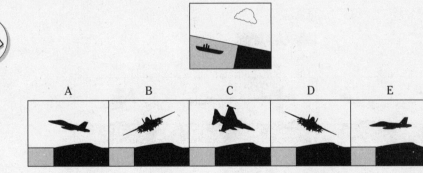

The correct answer is Choice (B).

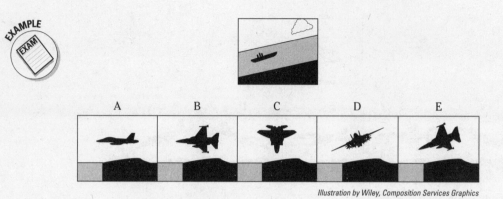

Illustration by Wiley, Composition Services Graphics

The correct answer is Choice (E).

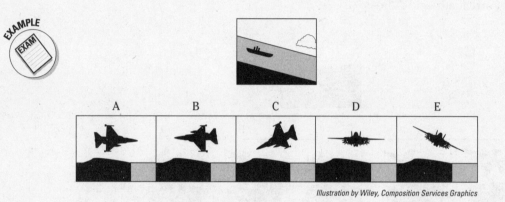

Illustration by Wiley, Composition Services Graphics

The correct answer is Choice (A).

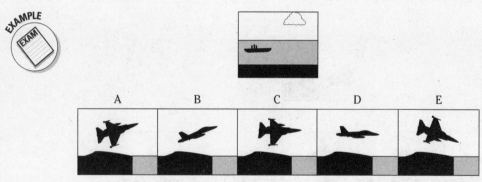

Illustration by Wiley, Composition Services Graphics

The correct answer is Choice (D).

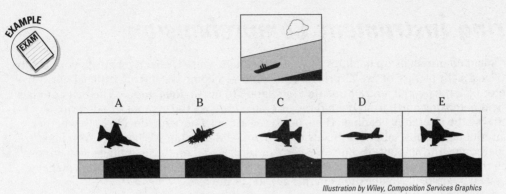

Illustration by Wiley, Composition Services Graphics

The correct answer is Choice (C).

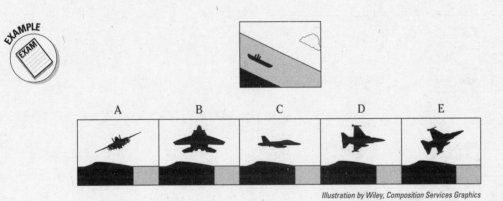

Illustration by Wiley, Composition Services Graphics

The correct answer is Choice (D).

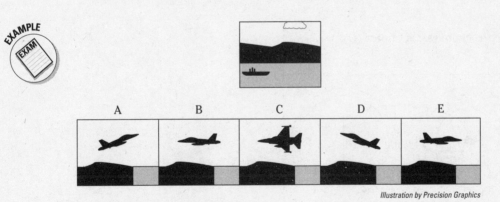

Illustration by Precision Graphics

The correct answer is Choice (B).

Conquering Instrument Comprehension

Instrument comprehension qualifies as a mental skill because it effectively tests your ability to utilize a sight picture of two aircraft instruments — a compass and an artificial horizon — to determine the overall aircraft position in relation to north. *Remember:* The test assumes that you're looking north from behind the aircraft. First, use the compass to determine which way the aircraft is heading. Then, using the artificial horizon, decide both whether the aircraft has its nose above or below the horizon and whether it's banking. You must also determine the amount of climb, descent, or turn. Based on these findings, you choose which three-dimensional aircraft picture given in the answer choices is correct. You have 5 minutes to complete 15 questions in this section of the test.

Here are some practice problems to test your skills:

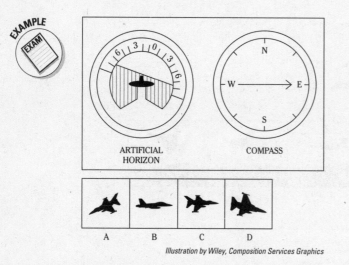

Illustration by Wiley, Composition Services Graphics

The correct answer is Choice (D).

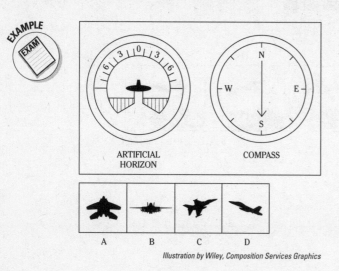

Illustration by Wiley, Composition Services Graphics

The correct answer is Choice (A).

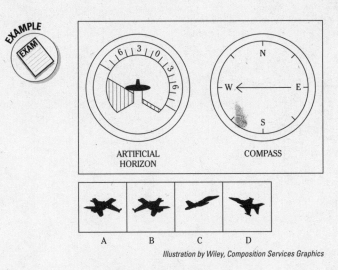

Illustration by Wiley, Composition Services Graphics

The correct answer is Choice (D).

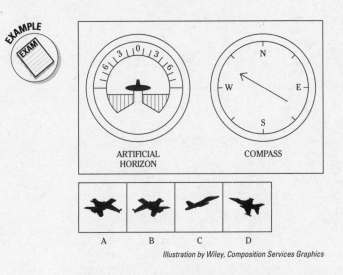

Illustration by Wiley, Composition Services Graphics

The correct answer is Choice (B).

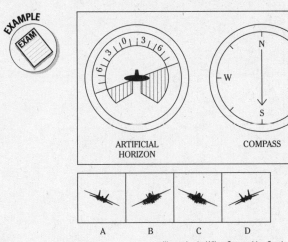

Illustration by Wiley, Composition Services Graphics

The correct answer is Choice (B).

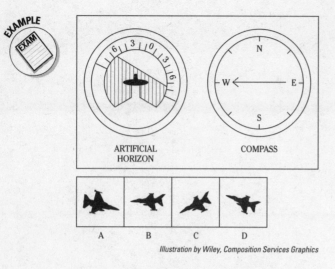

Illustration by Wiley, Composition Services Graphics

The correct answer is Choice (C).

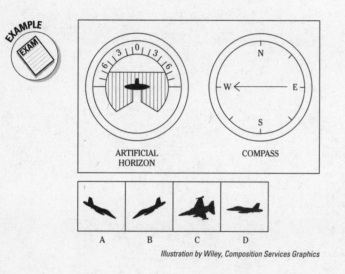

Illustration by Wiley, Composition Services Graphics

The correct answer is Choice (B).

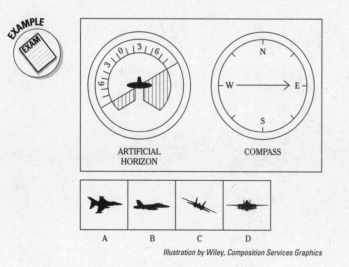

Illustration by Wiley, Composition Services Graphics

The correct answer is Choice (A).

Part IV
Practice Military Flight Aptitude Tests

The 5th Wave   By Rich Tennant

©RICHTENNANT

"The math portion of that test was so easy. I figure I've got a 7 in 5 chance of acing it."

In this part . . .

You may have heard the old saying that practice makes perfect. Although we can't guarantee that you'll get a perfect score on your flight aptitude test, the more you practice taking the test, the better your chances of doing well. In this part, we provide sample tests with answers and explanations for each of the three major military flight aptitude tests: the Air Force Officer Qualifying Test (AFOQT), the Navy and Marine Corps/Coast Guard Aviation Selection Test Battery (ASTB), and the Army Selection Instrument for Flight Training (SIFT).

Chapter 14

Air Force Officer Qualifying Test (AFOQT) Practice Test

⋯⋯⋯⋯⋯⋯⋯⋯⋯⋯⋯⋯⋯⋯⋯⋯⋯⋯⋯⋯

The United States Air Force utilizes just one test for all its officer candidates, regardless of whether those candidates want to become aviators. The Air Force Officer Qualifying Test consists of 12 timed subtests, and the qualifying scores are combined into 5 composite scores that are designed to predict your success in various fields within the Air Force, including aviation. In addition to the five composite scores, you also receive a percentile score for each of the five composite areas.

Currently, the Air Force allows a candidate to take the test twice — an original and one retest. You have to wait at least six months between tests. *Remember:* The Air Force uses your most recent score, not your highest score, for selection criteria scoring.

The Subtests of the AFOQT

The AFOQT takes approximately three and a half hours to complete, including administrative periods (pre-test instruction) and a break. The 12 subtests are broken down as follows:

Subtest	# of items	Time
1. Verbal Analogies (VA)	25	8 minutes
2. Arithmetic Reasoning (AR)	25	29 minutes
3. Word Knowledge (WK)	25	5 minutes
4. Math Knowledge (MK)	25	22 minutes
10-minute break		
5. Instrument Comprehension (IC)	20	6 minutes
6. Block Counting (BC)	20	3 minutes
7. Table Reading (TR)	40	7 minutes
8. Aviation Information (AI)	20	8 minutes
9. General Science (GS)	20	10 minutes
10. Rotated Blocks (RB)	15	13 minutes
11. Hidden Figures (HF)	15	8 minutes
12. Self-Description Inventory (SDI)	220	40 minutes

The five composite scores derived from the test are combined into the following categories. (*Note:* Various sections are weighted differently according to a secret formula, so you can't find your composite score by just adding up the number of correct answers for each section.)

- **Pilot (AR + MK + IC + TR + AI):** This score predicts your success in the aviation field by measuring the knowledge and abilities the Air Force feels you need to successfully complete Air Force pilot training. The subtests included in this score measure mathematical ability, aeronautical knowledge, spatial relation of the aircraft to its systems and instruments, and perceptual speed. If you're a pilot candidate, you must score at least 25 for this composite; if you're a navigator candidate, you need to score at least 10.

- **Navigator-technical (VA + AR + MK + BC + TR + GS):** This grouping measures the abilities required to successfully complete Air Force navigator training. Unlike the pilot composite, this score doesn't focus on aeronautical knowledge and spatial orientation. Pilot candidates need a minimum score of 10 for this composite; navigator candidates need a minimum score of 25.

- **Academic aptitude (VA + AR + WK + MK):** This grouping measures verbal and quantitative knowledge, which is an important aspect of your career as a military officer. Good news: You don't need a particular minimum score for this composite.

- **Verbal (VA + WK):** This grouping measures verbal knowledge and abilities. The combined subtest determines the officer candidate's ability to reason, understand synonyms, and recognize relationships between words. All candidates must achieve a minimum score of 15.

- **Quantitative (AR + MK):** This composite score measures the officer candidate's math-related abilities and knowledge. All candidates must achieve a minimum score of 10.

You receive a score for each of the five areas but not a total combined score. In addition to the minimum composite scores, all pilot and navigator candidates must have a combined pilot and navigator-technical score of at least 50. If you've been keeping track of the math, you'll realize that this requirement means that achieving the minimum scores in those sections isn't good enough for these programs. However, you can perform marginally on one section (as long as you don't go below the minimum) and make up the points in another, higher-scoring section. All commissioning sources determine how high these scores must be for the test-taker to be selected.

Answer Sheet

For Subtests 1 through 6 of the exam, use the following answer sheets and fill in the answer bubble for the corresponding number, using a #2 pencil.

Subtest 1: Verbal Analogies

1. Ⓐ Ⓑ Ⓒ Ⓓ Ⓔ	11. Ⓐ Ⓑ Ⓒ Ⓓ Ⓔ	21. Ⓐ Ⓑ Ⓒ Ⓓ Ⓔ
2. Ⓐ Ⓑ Ⓒ Ⓓ Ⓔ	12. Ⓐ Ⓑ Ⓒ Ⓓ Ⓔ	22. Ⓐ Ⓑ Ⓒ Ⓓ Ⓔ
3. Ⓐ Ⓑ Ⓒ Ⓓ Ⓔ	13. Ⓐ Ⓑ Ⓒ Ⓓ Ⓔ	23. Ⓐ Ⓑ Ⓒ Ⓓ Ⓔ
4. Ⓐ Ⓑ Ⓒ Ⓓ Ⓔ	14. Ⓐ Ⓑ Ⓒ Ⓓ Ⓔ	24. Ⓐ Ⓑ Ⓒ Ⓓ Ⓔ
5. Ⓐ Ⓑ Ⓒ Ⓓ Ⓔ	15. Ⓐ Ⓑ Ⓒ Ⓓ Ⓔ	25. Ⓐ Ⓑ Ⓒ Ⓓ Ⓔ
6. Ⓐ Ⓑ Ⓒ Ⓓ Ⓔ	16. Ⓐ Ⓑ Ⓒ Ⓓ Ⓔ	
7. Ⓐ Ⓑ Ⓒ Ⓓ Ⓔ	17. Ⓐ Ⓑ Ⓒ Ⓓ Ⓔ	
8. Ⓐ Ⓑ Ⓒ Ⓓ Ⓔ	18. Ⓐ Ⓑ Ⓒ Ⓓ Ⓔ	
9. Ⓐ Ⓑ Ⓒ Ⓓ Ⓔ	19. Ⓐ Ⓑ Ⓒ Ⓓ Ⓔ	
10. Ⓐ Ⓑ Ⓒ Ⓓ Ⓔ	20. Ⓐ Ⓑ Ⓒ Ⓓ Ⓔ	

Subtest 2: Arithmetic Reasoning

26. Ⓐ Ⓑ Ⓒ Ⓓ Ⓔ	36. Ⓐ Ⓑ Ⓒ Ⓓ Ⓔ	46. Ⓐ Ⓑ Ⓒ Ⓓ Ⓔ
27. Ⓐ Ⓑ Ⓒ Ⓓ Ⓔ	37. Ⓐ Ⓑ Ⓒ Ⓓ Ⓔ	47. Ⓐ Ⓑ Ⓒ Ⓓ Ⓔ
28. Ⓐ Ⓑ Ⓒ Ⓓ Ⓔ	38. Ⓐ Ⓑ Ⓒ Ⓓ Ⓔ	48. Ⓐ Ⓑ Ⓒ Ⓓ Ⓔ
29. Ⓐ Ⓑ Ⓒ Ⓓ Ⓔ	39. Ⓐ Ⓑ Ⓒ Ⓓ Ⓔ	49. Ⓐ Ⓑ Ⓒ Ⓓ Ⓔ
30. Ⓐ Ⓑ Ⓒ Ⓓ Ⓔ	40. Ⓐ Ⓑ Ⓒ Ⓓ Ⓔ	50. Ⓐ Ⓑ Ⓒ Ⓓ Ⓔ
31. Ⓐ Ⓑ Ⓒ Ⓓ Ⓔ	41. Ⓐ Ⓑ Ⓒ Ⓓ Ⓔ	
32. Ⓐ Ⓑ Ⓒ Ⓓ Ⓔ	42. Ⓐ Ⓑ Ⓒ Ⓓ Ⓔ	
33. Ⓐ Ⓑ Ⓒ Ⓓ Ⓔ	43. Ⓐ Ⓑ Ⓒ Ⓓ Ⓔ	
34. Ⓐ Ⓑ Ⓒ Ⓓ Ⓔ	44. Ⓐ Ⓑ Ⓒ Ⓓ Ⓔ	
35. Ⓐ Ⓑ Ⓒ Ⓓ Ⓔ	45. Ⓐ Ⓑ Ⓒ Ⓓ Ⓔ	

Subtest 3: Word Knowledge

51. Ⓐ Ⓑ Ⓒ Ⓓ Ⓔ	61. Ⓐ Ⓑ Ⓒ Ⓓ Ⓔ	71. Ⓐ Ⓑ Ⓒ Ⓓ Ⓔ
52. Ⓐ Ⓑ Ⓒ Ⓓ Ⓔ	62. Ⓐ Ⓑ Ⓒ Ⓓ Ⓔ	72. Ⓐ Ⓑ Ⓒ Ⓓ Ⓔ
53. Ⓐ Ⓑ Ⓒ Ⓓ Ⓔ	63. Ⓐ Ⓑ Ⓒ Ⓓ Ⓔ	73. Ⓐ Ⓑ Ⓒ Ⓓ Ⓔ
54. Ⓐ Ⓑ Ⓒ Ⓓ Ⓔ	64. Ⓐ Ⓑ Ⓒ Ⓓ Ⓔ	74. Ⓐ Ⓑ Ⓒ Ⓓ Ⓔ
55. Ⓐ Ⓑ Ⓒ Ⓓ Ⓔ	65. Ⓐ Ⓑ Ⓒ Ⓓ Ⓔ	75. Ⓐ Ⓑ Ⓒ Ⓓ Ⓔ
56. Ⓐ Ⓑ Ⓒ Ⓓ Ⓔ	66. Ⓐ Ⓑ Ⓒ Ⓓ Ⓔ	
57. Ⓐ Ⓑ Ⓒ Ⓓ Ⓔ	67. Ⓐ Ⓑ Ⓒ Ⓓ Ⓔ	
58. Ⓐ Ⓑ Ⓒ Ⓓ Ⓔ	68. Ⓐ Ⓑ Ⓒ Ⓓ Ⓔ	
59. Ⓐ Ⓑ Ⓒ Ⓓ Ⓔ	69. Ⓐ Ⓑ Ⓒ Ⓓ Ⓔ	
60. Ⓐ Ⓑ Ⓒ Ⓓ Ⓔ	70. Ⓐ Ⓑ Ⓒ Ⓓ Ⓔ	

Subtest 4: Math Knowledge

76. Ⓐ Ⓑ Ⓒ Ⓓ Ⓔ   86. Ⓐ Ⓑ Ⓒ Ⓓ Ⓔ   96. Ⓐ Ⓑ Ⓒ Ⓓ Ⓔ
77. Ⓐ Ⓑ Ⓒ Ⓓ Ⓔ   87. Ⓐ Ⓑ Ⓒ Ⓓ Ⓔ   97. Ⓐ Ⓑ Ⓒ Ⓓ Ⓔ
78. Ⓐ Ⓑ Ⓒ Ⓓ Ⓔ   88. Ⓐ Ⓑ Ⓒ Ⓓ Ⓔ   98. Ⓐ Ⓑ Ⓒ Ⓓ Ⓔ
79. Ⓐ Ⓑ Ⓒ Ⓓ Ⓔ   89. Ⓐ Ⓑ Ⓒ Ⓓ Ⓔ   99. Ⓐ Ⓑ Ⓒ Ⓓ Ⓔ
80. Ⓐ Ⓑ Ⓒ Ⓓ Ⓔ   90. Ⓐ Ⓑ Ⓒ Ⓓ Ⓔ   100. Ⓐ Ⓑ Ⓒ Ⓓ Ⓔ
81. Ⓐ Ⓑ Ⓒ Ⓓ Ⓔ   91. Ⓐ Ⓑ Ⓒ Ⓓ Ⓔ
82. Ⓐ Ⓑ Ⓒ Ⓓ Ⓔ   92. Ⓐ Ⓑ Ⓒ Ⓓ Ⓔ
83. Ⓐ Ⓑ Ⓒ Ⓓ Ⓔ   93. Ⓐ Ⓑ Ⓒ Ⓓ Ⓔ
84. Ⓐ Ⓑ Ⓒ Ⓓ Ⓔ   94. Ⓐ Ⓑ Ⓒ Ⓓ Ⓔ
85. Ⓐ Ⓑ Ⓒ Ⓓ Ⓔ   95. Ⓐ Ⓑ Ⓒ Ⓓ Ⓔ

Subtest 5: Instrument Comprehension

101. Ⓐ Ⓑ Ⓒ Ⓓ   109. Ⓐ Ⓑ Ⓒ Ⓓ   117. Ⓐ Ⓑ Ⓒ Ⓓ
102. Ⓐ Ⓑ Ⓒ Ⓓ   110. Ⓐ Ⓑ Ⓒ Ⓓ   118. Ⓐ Ⓑ Ⓒ Ⓓ
103. Ⓐ Ⓑ Ⓒ Ⓓ   111. Ⓐ Ⓑ Ⓒ Ⓓ   119. Ⓐ Ⓑ Ⓒ Ⓓ
104. Ⓐ Ⓑ Ⓒ Ⓓ   112. Ⓐ Ⓑ Ⓒ Ⓓ   120. Ⓐ Ⓑ Ⓒ Ⓓ
105. Ⓐ Ⓑ Ⓒ Ⓓ   113. Ⓐ Ⓑ Ⓒ Ⓓ
106. Ⓐ Ⓑ Ⓒ Ⓓ   114. Ⓐ Ⓑ Ⓒ Ⓓ
107. Ⓐ Ⓑ Ⓒ Ⓓ   115. Ⓐ Ⓑ Ⓒ Ⓓ
108. Ⓐ Ⓑ Ⓒ Ⓓ   116. Ⓐ Ⓑ Ⓒ Ⓓ

Subtest 6: Block Counting

121. Ⓐ Ⓑ Ⓒ Ⓓ Ⓔ   131. Ⓐ Ⓑ Ⓒ Ⓓ Ⓔ
122. Ⓐ Ⓑ Ⓒ Ⓓ Ⓔ   132. Ⓐ Ⓑ Ⓒ Ⓓ Ⓔ
123. Ⓐ Ⓑ Ⓒ Ⓓ Ⓔ   133. Ⓐ Ⓑ Ⓒ Ⓓ Ⓔ
124. Ⓐ Ⓑ Ⓒ Ⓓ Ⓔ   134. Ⓐ Ⓑ Ⓒ Ⓓ Ⓔ
125. Ⓐ Ⓑ Ⓒ Ⓓ Ⓔ   135. Ⓐ Ⓑ Ⓒ Ⓓ Ⓔ
126. Ⓐ Ⓑ Ⓒ Ⓓ Ⓔ   136. Ⓐ Ⓑ Ⓒ Ⓓ Ⓔ
127. Ⓐ Ⓑ Ⓒ Ⓓ Ⓔ   137. Ⓐ Ⓑ Ⓒ Ⓓ Ⓔ
128. Ⓐ Ⓑ Ⓒ Ⓓ Ⓔ   138. Ⓐ Ⓑ Ⓒ Ⓓ Ⓔ
129. Ⓐ Ⓑ Ⓒ Ⓓ Ⓔ   139. Ⓐ Ⓑ Ⓒ Ⓓ Ⓔ
130. Ⓐ Ⓑ Ⓒ Ⓓ Ⓔ   140. Ⓐ Ⓑ Ⓒ Ⓓ Ⓔ

Subtest 7: Table Reading

141. Ⓐ Ⓑ Ⓒ Ⓓ Ⓔ   151. Ⓐ Ⓑ Ⓒ Ⓓ Ⓔ   161. Ⓐ Ⓑ Ⓒ Ⓓ Ⓔ   171. Ⓐ Ⓑ Ⓒ Ⓓ Ⓔ
142. Ⓐ Ⓑ Ⓒ Ⓓ Ⓔ   152. Ⓐ Ⓑ Ⓒ Ⓓ Ⓔ   162. Ⓐ Ⓑ Ⓒ Ⓓ Ⓔ   172. Ⓐ Ⓑ Ⓒ Ⓓ Ⓔ
143. Ⓐ Ⓑ Ⓒ Ⓓ Ⓔ   153. Ⓐ Ⓑ Ⓒ Ⓓ Ⓔ   163. Ⓐ Ⓑ Ⓒ Ⓓ Ⓔ   173. Ⓐ Ⓑ Ⓒ Ⓓ Ⓔ
144. Ⓐ Ⓑ Ⓒ Ⓓ Ⓔ   154. Ⓐ Ⓑ Ⓒ Ⓓ Ⓔ   164. Ⓐ Ⓑ Ⓒ Ⓓ Ⓔ   174. Ⓐ Ⓑ Ⓒ Ⓓ Ⓔ
145. Ⓐ Ⓑ Ⓒ Ⓓ Ⓔ   155. Ⓐ Ⓑ Ⓒ Ⓓ Ⓔ   165. Ⓐ Ⓑ Ⓒ Ⓓ Ⓔ   175. Ⓐ Ⓑ Ⓒ Ⓓ Ⓔ
146. Ⓐ Ⓑ Ⓒ Ⓓ Ⓔ   156. Ⓐ Ⓑ Ⓒ Ⓓ Ⓔ   166. Ⓐ Ⓑ Ⓒ Ⓓ Ⓔ   176. Ⓐ Ⓑ Ⓒ Ⓓ Ⓔ
147. Ⓐ Ⓑ Ⓒ Ⓓ Ⓔ   157. Ⓐ Ⓑ Ⓒ Ⓓ Ⓔ   167. Ⓐ Ⓑ Ⓒ Ⓓ Ⓔ   177. Ⓐ Ⓑ Ⓒ Ⓓ Ⓔ
148. Ⓐ Ⓑ Ⓒ Ⓓ Ⓔ   158. Ⓐ Ⓑ Ⓒ Ⓓ Ⓔ   168. Ⓐ Ⓑ Ⓒ Ⓓ Ⓔ   178. Ⓐ Ⓑ Ⓒ Ⓓ Ⓔ
149. Ⓐ Ⓑ Ⓒ Ⓓ Ⓔ   159. Ⓐ Ⓑ Ⓒ Ⓓ Ⓔ   169. Ⓐ Ⓑ Ⓒ Ⓓ Ⓔ   179. Ⓐ Ⓑ Ⓒ Ⓓ Ⓔ
150. Ⓐ Ⓑ Ⓒ Ⓓ Ⓔ   160. Ⓐ Ⓑ Ⓒ Ⓓ Ⓔ   170. Ⓐ Ⓑ Ⓒ Ⓓ Ⓔ   180. Ⓐ Ⓑ Ⓒ Ⓓ Ⓔ

Subtest 8: Aviation Information

181. Ⓐ Ⓑ Ⓒ Ⓓ Ⓔ   191. Ⓐ Ⓑ Ⓒ Ⓓ Ⓔ
182. Ⓐ Ⓑ Ⓒ Ⓓ Ⓔ   192. Ⓐ Ⓑ Ⓒ Ⓓ Ⓔ
183. Ⓐ Ⓑ Ⓒ Ⓓ Ⓔ   193. Ⓐ Ⓑ Ⓒ Ⓓ Ⓔ
184. Ⓐ Ⓑ Ⓒ Ⓓ Ⓔ   194. Ⓐ Ⓑ Ⓒ Ⓓ Ⓔ
185. Ⓐ Ⓑ Ⓒ Ⓓ Ⓔ   195. Ⓐ Ⓑ Ⓒ Ⓓ Ⓔ
186. Ⓐ Ⓑ Ⓒ Ⓓ Ⓔ   196. Ⓐ Ⓑ Ⓒ Ⓓ Ⓔ
187. Ⓐ Ⓑ Ⓒ Ⓓ Ⓔ   197. Ⓐ Ⓑ Ⓒ Ⓓ Ⓔ
188. Ⓐ Ⓑ Ⓒ Ⓓ Ⓔ   198. Ⓐ Ⓑ Ⓒ Ⓓ Ⓔ
189. Ⓐ Ⓑ Ⓒ Ⓓ Ⓔ   199. Ⓐ Ⓑ Ⓒ Ⓓ Ⓔ
190. Ⓐ Ⓑ Ⓒ Ⓓ Ⓔ   200. Ⓐ Ⓑ Ⓒ Ⓓ Ⓔ

Subtest 9: General Science

201. Ⓐ Ⓑ Ⓒ Ⓓ Ⓔ   211. Ⓐ Ⓑ Ⓒ Ⓓ Ⓔ
202. Ⓐ Ⓑ Ⓒ Ⓓ Ⓔ   212. Ⓐ Ⓑ Ⓒ Ⓓ Ⓔ
203. Ⓐ Ⓑ Ⓒ Ⓓ Ⓔ   213. Ⓐ Ⓑ Ⓒ Ⓓ Ⓔ
204. Ⓐ Ⓑ Ⓒ Ⓓ Ⓔ   214. Ⓐ Ⓑ Ⓒ Ⓓ Ⓔ
205. Ⓐ Ⓑ Ⓒ Ⓓ Ⓔ   215. Ⓐ Ⓑ Ⓒ Ⓓ Ⓔ
206. Ⓐ Ⓑ Ⓒ Ⓓ Ⓔ   216. Ⓐ Ⓑ Ⓒ Ⓓ Ⓔ
207. Ⓐ Ⓑ Ⓒ Ⓓ Ⓔ   217. Ⓐ Ⓑ Ⓒ Ⓓ Ⓔ
208. Ⓐ Ⓑ Ⓒ Ⓓ Ⓔ   218. Ⓐ Ⓑ Ⓒ Ⓓ Ⓔ
209. Ⓐ Ⓑ Ⓒ Ⓓ Ⓔ   219. Ⓐ Ⓑ Ⓒ Ⓓ Ⓔ
210. Ⓐ Ⓑ Ⓒ Ⓓ Ⓔ   220. Ⓐ Ⓑ Ⓒ Ⓓ Ⓔ

Subtest 10: Rotated Blocks

221. Ⓐ Ⓑ Ⓒ Ⓓ Ⓔ   231. Ⓐ Ⓑ Ⓒ Ⓓ Ⓔ
222. Ⓐ Ⓑ Ⓒ Ⓓ Ⓔ   232. Ⓐ Ⓑ Ⓒ Ⓓ Ⓔ
223. Ⓐ Ⓑ Ⓒ Ⓓ Ⓔ   233. Ⓐ Ⓑ Ⓒ Ⓓ Ⓔ
224. Ⓐ Ⓑ Ⓒ Ⓓ Ⓔ   234. Ⓐ Ⓑ Ⓒ Ⓓ Ⓔ
225. Ⓐ Ⓑ Ⓒ Ⓓ Ⓔ   235. Ⓐ Ⓑ Ⓒ Ⓓ Ⓔ
226. Ⓐ Ⓑ Ⓒ Ⓓ Ⓔ
227. Ⓐ Ⓑ Ⓒ Ⓓ Ⓔ
228. Ⓐ Ⓑ Ⓒ Ⓓ Ⓔ
229. Ⓐ Ⓑ Ⓒ Ⓓ Ⓔ
230. Ⓐ Ⓑ Ⓒ Ⓓ Ⓔ

Subtest 11: Hidden Figures

236. Ⓐ Ⓑ Ⓒ Ⓓ Ⓔ   246. Ⓐ Ⓑ Ⓒ Ⓓ Ⓔ
237. Ⓐ Ⓑ Ⓒ Ⓓ Ⓔ   247. Ⓐ Ⓑ Ⓒ Ⓓ Ⓔ
238. Ⓐ Ⓑ Ⓒ Ⓓ Ⓔ   248. Ⓐ Ⓑ Ⓒ Ⓓ Ⓔ
239. Ⓐ Ⓑ Ⓒ Ⓓ Ⓔ   249. Ⓐ Ⓑ Ⓒ Ⓓ Ⓔ
240. Ⓐ Ⓑ Ⓒ Ⓓ Ⓔ   250. Ⓐ Ⓑ Ⓒ Ⓓ Ⓔ
241. Ⓐ Ⓑ Ⓒ Ⓓ Ⓔ
242. Ⓐ Ⓑ Ⓒ Ⓓ Ⓔ
243. Ⓐ Ⓑ Ⓒ Ⓓ Ⓔ
244. Ⓐ Ⓑ Ⓒ Ⓓ Ⓔ
245. Ⓐ Ⓑ Ⓒ Ⓓ Ⓔ

Subtest 12: Self-Description Inventory

251. Ⓐ Ⓑ Ⓒ Ⓓ Ⓔ
252. Ⓐ Ⓑ Ⓒ Ⓓ Ⓔ
253. Ⓐ Ⓑ Ⓒ Ⓓ Ⓔ
254. Ⓐ Ⓑ Ⓒ Ⓓ Ⓔ
255. Ⓐ Ⓑ Ⓒ Ⓓ Ⓔ
256. Ⓐ Ⓑ Ⓒ Ⓓ Ⓔ
257. Ⓐ Ⓑ Ⓒ Ⓓ Ⓔ
258. Ⓐ Ⓑ Ⓒ Ⓓ Ⓔ
259. Ⓐ Ⓑ Ⓒ Ⓓ Ⓔ
260. Ⓐ Ⓑ Ⓒ Ⓓ Ⓔ

Subtest 1

Verbal Analogies

Time: 8 minutes for 25 questions

Description: This part of the exam measures your ability to reason and see relationships between words. Choose the answer that best completes the analogy developed at the beginning of each question.

Examples:

RED is to PINK as

(A) YELLOW is to ORANGE

(B) PURPLE is to LAVENDER

(C) BLUE is to BLACK

(D) WHITE is to GRAY

(E) GREEN is to GRASS

The correct answer is Choice (B).

BROOM is to SWEEP as SPONGE is to

(A) MOP

(B) CLEAN

(C) DETERGENT

(D) SCRUB

(E) GERMS

The correct answer is Choice (D).

1. CONCAVE is to CONVEX as

(A) CAVITY is to MOUND

(B) HILL is to HOLE

(C) OVAL is to OBLONG

(D) ROUND is to POINTED

(E) SQUARE is to ROUND

2. PERJURE is to STATE as

(A) ABANDON is to DESERT

(B) CONCENTRATE is to FOCUS

(C) MARVEL is to WONDER

(D) ROB is to STEAL

(E) TRESPASS is to ENTER

3. ANARCHIST is to DISORDER as

(A) YAWN is to BOREDOM

(B) MONTH is to YEAR

(C) GOOD is to BEST

(D) PACIFIST is to PEACE

(E) CONSTELLATION is to STARS

4. DOCTOR is to HEALING as

(A) PRISON is to GUARD

(B) DINOSAURS is to PALEONTOLOGIST

(C) AUTHOR is to WRITING

(D) CLAP is to HANDS

(E) PLANET is to UNIVERSE

5. AIRCRAFT is to FLY as BOAT is to

(A) STEER

(B) SINK

(C) SHIP

(D) LAND

(E) SAIL

6. SHEEP is to LAMB as HORSE is to

(A) COLT

(B) DOE

(C) FAWN

(D) MARE

(E) RAM

Go on to next page

7. BIRTH is to LIFE as
   (A) RODENT is to SKUNK
   (B) GENTRY is to NOBILITY
   (C) PROLIFERATE is to CEASE
   (D) WINCE is to JOY
   (E) EXPOSURE is to INFECTION

8. HORIZONTAL is to VERTICAL as WARP is to
   (A) COUNT
   (B) PILE
   (C) SELVAGE
   (D) WEAVE
   (E) WOOF

9. ISOLATION is to LONELINESS as
   (A) SHORTEN is to NIP
   (B) QUIET is to TACIT
   (C) PROMOTION is to ADVANCEMENT
   (D) MONOTONY is to HOMOGENOUS
   (E) RUSTIC is to CITY

10. GROW is to MATURE as BLOOM is to
    (A) ROSE
    (B) PETAL
    (C) FLOURISH
    (D) DECAY
    (E) BLOSSOM

11. ACTOR is to STAGE as
    (A) PATIENT is to DOCTOR
    (B) OUTSIDE is to BENCH
    (C) GARAGE is to CAR
    (D) TEACHER is to CLASSROOM
    (E) METER is to ELECTRIC

12. CRUMB is to LOAF as
    (A) PAINTER is to CANVAS
    (B) PUDDLE is to OCEAN
    (C) SOUND is to MICROPHONE
    (D) PRIDE is to FALL
    (E) FEATHER is to QUILL

13. CARROT is to VEGETABLE as
    (A) DOGWOOD is to OAK
    (B) FOOT is to PAW
    (C) PEPPER is to SPICE
    (D) SHEEP is to LAMB
    (E) VEAL is to BEEF

14. IGNORE is to OVERLOOK as
    (A) AGREE is to CONSENT
    (B) ATTACH is to SEPARATE
    (C) CLIMB is to WALK
    (D) DULL is to SHARPEN
    (E) LEARN is to REMEMBER

15. HALLOWED is to SACRED as
    (A) SOLDIER is to ARMY
    (B) GAMUT is to PROVINCIAL
    (C) LIBEL is to PRAISE
    (D) NOMADIC is to WANDERING
    (E) OBLIVIOUS is to KEEN

16. GOWN is to GARMENT as GASOLINE is to
    (A) COOLANT
    (B) FUEL
    (C) GREASE
    (D) LUBRICANT
    (E) OIL

17. PUSH is to SHOVE as CLIMB is to
    (A) MOUNTAIN
    (B) FALL
    (C) WALK
    (D) LINGER
    (E) CLAMBER

18. FISHING ROD is to HOOK as KNIFE is to
    (A) BLADE
    (B) BULLET
    (C) CUT
    (D) STEAK
    (E) HANDLE

Go on to next page

19. SLOTH is to LAZINESS as
    (A) GENTEEL is to VULGAR
    (B) INSOMNIAC is to SLEEPLESSNESS
    (C) HACKNEYED is to UNIQUE
    (D) ACCEDE is to RESPECT
    (E) CRYPT is to TOMB

20. BOOK is to CHAPTER as BUILDING is to
    (A) ELEVATOR
    (B) LOBBY
    (C) ROOF
    (D) STORY
    (E) WING

21. BATHING is to CLEANLINESS as
    (A) MEDICINE is to HARM
    (B) SCHOOLING is to EDUCATION
    (C) SPITE is to KINDNESS
    (D) UTENSIL is to CHEF
    (E) SEW is to CLOTHING

22. ELEVATOR is to HEIGHT as THRUST is to
    (A) STAIRWAY
    (B) CLIMBING
    (C) ROCKET
    (D) ALTITUDE
    (E) FLIGHT

23. SANCTUARY is to REFUGE as
    (A) FINGER is to HAND
    (B) IMPRISONMENT is to PUNISHMENT
    (C) BANJO is to COUNTRY
    (D) BALLOON is to HELIUM
    (E) SADNESS is to BLUES

24. OBEY is to COMPLY as REPLY is to
    (A) QUESTION
    (B) STATEMENT
    (C) ANSWER
    (D) REPOSE
    (E) REWIND

25. SPEED is to DECELERATION as VELOCITY is to
    (A) DISTANCE
    (B) THRUST
    (C) RAPIDITY
    (D) BRAKING
    (E) URGENCY

STOP DO NOT TURN THE PAGE UNTIL TOLD TO DO SO.

Subtest 2

Arithmetic Reasoning

Time: 29 minutes for 25 questions

Description: This section tests your mathematic reasoning ability. Decide which answer choice is most correct.

26. Tommy receives $30 for his birthday and $15 for cleaning the yard. If he spends $16 on a CD, how much money does he have left?

    (A) $29

    (B) $27

    (C) $14

    (D) $1

    (E) $0.45

27. During a season, a high-school football quarterback attempted 82 passes and completed 57 of them. What was his completion percentage?

    (A) 30.4 percent

    (B) 69.5 percent

    (C) 43.8 percent

    (D) 81.7 percent

    (E) 143.9 percent

28. A pound of margarine contains four equal sticks of margarine. The wrapper of each stick has markings that indicate how to divide the stick into eight 1-tablespoon sections. If a recipe calls for four tablespoons of margarine, the amount to use is

    (A) 1/16 pound

    (B) 1/8 pound

    (C) 1/4 pound

    (D) 1/2 pound

    (E) 3/4 pound

29. George earns $8.40 an hour, plus an overtime rate equal to 1½ times his regular pay for each hour worked above 40 hours per week. What are his total gross earnings for a 45-hour workweek?

    (A) $336

    (B) $370

    (C) $399

    (D) $567

    (E) $599

30. Carrie earns an average of $22 an hour in tips as a waitress at a restaurant. If her hourly wage is $2.50 and she has to pay a 10-percent tip share to the hostesses and busboys, how much does she take home at the end of a day when she has worked from 10:30 a.m. to 5:30 p.m.?

    (A) $32.90

    (B) $121.11

    (C) $138.60

    (D) $156.10

    (E) $171.50

31. An athlete jogs 15 laps around a circular track. If the total distance she jogs is 3 kilometers, what's the distance around the track?

    (A) 0.2 meters

    (B) 2 meters

    (C) 20 meters

    (D) 200 meters

    (E) 2,000 meters

Go on to next page

32. Although an air assault infantry company has 131 soldiers authorized, B Company has only 125 total soldiers assigned, of whom 4 percent are officers. How many enlisted soldiers are assigned to B Company?

    (A) 114

    (B) 123

    (C) 120

    (D) 121

    (E) 126

33. The fuel tank of a gasoline generator has enough capacity to operate the generator for 1 hour and 15 minutes. About how many times must the fuel tank be filled to run the generator from 6:15 p.m. to 7:00 a.m.?

    (A) 9.4

    (B) 10.2

    (C) 10.8

    (D) 11.5

    (E) 12.0

34. On a map, 1 centimeter represents 4 miles. A distance of 10 miles would be how far on the map?

    (A) 1¾ centimeters

    (B) 2 centimeters

    (C) 2½ centimeters

    (D) 4 centimeters

    (E) 4½ centimeters

35. One phone plan charges a $20 monthly fee and $0.08 per minute on every phone call made. Another phone plan charges a $12 monthly fee and $0.12 per minute for every phone call made. After how many minutes would the charge be the same for each phone plan?

    (A) 60

    (B) 90

    (C) 120

    (D) 200

    (E) 320

36. A jar contains red, green, and yellow marbles, and 20 percent of these marbles are either red or green. What are the chances of randomly picking a yellow marble out of the jar?

    (A) 1 out of 3

    (B) 1 out of 5

    (C) 2 out of 3

    (D) 2 out of 5

    (E) 4 out of 5

37. John found a chandelier for the dining room for $1,400. However, because the model had been discontinued and the display had no factory packaging material, the store manager discounted the price to $1,150. What was the percentage of the reduction?

    (A) 1.78 percent

    (B) 13.0 percent

    (C) 15.0 percent

    (D) 17.9 percent

    (E) 21.7 percent

38. Tom donates 4/13 of his paycheck to his favorite charity. If he donates $26.80, what's the amount of his paycheck?

    (A) $8.25

    (B) $82.50

    (C) $87.10

    (D) $137.50

    (E) $348.40

39. A submarine sails x miles the first day, y miles the second day, and z miles the third day. What's the average number of miles sailed per day?

    (A) $3xyz$

    (B) $3(x + y + z)$

    (C) $(x + y + z) \div 3$

    (D) $(x + y + z)$

    (E) $xyz \div 3$

Go on to next page

40. A passenger plane can carry two tons of cargo. A freight plane can carry six tons of cargo. If an equal number of both kinds of planes are used to ship 160 tons of cargo and each plane carries its maximum cargo load, how many tons of cargo are shipped on the passenger planes?

    (A) 40 tons

    (B) 60 tons

    (C) 80 tons

    (D) 100 tons

    (E) 120 tons

41. When a highway was converted to a toll road, the traffic declined from 11,200 cars per day to 10,044. What was the percentage of the decline in traffic?

    (A) 10.3 percent

    (B) 11.5 percent

    (C) 10.1 percent

    (D) 8.9 percent

    (E) 79.3 percent

42. If the weight of water is 62.4 pounds per cubic foot, the weight of the water that fills a 6-inch-x-6-inch-x-1 foot rectangular container is

    (A) 3.9 pounds

    (B) 7.8 pounds

    (C) 15.6 pounds

    (D) 31.2 pounds

    (E) 62.4 pounds

43. What's the volume of a container that is 23 feet long, 15 feet wide, and 11 feet high?

    (A) 2,530 square feet

    (B) 3,450 cubic feet

    (C) 3,795 square feet

    (D) 3,795 cubic feet

    (E) 5,280 cubic feet

44. The area of circle A is four times as large as circle B (which has a radius of 3 inches). The radius of circle A is

    (A) 12 inches

    (B) 9 inches

    (C) 8 inches

    (D) 6 inches

    (E) 4 inches

45. A theater contains x rows, with y seats in each row. How many total seats are in the theater?

    (A) $x + y$

    (B) $x - y$

    (C) xy

    (D) $y - x$

    (E) $2x + y$

46. Two runners finish a race in 80 seconds, another runner finishes the race in 72 seconds, and a fourth runner finishes the race in 68 seconds. The average of the runners' times is

    (A) 73 seconds

    (B) 74 seconds

    (C) 75 seconds

    (D) 76 seconds

    (E) 77 seconds

47. Mr. Jones earns a weekly salary of $300 plus a 10-percent commission on all sales. If he had $8,350 in sales last week, what were his total earnings?

    (A) $835

    (B) $865

    (C) $1,135

    (D) $1,835

    (E) $1,925

Go on to next page

48. When 550 gallons of oil are added to an oil tank that is 1/8 full, the tank becomes 1/2 full. The capacity of the oil tank is

    (A) 1,350 gallons

    (B) 1,390 gallons

    (C) 1,430 gallons

    (D) 1,470 gallons

    (E) 1,510 gallons

49. A wheel has a 1-meter radius. How many meters will a point on the rim of that wheel travel if the wheel makes 35 rotations?

    (A) 110

    (B) 120

    (C) 210

    (D) 220

    (E) 240

50. In the city of Trenton, houses are assessed at 80 percent of the purchase price. If Mr. Hall buys a home in Trenton for $120,000 and real estate taxes are $4.75 per $100 of assessed value, how much property tax must he pay each year?

    (A) $3,648

    (B) $5,472

    (C) $4,560

    (D) $4,845

    (E) $5,700

STOP DO NOT TURN THE PAGE UNTIL TOLD TO DO SO.

Subtest 3
Word Knowledge

Time: 5 minutes for 25 questions

Description: This test measures your verbal comprehension and ability to understand written language. Select the best answer that means the same as the word given.

51. Tedious
    - (A) Demanding
    - (B) Dull
    - (C) Hard
    - (D) Simple
    - (E) Surprising

52. Assent
    - (A) Acquire
    - (B) Climb
    - (C) Consent
    - (D) Emphasize
    - (E) Participate

53. Equivalent
    - (A) Complicated
    - (B) Inferior
    - (C) Superior
    - (D) Evident
    - (E) Equal

54. Telemetry
    - (A) Mental communication
    - (B) Marketing goods or services by telephone
    - (C) Transmission of measurements made by automatic instruments
    - (D) Study of climactic variations
    - (E) Rashness

55. Succinct
    - (A) Concise
    - (B) Helpful
    - (C) Important
    - (D) Misleading
    - (E) Sweet

56. Centripetal
    - (A) Away from a center or axis
    - (B) Relating to the feet
    - (C) Having more than 100 petals
    - (D) Toward a center or an axis
    - (E) Circular

57. Counteract
    - (A) Criticize
    - (B) Conserve
    - (C) Erode
    - (D) Neutralize
    - (E) Retreat

58. Redundant
    - (A) Brilliant
    - (B) Held back
    - (C) Repetitive
    - (D) Unruly
    - (E) Isolated

Go on to next page

59. Verify

(A) Alarm

(B) Confirm

(C) Explain

(D) Guarantee

(E) Question

60. Tacit

(A) Silent

(B) Sour

(C) Ornament

(D) Talkative

(E) Pleasing

61. Itinerary

(A) Migrant

(B) Not permanent

(C) Cure-all

(D) Schedule

(E) Character

62. Rebuff

(A) Forget

(B) Ignore

(C) Recover

(D) Polish

(E) Snub

63. Indolent

(A) Hopeless

(B) Lazy

(C) Lenient

(D) Rude

(E) Selfish

64. Mercurial

(A) Having compassion

(B) Specious

(C) Unpredictably changeable

(D) Metallic

(E) Containing mercury

65. Flexible

(A) Flammable

(B) Fragile

(C) Pliable

(D) Rigid

(E) Separable

66. Diagnose

(A) Predict the outcome

(B) Cut in two

(C) Identify a situation

(D) Antagonize

(E) Speak about

67. Altercation

(A) Controversy

(B) Defeat

(C) Irritation

(D) Substitution

(E) Vexation

68. Rectify

(A) Dealing with the digestive system

(B) Cause trouble or havoc

(C) Get back

(D) Correct

(E) Give fresh life to

69. Anachronistic

(A) Chronologically out of place

(B) Cursed

(C) Dealing with organism structure

(D) Attribution of conscious thoughts to inanimate objects or animals

(E) Existing before a war

70. Conducive

(A) Confusing

(B) Cooperative

(C) Energetic

(D) Helpful

(E) Respectful

Go on to next page

71. Terse

    (A) Faulty

    (B) Lengthy

    (C) Oral

    (D) Pointed

    (E) Written

72. Dilated

    (A) Cleared

    (B) Clouded

    (C) Decreased

    (D) Enlarged

    (E) Tightened

73. Picayune

    (A) Unnoticed

    (B) Insignificant

    (C) Intense

    (D) Hot

    (E) Unfortunate

74. Kinetic

    (A) Relating to the motion of material bodies

    (B) Referring to motion pictures

    (C) Moving at a high speed

    (D) Relating to a sensory experience

    (E) Referring to a relative

75. Sullen

    (A) Angrily silent

    (B) Grayish yellow

    (C) Mildly nauseated

    (D) Soaking wet

    (E) Very dirty

STOP DO NOT TURN THE PAGE UNTIL TOLD TO DO SO.

Subtest 4

Math Knowledge

Time: 22 minutes for 25 questions

Description: This subtest deals with your general understanding of and ability to use mathematical relationships in problem solving. Each problem is followed by five possible answers, and you must determine which answer is most correct. Use scratch paper to do your calculations and then mark the correct answer. (*Note:* We don't provide any scratch paper with this book, but you'll receive paper at your test site.)

76. John took five midterm tests for five different college classes; his average for all five tests was 88. That night at home, he could only remember his first 4 scores: 78, 86, 94, and 96. What was his score on the fifth test?

    (A) 82

    (B) 86

    (C) 84

    (D) 88

    (E) 87

77. Solve for z: $3z - 5 + 2z = 25 - 5z$

    (A) $z = 1$

    (B) $z = 3$

    (C) $z = -3$

    (D) $z = 0$

    (E) No solution

78. The expression $\sqrt{28} - \sqrt{7}$ reduces to

    (A) $\sqrt{4}$

    (B) $\sqrt{7}$

    (C) $3\sqrt{7}$

    (D) $\sqrt{21}$

    (E) $-\sqrt{35}$

79. If $5x + 3y = 29$ and $x - y = 1$, x equals

    (A) 1

    (B) 2

    (C) 3

    (D) 4

    (E) 5

80. Find the square root of 85, correct to the nearest tenth.

    (A) 9.1

    (B) 9.2

    (C) 9.3

    (D) 9.4

    (E) 9.5

81. The volume of a cylinder with a radius of r and a height of h is

    (A) πrh

    (B) $2\pi rh$

    (C) $2\pi r^2 h$

    (D) $4\pi r^2 h$

    (E) None of the above

82. An airplane is flying a circular or "racetrack" orbit around a 4,000-meter-high mountaintop. Assuming the pilot flies a perfectly circular course, how far does he need to travel in kilometers for each orbit if the distance between the mountaintop and the outer edge of his orbit is 40 kilometers?

    (A) 13 kilometers

    (B) 25 kilometers

    (C) 126 kilometers

    (D) 251 kilometers

    (E) 503 kilometers

Go on to next page ⟹

83. If x is an odd integer, which of the following is an even integer?

    (A) $2x + 1$

    (B) $2x - 1$

    (C) $x(2 + x)$

    (D) $(2 + x - 1)$

    (E) None of the above

84. A new wildlife preserve is laid out in a perfect circle with a radius of 14 kilometers. The lion habitat is shaped like a wedge and has an 8-foot-high razor wire fence around its two inner sides that meet at a 90-degree angle in the center of the preserve. What's the area of the lion habitat?

    (A) 140 square kilometers

    (B) 3.5 square kilometers

    (C) 210 square kilometers

    (D) 154 square kilometers

    (E) 35 square kilometers

85. The sum of the angle measures of a pentagon is

    (A) 360 degrees

    (B) 540 degrees

    (C) 720 degrees

    (D) 900 degrees

    (E) 1,180 degrees

86. $2(a - b) + 4(a + 3b) =$

    (A) $6a - 10b$

    (B) $6a + 2b$

    (C) $8a + 2b$

    (D) $6a - 2b$

    (E) $6a + 10b$

87. The area of a square with a perimeter of 40 yards is

    (A) 100 square feet

    (B) 180 square feet

    (C) 900 square feet

    (D) 300 square yards

    (E) 1,600 square feet

88. If $3^n = 9$, what's the value of $4^{n + 1}$?

    (A) 24

    (B) 48

    (C) 64

    (D) 108

    (E) None of the above

89. Two circles have the same center. If their radii are 7 centimeters and 10 centimeters, find the area that is part of the larger circle but not part of the smaller one.

    (A) 3 square centimeters

    (B) 17 square centimeters

    (C) 51π square centimeters

    (D) 71π square centimeters

    (E) 91π square centimeters

90. The ratio of $3x$ to $5y$ is 1:2. What's the ratio of x to y?

    (A) 1:2

    (B) 2:3

    (C) 3:4

    (D) 4:5

    (E) 5:6

91. The reciprocal of 7 to the nearest thousandth is

    (A) 0.143

    (B) 1.428

    (C) 14

    (D) 21

    (E) 49

92. Which of the following is the smallest prime number greater than 200?

    (A) 201

    (B) 205

    (C) 211

    (D) 214

    (E) 223

Go on to next page

93. One million may be represented as

    (A) 10^4

    (B) 10^5

    (C) 10^6

    (D) 10^7

    (E) 10^8

94. 10^x divided by 10^y equals

    (A) $10^{\frac{x}{y}}$

    (B) 10^{xy}

    (C) 10^{x+y}

    (D) 10^{x-y}

    (E) None of the above

95. The cube root of 729 is equal to the square of

    (A) 11

    (B) 9

    (C) 7

    (D) 5

    (E) 3

96. A cook is mixing fruit juice from concentrate for a catered event. Ten ounces of liquid contain 20 percent fruit juice and 80 percent water. He then further dilutes the mixture by adding 40 additional ounces of water. What's the percent of fruit juice in the new solution?

    (A) 4 percent

    (B) 10 percent

    (C) 14 percent

    (D) 18 percent

    (E) 20 percent

97. A cylindrical container has a radius of 7 inches and a height of 15 inches. How many gallons of hydraulic fluid can it hold? (***Note:*** There are 231 cubic inches in a gallon.)

    (A) 15 gallons

    (B) 14 gallons

    (C) 140 gallons

    (D) 10 gallons

    (E) 23.1 gallons

98. If one angle of a triangle measures 115 degrees, the degree sum of the other two angles is

    (A) 245

    (B) 75

    (C) 195

    (D) 65

    (E) None of the above

99. An equilateral triangle has a perimeter divisible by both 3 and 5. Which of the following can be the length of each of its sides?

    (A) 3

    (B) 4

    (C) 5

    (D) 6

    (E) 7

100. If one of the angles of a right triangle is 30 degrees, what are the degree measurements of the other two angles?

    (A) 30 and 120

    (B) 60 and 45

    (C) 60 and 90

    (D) 45 and 90

    (E) 45 and 120

 STOP DO NOT TURN THE PAGE UNTIL TOLD TO DO SO.

Subtest 5

Instrument Comprehension

Time: 6 minutes for 20 questions

Description: In this subtest, you have to determine the position of an airplane in flight by looking at two dials: one showing the artificial horizon and the other showing the compass heading. From these dials, you have to determine the amount of climb or dive, the degree of bank to left or right, and the heading. Choose the airplane silhouette from the answer choices (A) through (D) that most nearly represents the position indicated on the dials.

Directions: Below are shown two sets of dials, labeled artificial horizon and compass. The heavy black line on the artificial horizon represents the horizon line. If the airplane is above the horizon, it's climbing. If it's below the horizon, it's diving. The greater amount of climb or dive, the farther up or down the horizon line is seen. The artificial horizon dial also has a black arrowhead showing the degree of bank to left or right. If the airplane has no bank, the arrowhead points to zero. If it's banked to the left, the arrowhead points to the right of zero. If the airplane is banked to the right, the arrowhead points to the left of zero.

101.

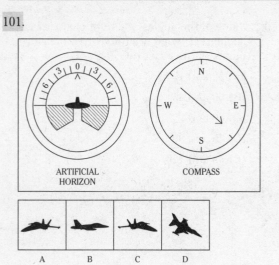

102.

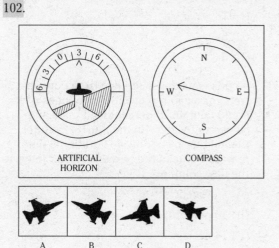

Go on to next page

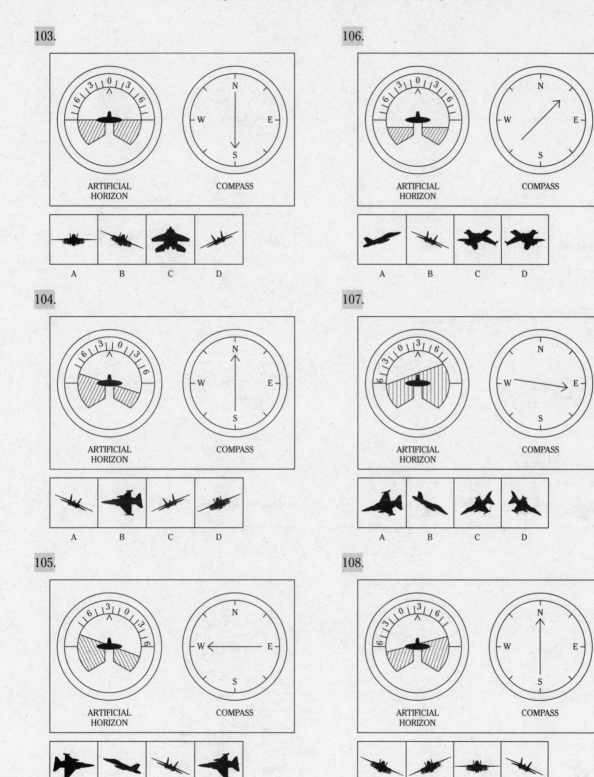

103.

ARTIFICIAL HORIZON   COMPASS

A   B   C   D

104.

ARTIFICIAL HORIZON   COMPASS

A   B   C   D

105.

ARTIFICIAL HORIZON   COMPASS

A   B   C   D

106.

ARTIFICIAL HORIZON   COMPASS

A   B   C   D

107.

ARTIFICIAL HORIZON   COMPASS

A   B   C   D

108.

ARTIFICIAL HORIZON   COMPASS

A   B   C   D

Go on to next page

109.

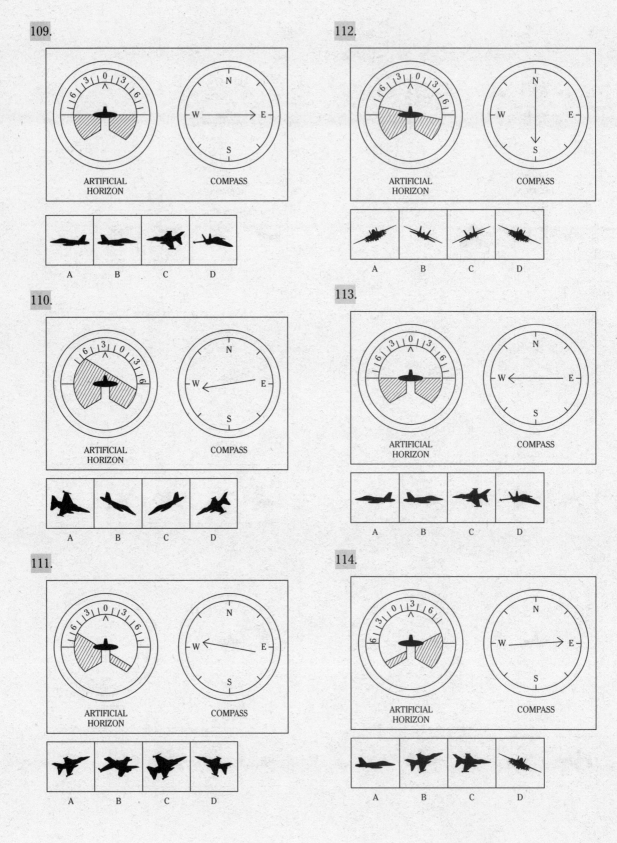

110.

111.

112.

113.

114.

Go on to next page

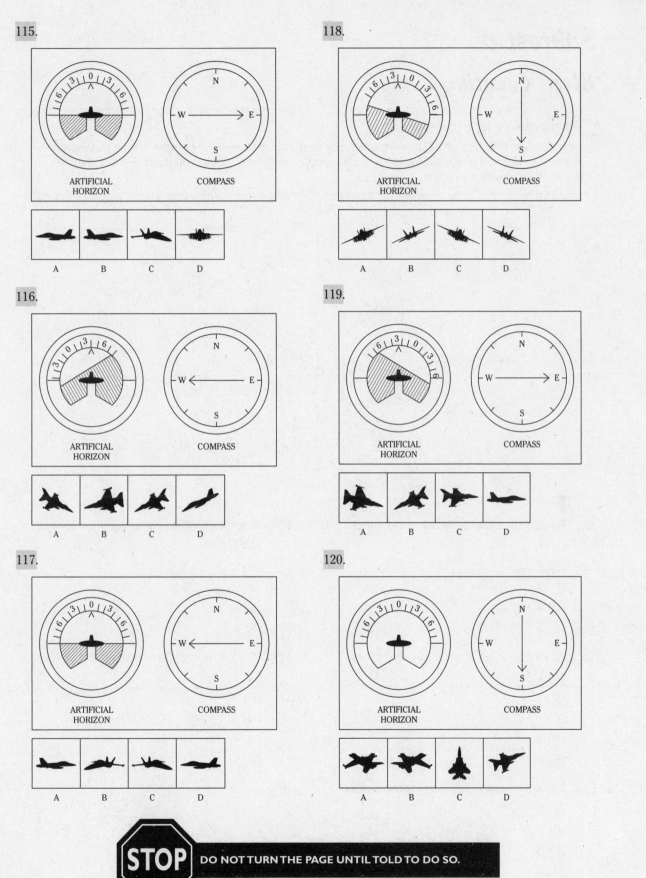

115.

ARTIFICIAL HORIZON

COMPASS

A   B   C   D

116.

ARTIFICIAL HORIZON

COMPASS

A   B   C   D

117.

ARTIFICIAL HORIZON

COMPASS

A   B   C   D

118.

ARTIFICIAL HORIZON

COMPASS

A   B   C   D

119.

ARTIFICIAL HORIZON

COMPASS

A   B   C   D

120.

ARTIFICIAL HORIZON

COMPASS

A   B   C   D

STOP DO NOT TURN THE PAGE UNTIL TOLD TO DO SO.

Subtest 6

Block Counting

Time: 3 minutes for 20 questions

Description: This section of the test measures your ability to see and comprehend a three-dimensional viewpoint of a pile of blocks. Given a specific numbered block, you must determine how many other blocks it touches.

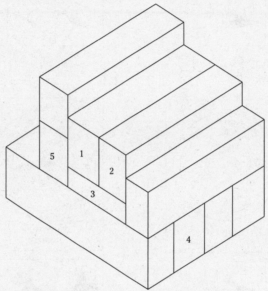

121. Block 1 touches how many other blocks?
    (A) 1
    (B) 2
    (C) 3
    (D) 4
    (E) 5

122. Block 2 touches how many other blocks?
    (A) 1
    (B) 2
    (C) 3
    (D) 4
    (E) 5

123. Block 3 touches how many other blocks?
    (A) 8
    (B) 7
    (C) 3
    (D) 4
    (E) 5

124. Block 4 touches how many other blocks?
    (A) 1
    (B) 2
    (C) 3
    (D) 4
    (E) 5

125. Block 5 touches how many other blocks?
    (A) 1
    (B) 7
    (C) 3
    (D) 4
    (E) 5

Go on to next page

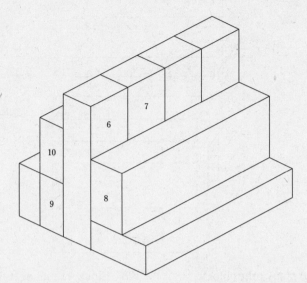

126. Block 6 touches how many other blocks?

    (A) 6

    (B) 2

    (C) 3

    (D) 4

    (E) 5

127. Block 7 touches how many other blocks?

    (A) 7

    (B) 6

    (C) 3

    (D) 4

    (E) 5

128. Block 8 touches how many other blocks?

    (A) 1

    (B) 2

    (C) 5

    (D) 4

    (E) 7

129. Block 9 touches how many other blocks?

    (A) 7

    (B) 6

    (C) 3

    (D) 4

    (E) 5

130. Block 10 touches how many other blocks?

    (A) 1

    (B) 2

    (C) 3

    (D) 4

    (E) 5

Go on to next page

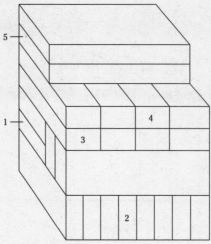

131. Block 1 touches how many other blocks?

    (A) 6

    (B) 10

    (C) 7

    (D) 4

    (E) 5

132. Block 2 touches how many other blocks?

    (A) 1

    (B) 2

    (C) 3

    (D) 4

    (E) 5

133. Block 3 touches how many other blocks?

    (A) 6

    (B) 5

    (C) 7

    (D) 4

    (E) 3

134. Block 4 touches how many other blocks?

    (A) 1

    (B) 2

    (C) 3

    (D) 4

    (E) 5

135. Block 5 touches how many other blocks?

    (A) 1

    (B) 2

    (C) 3

    (D) 4

    (E) 5

Go on to next page

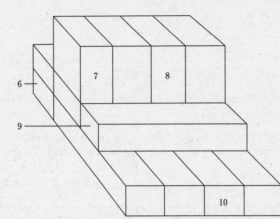

136. Block 6 touches how many other blocks?

    (A) 1

    (B) 2

    (C) 3

    (D) 4

    (E) 5

137. Block 7 touches how many other blocks?

    (A) 1

    (B) 2

    (C) 3

    (D) 4

    (E) 5

138. Block 8 touches how many other blocks?

    (A) 1

    (B) 2

    (C) 3

    (D) 4

    (E) 5

139. Block 9 touches how many other blocks?

    (A) 1

    (B) 2

    (C) 3

    (D) 4

    (E) 5

140. Block 10 touches how many other blocks?

    (A) 1

    (B) 2

    (C) 3

    (D) 4

    (E) 5

STOP DO NOT TURN THE PAGE UNTIL TOLD TO DO SO.

Subtest 7

Table Reading

Time: 7 minutes for 40 questions

Description: This test gauges your ability to read a table quickly and accurately. For this test, you use the given value to find the entry that occurs at the intersections of the corresponding row and column.

For questions 141 to 145, use the following table. Note that the x values are shown at the bottom of the table and the y values are shown at the left side of the table. Given x and y, choose the answer that represents the intersecting value.

y										
10	29	6	7	9	27	27	6	12	28	11
9	11	14	17	21	28	21	8	28	24	2
8	4	10	18	25	21	23	12	9	4	14
7	20	8	16	30	29	4	6	29	18	25
6	18	6	15	8	9	5	29	17	28	18
5	7	22	19	16	7	5	21	5	15	5
4	30	15	16	23	26	22	3	12	8	24
3	12	23	7	28	28	10	30	3	9	11
2	1	5	9	20	2	8	12	29	13	16
1	28	11	5	30	16	15	23	9	14	9
	1	2	3	4	5	6	7	8	9	10

x

141. $x = 4; y = 6$
(A) 16
(B) 8
(C) 24
(D) 4
(E) 32

142. $x = 2; y = 8$
(A) 16
(B) 12
(C) 24
(D) 28
(E) 10

143. $x = 3; y = 3$
(A) 10
(B) 6
(C) 7
(D) 42
(E) 16

144. $x = 5; y = 1$
(A) 16
(B) 22
(C) 9
(D) 25
(E) 7

145. $x = 9; y = 6$
(A) 28
(B) 22
(C) 21
(D) 18
(E) 9

Go on to next page

Questions 146 to 150 are based on the following table of commuter train schedules.

	Wilks Station		Canton Station		Plymouth Station		Central Station		Holman Station	
Metro A	4:10 P	4:14 P	4:24 P	4:28 P	4:40 P	4:44 P	4:46 P	4:50 P	4:10 P	4:10 P
Metro B	4:18 P	4:22 P	4:32 P	4:36 P	4:48 P	4:52 P	4:54 P	4:58 P	4:10 P	4:10 P
Metro C	4:21 P	4:25 P	4:35 P	4:39 P	4:51 P	4:55 P	4:57 P	5:01 P	4:10 P	4:10 P

146. The metro line A is scheduled to arrive at Wilks Station at

(A) 3:15 p.m.

(B) 3:16 p.m.

(C) 4:10 p.m.

(D) 3:46 p.m.

(E) 3:55 p.m.

147. The metro line B is scheduled to arrive at Wilks Station at

(A) 4:22 p.m.

(B) 4:11 p.m.

(C) 4:16 p.m.

(D) 3:10 p.m.

(E) 4:18 p.m.

148. The metro line B will arrive at Plymouth Station at

(A) 4:21 p.m.

(B) 3:55 p.m.

(C) 4:48 p.m.

(D) 4:35 p.m.

(E) 4:55 p.m.

149. Metro line C departs Plymouth Station at

(A) 4:55 p.m.

(B) 4:28 p.m.

(C) 4:44 p.m.

(D) 4:52 p.m.

(E) 4:21 p.m.

150. Metro line C arrives at Central Station at

(A) 5:01 p.m.

(B) 4:52 p.m.

(C) 4:57 p.m.

(D) 5:58 p.m.

(E) 4:48 p.m.

Go on to next page

Questions 151 to 155 are based on the following mileage chart listed in the back of a U.S. travel atlas.

	Atlanta	Boston	Dallas	Denver	Detroit	New York City	Los Angeles	Salt Lake City
Atlanta	NA	1107	790	1400	725	860	2175	1875
Boston	1107	NA	1795	1970	705	215	3080	2365
Dallas	790	1795	NA	815	1190	1550	1430	1305
Denver	1400	1970	815	NA	1270	1780	1015	560
Detroit	725	705	1190	1270	NA	615	2285	1665
New York City	860	215	1550	1780	615	NA	2795	2175
Los Angeles	2175	3080	1430	560	2285	2795	NA	690
Salt Lake City	1875	2365	1305	560	1665	2175	690	NA

151. How far is it from Dallas to Detroit?

(A) 849 miles

(B) 1,500 miles

(C) 1,722 miles

(D) 1,640 miles

(E) 1,190 miles

152. How far is it from Atlanta to New York City?

(A) 970 miles

(B) 1,213 miles

(C) 860 miles

(D) 775 miles

(E) 1,055 miles

153. How far is it from Atlanta to Denver if you first go to Dallas and then to Denver?

(A) 1,230 miles

(B) 1,547 miles

(C) 1,449 miles

(D) 1,605 miles

(E) 1,190 miles

154. How far is it from Salt Lake City to Denver?

(A) 777 miles

(B) 640 miles

(C) 560 miles

(D) 305 miles

(E) 435 miles

155. How far is it from Boston to Los Angeles?

(A) 3,080 miles

(B) 3,410 miles

(C) 2,905 miles

(D) 2,490 miles

(E) 3,216 miles

Go on to next page

Questions 156 to 160 cover the military compensation tables.

Grade	2 or less	Over 2	Over 3	Over 4	Over 6	Over 8	Over 10	Over 12	Over 14	Over 16	Over 18	Over 20	Over 22	Over 24	Over 26	Over 28	Over 30	Over 32	Over 34	Over 36	Over 38	Over 40
0-10[1]												15913.2	15990.6	16323.6	16902.6	16902.6	17747.7	17747.7	18634.8	18634.8	19566.9	19566.9
0-9[1]												13917.6	14118.6	14408.1	14913.3	14913.3	15659.4	15659.4	16442.4	16442.4	17264.4	17264.4
0-8[1]	9847.8	10170.3	10384.5	10444.2	10711.5	11157.6	11261.4	11685	11806.5	12171.6	12700.2	13187.1	13512.3	13512.3	13512.3	13512.3	13850.4	13850.4	14196.6	14196.6	14196.6	14196.6
0-7[1]	8182.5	8562.9	8738.7	8878.5	9131.7	9381.9	9671.1	9959.4	10248.6	11157.6	11924.7	11924.7	11924.7	11924.7	11985.6	11985.6	12225.3	12225.3	12225.3	12225.3	12225.3	12225.3
0-6[2]	6064.8	6663	7100.1	7100.1	7127.1	7432.8	7473	7473	7897.8	8648.7	9089.4	9529.8	9780.6	10034.4	10526.7	10526.7	10736.7	10736.7	10736.7	10736.7	10736.7	10736.7
0-5	5055.9	5695.5	6089.7	6164.1	6410.1	6557.1	6880.8	7118.4	7425.3	7895.1	8118	8338.8	8589.9	8589.9	8589.9	8589.9	8589.9	8589.9	8589.9	8589.9	8589.9	8589.9
0-4	4362.3	5049.9	5386.8	5461.8	5774.7	6109.8	6527.7	6852.9	7078.8	7208.7	7283.7	7283.7	7283.7	7283.7	7283.7	7283.7	7283.7	7283.7	7283.7	7283.7	7283.7	7283.7
0-3	3835.5	4347.9	4692.9	5116.5	5361.6	5630.7	5804.7	6090.6	6240	6240	6240	6240	6240	6240	6240	6240	6240	6240	6240	6240	6240	6240
0-2	3314.1	3774.3	4347	4493.7	4586.4	4586.4	4586.4	4586.4	4586.4	4586.4	4586.4	4586.4	4586.4	4586.4	4586.4	4586.4	4586.4	4586.4	4586.4	4586.4	4586.4	4586.4
0-1	2876.4	2994	3619.2	3619.2	3619.2	3619.2	3619.2	3619.2	3619.2	3619.2	3619.2	3619.2	3619.2	3619.2	3619.2	3619.2	3619.2	3619.2	3619.2	3619.2	3619.2	3619.2
0-3[3]				5116.5	5361.6	5630.7	5804.7	6090.6	6332.1	6470.7	6659.4	6659.4	6659.4	6659.4	6659.4	6659.4	6659.4	6659.4	6659.4	6659.4	6659.4	6659.4
0-2[3]				4493.7	4586.4	4732.5	4978.8	5169.3	5311.2	5311.2	5311.2	5311.2	5311.2	5311.2	5311.2	5311.2	5311.2	5311.2	5311.2	5311.2	5311.2	5311.2
0-1[3]		3619.2	3864.6	4007.1	4153.8	4297.2	4493.7	4493.7	4493.7	4493.7	4493.7	4493.7	4493.7	4493.7	4493.7	4493.7	4493.7	4493.7	4493.7	4493.7	4493.7	4493.7

Grade	2 or less	Over 2	Over 3	Over 4	Over 6	Over 8	Over 10	Over 12	Over 14	Over 16	Over 18	Over 20	Over 22	Over 24	Over 26	Over 28	Over 30	Over 32	Over 34	Over 36	Over 38	Over 40
w-5												7047.9	7405.5	7671.6	7966.5	7966.5	8365.2	8365.2	8783.1	8783.1	9222.9	9222.9
w-4	3963.9	4263.9	4386	4506.6	4713.9	4919.1	5126.7	5439.6	5713.5	5974.2	6187.5	6395.4	6701.1	6952.2	7238.7	7238.7	7383.3	7383.3	7383.3	7383.3	7383.3	7383.3
w 3	3619.5	3770.4	3924.2	3975.9	4137.2	4457.1	4789.2	4945.5	5126.4	5313	5648.1	5874.46	6009.92	6153.75	6349.35	6349.35	6349.35	6349.35	6349.35	6349.35	6349.35	6349.35
w-2	3202.8	3505.8	3599.4	3663.3	3871.2	4194	4353.9	4511.4	4704	4854.3	4990.8	5153.7	5261.1	5346.3	5346.3	5346.3	5346.3	5346.3	5346.3	5346.3	5346.3	5346.3
w-1	2811.6	3114	3195.3	3367.5	3570.9	3870.6	4010.4	4205.7	4398.3	4549.8	4689	4858.2	4858.2	4858.2	4858.2	4858.2	4858.2	4858.2	4858.2	4858.2	4858.2	4858.2

Grade	2 or less	Over 2	Over 3	Over 4	Over 6	Over 8	Over 10	Over 12	Over 14	Over 16	Over 18	Over 20	Over 22	Over 24	Over 26	Over 28	Over 30	Over 32	Over 34	Over 36	Over 38	Over 40
E-9[4]							4788.9	4897.5	5034.3	5194.8	5357.4	5617.4	5837.26	6068.82	6422.51	6422.51	6743.34	6743.34	7080.91	7080.91	7435.22	7435.22
E-8						3920.1	4093.5	4200.9	4329.6	4469.1	4720.5	4847.8	5064.79	5184.75	5481.09	5481.09	5591.14	5591.14	5591.14	5591.14	5591.14	5591.14
E-7	2725.2	2974.5	3088.2	3239.1	3357	3559.2	3673.2	3875.7	4043.7	4158.6	4281	4328.58	4487.29	4572.85	4897.71	4897.71	4897.71	4897.71	4897.71	4897.71	4897.71	4897.71
E-6	2357.1	2593.8	2708.1	2819.4	2935.5	3196.5	3298.5	3495.3	3555.6	3599.7	3650.7	3650.96	3650.96	3650.96	3650.96	3650.96	3650.96	3650.96	3650.96	3650.96	3650.96	3650.96
E-5	2159.4	2304.3	2415.9	2529.9	2707.5	2893.5	3045.6	3064.2	3064.2	3064.2	3064.2	3064.2	3064.2	3064.2	3064.2	3064.2	3064.2	3064.2	3064.2	3064.2	3064.2	3064.2
E-4	1979.7	2081.1	2193.9	2304.9	2403.3	2403.3	2403.3	2403.3	2403.3	2403.3	2403.3	2403.3	2403.3	2403.3	2403.3	2403.3	2403.3	2403.3	2403.3	2403.3	2403.3	2403.3
E-3	1787.4	1899.9	2014.8	2014.8	2014.8	2014.8	2014.8	2014.8	2014.8	2014.8	2014.8	2014.8	2014.8	2014.8	2014.8	2014.8	2014.8	2014.8	2014.8	2014.8	2014.8	2014.8
E-2	1699.8	1699.8	1699.8	1699.8	1699.8	1699.8	1699.8	1699.8	1699.8	1699.8	1699.8	1699.8	1699.8	1699.8	1699.8	1699.8	1699.8	1699.8	1699.8	1699.8	1699.8	1699.8
E-1	1516.2	1516.2	1516.2	1516.2	1516.2	1516.2	1516.2	1516.2	1516.2	1516.2	1516.2	1516.2	1516.2	1516.2	1516.2	1516.2	1516.2	1516.2	1516.2	1516.2	1516.2	1516.2

156. What does an 0-2 (1st Lieutenant in the Air Force) with 3 years of service earn per month for base pay?

(A) $4,216.50

(B) $4,347.00

(C) $3,990.22

(D) $4,479.00

(E) $3,660.76

157. When you first get your commission and enter flight school (less than 1 year of service), what is your base pay?

(A) $2,876.40

(B) $2,890.84

(C) $2,858.00

(D) $3,163.50

(E) $3,216.63

158. What does a Captain (0-3) make in base pay after 6 years of service in the Air Force?

(A) $4,895.52

(B) $5,572.48

(C) $5,101.00

(D) $5,361.60

(E) $4,790.25

159. You're a 2nd Lieutenant with 6 years of prior enlisted service. What's your base pay per month?

(A) $4,290.60

(B) $3,455.00

(C) $3,864.60

(D) $3,910.23

(E) $3,245.75

160. A Lieutenant Colonel (0-5) with more than 16 years of service makes how much base pay per month?

(A) $7,216.00

(B) $7,086.20

(C) $8,254.46

(D) $8,045.10

(E) $7,895.10

Go on to next page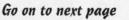

Questions 161 to 165 involve data from the acceptable military height and weight tables.

Male

HEIGHT IN INCHES	MINIMUM WEIGHT	MAX WEIGHT AGE 17-20	MAX WEIGHT AGE 21-27	MAX WEIGHT AGE 28-39	MAX WEIGHT AGE 40 +
58	91				
59	94				
60	97	132	136	139	141
61	100	136	140	144	146
62	104	141	144	148	150
63	107	145	149	153	155
64	110	150	154	158	160
65	114	155	159	163	165
66	117	160	163	168	170
67	121	165	169	174	178
68	125	170	174	179	181
69	128	175	179	184	186
70	132	180	185	189	192
71	136	185	189	194	197
72	140	190	195	200	203
73	144	195	200	205	208
74	148	201	206	211	214
75	152	206	212	217	220
76	156	212	217	223	226
77	160	218	223	229	232
78	164	223	229	235	238
79	168	229	235	241	244
80	173	234	240	247	250

Go on to next page

Female

HEIGHT IN INCHES	MINIMUM WEIGHT	MAX WEIGHT AGE 17-20	MAX WEIGHT AGE 21-27	MAX WEIGHT AGE 28-39	MAX WEIGHT AGE 40 +
58	91	119	121	122	123
59	94	124	125	126	128
60	97	128	129	131	133
61	100	132	134	135	137
62	104	136	138	140	142
63	107	141	143	144	146
64	110	145	147	149	151
65	114	150	152	154	156
66	117	155	156	158	161
67	121	159	161	163	166
68	125	164	166	168	171
69	128	169	171	176	176
70	132	174	176	178	181
71	136	179	181	183	186
72	140	184	186	188	191
73	144	189	191	194	197
74	148	194	197	199	202
75	152	200	202	204	208
76	156	205	207	210	213
77	160	210	213	215	219
78	164	216	218	221	225
79	168	221	224	227	230
80	173	227	230	233	236

161. A 27-year-old male who is 74 inches tall can weigh up to

(A) 202 pounds

(B) 206 pounds

(C) 198 pounds

(D) 201 pounds

(E) 212 pounds

162. A 42-year-old male who is 71 inches tall can weigh up to

(A) 199 pounds

(B) 204 pounds

(C) 189 pounds

(D) 197 pounds

(E) 199 pounds

Go on to next page

163. A 32-year-old female who is 66 inches tall can weight up to

    (A) 158 pounds

    (B) 151 pounds

    (C) 148 pounds

    (D) 160 pounds

    (E) 164 pounds

164. A 38-year-old male who is 70 inches tall can weigh up to

    (A) 188 pounds

    (B) 189 pounds

    (C) 192 pounds

    (D) 204 pounds

    (E) 212 pounds

165. A 22-year-old female who is 62 inches tall can weigh up to

    (A) 108 pounds

    (B) 126 pounds

    (C) 144 pounds

    (D) 130 pounds

    (E) 138 pounds

Questions 166 to 170 are based on the following table. The x values are shown along the horizontal plane, and the y values are on the vertical plane. Given the x and y values, determine the appropriate value.

y	8	−23	−15	25	5	−20	−20	−20	−20
	7	15	1	−17	−8	−4	−7	13	22
	6	18	24	−16	3	13	−9	2	−9
	5	13	−14	−15	−7	24	−18	−5	10
	4	−12	−23	19	18	−7	7	−19	12
	3	19	16	−18	−1	6	16	−4	−15
	2	−24	2	19	6	−18	19	−14	6
	1	13	16	−6	−8	6	25	−8	17
		1	2	3	4	5	6	7	8

x

166. $x = 2; y = 3$

    (A) 16

    (B) −22

    (C) −16

    (D) 8

    (E) 24

167. $x = 6; y = 7$

    (A) −1

    (B) −21

    (C) −7

    (D) 7

    (E) 48

168. $x = 1; y = 6$

    (A) 15

    (B) 18

    (C) −1

    (D) 11

    (E) −11

Go on to next page

169. $x = 4; y = 1$

(A) 4

(B) 6

(C) 8

(D) 12

(E) –8

170. $x = 5; y = 4$

(A) 6

(B) 14

(C) –7

(D) –5

(E) 3

Questions 171 to 175 concern the calculations of federal tax with the following table and criteria given.

Tax Table 2011

Marginal Tax Rate	Single	Married Filing Jointly of Qualified Widow(er)	Married Filing Separately	Head of Household
10%	$0–$8,500	$0–$17,000	$0–$8,500	$0–12,150
15%	$8,501–$34,500	$17,001–$69,000	$8,501–$34,500	$12,151–$46,250
25%	$34,501–$83,600	$69,001–$139,350	$34,501–$69,675	$46,251–$119,400
28%	$83,601–$174,400	$139,351–$212,300	$69,676–$106,150	$119,401–$193,350
33%	$174,401–$379,150	$212,301–$379,150	$106,151–$189,575	$193,351–$379,150
35%	$379,151+	$379,151+	$189,576+	$379,151+

171. You're a married head of a household with two children; after deductions, your income is $46,280. What tax bracket do you fall in?

(A) 15 percent

(B) 28 percent

(C) 33 percent

(D) 0 percent

(E) 25 percent

172. You're single with no dependents and have an after-deduction taxable amount of $22,500. What tax bracket do you fall in?

(A) 15 percent

(B) 28 percent

(C) 33 percent

(D) 0 percent

(E) 25 percent

173. You're married with no children, are filing jointly, and have an after-deduction earnings of $82,300. What tax bracket do you fall in?

(A) 15 percent

(B) 28 percent

(C) 33 percent

(D) 35 percent

(E) 25 percent

174. You're the head of a household and earn $126,200 after deductions. What tax bracket do you fall in?

(A) 15 percent

(B) 28 percent

(C) 33 percent

(D) 35 percent

(E) 25 percent

Go on to next page

175. You're single and, after all deductions, you have taxable earnings of $10,150. What tax bracket do you fall in?

(A) 15 percent

(B) 28 percent

(C) 33 percent

(D) 35 percent

(E) 25 percent

Questions 176 to 180 deal with the grading cutoff for a recently taken course with an assigned instructor curve. Given your score in both the lab course and classroom, find your overall grade

All Test + LAB Final Score Count

Each 1/6th of Total Score

Test 1	Test 2	Test 3	Test 4	LAB	Final
91	93	89	94	93	?

Final Grade = Total Points

A	92%+	549+
A -	90–91%	537–548
B +	87–89%	519–536
B	84–86%	501–518
B -	80–83%	477–500
C +	77–79%	459–476
C	74–76%	441–458
C -	70–73%	417–440
D +	67–69%	399–416
D	64–66%	381–398
D -	60–63%	357–380
F	59% and below	356 and below

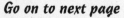
Go on to next page

176. Last test equals 88 percent
    (A) A–
    (B) A
    (C) B+
    (D) B
    (E) B–

177. Last test equals 74 percent
    (A) A–
    (B) A
    (C) B+
    (D) B
    (E) B–

178. Last test equals 96 percent
    (A) A–
    (B) A
    (C) B+
    (D) B
    (E) B–

179. Last test equals 92 percent
    (A) A–
    (B) A
    (C) B+
    (D) B
    (E) B–

180. Last test equals 84 percent
    (A) A–
    (B) A
    (C) B+
    (D) B
    (E) B–

Subtest 8

Aviation Information

Time: 8 minutes for 20 questions

Description: This section is a test of your aeronautical knowledge. You will be given questions or incomplete statements with five possible choices. Pick the most-correct answer.

181. What's the critical angle of attack?

   (A) The angle of attack required for lifting action on the wing

   (B) The angle of attack that is critical to achieve during takeoff

   (C) The angle at which the wing on an aircraft will stall

   (D) The angle of attack that is critical to achieve during approach

   (E) The angle in which the aircraft will have the lowest amount of parasite drag

182. When flaps are extended, or lowered, the aircraft experiences

   (A) Less lift and less drag

   (B) Less lift and more drag

   (C) More lift and less drag

   (D) More lift and more drag

   (E) No change in lift or drag

183. The four forces acting on an airplane are

   (A) Lift, pressure, drag, and power

   (B) Drag, thrust, acceleration, and weight

   (C) Drag, airspeed, gravity, and friction

   (D) Lift, drag, power, and thrust

   (E) Lift, drag, power, and weight

184. Induced drag is greatest at

   (A) High airspeeds

   (B) Low airspeeds

   (C) Diving flight

   (D) Shallow turns

   (E) Straight and level flight

185. Which doesn't affect density altitude?

   (A) Altitude

   (B) Temperature

   (C) Humidity

   (D) Aircraft gross weight

   (E) Atmospheric pressure

186. *Va* is defined as the

   (A) Stall speed

   (B) Best rate of climb airspeed

   (C) Minimum rate of descent airspeed

   (D) Maneuvering airspeed

   (E) Takeoff airspeed

187. Flying with a CG that is aft results in

   (A) No difference

   (B) Less stability at slow airspeeds

   (C) Less stability at all airspeeds

   (D) Less stability at high airspeeds

   (E) A higher angle of attack

188. Which of the following statements is true in respect to the forces acting on an aircraft in stable, straight, and level flight?

   (A) Lift equals drag; thrust equals weight.

   (B) Lift equals weight; thrust equals drag.

   (C) Lift is greater than drag; thrust equals weight.

   (D) Lift equals drag; thrust is greater than weight.

   (E) Lift is greater than weight; thrust is greater than drag.

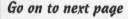 *Go on to next page*

189. On a final approach aligned with the runway, you see both rows of VASI approach lights indicating white. This display means that

    (A) You're above the glide path.

    (B) You're below the glide path.

    (C) You're slightly to the left of the centerline.

    (D) You're slightly to the right of the centerline.

    (E) You're cleared for landing.

190. The wings of an airplane are curved on the top and flat on the bottom in order to

    (A) Reduce drag

    (B) Increase drag

    (C) Produce lift

    (D) Decrease noise

    (E) Increase rotational turn rate

191. Nighttime airport taxiway identifiers are what color?

    (A) Red

    (B) White

    (C) Green

    (D) Blue

    (E) Orange

192. Bernoulli's principle indicates that

    (A) The faster airflow over the greater curvature of the upper wing decreases pressure and lift.

    (B) The slower airflow over the greater curvature of the upper wing increases pressure and lift.

    (C) The faster airflow over the flat surface of the bottom of the wing increases pressure and lift.

    (D) The faster airflow over the flat surface of the bottom of the wing decreases pressure and lift.

    (E) The faster airflow over the greater curvature of the upper wing decreases pressure and increases lift.

193. On a conventional aircraft, what primary flight control produces motion around the longitudinal axis?

    (A) The rudder

    (B) The aircraft trim tab

    (C) The elevators

    (D) The ailerons

    (E) The flaps

194. A solid green light signal from the tower to an aircraft in flight means

    (A) You're cleared to land.

    (B) Caution for other traffic.

    (C) Depart the air traffic area.

    (D) Go around for another approach.

    (E) Contact the tower on standard frequency.

195. How is a closed runway identified?

    (A) The runway has stripes painted every 500 feet.

    (B) The runway has a large yellow *X* painted on both approach ends.

    (C) The runway has obstacles placed at either approach end.

    (D) Large "Closed" signs are painted on the runway.

    (E) Large red "Do not land" signs are painted on the runway.

196. What's the transponder code for "emergency"?

    (A) 1200

    (B) 7667

    (C) 7777

    (D) 7700

    (E) 6666

Go on to next page

197. Displaced thresholds are for what type of airport operations?

    (A) Takeoffs only

    (B) Landings only

    (C) Aircraft pre-takeoff checks

    (D) Takeoffs, landings, and taxi operations

    (E) Takeoffs and taxi operations only

198. The ratio of aircraft speed in relation to the speed of sound is the

    (A) Mach number

    (B) Warp number

    (C) Air/sound speed

    (D) Aerodynamic velocity

    (E) True airspeed

199. An airport windsock tells you

    (A) The direction the wind is coming from

    (B) The airport density altitude

    (C) The wind direction, a rough idea of velocity, and gusts

    (D) Whether the runway is open

    (E) Which runway is the only legal one to operate on

200. Induced drag has the least effect at

    (A) Cruise flight

    (B) Slow airspeeds

    (C) High airspeeds

    (D) During steep turns

    (E) In a dive

STOP DO NOT TURN THE PAGE UNTIL TOLD TO DO SO.

Subtest 9
General Science

Time: 10 minutes for 20 questions

Description: This section tests your knowledge of general scientific principles. You will be given questions or incomplete statements with five possible choices. Pick the most-correct answer.

201. Fats and oils that are found in foods are called

    (A) Carbohydrates

    (B) Lipids

    (C) Amino acids

    (D) Proteins

    (E) Trace elements

202. When a substance transfers directly from a solid to a gas, it's called

    (A) Condensation

    (B) Reduction

    (C) Boyle's melting

    (D) Sublimation

    (E) Direct transformation

203. Which organ is responsible for detoxification and protein synthesis?

    (A) Liver

    (B) Heart

    (C) Lungs

    (D) Bladder

    (E) Pancreas

204. What type of energy is derived from the core heating ability, or stored energy, of the earth?

    (A) Fossil

    (B) Solar

    (C) Geothermal

    (D) Volcanic

    (E) Hydroelectric

205. The study of interactions between organisms and their physical environment is known as

    (A) Biology

    (B) Embryology

    (C) Ecology

    (D) Cytology

    (E) Physiology

206. The function of an enzyme is to

    (A) Speed up a chemical reaction

    (B) Slow down a chemical reaction

    (C) Absorb energy during a chemical reaction

    (D) Transfer energy during a chemical reaction

    (E) Be the by-product of a chemical reaction

207. A woman with type O blood and a man with type AB blood can have an offspring with what blood type?

    (A) Type AB

    (B) Type B

    (C) Type A

    (D) Type O

    (E) Type A or B

Go on to next page

208. Which of the following animals has the highest metabolic rate?

    (A) Lion

    (B) Elephant

    (C) Sloth

    (D) Rabbit

    (E) Cheetah

209. In the electromagnetic spectrum, which has the longest wavelength and the lowest frequency?

    (A) X-rays

    (B) Radio waves

    (C) Sunlight

    (D) Microwaves

    (E) Gamma rays

210. Most of the nutrients in food are absorbed in the body's

    (A) Stomach

    (B) Gall bladder

    (C) Large intestine

    (D) Small intestine

    (E) Kidneys

211. The measurement of electrical resistance to oppose the current or flow of electrons is

    (A) Watts

    (B) Amperes

    (C) Volts

    (D) Joules

    (E) Ohms

212. Lack of vitamin C, or ascorbic acid, causes which disease?

    (A) Goiter

    (B) Alzheimer's

    (C) Scurvy

    (D) Epilepsy

    (E) Rickets

213. After salt is added to water, the water's freezing level

    (A) Increases

    (B) Stays the same

    (C) Becomes variable

    (D) Increases and then decreases

    (E) Decreases

214. Inside a cell, DNA is located within the

    (A) Nucleus

    (B) Golgi apparatus

    (C) Lysosome

    (D) Endoplasmic reticulum

    (E) Centriole

215. The International System (SI) standard uses what base unit for weight?

    (A) Pound

    (B) Ton

    (C) Joule

    (D) Gram

    (E) Kilogram

216. If one parent has a dominant trait gene (dD) and the other parent doesn't have the trait (dd), what's the chance that their offspring will have the dominant trait?

    (A) 25 percent

    (B) 50 percent

    (C) 75 percent

    (D) 100 percent

    (E) Varies

217. When heat is given off during a chemical reaction, the process is called

    (A) Hot

    (B) Thermal

    (C) Endothermic

    (D) Exothermic

    (E) A reduction

Go on to next page

218. Of the various elements in the air, the most abundant is

    (A) Helium

    (B) Nitrogen

    (C) Oxygen

    (D) Carbon dioxide

    (E) Argon

219. A 120-volt power source results in 3 amps to the load. The total power delivered is

    (A) 100 watts

    (B) 300 watts

    (C) 360 watts

    (D) 240 watts

    (E) 120 watts

220. The process of dividing one cell nucleus into two nuclei is called

    (A) Division

    (B) Subtration

    (C) Cytokinesis

    (D) Cell division

    (E) Mitosis

STOP DO NOT TURN THE PAGE UNTIL TOLD TO DO SO.

Subtest 10

Rotated Blocks

Time: 13 minutes for 15 questions

Description: This section tests your ability to visualize and manipulate objects. In each initial picture, you see a 3-D representation of a block. Identify which of the five possible choices best represents the same block.

221.

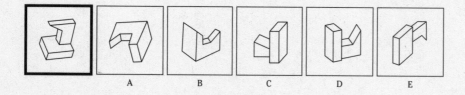

222.

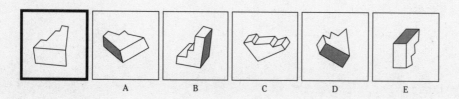

223.

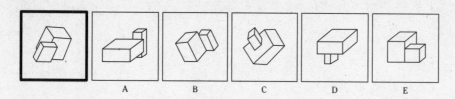

224.

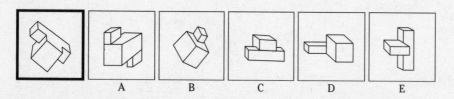

Go on to next page

225.

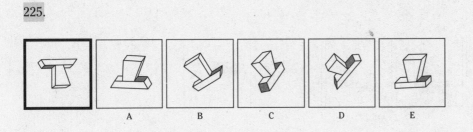

226.

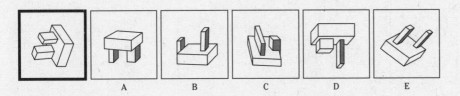

227.

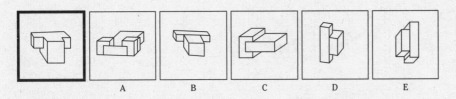

228.

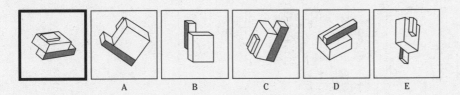

229.

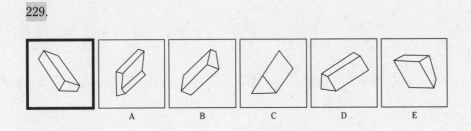

230.

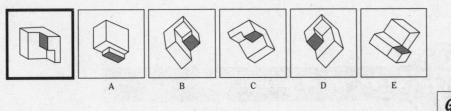

Go on to next page

231.

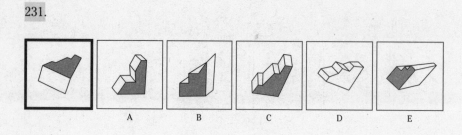

A   B   C   D   E

232.

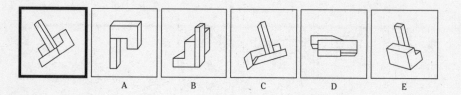

A   B   C   D   E

233.

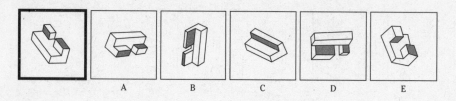

A   B   C   D   E

234.

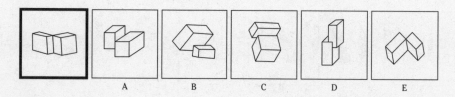

A   B   C   D   E

235.

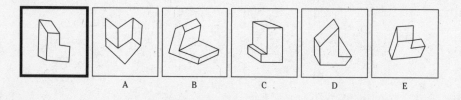

A   B   C   D   E

STOP DO NOT TURN THE PAGE UNTIL TOLD TO DO SO.

Subtest 11

Hidden Figures

Time: 8 minutes for 15 questions

Description: This section tests your ability to recognize a simple figure in a complex drawing. Before each set of questions, you see five figures lettered A, B, C, D, and E. For each question, identify which simple figure (A through E) is in the complex drawing.

236.–240.

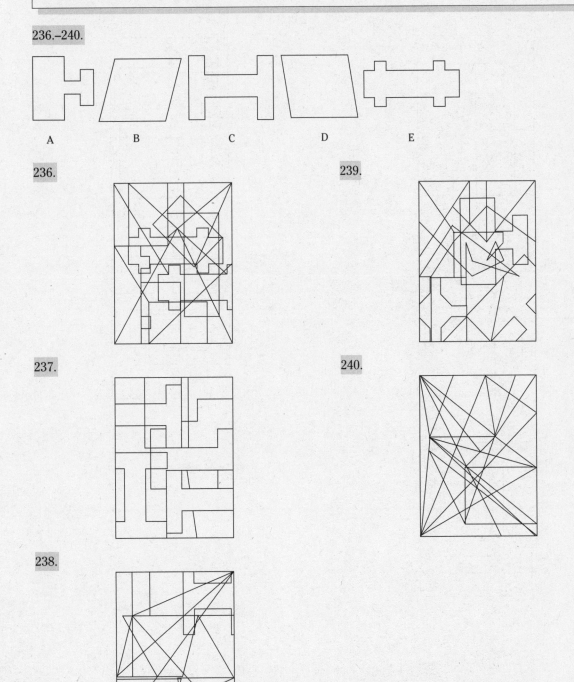

A   B   C   D   E

236.

237.

238.

239.

240.

Go on to next page

241.–245.

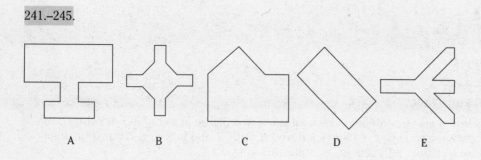

A   B   C   D   E

241.

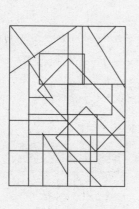

242.

243.

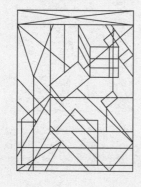

244.

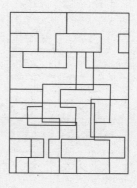

245.

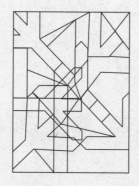

Go on to next page

246.–250.

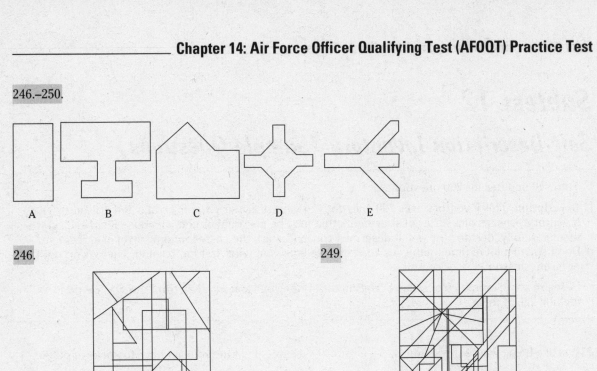

A   B   C   D   E

246.

249.

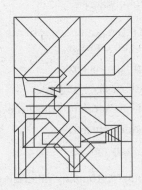

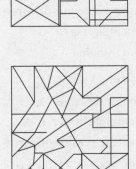

247.

250.

248.

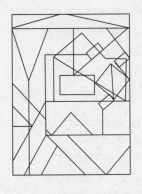

Subtest 12

Self-Description Inventory (Sample Questions)

Time: 40 minutes for 220 questions

Description: This inventory uses 220 questions to measure your personal traits and attitudes. The inventory consists of a series of statements that may be personal or controversial. Read each statement carefully, decide how well it describes you, and mark the corresponding level of agreement. Don't spend a lot of time on the answers; choose based on your first impression. There is no right or wrong answer.

Here are some examples of self-description questions your test may ask (don't worry, we don't include 220 of them):

251. I like being where the action is.
    (A) Strongly disagree
    (B) Moderately disagree
    (C) Neither agree nor disagree
    (D) Moderately agree
    (E) Strongly agree

252. I like new challenges.
    (A) Strongly disagree
    (B) Moderately disagree
    (C) Neither agree nor disagree
    (D) Moderately agree
    (E) Strongly agree

253. I always try to finish what I start.
    (A) Strongly disagree
    (B) Moderately disagree
    (C) Neither agree nor disagree
    (D) Moderately agree
    (E) Strongly agree

254. I generally get along well with most people.
    (A) Strongly disagree
    (B) Moderately disagree
    (C) Neither agree nor disagree
    (D) Moderately agree
    (E) Strongly agree

255. I get nervous if I have to speak in public.
    (A) Strongly disagree
    (B) Moderately disagree
    (C) Neither agree nor disagree
    (D) Moderately agree
    (E) Strongly agree

256. People often get upset with me for not showing up on time.
    (A) Strongly disagree
    (B) Moderately disagree
    (C) Neither agree nor disagree
    (D) Moderately agree
    (E) Strongly agree

257. I like to listen to many different kinds of music.
    (A) Strongly disagree
    (B) Moderately disagree
    (C) Neither agree nor disagree
    (D) Moderately agree
    (E) Strongly agree

258. I usually let my work goals take priority over my personal interests.
    (A) Strongly disagree
    (B) Moderately disagree
    (C) Neither agree nor disagree
    (D) Moderately agree
    (E) Strongly agree

Go on to next page

259. I am not comfortable supervising others.

    (A) Strongly disagree

    (B) Moderately disagree

    (C) Neither agree nor disagree

    (D) Moderately agree

    (E) Strongly agree

260. I am pleased when friends drop in to see me.

    (A) Strongly disagree

    (B) Moderately disagree

    (C) Neither agree nor disagree

    (D) Moderately agree

    (E) Strongly agree

Here are other sample questions that may appear in this test section:

- I don't like to be involved in group activities.
- I have higher work standards than do most people.
- I am neater than most people I know.
- I keep my promises.
- I sympathize with those who are worse off than me.
- I love life.
- I look at the bright side of life.
- I tend to make rash decisions.
- I excel in what I do.
- I would cheat to get ahead.
- I keep my emotions under control.
- I am easily hurt.
- I enjoy being the center of attention.
- I act wild and crazy.
- I rarely notice my emotional reactions.

Chapter 15

Air Force Officer Qualifying Test (AFOQT) Answers/Explanations

. . . .

*I*t's the moment you've been waiting for: time to check your answers on the sample Air Force Officer Qualifying Test (AFOQT) in Chapter 14. We present the answers in two different formats: with more-detailed explanations and in a simple answer key. If you're in a rush, you can get your answers quickly and easily by simply turning to the answer key at the end of this chapter. However (and this is our recommendation), if you really want to understand the "why" behind each answer, read through the explanations. By taking the time to do so, you have a better chance of increasing your score on the AFOQT.

Subtest 1: Verbal Analogies

1. **A.** *Concave* is hollow and curves inward, while *convex* curves outward. A *cavity* is hollow and curves inward, while a *mound* curves outward.

2. **E.** *Perjure* is to state something falsely under a legal oath; *trespass* is to wrongfully enter.

3. **D.** An *anarchist* by definition is committed to disorder, and a pacifist is committed to peace.

4. **C.** A doctor uses his or her skill to heal, while an author uses his or her skill to write.

5. **E.** An aircraft flies, while a boat sails.

6. **A.** A lamb is a very young sheep, and a colt is a very young horse.

7. **E.** A birth results in life, while exposure results in infection.

8. **E.** Horizontal is perpendicular to vertical; in weaving, *woof* is perpendicular to the *warp* threads.

9. **C.** Isolation results in loneliness, while a promotion results in advancement.

10. **E.** *Grow* and *mature* are both components of development, as are bloom and blossom.

11. **D.** An actor works on a stage, while a teacher works in a classroom.

12. **B.** A crumb is a very small amount of bread compared to a loaf, while a puddle is a very small amount of water compared to an ocean.

13. **C.** A carrot is a type of vegetable, while pepper is a type of spice.

14. **A.** *Ignore* means nearly the same as *overlook*, while *agree* means basically the same as *consent*.

15. **D.** *Hallowed* means to hold something precious or sacred, while *nomadic* means, in effect, wandering.

16. **B.** A gown is a type of garment, while gasoline is a type of fuel.

17. **E.** *Push* means the same as *shove*, while *clamber* means the same as *climb*.

18. **A.** The metal tip or end of a fishing rod is the hook, while the metal end of a knife is the blade.

19. **B.** Someone who is said to be a *sloth* is prone to laziness, while someone who is an *insomniac* is prone to sleeplessness.

20. **D.** Chapters are components of a book, just as stories are components of a building.

21. **B.** Bathing leads to cleanliness as schooling leads to education.

22. **D.** An elevator ascends to a height, while *thrust* helps a vehicle ascend to an altitude.

23. **B.** When you give someone *sanctuary,* you give refuge; when you imprison someone, you give punishment.

24. **C.** *Obey* means the same as *comply,* while *reply* is the same as *answer.*

25. **D.** Deceleration reduces speed, while braking reduces velocity.

Subtest 2: Arithmetic Reasoning

26. **A.** $30 + $15 = $45; $45 – $16 = $29.

27. **B.** $57 \div 82 = 0.69512$ or 69.5 percent.

28. **B.** 1 pound equals 32 tablespoons (4 sticks with 8 tablespoons each). 4 tablespoons ÷ 32 tablespoons per pound = 1/8 pound.

29. **C.** (40 hours × $8.40) + (1.5 × 5 hours × $8.40) = $336 + $63 = $399.

30. **D.** 10:30 a.m. till 5:30 p.m. = 7 hours. 7 × $2.50 = $17.50 wage. 7 × $22 = $154 in tips. $154 – $15.40 (tip to staff) = $138.60. $17.50 + $138.60 = $156.10 before taxes.

31. **D.** 3 kilometers = 3,000 meters. 3,000 ÷ 15 laps = 200 meters per lap.

32. **C.** 125 total soldiers × .04 = 5 officers in the company. 125 – 5 = 120 enlisted in the company.

33. **B.** The total time from 6:15 p.m. until 7:00 a.m. is 12 hours and 45 minutes, or 765 minutes. The tank will last 1 hour and 15 minutes, or 75 minutes, so 765 ÷ 75 = 10.2 tank fills.

34. **C.** 10 ÷ 4 = 2.5 centimeters.

35. **D.** Set x as a variable for the number of minutes. Use the formula $20 + .08x = 12 + .12x$. Rearrange the equation to group like terms: $20 – 12 = .12x – .08x$. Therefore, $8 = .04x$; $8 \div .04 = x$. $x = 200$.

36. **E.** If the red and green marbles total 20 percent of the jar's contents, the remaining yellow marbles make up 80 percent of the jar. If you reach in and pull out a random marble, you have an 80-percent chance of its being yellow. Eighty percent is 80/100, or 4/5 (4 out of 5).

37. **D.** Divide the discounted price ($1,150) by the original price ($1,400), and you see that John bought the chandelier for 82.1 percent of its original price. 100 – 82.1 = 17.9-percent savings.

38. **C.** Multiply the donated amount of $26.80 by 13/4, the inverse of the 4/13 donation. $26.80 × 13 = $348.40; $348.40 ÷ 4 = $87.10.

39. **C.** Add up the mileage and divide it by 3 days, or $(x + y + z) \div 3$.

40. **A.** Here you must pay attention to the details of exactly what the question is asking for. Let x equal the number of each kind of plane (the problem tells you that you have equal numbers of both types of planes, so you can use the same variable for each type). Use the formula $2x + 6x = 160$ tons. $8x = 160$ tons, so $x = 160$ tons ÷ 8. Therefore, you need 20 passenger planes. But the question asks for the amount of cargo shipped, so you have to multiply each of those planes by the 2 tons it carries for a total of 40 tons.

41. **A.** The highway experienced a decline of 1,156 cars per day (11,200 – 10,044). To get the percentage, divide 1,156 by 11,200; you get 10.3 percent.

42. **C.** 1 cubic foot is 1 foot x 1 foot x 1 foot. You have a container that's 1/2 foot x 1/2 foot x 1 foot, or 1/4 cubic foot. The weight of the water is 62.4 pounds per cubic foot × 1/4 cubic foot or 15.6 pounds.

43. **D.** $23 \times 15 \times 11 = 3{,}795$ cubic feet. Choice (C) is incorrect because the units are incorrect.

44. **D.** In this question, the area of circle A is 4 times the area of circle B. The equation to use is area$_A$ = 4 × area$_B$. Therefore, $\pi r^2_A = 4 \times \pi r^2_B$. π cancels out on both sides, giving you $r^2_A = 4 \times r^2_B$. Now, $r^2_A = 4 \times 3^2 = 4 \times 9 = 36$. Therefore, $r^2_A = 36$, and r_A equals the square root of 36, which is 6.

45. **C.** To get the total, multiply the seats per row by number of rows, or xy.

46. **C.** Add up all the times and divide by four to get the average. $80 + 80 + 72 + 68 = 300$; $300 \div 4 = 75$

47. **C.** $300 + (.1 \times \$8{,}350) = \$300 + \$835 = \$1{,}135$.

48. **D.** Let x equal the capacity of the tank. You added 550 gallons to one-eighth of a tank to get half a tank, so $1/2x – 1/8x = 550$ gallons. You can rewrite 1/2 as 4/8, so $4/8x – 1/8x = 550$ gallons. Therefore, $3/8x = 550$ gallons. Multiply by the reciprocal of the fraction (8/3) to isolate the variable: $550 \times 8/3 = 1{,}467$ gallons. Round up to 1,470 gallons for the closest answer.

49. **D.** Use the formula for circumference: $C = d \times \pi$. You know the radius (1 meter), so double it to get the diameter, d, and then plug it into the formula: $C = 2$ meters $\times 3.14$, or 6.28 meters. If the wheel travels 35 rotations, any given point on the wheel travels 6.28 meters 35 times; $6.28 \times 35 = 219.8$, so Choice (D), 220 meters, is the best answer.

50. **C.** $\$120{,}000 \times 0.80 = \$96{,}000$. $\$96{,}000 \div \$100 = 960$; $960 \times \$4.75 = \$4{,}560$.

Subtest 3: Word Knowledge

51. **B.**	58. **C.**	65. **C.**	72. **D.**
52. **C.**	59. **B.**	66. **C.**	73. **B.**
53. **E.**	60. **A.**	67. **A.**	74. **A.**
54. **C.**	61. **D.**	68. **D.**	75. **A.**
55. **A.**	62. **E.**	69. **A.**	
56. **D.**	63. **B.**	70. **D.**	
57. **D.**	64. **C.**	71. **D.**	

Subtest 4: Math Knowledge

76. **B.** Use the equation $(78 + 86 + 94 + 96 + x) \div 5 = 88$. Simplifying, you get $(354 + x) \div 5 = 88$. Multiply both sides by 5 to get $354 + x = 440$, and then subtract 354 to find that $x = 86$.

77. **B.** First, combine the like terms on the left side of the equation to get $5z – 5 = 25 – 5z$. You can then simplify the equation to determine that $5z + 5z = 25 + 5$ or $10z = 30$. Therefore $z = 30 \div 10 = 3$.

78. **B.** The square root of 28 is 5.29, and the square root of 7 is 2.65. $5.29 – 2.65 = 2.64$. $2.64^2 =$ about 7. The closest answer is the square root of 7.

79. **D.** First, solve for y. You know that $x - y = 1$; therefore, you can rearrange the equation to $y = x - 1$. Plug this result into the original equation to get $5x + 3(x - 1) = 29$. Simplify to $5x + 3x - 3 = 29$, and then simplify again to $8x - 3 = 29$. $8x = 29 + 3 = 32$. Finally, a bit more math gives you $x = 32 \div 8 = 4$.

80. **B.** The square root of 85 is 9.21, rounded to 9.2.

81. **E.** The volume is the height times the area of the base. The area of the base is πr^2. Therefore, the answer is the height (h) times πr^2. None of the choices lists that answer, so the answer is Choice (E).

82. **D.** The formula for circumference is $C = 2\pi r$. The radius of the pilot's orbit is 40 kilometers, so you plug that into the formula to get $C = 2\pi(40 \text{ kilometers}) = 251$ kilometers.

83. **D.** Adding 2 to an odd integer and then subtracting 1 will always result in the net addition of 1 to an odd integer. This results in an even integer.

84. **D.** The lion habitat has the outer ring of the main habitat as one boundary and two inner fences as its other boundaries that arrive at the center at a 90-degree angle. This setup implies that the area of the lion habitat is one quarter of the preserve's total area. The total area is πr^2, or $3.14 \times (14 \text{ kilometers})^2 = 3.14 \times 196 \text{ kilometers}^2 = 615.44$. Divide your answer by 4: $615.44 \div 4 = 153.86 = 154$ square kilometers.

85. **B.** A pentagon has five sides. Use the formula (side total – 2) × 180 degrees = total sum of angle measurements. $(5 - 2) \times 180$ degrees = 3×180 degrees = 540 degrees.

86. **E.** $2(a - b) + 4(a + 3b) = 2a - 2b + 4a + 12b = 6a + 10b$.

87. **C.** The first thing to notice in this question is that the answer choices contain different units (square feet) from the units given in the question (yards). Therefore, you have to convert the side lengths to feet. The square has a perimeter of 40 yards, so that means each equal side is 10 yards; multiply that by 3 feet per yard to get side lengths of 30 feet. The area is the square of the side length, or 900 square feet. ***Remember:*** The test makers often try to trick you by switching up the units to be sure you're paying attention, so always make sure you know what the question is asking for.

88. **C.** $3^n = 9$, so n equals 2; therefore, $4^{n+1} = 4^{(2+1)} = 4^3 = 64$.

89. **C.** Take the large area and subtract the smaller area. Large = $\pi(10 \text{ centimeters})^2 = \pi(100 \text{ centimeters}^2) = 314$ square centimeters. Small = $\pi(7 \text{ centimeters})^2 = \pi(49 \text{ centimeters}^2) = 153.9$ square centimeters. 314 square centimeters – 153.9 square centimeters = 160.1 square centimeters. Because the answer choices have π or 3.14 left in the equation, simply divide 160.1 by π or 3.14: 160.1 square centimeters $\div 3.14 = 50.98$ centimeters^2 to get the answer 51π centimeters^2 or 51π square centimeters.

90. **E.** From the question, you know that $3x/5y = 1/2$. You can cross-multiply this equation to get $6x = 5y$ and then simplify to get $6x/y = 5$. Divide each side by 6 to get $x/y = 5/6$, so the ratio is 5:6.

91. **A.** The reciprocal of 7 is just 1/7 or 0.1428, which rounds to 0.143.

92. **C.** A *prime number* is a number that is only divisible by 1 and itself. 211 is the first number that fits that criterion. 201 can be divided by 3, and 205 can be divided by 5.

93. **C.** One million is 1,000,000 and is represented by 1×10^6. That number indicates a *1* followed by six zeros.

94. **D.** To divide, you simply subtract the exponents. Therefore the answer is 10^{x-y}.

95. **E.** The cube root of 729 is 9, and the square root of 9 is 3. Therefore, the square of 3 equals the cube root of 729.

96. **A.** In the first concentration, the cook had 10 ounces of liquid that were 20 percent juice, for a total of 2 ounces of juice. He adds an additional 40 ounces of water for a total of 50 ounces of liquid, but the mixture still contains only the 2 ounces of juice, so the concentration is now 2/50, or 4 percent.

97. **D.** To get the volume, use the formula of height × area of the base, or 15 inches × $[\pi(7 \text{ inches})^2]$ = 15 inches × π(49 square inches) = 15 inches × 153.86 square inches = 15 inches × 154 square inches = 2,310 cubic inches. Divide 2,310 cubic inches by 231 cubic inches per gallon to get 10 gallons.

98. **D.** A triangle has three sides; to get the total sum of the angles, take the number of sides – 2 and multiply by 180. In this case, it comes to 1 × 180 degrees or 180 degrees. 180 degrees minus the 115 degrees that are already accounted for in the problem leaves a total of 65 degrees for the other two angles.

99. **C.** 3 × 5 equals 15, which is thus divisible by both 3 and 5. The side lengths of an equilateral triangle are all the same, so 15 ÷ 3 = 5.

100. **C.** A right triangle means that one angle is 90 degrees. The total sum of the degrees is 180 degrees, and you have a given angle of 30 degrees, so you have 150 degrees left over. You can also subtract the known 90-degree angle, so 150 degrees – 90 degrees = 60 degrees for the last angle. Therefore, the answer is 60 degrees and 90 degrees.

Subtest 5: Instrument Comprehension

101. **C.**	106. **C.**	111. **D.**	116. **B.**
102. **B.**	107. **D.**	112. **D.**	117. **D.**
103. **A.**	108. **D.**	113. **A.**	118. **C.**
104. **C.**	109. **B.**	114. **B.**	119. **A.**
105. **D.**	110. **D.**	115. **B.**	120. **C.**

Subtest 6: Block Counting

121. **D.**	126. **E.**	131. **B.**	136. **E.**
122. **C.**	127. **B.**	132. **E.**	137. **B.**
123. **A.**	128. **C.**	133. **B.**	138. **C.**
124. **E.**	129. **B.**	134. **D.**	139. **E.**
125. **B.**	130. **E.**	135. **E.**	140. **E.**

Subtest 7: Table Reading

141. **B.**	151. **E.**	161. **B.**	171. **E.**
142. **E.**	152. **C.**	162. **D.**	172. **A.**
143. **C.**	153. **D.**	163. **A.**	173. **E.**
144. **A.**	154. **C.**	164. **B.**	174. **B.**
145. **A.**	155. **A.**	165. **E.**	175. **A.**
146. **C.**	156. **B.**	166. **A.**	176. **A.**
147. **E.**	157. **A.**	167. **C.**	177. **C.**
148. **C.**	158. **D.**	168. **B.**	178. **B.**
149. **A.**	159. **C.**	169. **E.**	179. **B.**
150. **C.**	160. **E.**	170. **C.**	180. **A.**

Subtest 8: Aviation Information

181. **C.** When you exceed the critical angle of attack, the wing loses lift, and the aircraft stalls.

182. **D.** Lowering the flaps increases both lift and drag.

183. **E.** The four forces acting on an aircraft are lift, drag, power, and weight. (**Remember:** Sometimes power is known as *thrust.*)

184. **B.** Induced drag is greatest at low airspeeds.

185. **D.** Of the choices, only aircraft gross weight doesn't affect density altitude.

186. **D.** *Va* is maneuvering speed.

187. **C.** An aft CG makes your aircraft less stable at all airspeeds.

188. **B.** During steady state flight, lift equals weight and thrust equals drag.

189. **A.** Two rows of whites indicate you are too high. "A row of red over a row of white, you're all right." and "Red over red, you'll soon be dead." are common sayings.

190. **C.** Bernoulli's principle comes into play here. The greater curvature on the top increases airflow and reduces pressure, resulting in lift. See Chapter 11 for more on Bernoulli's principle.

191. **D.** Taxiways are blue. Don't land there (it has happened).

192. **E.** Bernoulli's principle is the basic fundamental for flight.

193. **D.** In a turn, or roll, the ailerons turn in opposite directions; if you can visualize the aircraft as flying through water, you can see how this motion increases one wing and decreases the other.

194. **A.** While you're in the air, a steady or solid green light signal means you are cleared to land. The most common usage of this signal occurs during a complete radio failure. (This situation actually happened to coauthor Terry during bad weather at Thunder Bay, Ontario.)

195. **B.** Runway closures have huge Xs painted on them.

196. **D.** 7700 is the standard code for "emergency," although certain specific emergencies, such as lost communication or hijacking, have their own transponder codes.

197. **E.** Runways typically have displaced thresholds to alert pilots to some sort of obstacle that changes where on the runway the pilots can land. You can still take off or taxi on those runways, but using that portion of a runway for landing is prohibited.

198. **A.** *Mach number* is a common number for fast-moving aircraft. The number can change based on ambient conditions.

199. **C.** A windsock is a simple, common system located at most airports. The standard 30-knot windsock can tell you which runway you are supposed to land on at uncontrolled fields and gives you a rough idea of wind velocity and any wind gusts or shifts present.

200. **C.** Induced drag has the least effect at high airspeeds.

Subtest 9: General Science

201. **B.** Lipids are a broad group of molecules that includes fats and oils.

202. **D.** *Sublimation* is the process of passing from a solid directly to a gas without becoming a liquid.

203. **A.** The liver is responsible for detoxification and protein synthesis (among other things).

204. **C.** *Geothermal* heat is heat produced within the earth's inner core.

205. **C.** *Ecology* is the study of organisms and how they react within their physical environment.

206. **A.** An enzyme speeds up a chemical reaction without being changed.

207. **E.** A and B blood types are dominant traits, so standard biological cross-matching indicates that this couple's offspring will have one of these blood types.

208. **D.** The smaller the animal, the higher the metabolic rate, so the rabbit is your best choice here.

209. **B.** Of the answer choices provided, the radio wavelength is the longest with the shortest frequency.

210. **D.** Most nutrients are absorbed through the small intestine. The stomach processes the food for digestion and then absorption.

211. **E.** The accepted measure of electrical resistance is ohms; the higher the resistance, the greater the number of ohms.

212. **C.** Lack of vitamin C causes scurvy. Fun fact: English sailors started carrying limes to prevent that disease on long voyages, which is where the slang term "limeys" comes from.

213. **E.** Salt decreases water's freezing level (that is, lowers the temperature at which it freezes), which is why street crews salt the roads during the winter to keep them from becoming icy.

214. **A.** DNA is located in the cell nucleus. (Actually, you can find a small amount in the mitochondria, but that's not one of the listed choices.)

215. **E.** The kilogram is the standard, accepted SI measurement of weight. (Don't let the prefix fool you into thinking gram is the base unit.) The International System, or System International, unit system for measurements was derived from the metric system in the 1960s.

216. **B.** Draw a cross chart, and you see that two of the four potential offspring will have Dd markers. Because the *D* is dominant, the chance is 2/4 or 50 percent that the children will have this trait.

217. **D.** *Exothermic* means to give off heat, so that's the correct answer. *Endothermic* means to take in or absorb heat.

218. **B.** Nitrogen is by far the most common element in the air.

219. **C.** Use the formula of power (based on Ohm's and Watt's laws) — $W = V \times I$ — to find that $W = 120 \times 3 = 360$ watts.

220. **E.** The process of cell division is called *mitosis*.

Subtest 10: Rotated Blocks

221. **C.**	225. **A.**	229. **B.**	233. **A.**
222. **D.**	226. **A.**	230. **C.**	234. **E.**
223. **B.**	227. **B.**	231. **C.**	235. **C.**
224. **C.**	228. **C.**	232. **B.**	

Subtest 11: Hidden Figures

236. **E.**

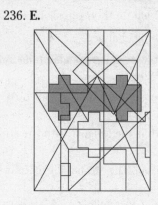

240. **B.**

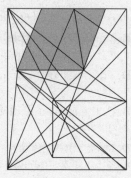

237. **C.**

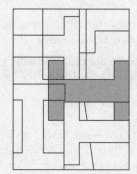

241. **D.**

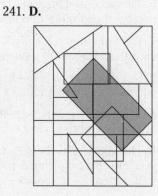

238. **D.**

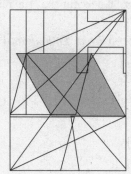

242. **E.**

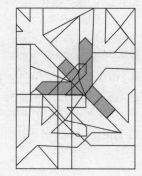

239. **A.**

243. **C.**

244. **B.**

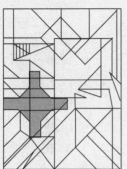

248. **C.**

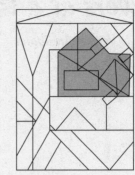

245. **A.**

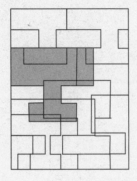

249. **B.**

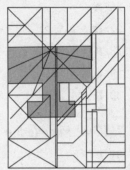

246. **A.**

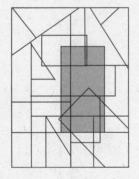

250. **E.**

247. **D.**

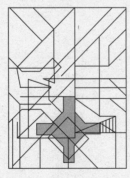

Subtest 12: Self-Description Inventory

251 to 470. This section's questions have no correct or incorrect answers. See Chapter 14 for more on the self-description portion of the test.

Answers at a Glance

Subtest 1: Verbal Analogies

1. A	6. A	11. D	16. B	21. B
2. E	7. E	12. B	17. E	22. D
3. D	8. E	13. C	18. A	23. B
4. C	9. C	14. A	19. B	24. C
5. E	10. E	15. D	20. D	25. D

Subtest 2: Arithmetic Reasoning

26. A	31. D	36. E	41. A	46. C
27. B	32. C	37. D	42. C	47. C
28. B	33. B	38. C	43. D	48. D
29. C	34. C	39. C	44. D	49. D
30. D	35. D	40. A	45. C	50. C

Subtest 3: Word Knowledge

51. B	56. D	61. D	66. C	71. D
52. C	57. D	62. E	67. A	72. D
53. E	58. C	63. B	68. D	73. B
54. C	59. B	64. C	69. A	74. A
55. A	60. A	65. C	70. D	75. A

Subtest 4: Math Knowledge

76. B	81. E	86. E	91. A	96. A
77. B	82. D	87. C	92. C	97. D
78. B	83. D	88. C	93. C	98. D
79. D	84. D	89. C	94. D	99. C
80. B	85. B	90. E	95. E	100. C

Subtest 5: Instrument Comprehension

101. C	105. D	109. B	113. A	117. D
102. B	106. C	110. D	114. B	118. C
103. A	107. D	111. D	115. B	119. A
104. C	108. D	112. D	116. B	120. C

Subtest 6: Block Counting

121. D	125. B	129. B	133. B	137. B
122. C	126. E	130. E	134. D	138. C
123. A	127. B	131. B	135. E	139. E
124. E	128. C	132. E	136. E	140. E

Subtest 7: Table Reading

141. B	149. A	157. A	165. E	173. E
142. E	150. C	158. D	166. A	174. B
143. C	151. E	159. C	167. C	175. A
144. A	152. C	160. E	168. B	176. A
145. A	153. D	161. B	169. E	177. C
146. C	154. C	162. D	170. C	178. B
147. E	155. A	163. A	171. E	179. B
148. C	156. B	164. B	172. A	180. A

Subtest 8: Aviation Information

181. C	185. D	189. A	193. D	197. E
182. D	186. D	190. C	194. A	198. A
183. E	187. C	191. D	195. B	199. C
184. B	188. B	192. E	196. D	200. C

Subtest 9: General Science

201. B	205. C	209. B	213. E	217. D
202. D	206. A	210. D	214. A	218. B
203. A	207. E	211. E	215. E	219. C
204. C	208. D	212. C	216. B	220. E

Subtest 10: Rotated Blocks

221. C	224. C	227. B	230. C	233. A
222. D	225. A	228. C	231. C	234. E
223. B	226. A	229. B	232. B	235. C

Subtest 11: Hidden Figures

236. E	239. A	242. E	245. A	248. C
237. C	240. B	243. C	246. A	249. B
238. D	241. D	244. B	247. D	250. E

Chapter 16

Navy/Marine Corps/Coast Guard Aviation Selection Test Battery (ASTB) Practice Test

. . . .

*W*hen it comes to military flight aptitude tests, the U.S. government really gets its money's worth out of the Aviation Selection Test Battery. The U.S. Navy, Marine Corps, and Coast Guard all use the *Aviation Selection Test Battery* (ASTB) to help select officer aviation program applicants for training. The Navy also uses selected sections of the test to choose among candidates for Officer Candidate School (OCS), and the Coast Guard uses the ASTB to select its pilot trainees. In addition, the Coast Guard makes selections for its non-aviation officer commissioning program using a subcomponent score from the ASTB (that is, scores from specific test sections only).

The ASTB is periodically updated and modified to suit the needs of the services that depend on it to make pilot and officer selections. For example, the Naval Operational Medicine Institute (NOMI) performed a complete update of the ASTB in 1992, and in 2004 the organization released three new versions of the ASTB (Forms 3, 4, and 5) while suspending two earlier versions (Forms 1 and 2) that had been in use from 1992 to 2004. Each of these versions is identical in format but uses different questions.

The ASTB is administered by numerous organizations across the country. For example, you can take the test within NROTC units, Marine Corps Officer Selection Offices (OSOs), and Navy Recruiting Districts (NRDs). Although paper-based tests are still the norm, you can also take the test in select locations by way of a web-based system (APEX.NET).

ASTB retests are allowable, but restrictions apply. You only get two retests; you can only take each version of the test once, so if you take Form 5 the first time, you have to take Form 3 or Form 4 the next time. You have to wait until the 31st day following the date of your first attempt before you can take a retest. You can take the second (and final) retest on the 91st day following the first retest.

Because you can take each version of the test only once, you're limited to no more than three tests over your lifetime. If you've taken an obsolete version of the test (Forms 1 and 2) that's now out of circulation, however, that test doesn't count toward the three-test lifetime limit.

An illegal test can occur when you either take a form of the test that you've already taken or retake a test too early. If this happens, you can't use the scores from the illegal test, but it still counts toward your lifetime limit.

ASTB Test Structure

The ASTB was specifically designed and validated to predict success in aviation training. The test comprises six subtests and takes about 2 hours and 30 minutes (including administrative time) to complete.

The six subtests for the Aviation Selection Test Battery are as follows:

Subtest	# of items	Time
1. Math Skills Test (MST)	30	25 minutes
2. Reading Skills Test (RST)	27	25 minutes
3. Mechanical Comprehension Test (MCT)	30	15 minutes
4. Spatial Apperception Test (SAT)	25	10 minutes
5. Aviation and Nautical Information Test (ANIT)	30	15 minutes
6. Aviation Supplemental Test (AST)	34	25 minutes

Note: You can't use a calculator on this test. The math problems on the exam are designed to be completed without a calculator, but a few formulas are provided. You receive scrap paper to work problems on at the test site.

Answer Sheet

For Subtests 1 through 6 of the exam, use the following answer sheets and fill in the answer bubble for the corresponding number, using a #2 pencil.

Subtest 1: Math Skills Test

1. Ⓐ Ⓑ Ⓒ Ⓓ	9. Ⓐ Ⓑ Ⓒ Ⓓ	17. Ⓐ Ⓑ Ⓒ Ⓓ	25. Ⓐ Ⓑ Ⓒ Ⓓ
2. Ⓐ Ⓑ Ⓒ Ⓓ	10. Ⓐ Ⓑ Ⓒ Ⓓ	18. Ⓐ Ⓑ Ⓒ Ⓓ	26. Ⓐ Ⓑ Ⓒ Ⓓ
3. Ⓐ Ⓑ Ⓒ Ⓓ	11. Ⓐ Ⓑ Ⓒ Ⓓ	19. Ⓐ Ⓑ Ⓒ Ⓓ	27. Ⓐ Ⓑ Ⓒ Ⓓ
4. Ⓐ Ⓑ Ⓒ Ⓓ	12. Ⓐ Ⓑ Ⓒ Ⓓ	20. Ⓐ Ⓑ Ⓒ Ⓓ	28. Ⓐ Ⓑ Ⓒ Ⓓ
5. Ⓐ Ⓑ Ⓒ Ⓓ	13. Ⓐ Ⓑ Ⓒ Ⓓ	21. Ⓐ Ⓑ Ⓒ Ⓓ	29. Ⓐ Ⓑ Ⓒ Ⓓ
6. Ⓐ Ⓑ Ⓒ Ⓓ	14. Ⓐ Ⓑ Ⓒ Ⓓ	22. Ⓐ Ⓑ Ⓒ Ⓓ	30. Ⓐ Ⓑ Ⓒ Ⓓ
7. Ⓐ Ⓑ Ⓒ Ⓓ	15. Ⓐ Ⓑ Ⓒ Ⓓ	23. Ⓐ Ⓑ Ⓒ Ⓓ	
8. Ⓐ Ⓑ Ⓒ Ⓓ	16. Ⓐ Ⓑ Ⓒ Ⓓ	24. Ⓐ Ⓑ Ⓒ Ⓓ	

Subtest 2: Reading Skills Test

31. Ⓐ Ⓑ Ⓒ Ⓓ	39. Ⓐ Ⓑ Ⓒ Ⓓ	47. Ⓐ Ⓑ Ⓒ Ⓓ	55. Ⓐ Ⓑ Ⓒ Ⓓ
32. Ⓐ Ⓑ Ⓒ Ⓓ	40. Ⓐ Ⓑ Ⓒ Ⓓ	48. Ⓐ Ⓑ Ⓒ Ⓓ	56. Ⓐ Ⓑ Ⓒ Ⓓ
33. Ⓐ Ⓑ Ⓒ Ⓓ	41. Ⓐ Ⓑ Ⓒ Ⓓ	49. Ⓐ Ⓑ Ⓒ Ⓓ	57. Ⓐ Ⓑ Ⓒ Ⓓ
34. Ⓐ Ⓑ Ⓒ Ⓓ	42. Ⓐ Ⓑ Ⓒ Ⓓ	50. Ⓐ Ⓑ Ⓒ Ⓓ	
35. Ⓐ Ⓑ Ⓒ Ⓓ	43. Ⓐ Ⓑ Ⓒ Ⓓ	51. Ⓐ Ⓑ Ⓒ Ⓓ	
36. Ⓐ Ⓑ Ⓒ Ⓓ	44. Ⓐ Ⓑ Ⓒ Ⓓ	52. Ⓐ Ⓑ Ⓒ Ⓓ	
37. Ⓐ Ⓑ Ⓒ Ⓓ	45. Ⓐ Ⓑ Ⓒ Ⓓ	53. Ⓐ Ⓑ Ⓒ Ⓓ	
38. Ⓐ Ⓑ Ⓒ Ⓓ	46. Ⓐ Ⓑ Ⓒ Ⓓ	54. Ⓐ Ⓑ Ⓒ Ⓓ	

Subtest 3: Mechanical Comprehension Test

58. Ⓐ Ⓑ Ⓒ Ⓓ	66. Ⓐ Ⓑ Ⓒ Ⓓ	74. Ⓐ Ⓑ Ⓒ Ⓓ	82. Ⓐ Ⓑ Ⓒ Ⓓ
59. Ⓐ Ⓑ Ⓒ Ⓓ	67. Ⓐ Ⓑ Ⓒ Ⓓ	75. Ⓐ Ⓑ Ⓒ Ⓓ	83. Ⓐ Ⓑ Ⓒ Ⓓ
60. Ⓐ Ⓑ Ⓒ Ⓓ	68. Ⓐ Ⓑ Ⓒ Ⓓ	76. Ⓐ Ⓑ Ⓒ Ⓓ	84. Ⓐ Ⓑ Ⓒ Ⓓ
61. Ⓐ Ⓑ Ⓒ Ⓓ	69. Ⓐ Ⓑ Ⓒ Ⓓ	77. Ⓐ Ⓑ Ⓒ Ⓓ	85. Ⓐ Ⓑ Ⓒ Ⓓ
62. Ⓐ Ⓑ Ⓒ Ⓓ	70. Ⓐ Ⓑ Ⓒ Ⓓ	78. Ⓐ Ⓑ Ⓒ Ⓓ	86. Ⓐ Ⓑ Ⓒ Ⓓ
63. Ⓐ Ⓑ Ⓒ Ⓓ	71. Ⓐ Ⓑ Ⓒ Ⓓ	79. Ⓐ Ⓑ Ⓒ Ⓓ	87. Ⓐ Ⓑ Ⓒ Ⓓ
64. Ⓐ Ⓑ Ⓒ Ⓓ	72. Ⓐ Ⓑ Ⓒ Ⓓ	80. Ⓐ Ⓑ Ⓒ Ⓓ	
65. Ⓐ Ⓑ Ⓒ Ⓓ	73. Ⓐ Ⓑ Ⓒ Ⓓ	81. Ⓐ Ⓑ Ⓒ Ⓓ	

Subtest 4: Spatial Apperception Test

88. Ⓐ Ⓑ Ⓒ Ⓓ	96. Ⓐ Ⓑ Ⓒ Ⓓ	104. Ⓐ Ⓑ Ⓒ Ⓓ	112. Ⓐ Ⓑ Ⓒ Ⓓ
89. Ⓐ Ⓑ Ⓒ Ⓓ	97. Ⓐ Ⓑ Ⓒ Ⓓ	105. Ⓐ Ⓑ Ⓒ Ⓓ	
90. Ⓐ Ⓑ Ⓒ Ⓓ	98. Ⓐ Ⓑ Ⓒ Ⓓ	106. Ⓐ Ⓑ Ⓒ Ⓓ	
91. Ⓐ Ⓑ Ⓒ Ⓓ	99. Ⓐ Ⓑ Ⓒ Ⓓ	107. Ⓐ Ⓑ Ⓒ Ⓓ	
92. Ⓐ Ⓑ Ⓒ Ⓓ	100. Ⓐ Ⓑ Ⓒ Ⓓ	108. Ⓐ Ⓑ Ⓒ Ⓓ	
93. Ⓐ Ⓑ Ⓒ Ⓓ	101. Ⓐ Ⓑ Ⓒ Ⓓ	109. Ⓐ Ⓑ Ⓒ Ⓓ	
94. Ⓐ Ⓑ Ⓒ Ⓓ	102. Ⓐ Ⓑ Ⓒ Ⓓ	110. Ⓐ Ⓑ Ⓒ Ⓓ	
95. Ⓐ Ⓑ Ⓒ Ⓓ	103. Ⓐ Ⓑ Ⓒ Ⓓ	111. Ⓐ Ⓑ Ⓒ Ⓓ	

Subtest 5: Aviation and Nautical Information

113. Ⓐ Ⓑ Ⓒ Ⓓ Ⓔ	123. Ⓐ Ⓑ Ⓒ Ⓓ Ⓔ	133. Ⓐ Ⓑ Ⓒ Ⓓ Ⓔ
114. Ⓐ Ⓑ Ⓒ Ⓓ Ⓔ	124. Ⓐ Ⓑ Ⓒ Ⓓ Ⓔ	134. Ⓐ Ⓑ Ⓒ Ⓓ Ⓔ
115. Ⓐ Ⓑ Ⓒ Ⓓ Ⓔ	125. Ⓐ Ⓑ Ⓒ Ⓓ Ⓔ	135. Ⓐ Ⓑ Ⓒ Ⓓ Ⓔ
116. Ⓐ Ⓑ Ⓒ Ⓓ Ⓔ	126. Ⓐ Ⓑ Ⓒ Ⓓ Ⓔ	136. Ⓐ Ⓑ Ⓒ Ⓓ Ⓔ
117. Ⓐ Ⓑ Ⓒ Ⓓ Ⓔ	127. Ⓐ Ⓑ Ⓒ Ⓓ Ⓔ	137. Ⓐ Ⓑ Ⓒ Ⓓ Ⓔ
118. Ⓐ Ⓑ Ⓒ Ⓓ Ⓔ	128. Ⓐ Ⓑ Ⓒ Ⓓ Ⓔ	138. Ⓐ Ⓑ Ⓒ Ⓓ Ⓔ
119. Ⓐ Ⓑ Ⓒ Ⓓ Ⓔ	129. Ⓐ Ⓑ Ⓒ Ⓓ Ⓔ	139. Ⓐ Ⓑ Ⓒ Ⓓ Ⓔ
120. Ⓐ Ⓑ Ⓒ Ⓓ Ⓔ	130. Ⓐ Ⓑ Ⓒ Ⓓ Ⓔ	140. Ⓐ Ⓑ Ⓒ Ⓓ Ⓔ
121. Ⓐ Ⓑ Ⓒ Ⓓ Ⓔ	131. Ⓐ Ⓑ Ⓒ Ⓓ Ⓔ	141. Ⓐ Ⓑ Ⓒ Ⓓ Ⓔ
122. Ⓐ Ⓑ Ⓒ Ⓓ Ⓔ	132. Ⓐ Ⓑ Ⓒ Ⓓ Ⓔ	142. Ⓐ Ⓑ Ⓒ Ⓓ Ⓔ

Subtest 6: Aviation Supplemental Test

143. Ⓐ Ⓑ Ⓒ Ⓓ	152. Ⓐ Ⓑ Ⓒ Ⓓ	161. Ⓐ Ⓑ Ⓒ Ⓓ	170. Ⓐ Ⓑ Ⓒ Ⓓ
144. Ⓐ Ⓑ Ⓒ Ⓓ	153. Ⓐ Ⓑ Ⓒ Ⓓ	162. Ⓐ Ⓑ Ⓒ Ⓓ	171. Ⓐ Ⓑ Ⓒ Ⓓ
145. Ⓐ Ⓑ Ⓒ Ⓓ	154. Ⓐ Ⓑ Ⓒ Ⓓ	163. Ⓐ Ⓑ Ⓒ Ⓓ	172. Ⓐ Ⓑ Ⓒ Ⓓ
146. Ⓐ Ⓑ Ⓒ Ⓓ	155. Ⓐ Ⓑ Ⓒ Ⓓ	164. Ⓐ Ⓑ Ⓒ Ⓓ	173. Ⓐ Ⓑ Ⓒ Ⓓ
147. Ⓐ Ⓑ Ⓒ Ⓓ	156. Ⓐ Ⓑ Ⓒ Ⓓ	165. Ⓐ Ⓑ Ⓒ Ⓓ	174. Ⓐ Ⓑ Ⓒ Ⓓ
148. Ⓐ Ⓑ Ⓒ Ⓓ	157. Ⓐ Ⓑ Ⓒ Ⓓ	166. Ⓐ Ⓑ Ⓒ Ⓓ	175. Ⓐ Ⓑ Ⓒ Ⓓ
149. Ⓐ Ⓑ Ⓒ Ⓓ	158. Ⓐ Ⓑ Ⓒ Ⓓ	167. Ⓐ Ⓑ Ⓒ Ⓓ	176. Ⓐ Ⓑ Ⓒ Ⓓ
150. Ⓐ Ⓑ Ⓒ Ⓓ	159. Ⓐ Ⓑ Ⓒ Ⓓ	168. Ⓐ Ⓑ Ⓒ Ⓓ	
151. Ⓐ Ⓑ Ⓒ Ⓓ	160. Ⓐ Ⓑ Ⓒ Ⓓ	169. Ⓐ Ⓑ Ⓒ Ⓓ	

Subtest 1

Math Skills Test

The Math Skills subtest checks your arithmetic and algebra skills, plus some geometry, by using equations and word problems. You can expect questions that require solving for variables, working with time and distance, and estimating simple probabilities.

Time: 25 minutes for 30 questions

Directions: This subtest deals with your general understanding and ability to use mathematical relationships in problem solving. Each problem is followed by four possible answers, and you must determine which answer is most correct. Use scratch paper (provided) to do your calculations and then mark the correct answer. (*Note:* We don't provide scratch paper here, but you'll get paper at the test site.)

1. A 5-foot-tall fence post casts a 10-foot shadow. A nearby building casts a 60-foot shadow. How tall is the building?

   (A) 25 feet

   (B) 40 feet

   (C) 30 feet

   (D) 50 feet

2. A Navy Special Operations unit of six members has enough rations to last for a seven-day period. Immediately upon insertion, they capture four suspected insurgents. How long will the rations now last?

   (A) 4.2 days

   (B) 6 days

   (C) 3.5 days

   (D) 5.1 days

3. An item in a store has been marked down to 75 percent of its initial sale price. The store is running a weekend sale and has advertised that everything in the store is an additional 25 percent off. What is the final discount applied to the item in relation to the initial sales price?

   (A) 50.0 percent

   (B) 43.75 percent

   (C) 62.1 percent

   (D) 38.0 percent

4. Tom ordered a pizza, ate 5/16 of it, and then gave away the rest to three friends in his barracks. How much of the pizza did each of the three friends receive if each got an equal share?

   (A) 0.229

   (B) 0.3

   (C) 0.32

   (D) 0.25

5. The scale on a particular map is 1 inch equals 60 miles. On this map, two locations are 6 centimeters apart. What is the distance between the locations in miles?

   (A) 223.4 miles

   (B) 145.7 miles

   (C) 141.6 miles

   (D) 124.8 miles

6. A shipment of 10,000 pounds of corn meal is destined for a developing nation. The meal is packaged in 80-ounce bags. How many bags are shipped?

   (A) 1,500 bags

   (B) 4,400 bags

   (C) 2,500 bags

   (D) 2,000 bags

Go on to next page

7. At a factory, three workers earn $675 per week, two workers earn $600 per week, and four workers earn $595 per week. Assume that every employee works 40 hours per week. What is the average cost per hour the company pays its employees?

   (A) $16.50 per hour

   (B) $15.57 per hour

   (C) $14.89 per hour

   (D) $13.25 per hour

8. A man donates $225,000 to two favorite universities. The ratio of the amount that university A receives to the amount university B receives is 4:3. How much does university A receive?

   (A) $128,571.44

   (B) $129,447.27

   (C) $134,234.17

   (D) $96,428.88

9. A student receives the following test scores on four of five tests: 88, 84, 92, and 96. If the class she attends requires an average score of 90 on the five tests to receive an *A* for the course, what must her final test score be to receive an *A?*

   (A) 88

   (B) 92

   (C) 91

   (D) 90

10. If $a = 5b$ and $10b = 4c$, $a =$

    (A) $b + c$

    (B) $2c$

    (C) $4c$

    (D) $b - c$

11. 1,000,000 can be represented by

    (A) 10^3

    (B) 10^6

    (C) 10^5

    (D) 10^4

12. Two aircraft are 900 miles apart and heading toward each other. One aircraft flies at 680 miles per hour, and the other flies at 630 miles per hour. At a 10-mile separation, the pilots will be able to visually acquire each other. How long until the pilots will be able to visually acquire one another?

    (A) 38 minutes

    (B) 25 minutes

    (C) 41 minutes

    (D) 19 minutes

13. As Ensign Taylor drove 7 hours to a new duty station, her average speed was 61 miles per hour. If her gas mileage was 27 miles per gallon, how much fuel did she burn?

    (A) 15.8 gallons

    (B) 16.1 gallons

    (C) 15.4 gallons

    (D) 16.5 gallons

14. A 600-gallon tank of water can be filled with one hose in 30 minutes and drained completely with another, different-sized hose in 60 minutes. If both hoses are opened on the empty tank, how long until the tank fills?

    (A) 45 minutes

    (B) 110 minutes

    (C) 30 minutes

    (D) 60 minutes

15. What is the perimeter of a right triangle that has two base side lengths of 8 and 12 feet?

    (A) 32 feet, 1 inch

    (B) 34 feet, 5 inches

    (C) 33 feet, 8 inches

    (D) 34 feet, 1 inch

16. If you need five bags of salt crystals to de-ice a 2-acre parking lot, how many bags of salt do you need to de-ice a 6⅓ acre lot?

    (A) 17.75 bags

    (B) 16.25 bags

    (C) 19.1 bags

    (D) 15.83 bags

Go on to next page

17. You have 16 ounces of a mixture containing 40 percent juice. You add 2 ounces of pure juice to the mixture. What percentage of the mixture is juice now?

    (A) 47 percent

    (B) 46 percent

    (C) 49 percent

    (D) 53 percent

18. You have red, green, and blue straws in a bin. The red and green straws combined equal 25 percent of the total number of straws. If you blindly reach in and grab a straw, what is the probability that it will be blue?

    (A) 2 out of 4

    (B) 3 out of 4

    (C) 1 out of 3

    (D) 2 out of 5

19. One of the angles of a right triangle is 25 degrees; what are the other two angles?

    (A) 75 degrees; 105 degrees

    (B) 80 degrees; 75 degrees

    (C) 90 degrees; 65 degrees

    (D) 70 degrees; 85 degrees

20. The reciprocal of 5 is

    (A) 15 percent

    (B) 18 percent

    (C) 20 percent

    (D) 22 percent

21. A 22-foot-tall ladder is resting against the 16-foot upper wall of a building. The top of the ladder is completely even with the top of the wall. How far out from the building is the base of the ladder?

    (A) 15.1 feet

    (B) 8.9 feet

    (C) 13.9 feet

    (D) 12.0 feet

22. A rectangular enclosure's length is two times its width, and the enclosure's perimeter is 150 feet. What is the area of the enclosure?

    (A) 1,350 square feet

    (B) 1,250 square feet

    (C) 1,125 square feet

    (D) 1,500 square feet

23. A cylinder has a diameter of 100 centimeters and a height of 2.5 meters. What is the volume of the cylinder? (One gallon equals 3,781.4 cubic centimeters)

    (A) 532 gallons

    (B) 219 gallons

    (C) 375 gallons

    (D) 519 gallons

24. Last year, fertilizer cost $24.75 per bag. This year, it costs $25.11 per bag. How much did fertilizer prices increase?

    (A) 1.6 percent

    (B) 1.5 percent

    (C) 2.1 percent

    (D) 3.1 percent

25. If a train travels 550 miles in 6 hours, how far does it travel in 22 minutes?

    (A) 25.50 miles

    (B) 18.27 miles

    (C) 33.61 miles

    (D) 41.74 miles

26. Carpet costs $3.99 per square foot. What is the cost to carpet a room that is 4 yards by 7 yards?

    (A) $1,005.48

    (B) $1,276.18

    (C) $1,345.89

    (D) $1,299.01

Go on to next page

27. A family is moving to a new duty station 2,900 miles away and has 6 days to make the trip. On the first day, the family drove 1/5 of the total distance; on the second day, it completed 1/7 of the total distance. How many miles does the family have to average each of the remaining days to arrive on time?

    (A) 521.8 miles per day

    (B) 432.2 miles per day

    (C) 502.1 miles per day

    (D) 476.5 miles per day

28. Eight helicopters can search an area of the ocean in 2.7 hours. Three of the 8 helicopters are down for maintenance. How long will the remaining helicopters need to search the same section of the ocean?

    (A) 3.14 hours

    (B) 4.32 hours

    (C) 6.7 hours

    (D) 4.15 hours

29. John makes $21.50 per hour and time and a half for any time over 40 hours per week. John worked 53 hours this week. How much did he earn before taxes?

    (A) $1,300.50

    (B) $1,289.10

    (C) $1,244.75

    (D) $1,279.25

30. Tom made $360 this week working as a handyman. He received an additional $50 tip and spent $27 on lunches. He owes a car payment this week of $250. How much does he have left over for spending?

    (A) $133

    (B) $122

    (C) $176

    (D) $144

Subtest 2

Reading Skills Test

Reading comprehension items ask you to make inferences based on given text passages. Remember that multiple answer choices may look accurate; your job is to choose the one that can be derived only from the given information.

Time: 25 minutes for 27 questions

Directions: Read the short passages and pick the most-correct answers for the corresponding questions.

The state of Georgia, which has 159 counties, is located within the borders of the United States of America. Georgia is bordered by South Carolina to the east, North Carolina and Tennessee to the north, Alabama to the west, and Florida to the south. On its southeastern coast, Georgia is bordered by the Atlantic Ocean.

31. How many states share a border with Georgia?

    (A) 1

    (B) 5

    (C) 4

    (D) 2

32. What ocean borders Georgia?

    (A) Pacific

    (B) Atlantic

    (C) Indian

    (D) Gulf of Mexico

Dispensing with the traditional model of an orchestra led by a conductor, Orpheus Chamber Orchestra sets out to achieve excellence through teambuilding and collaboration. For each piece to be performed by Orpheus, an elected committee of musicians selects a concertmaster, and each instrumental section chooses a representative. These chosen representatives (the *core group*) develop an overall interpretive approach to the music (including tempi, phrasing, and articulation) before the entire orchestra comes together to rehearse. The core also structures the rehearsal process for the entire orchestra. This setup provides clear leadership while ensuring that every member has a real stake in the artistic outcome of every piece the orchestra performs.

33. According to the passage,

    (A) Orpheus uses the traditional model of an orchestra led by a conductor.

    (B) Orpheus sells many thousands of music CDs every year.

    (C) Orpheus is not led by a conductor.

    (D) A conductor is essential for an orchestra to function properly.

34. According to the passage, the overall interpretive approach to the music includes:

    (A) Core, phrasing, and articulation

    (B) Phrasing, metrics, and feeling

    (C) Tempi, phrasing, and articulation

    (D) Tempi, phrasing, and rehearsal

Go on to next page

Many seasoned racers consider one race to be the Mount Everest of offshore ocean racing. This competition is the 628-nautical-mile Sydney Hobart Yacht Race. Nicknamed "hell on high water" by sailors, this race offers participants a taste of both hell and high water because the racers are required to cross the eastern end of the infamous Bass Strait, which lies between the coasts of the state of Victoria, Australia, and the island of Tasmania.

35. How long is the Sydney Hobart Yacht Race?
    (A) 350 miles
    (B) 4,000 kilometers
    (C) 600 meters
    (D) 628 nautical miles

36. The Bass Strait is located between
    (A) New South Wales and Tasmania
    (B) Victoria, Australia and New Zealand
    (C) Tasmania and Victoria, Australia
    (D) Antarctica and Tasmania

The district of country known geographically as Upper California is bounded on the north by Oregon, the 42nd degree of north latitude being the boundary line between the two territories; on the east by the Rocky Mountains and the Sierra de los Mimbres, a continuation of the same range; on the south by Sonora and Old or Lower California; and on the west by the Pacific Ocean. Its extent from north to south is about 700 miles and from east to west [is] from 600 to 800 miles, with an area of about 400,000 square miles. A small portion only of this extensive territory is fertile or inhabitable by civilized man, and this portion consists chiefly in the strip of country along the Pacific Ocean, about 700 miles in length and from 100 to 150 miles in breadth, bounded on the east by the Sierra Nevada and on the west by the Pacific. In speaking of Upper California, this strip of country is what is generally referred to.

37. Upper California is bounded on the north by what territory?
    (A) Washington
    (B) Oregon
    (C) Lower California
    (D) Pacific

38. The length of Upper California from north to south is approximately how many miles?
    (A) 600
    (B) 150
    (C) 800
    (D) 700

39. What body of water forms the western boundary of Upper California?
    (A) Gulf of California
    (B) Pacific Ocean
    (C) Sierra de los Mimbres
    (D) Salton Sea

Go on to next page

The largest river of Upper California is the Colorado or Red, which has a course of about 1,000 miles and empties into the Gulf of California in latitude about 32 degrees north. But little is known of the region through which this stream flows. The report of trappers, however, is that the river is canoned between high mountains and precipices a large portion of its course, and that its banks and the country generally through which it flows are arid, sandy, and barren. Green and Grand Rivers are its principal upper tributaries, both of which rise in the Rocky Mountains, and within the territories of the United States. The Gila is its lowest and largest branch, emptying into the Colorado just above its mouth. Sevier and Virgin Rivers are also tributaries of the Colorado. Mary's River rises near latitude 42 degrees north, and has a course of about 400 miles, when its waters sink in the sands of the desert. This river is not laid down on any map which I have seen. The Sacramento and San Joaquin Rivers have each a course of from 300 to 400 miles, the first flowing from the north and the last from the south, and both emptying into the Bay of St. Francisco at the same point. They water the large and fertile valley lying between the Sierra Nevada and the coast range of mountains. I subjoin a description of the valley and river San Joaquin, from the pen of a gentleman (Dr. Marsh) who has explored the river from its source to its mouth.

40. Into what body of water does the Colorado River empty?

(A) Gulf of California

(B) Green River

(C) Bay of St. Francisco

(D) Pacific Ocean

41. The largest branch of the Red River is the

(A) Virgin River

(B) Gila River

(C) Green River

(D) San Joaquin River

42. Dr. Marsh explored what body of water?

(A) Bay of St. Francisco

(B) Sierra Nevada

(C) San Joaquin River

(D) Sevier River

Go on to next page

The principal mountains west of the eastern boundary of California (the Rocky Mountains) are the Bear River, Wahsatch, Utah, the Sierra Nevada, and the Coast range. The Wahsatch Mountains form the eastern rim of the great interior basin. There are numerous ranges in this desert basin, all of which run north and south and are separated from each other by spacious and barren valleys and plains. The Sierra Nevada range is of greater elevation than the Rocky Mountains. The summits of the most elevated peaks are covered with perpetual snow. This and the Coast range run nearly parallel with the shore of the Pacific. The first is from 100 to 200 miles from the Pacific, and the last [is] from 40 to 60 miles. The valley between them is the most fertile portion of California.

43. The eastern rim of the great interior basin is comprised of the

    (A) Rocky Mountains

    (B) Sierra Nevada

    (C) Bear River

    (D) Wahsatch Mountains

44. The summits of the most elevated peaks of the Sierra Nevada range are covered with

    (A) Perpetual snow

    (B) Fertile plains

    (C) Rocks

    (D) Meadows

45. The Sierra Nevada range parallels what other range?

    (A) Rocky Mountains

    (B) Coast

    (C) Great Interior

    (D) Wahsatch

Upper California was discovered in 1548 by Cabrillo, a Spanish navigator. In 1578, the northern portion of it was visited by Sir Francis Drake, who called it New Albion. It was first colonized by the Spaniards in 1768 and formed a province of Mexico until after the revolution in that country. There have been numerous revolutions and civil wars in California within the last 20 years, but up to the conquest of the country by the United States in 1846, Mexican authority has generally been exercised over it.

46. The United States' conquest of Upper California occurred in what year?

    (A) 1846

    (B) 1548

    (C) 1768

    (D) 1492

47. Upper California was discovered by

    (A) Sir Francis Drake

    (B) New Albion

    (C) A Dutch navigator

    (D) Cabrillo

48. Upper California was first colonized by

    (A) Mexicans

    (B) Spaniards

    (C) Americans

    (D) The English

Go on to next page

The Indians reside about two hundred yards distant from the above-mentioned edifice. This place is called the rancheria. Most of the missions are made up of very reduced quarters built with mud-bricks, forming streets, while in others the Indians have been allowed to follow their customs, their dwellings being a sort of huts in a conical shape, which at the most do not exceed four yards in diameter, and the top of the cone may be elevated three yards. They are built of rough sticks, covered with bulrushes or grass in such a manner as to completely protect the inhabitants from all the inclemencies of the weather. Opposite the rancherias, and near to the mission, is to be found a small garrison, with proportionate rooms, for a corporal and five soldiers with their families. This small garrison is quite sufficient to prevent any attempt of the Indians from taking effect, there having been some examples made, which causes the Indians to respect this small force. One of these pickets in a mission has a double object; besides keeping the Indians in subjection, they run post with a monthly correspondence, or with any extraordinaries that may be necessary for government.

49. How many corporals are assigned to a garrison?

(A) Three

(B) Two

(C) One

(D) Four

50. Most Indian huts do not exceed how many yards in diameter?

(A) Two

(B) One

(C) Four

(D) Three

51. Most missions are built with

(A) Mud-bricks

(B) Rough sticks

(C) Bulrushes

(D) Grass

The general productions of the missions are the breed of the larger class of cattle, and sheep, horses, wheat, maize or Indian corn, beans, peas, and other vegetables. The productions of the missions situated more to the southward are more extensive, these producing the grape and olive in abundance. Of all these articles of production, the most lucrative is the large cattle, their hides and tallow affording an active commerce with foreign vessels on this coast. This being the only means the inhabitants, missionaries, or private individuals have of supplying their actual necessities, for this reason they generally give it all their attention.

52. The most lucrative mission article of production is

(A) Sheep

(B) Large cattle

(C) Grapes

(D) Horses

53. The more southward missions produce what in abundance?

(A) Peas and maize

(B) Horses and Indian corn

(C) Grape and wheat

(D) Olive and grape

54. Foreign commerce is active for what mission products?

(A) Beans

(B) Grape and olive

(C) Sheep

(D) Hides and tallow

Go on to next page

There are four ports, principal bays, in this territory, which take the names of the corresponding presidios. The best guarded is that of San Diego. That of San Francisco has many advantages. Santa Barbara is but middling in the best part of the season; at other times, always bad. Besides the above-mentioned places, vessels sometimes anchor at Santa Cruz, San Luis Obispo, El Refugio, San Pedro, and San Juan [so] that they may obtain the productions of the missions nearest these last-mentioned places; but from an order sent by the minister of war and circulated by the commandante-general, we are given to understand that no foreign vessel is permitted to anchor at any of these places, Monterey only excepted, notwithstanding the commandante-general has allowed the first three principal ports to remain open provisionally. Were it not so, there would undoubtedly be an end to all commerce with California, as I will quickly show.

55. Whose order excluded foreign vessels from anchoring at most ports?

(A) The commandante-general

(B) The minister of war

(C) San Pedro

(D) San Juan

56. Which port was excepted from the order excluding foreign vessels from anchoring at most ports?

(A) San Diego

(B) Santa Cruz

(C) Monterey

(D) San Luis Obispo

57. Which of the four principal bays is best guarded?

(A) San Diego

(B) Santa Barbara

(C) San Francisco

(D) El Refugio

STOP DO NOT TURN THE PAGE UNTIL TOLD TO DO SO.

Subtest 3

Mechanical Comprehension Test

The mechanical comprehension portion of the ASTB asks you to apply topics common to introductory high school physics courses in various situations. Possible topics include principles related to gases and liquids and how these properties affect pressure, volume, and velocity, as well as questions about engine components and performance; principles of electricity; gears; weight distribution; and the operation of simple machines, such as pulleys and fulcrums.

Time: 15 minutes for 30 questions

Directions: You see a series of questions with given conditions. Most questions will be depicted with a graphical representation of the problem. Use the scratch paper provided to do your calculations and choose the best answer to the problem. (*Note:* We don't provide scratch paper here, but you'll get paper at the test site.)

58. A 300-pound barrel must be lifted 3 feet to the bed of a truck. An inclined plane will reduce the amount of effort required to move the barrel by half if the inclined plane is

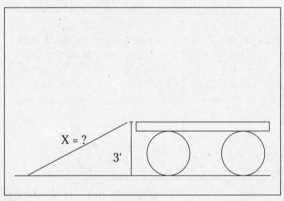

- Illustration by Wiley, Composition Services Graphics

(A) 4 feet

(B) 6 feet

(C) 8 feet

(D) 10 feet

59. Two people are carrying a 200-pound crate on a 12-foot-long, 2-x-8-inch board. To distribute the load evenly between the two people, the crate should be placed

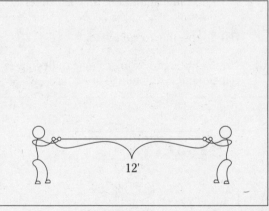

Illustration by Wiley, Composition Services Graphics

(A) 4 feet from one end of the board

(B) 5 feet from one end of the board

(C) 6 feet from one end of the board

(D) 7 feet from one end of the board

Go on to next page

60. Wheel A has a diameter of 22 feet; wheel B has a diameter of 11 feet. If both wheels revolve at the same rate, wheel B will cover a given linear distance in

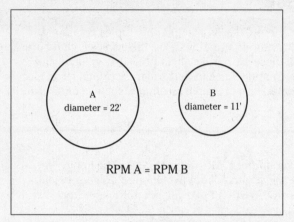

Illustration by Wiley, Composition Services Graphics

(A) Twice the amount of time that wheel A does

(B) One-half the amount of time that wheel A does

(C) The same amount of time as wheel A does

(D) Impossible to calculate

61. Not including friction, a single pulley gives a mechanical advantage of

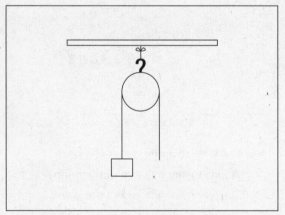

Illustration by Wiley, Composition Services Graphics

(A) 2

(B) 1

(C) 2.5

(D) 3

62. Four gears are turning in motion in a series. If gear A is turning clockwise, gear D will turn

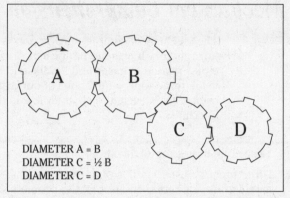

DIAMETER A = B
DIAMETER C = ½ B
DIAMETER C = D

Illustration by Wiley, Composition Services Graphics

(A) Clockwise and at the same speed as gear A

(B) Counterclockwise and more slowly than gear A

(C) Counterclockwise and more quickly than gear A

(D) Clockwise and more quickly than gear A

63. You balance a wooden beam on a fulcrum and then cut the beam exactly at the CG point into two sections A and B. Which section will be heavier?

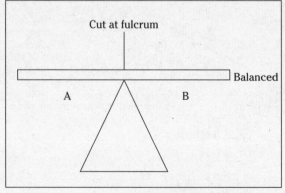

Illustration by Wiley, Composition Services Graphics

(A) A is heavier than B.

(B) B is heavier than A.

(C) Impossible to calculate.

(D) A is the same weight as B.

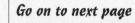

Go on to next page

64. If gear A has 14 teeth and makes four revolutions, gear B, which has 20 teeth, will make how many revolutions?

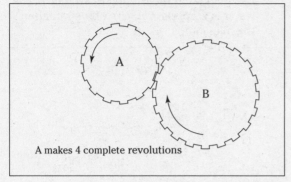

A makes 4 complete revolutions

Illustration by Wiley, Composition Services Graphics

(A) 6.1 revolutions

(B) 2.8 revolutions

(C) 7.5 revolutions

(D) 4.9 revolutions

65. The wheelbarrow is an example of

Illustration by Wiley, Composition Services Graphics

(A) A second-class lever

(B) A first-class lever

(C) A third-class lever

(D) A fourth-class lever

66. The pulley arrangement in the diagram shows a 50-pound force pulling on the rope attached to pulley A. How much weight can this pulley arrangement lift?

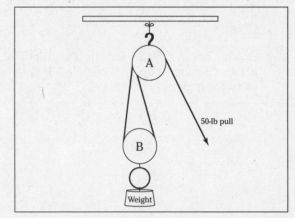

50-lb pull

Weight

Illustration by Wiley, Composition Services Graphics

(A) 50 pounds

(B) 120 pounds

(C) 100 pounds

(D) 80 pounds

67. An object can accelerate by

Illustration by Wiley, Composition Services Graphics

(A) Changing speed

(B) Changing the initial velocity

(C) Changing the direction of its velocity but not the magnitude

(D) All the above

Go on to next page

68. 115 degrees equals how many radians?

    (A) 1

    (B) 2

    (C) 3

    (D) 4

69. Floats A and B measure the specific gravity of two different samples. Which float indicates the higher specific gravity?

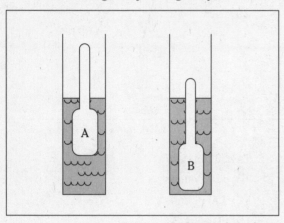

Illustration by Wiley, Composition Services Graphics

    (A) Float A.

    (B) Float B.

    (C) Neither A nor B is higher in specific gravity.

    (D) Impossible to calculate.

70. A 100-kilogram man jumps off a raft that weighs 150 kilograms. His initial velocity from jumping is 5 meters per second. Assuming that the friction resistance of the water is zero, the velocity of the raft after the man jumps will be

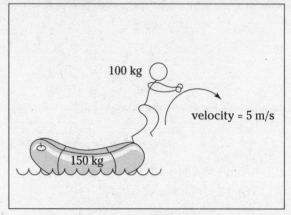

Illustration by Wiley, Composition Services Graphics

    (A) 3.33 meters per second

    (B) 2.7 meters per second

    (C) –3.33 meters per second

    (D) –2.7 meters per second

71. A given wheel rotates at a constant speed. The outside of the wheel has a _____ linear speed and a(n) _____ angular speed compared to the inside of the wheel.

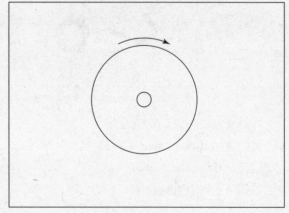

Illustration by Wiley, Composition Services Graphics

    (A) Lesser; greater

    (B) Lesser; equal

    (C) Greater; lesser

    (D) Greater; equal

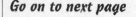

Go on to next page

72. Two objects traveling in opposite directions collide with one another. Object A weighs 5 kilograms and is traveling at 10 meters per second, and object B weighs 10 kilograms and is traveling at 5 meters per second. If the two objects remain attached following the collision, what is their combined speed?

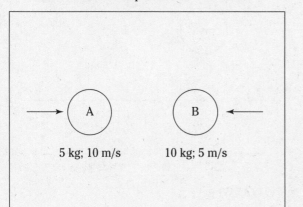

Illustration by Wiley, Composition Services Graphics

(A) 2 meters per second

(B) 0 meters per second

(C) 1 meter per second

(D) 3 meters per second

73. Given that both anvils in the diagram are the same weights, what will happen when anvil B is placed on the seesaw?

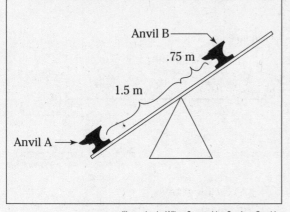

Illustration by Wiley, Composition Services Graphics

(A) Nothing.

(B) Anvil A will rise up and then settle back to the ground.

(C) Anvil B will go to the ground.

(D) Anvils A and B will reach an equilibrium at the same elevation.

74. Ambient air pressure is roughly 14.7 pounds per square inch at sea level. The total area of the top of your model airplane is 145 square inches. What is the amount of force exerted on the top of your motionless, grounded airplane at sea level?

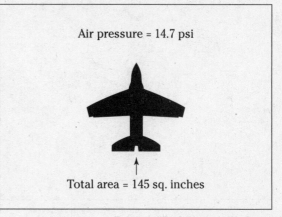

Illustration by Wiley, Composition Services Graphics

(A) 2,132 pounds

(B) 230 pounds

(C) 1,675 pounds

(D) 1,790 pounds

75. What mechanical advantage does this block and tackle arrangement have?

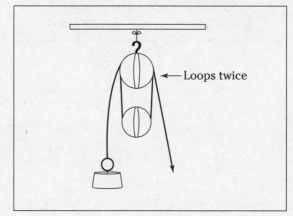

Illustration by Wiley, Composition Services Graphics

(A) 1

(B) 3

(C) 2

(D) 5

Go on to next page
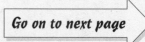

76. Gear 1 moves in a clockwise direction. Which other gear(s) move(s) in a clockwise direction?

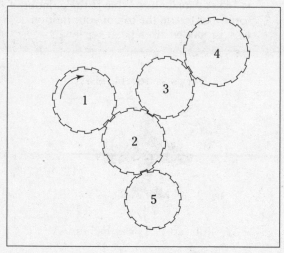

Illustration by Wiley, Composition Services Graphics

(A) 2 and 4

(B) 3 and 5

(C) 3, 4, and 5

(D) 3

77. A cubic foot of water weighs approximately 62.5 pounds. If an aquarium is 5 feet long, 3 feet deep, and 2 feet wide, what is the approximate pressure in pounds per square inch on the bottom of the tank?

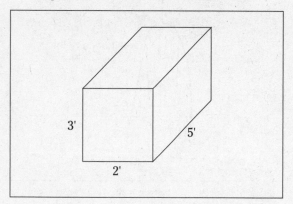

Illustration by Wiley, Composition Services Graphics

(A) 1.5 pounds per square inch

(B) 1.9 pounds per square inch

(C) 1.7 pounds per square inch

(D) 1.3 pounds per square inch

78. Wheel A and wheel B are the same distance from the bottom of the incline in the diagram. If both wheel A and wheel B revolve at the same rate, which will reach the bottom first?

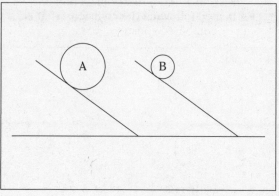

Illustration by Wiley, Composition Services Graphics

(A) Wheel B.

(B) Wheel A and B will reach the bottom at the same time.

(C) Wheel A.

(D) Impossible to calculate.

79. If a ramp is 10 meters long and has a total incline height of 3 meters, an object weighing 100 kilograms requires how much effort to move on the ramp?

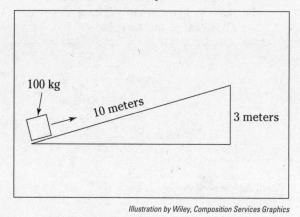

Illustration by Wiley, Composition Services Graphics

(A) 30 kilograms

(B) 40 kilograms

(C) 45 kilograms

(D) 62.5 kilograms

Go on to next page

80. In the diagram, assume all the valves are closed. Which valves must be opened to ensure that the tank fills to and remains at approximately 3/4 volume?

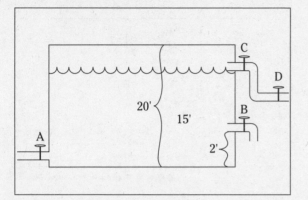

Illustration by Wiley, Composition Services Graphics

(A) A, B, and C

(B) A, C, and D

(C) B, C, and D

(D) B and C

81. If gear 1 makes five counterclockwise revolutions per minute in the diagram,

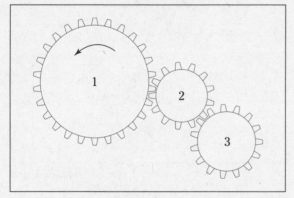

Illustration by Wiley, Composition Services Graphics

(A) Gear 3 moves clockwise 8.33 revolutions.

(B) Gear 2 moves clockwise 5 revolutions.

(C) Gear 3 moves counterclockwise 8.33 revolutions.

(D) Gear 2 moves counterclockwise 5 revolutions.

82. At which point is the baseball throw the slowest?

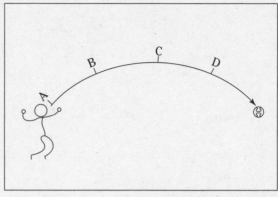

Illustration by Wiley, Composition Services Graphics

(A) A

(B) B

(C) C

(D) D

83. Water is flowing through the pipe depicted in the diagram at a rate of 100 gallons per hour. The water flow starts at point A, becomes constricted to about 50 percent at point B, and then opens back up to the circumference of the entire pipe at point C. Which statement is true?

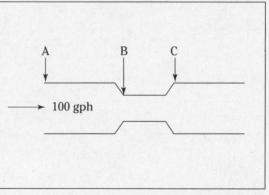

Illustration by Wiley, Composition Services Graphics

(A) The volume of water at point B is half of what it is at point A.

(B) The volume of water at point B is double what it is at point A.

(C) The velocity of the water flow is reduced at point B.

(D) The volume of water passing point B is the same as the volume of water passing points A and C.

Go on to next page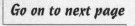

84. Pulley B is the driver in the arrangement. The pulley that turns the fastest is

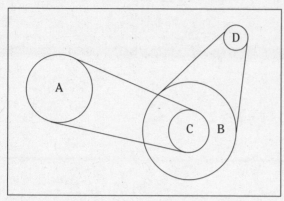

Illustration by Wiley, Composition Services Graphics

(A) A

(B) B

(C) C

(D) D

85. Which brace is more secure?

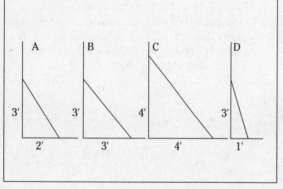

Illustration by Wiley, Composition Services Graphics

(A) A

(B) B

(C) C

(D) D

86. Which pendulum takes more time to make a complete swing?

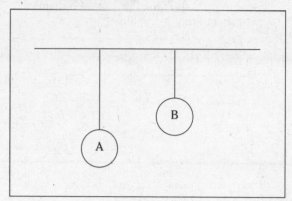

Illustration by Wiley, Composition Services Graphics

(A) Neither A nor B

(B) A

(C) B

(D) Impossible to calculate

87. Given the diagrams, which has the greatest resistance if all resistors are equal?

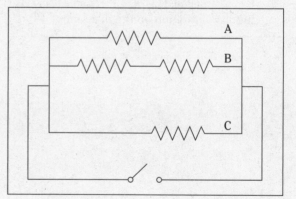

Illustration by Wiley, Composition Services Graphics

(A) A

(B) B

(C) C

(D) Impossible to calculate

STOP DO NOT TURN THE PAGE UNTIL TOLD TO DO SO.

Subtest 4
Spatial Apperception Test

This subtest checks your ability to match external and internal views of aircraft when given visual information about the aircraft's direction and orientation relative to the ground. Each question provides a view from inside the cockpit; you then have to match that diagram to one of five external views.

Time: 10 minutes for 25 questions

Directions: In each question, you see a pilot's view from the crew member station. Next, you see a series of five outside 3-D viewpoints of various aircraft, and you must select which aircraft best represents what's shown in the first picture.

88.

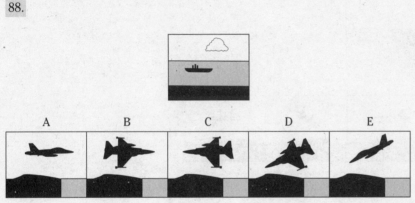

Illustration by Wiley, Composition Services Graphics

89.

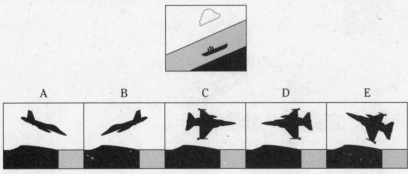

Illustration by Wiley, Composition Services Graphics

Go on to next page

90.

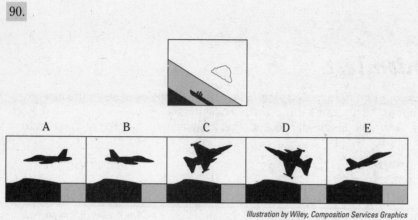

Illustration by Wiley, Composition Services Graphics

91.

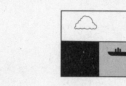

Illustration by Wiley, Composition Services Graphics

92.

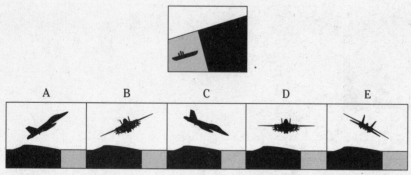

Illustration by Wiley, Composition Services Graphics

Go on to next page

93.

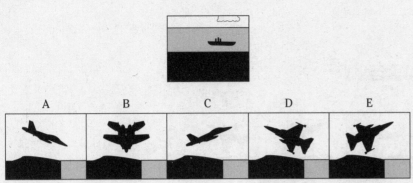

Illustration by Wiley, Composition Services Graphics

94.

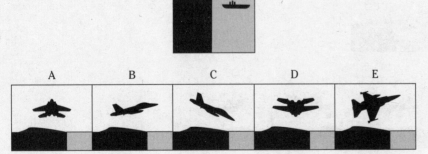

Illustration by Wiley, Composition Services Graphics

95.

Illustration by Wiley, Composition Services Graphics

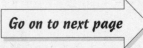
Go on to next page

96.

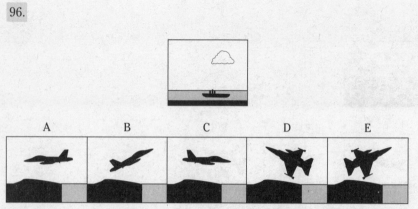

Illustration by Wiley, Composition Services Graphics

97.

Illustration by Wiley, Composition Services Graphics

98.

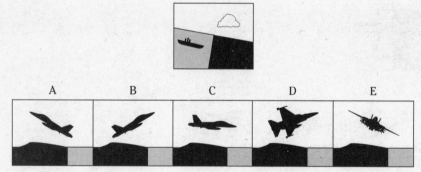

Illustration by Wiley, Composition Services Graphics

Go on to next page

99.

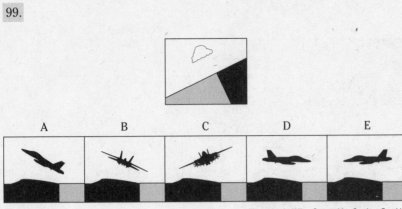

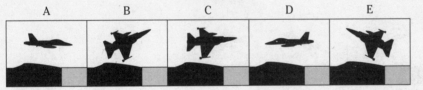

Illustration by Wiley, Composition Services Graphics

100.

Illustration by Wiley, Composition Services Graphics

101.

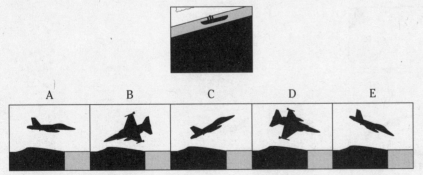

Illustration by Wiley, Composition Services Graphics

Go on to next page

102.

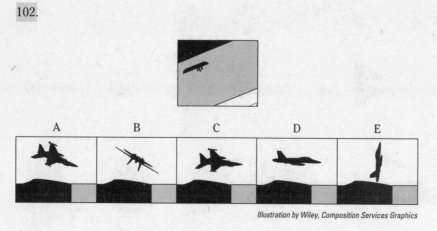

Illustration by Wiley, Composition Services Graphics

103.

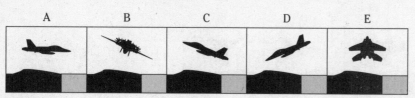

Illustration by Wiley, Composition Services Graphics

104.

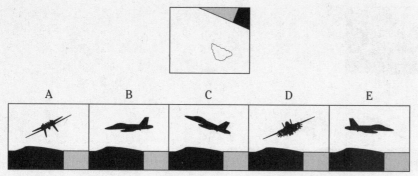

Illustration by Wiley, Composition Services Graphics

Go on to next page

105.

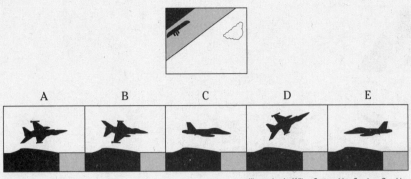

Illustration by Wiley, Composition Services Graphics

106.

Illustration by Wiley, Composition Services Graphics

107.

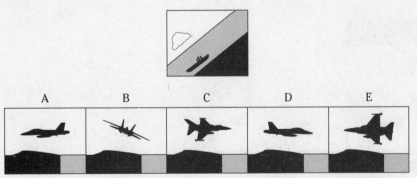

Illustration by Wiley, Composition Services Graphics

Go on to next page

108.

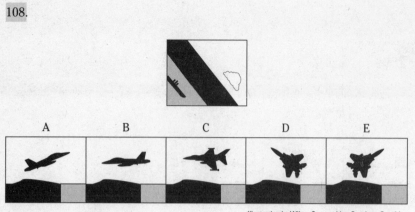

Illustration by Wiley, Composition Services Graphics

109.

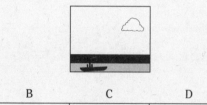

Illustration by Wiley, Composition Services Graphics

110.

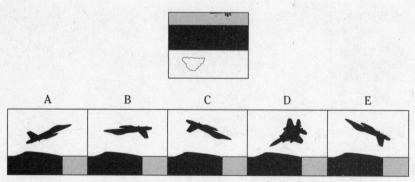

Illustration by Wiley, Composition Services Graphics

Go on to next page

111.

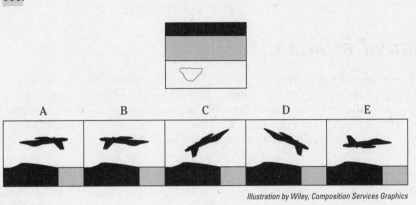

Illustration by Wiley, Composition Services Graphics

112.

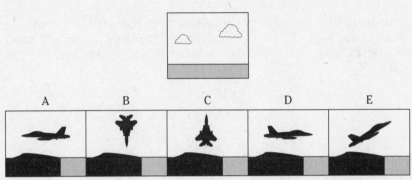

Illustration by Wiley, Composition Services Graphics

Subtest 5

Aviation and Nautical Information

This section gauges your knowledge of aviation history, nautical terminology and procedures, and aviation topics such as aircraft components, aerodynamic principles, and flight rules and regulations. Of all the ASTB subtests, this score is the easiest to improve through study because it focuses more on knowledge than on skills. Good study materials for this test include general reference materials (such as encyclopedias), FAA and civilian aviation books, and this book.

Time: 15 minutes for 30 questions

Directions: Read the questions and choose the best answer.

113. You're telling your spouse that you have a meeting at 1800, but your spouse doesn't understand the 24-hour clock system. What time do you say the meeting is?

    (A) 4:00 p.m.

    (B) 5:00 p.m.

    (C) 6:00 p.m.

    (D) 7:00 p.m.

    (E) 8:00 p.m.

114. The pilot banks the aircraft by using which flight control?

    (A) Power settings

    (B) Ailerons

    (C) Elevators

    (D) Flaps

    (E) Rudder

115. Which of these flight controls works by moving in opposite directions?

    (A) Power settings

    (B) Ailerons

    (C) Elevators

    (D) Flaps

    (E) Rudder

116. If you see the large number 36 on a hard surface runway, the same runway will have which number at the opposite end?

    (A) 36

    (B) 27

    (C) 20

    (D) 18

    (E) 9

117. When the pilot pulls back on the control stick or yoke, what happens to the elevators?

    (A) In unison, the trailing edges point down.

    (B) Nothing; this action has no effect on the elevators.

    (C) The elevators move in opposite directions with the left leading edge pointing up and the trailing edges pointing down.

    (D) In unison, the trailing edges point up.

    (E) The elevator automatically drops the flaps.

118. Five statute miles are equal to _____ nautical miles

    (A) 4.35

    (B) 5

    (C) 7.5

    (D) 5.75

    (E) 2.5

Go on to next page

119. You're traveling on the open water at night and see the lights of a boat that appears to be coming closer. You see a red light on the boat, so you know you're seeing which side of the boat?

    (A) The bow

    (B) Port side

    (C) Starboard side

    (D) The stern

    (E) The rear

120. A nautical mile is approximately

    (A) 1,840 meters

    (B) 1,910 meters

    (C) 6,076 feet

    (D) 5,276 feet

    (E) .97 statue miles

121. The wingspan is the distance from

    (A) Wingtip to wingtip

    (B) The nose of the aircraft to the tail

    (C) The highest point of the aircraft to the lowest point

    (D) The leading edge of the wing to the trailing edge

    (E) The wingtip to where the wing attaches to the fuselage

122. The tail section of the plane is referred to as the

    (A) Rudder

    (B) Stern

    (C) Fuselage

    (D) Empennage

    (E) Storage area

123. Which of the following engines can operate outside the earth's atmosphere?

    (A) Piston-driven engine

    (B) Turbo-charged engine

    (C) Gasoline-powered engine

    (D) Rocket engine

    (E) Jet engine

124. During takeoff, a tailwind

    (A) Decreases the takeoff roll

    (B) Increases the takeoff roll

    (C) Reduces the Vr speed

    (D) Increases the Vr speed

    (E) Has no effect on the takeoff

125. The outer walls of a ship are called the

    (A) Foredeck

    (B) Aftdeck

    (C) Keel

    (D) Bow

    (E) Hull

126. In sailing, it's possible to reach a speed

    (A) Slightly less than the windspeed

    (B) Equal to the windspeed

    (C) Equal to the crosswind component of the windspeed

    (D) Greater than the windspeed

    (E) Approximately 3/4 of the windspeed

127. A ship's windlass is for handling the

    (A) Anchor chain

    (B) Steerage

    (C) Loading cargo

    (D) Autopilot

    (E) Propeller shaft direction

128. Normally, restricted airspace

    (A) Is open to flight at any time without approval

    (B) Can have hidden hazards to aircraft such as artillery or aerial gunnery ranges

    (C) Prohibits flight by all aircraft at all times

    (D) Is above cities

    (E) Is above the White House and Capitol building

Go on to next page

129. An uncontrolled airfield is one that
    (A) Has an operation control tower
    (B) Has a published instrument approach
    (C) Has a GPS approach
    (D) Doesn't have an operating control tower
    (E) Doesn't have an airport manager

130. IFR stands for
    (A) Visual flight rules
    (B) I follow roads
    (C) Instrument flight rules
    (D) Initial flight recorder
    (E) Inability to follow rules violation

131. Above 18,000 feet Mean Sea Level, altimeters are set to
    (A) 28.85
    (B) 29.00
    (C) 27.72
    (D) 18.00
    (E) 29.92

132. The bridge of a ship
    (A) Is where the ship is controlled
    (B) Is where the chow hall is
    (C) Is the new term for the crow's nest
    (D) Is where the ship engineers work
    (E) Is sleeping quarters for the admiral

133. On-board ship, soundings determine
    (A) The attitude of the crew
    (B) Direction in relation to true north
    (C) The ship's position
    (D) The depth of the water
    (E) Call to quarters

134. Fog is formed when
    (A) Cold air travels over warm water.
    (B) Warm air moves over cold water.
    (C) Rain is imminent.
    (D) Warm air moves over warm water.
    (E) Cold air moves over cold water.

135. Which of the following is a flight instrument?
    (A) Oil pressure gauges
    (B) Pitot tube heat indicator
    (C) Altimeter
    (D) Control stick
    (E) Flap switch

136. Above flight level 180, you must always operate under
    (A) IFR
    (B) VFR
    (C) Negative control
    (D) Direct authority of an admiral
    (E) The two-pilot rule

137. The tailhook
    (A) Is designed to secure the aircraft to the deck during transport
    (B) Is designed to grapple arresting cables and slow the aircraft upon landing
    (C) Assists with launching the aircraft
    (D) Is a code of conduct
    (E) Is an in-flight aircraft trim device

138. A wall or vertical surface within a ship is called
    (A) A bulkhead
    (B) A ship wall
    (C) The privy
    (D) The galley
    (E) The gangway

139. The angle at which the wing is adjoined to the fuselage is called the
    (A) Angle of attack
    (B) Angle of incidence
    (C) Joint plane angle
    (D) Surface attack
    (E) Chord line

Go on to next page

140. While you're on final approach, the control tower advises you that you have a fast-moving inbound aircraft approaching and asks you to increase your approach speed to accommodate the faster aircraft. Which of the following is true?

    (A) The tower instructions are a request, not an order.

    (B) The tower instructions are an order.

    (C) If the tower instructions make you feel unsafe, you still must comply.

    (D) You don't have to comply with the tower instructions, and you don't have to respond to the tower.

    (E) You're at an uncontrolled airfield.

141. At night, you can identify a military airfield by what beacon signal?

    (A) A rotating white light

    (B) A rotating green light

    (C) A rotating green and white light

    (D) One rotating green light and two white lights

    (E) A rotating green and amber light

142. A high-G maneuver results in

    (A) Decreased blood flow to the brain

    (B) Increased blood flow to the brain

    (C) No effect on the blood flow

    (D) Slowed breathing

    (E) Decreased aileron effectiveness

STOP DO NOT TURN THE PAGE UNTIL TOLD TO DO SO.

Subtest 6

Aviation Supplemental Test

The final ASTB subtest consists of questions in the format of the questions in the preceding subtests and covers the same content.

Time: 25 minutes for 34 questions

Directions: Use scrap paper to determine the most-correct answer for each question.

143. $\left(\frac{1}{2} \div \frac{1}{2}\right) \times \sqrt{4} =$

  (A) 1

  (B) 2

  (C) 3

  (D) 4

144. *Abdicate* means to

  (A) Control through subversion

  (B) Produce more than expected

  (C) Give up a position of authority or power

  (D) Be self-absorbed

145. What is the product of $(5a - 2)(2a + 2)$?

  (A) $10a + 4$

  (B) $5a^2 + 2a + 6$

  (C) $10a^2 + 4a + 4$

  (D) $10a^2 + 6a - 4$

146. John drove a trip in three days. The first day he traveled 343 miles, and his average speed was 55 miles per hour. The second day, he traveled 380 miles and had an average speed of 63 miles per hour, and the third day, he traveled 224 miles and had an average speed of 61 miles per hour. What was his average speed for the entire trip?

  (A) 59.4 miles per hour

  (B) 60.7 miles per hour

  (C) 57.8 miles per hour

  (D) 59.0 miles per hour

147. Newton's third law states that for every action,

  (A) There is motion.

  (B) There must be an equal and opposite reaction.

  (C) There is a payback.

  (D) Gravity is offset.

A deficient intake of certain vitamins can cause all sorts of problems for both children and adults because these vitamins play a vital role in many human biological processes. For example, a lack of vitamin C has long been known to cause the disease scurvy; a lack of vitamin D (found in milk) can lead to the bone-softening disease rickets. Researchers have recently learned that in addition to the link between vitamin D and rickets, vitamin D is essential for the human disease-fighting immune system to function properly.

148. According to this paragraph, vitamin D

  (A) Is found in milk

  (B) Is not as important as vitamin C

  (C) Is related to vitamin C

  (D) Plays a role in the disease scurvy

149. If something is *essential,* it is

  (A) Bad

  (B) Luxurious

  (C) Unwanted

  (D) Needed

Go on to next page

150. Three lines intersect at a point. What is the value of $x + y + z$?

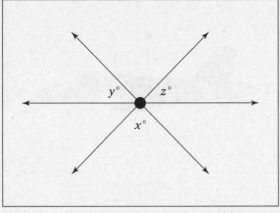

Illustration by Wiley, Composition Services Graphics

(A) 100°

(B) 180°

(C) 135°

(D) 240°

151. What is the quotient of 6 and 6?

(A) 1

(B) 3

(C) 6

(D) 9

152. Solve for x: $2x + 4(2x + 7) = 3(2x + 4)$.

(A) 2

(B) 4

(C) –4

(D) –1

153. If gear A is rotating clockwise, which way is gear B rotating? Is gear B rotating more quickly or more slowly than gear A?

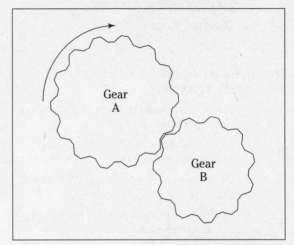

Illustration by Wiley, Composition Services Graphics

(A) Clockwise and more slowly

(B) Counterclockwise and more quickly

(C) Clockwise and more quickly

(D) Counterclockwise and more slowly

A major cable television news network recently reported that NASA astrobiologist Dr. Richard Hoover has discovered evidence of a new form of life in space. Specifically, Dr. Hoover claims to have discovered the presence of fossil bacteria in meteorites. This announcement was met with much controversy within the scientific community. As a result, Dr. Hoover asked a group of more than 5,000 scientists to review his work and then report their findings to the public. His hope is that further research will either confirm his own findings or definitively disprove them.

154. Bacteria are a

(A) Team of researchers

(B) Kind of virus

(C) Result of stellar evolution

(D) Form of life

Go on to next page

155. When something is *controversial,* people
    (A) Get ill from it
    (B) Strongly believe it is true
    (C) Disagree about it
    (D) Like it

156. Based on the reading selection, which statement is true?
    (A) No one believes Dr. Hoover discovered fossil bacteria.
    (B) Astrobiologists are better educated than astrogeologists.
    (C) Dr. Hoover believes he has discovered bacteria fossils from space.
    (D) Dr. Hoover discovered the bacteria by using a telescope.

157. A circle has a radius of 12 inches. What is its area?
    (A) 259.7 square centimeters
    (B) 259.7 square inches
    (C) 452.4 square centimeters
    (D) 452.4 square inches

158. What is the volume of a cylinder that is 2 feet tall and has a diameter of 8 inches?
    (A) 1,206 cubic inches
    (B) 1,206 square inches
    (C) 2,412 cubic inches
    (D) 603 cubic inches

159. The four forces acting on an aircraft are

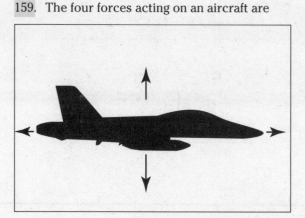

Illustration by Wiley, Composition Services Graphics

    (A) Drag, power, acceleration, and weight
    (B) Lift, drag, weight, and power
    (C) Lift, descent, thrust, and climb
    (D) Climb, descent, turn, and weight

160. A ship has 380 Navy personnel on-board, and 85 percent of the personnel on-board are enlisted. How many officers serve on the ship?
    (A) 24
    (B) 61
    (C) 52
    (D) 57

161. One unidentified plane is flying on a heading of 180 degrees at 160 miles per hour. A tactical jet is airborne and exactly 200 miles north of the unidentified aircraft. The tactical jet immediately turns to a heading of 180 degrees, and its speed is 582 miles per hour. How long does the tactical jet take to catch up with the unidentified aircraft?
    (A) 15 minutes
    (B) 28 minutes
    (C) 20 minutes
    (D) 10 minutes

Go on to next page

162. A cube has a volume of 216 cubic inches. What is the length of each side?

    (A) 2 inches

    (B) 4 inches

    (C) 6 inches

    (D) 8 inches

163. Which of the following statements is true?

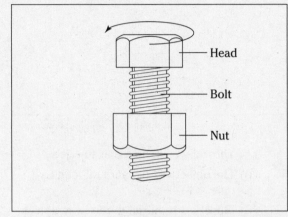

Illustration by Wiley, Composition Services Graphics

    (A) If the nut is held stationary and the head is turned counterclockwise, the head will move up.

    (B) If the nut is held stationary and the head is turned counterclockwise, the head will move down.

    (C) If the bolt is held stationary and the nut is rotated clockwise, the nut will move up.

    (D) If the bolt is held stationary and the nut is rotated counterclockwise, the nut will move down.

164. To control a light fixture from two different locations that each has its own switch, you need

    (A) A single-pole switch and a three-way switch

    (B) One single-pole and one double-pole switch

    (C) Two three-way switches

    (D) Two single-pole switches

In 1850, Alfred, Lord Tennyson's poem *In Memoriam A.H.H.* was published. The poem gives tribute to the author's friend, who died in early adulthood.

> Ring out, wild bells, to the wild sky,
> The flying cloud, the frosty light:
> The year is dying in the night;
> Ring out, wild bells, and let him die.
>
> Ring out the old, ring in the new,
> Ring, happy bells, across the snow:
> The year is going, let him go;
> Ring out the false, ring in the true.
>
> Ring out the grief that saps the mind,
> For those that here we see no more;
> Ring out the feud of rich and poor,
> Ring in redress to all mankind.
>
> Ring out a slowly dying cause,
> And ancient forms of party strife;
> Ring in the nobler modes of life,
> With sweeter manners, purer laws.

165. What holiday does this poem most likely refer to?

    (A) Thanksgiving

    (B) New Year's

    (C) Christmas

    (D) Labor Day

166. What does *redress* mean in this poem?

    (A) The lifeblood of a tree

    (B) To strike

    (C) Making up for wrong or injustice

    (D) Making merry

167. What does *feud* mean in this poem?

    (A) An ongoing quarrel

    (B) A small body of water

    (C) A celebration

    (D) Hitting one object with another

Go on to next page ⟹

168. Pliers are an example of a

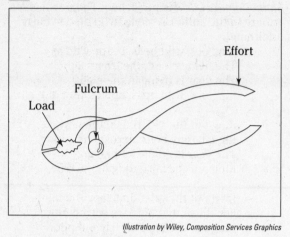

Illustration by Wiley, Composition Services Graphics

(A) Third class lever

(B) Second class lever

(C) Reduce load lever

(D) First class lever

169. You're flying out to find and rescue a sinking vessel. The last position of the ship was 120 nautical miles away, and you're flying at 150 knots. Assume there are no winds. You're burning a total of 812 pounds per hour of JP8. JP8 weighs 6.7 pounds per gallon; you have just refueled and have 360 gallons of fuel on board. You need at least 45 minutes of reserve fuel when you get back to your air station. After you get to the ship's last known position, how much time can you spend on station looking for survivors?

(A) 45 minutes

(B) 52 minutes

(C) 37 minutes

(D) 42 minutes

170. An enemy tactical ground radar installation can pick up any objects higher than 200 feet for approximately 48 kilometers. What surface area can the radar installation cover before being neutralized by U.S. forces?

(A) 6,355 square kilometers

(B) 7,238 square kilometers

(C) 6,355 square miles

(D) 7,238 square miles

171. If the fulcrum is moved away from the object on the board, how will that positioning affect the object?

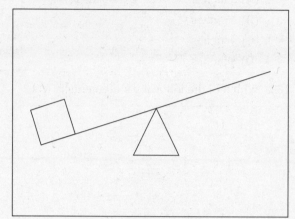

Illustration by Wiley, Composition Services Graphics

(A) The object will be easier to raise.

(B) The object will be more difficult to raise.

(C) The effort required to raise the object won't change.

(D) Impossible to calculate.

172. Angle θ is important because

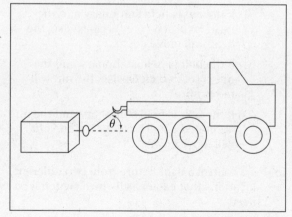

Illustration by Wiley, Composition Services Graphics

(A) At zero degrees, the entire force is dragging the weight.

(B) At 90 degrees, the entire force is lifting the weight.

(C) At 45 degrees, the force is equally divided between lifting and dragging the weight.

(D) All of the above.

Go on to next page
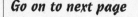

173. The length of a caged rectangular enclosure is 200 meters, and the width is 100 meters. What is the perimeter?

    (A) 300 meters

    (B) 400 meters

    (C) 500 meters

    (D) 600 meters

174. How much force must be applied at point A to move the 100-lb weight at point B?

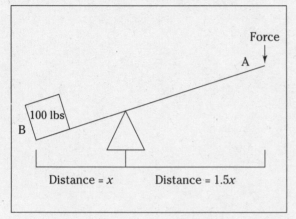

Illustration by Wiley, Composition Services Graphics

    (A) 25.0 lbs

    (B) 66.7 lbs

    (C) 62.4 lbs

    (D) 100.0 lbs

175. Not including any friction factor, what mechanical advantage does a single pulley give you?

    (A) 1

    (B) 2

    (C) 3

    (D) 4

176. If you push your left rudder pedal, what happens to the aircraft?

    (A) The trailing edge of the rudder moves to your left.

    (B) The trailing edge of the rudder moves to the right.

    (C) Nothing happens.

    (D) The nose of the aircraft shifts to the right.

Chapter 17

Navy/Marine Corps/Coast Guard Aviation Selection Test Battery (ASTB) Answers/Explanations

· ·

Now that you've completed the Navy/Marine Corps/Coast Guard Aviation Selection Test Battery (ASTB) in Chapter 16, you're ready to find out how you did. To help you get the most from this exercise, we present the answers and explanations in two different formats: the first with more-detailed explanations, and the second as a bare-bones answer key. If you really want to understand the *why* behind each answer, we recommend you read through the explanations. By taking the time to do so, you'll have a better understanding of the questions you'll be asked on the ASTB and a better chance of increasing your score.

Subtest 1: Math Skills Test

1. **C.** (5 feet ÷ 10 feet) × 60 feet = 30 feet.

2. **A.** Seven days of rations for 6 people equals a total of 42 ration portions. Next, add the 4 insurgents to equal a total of 10 people to feed and divide the total number of rations by the number of people. 42 ÷ 10 = 4.2 days.

3. **B.** 100 percent of the initial price minus 25 percent = 75 percent. Multiply this result by .75 (to figure in an additional 25 percent markdown) to get a total price of 56.25 percent of the initial price. This answer means your savings is 100 percent − 56.25 percent = 43.75 percent off.

4. **A.** Subtract 5 ÷ 16 from 1, and you have a total of 11/16 of the pizza left over. Convert this result to a decimal by dividing 11 by 16 to get 0.6875 of the pizza left over, and divide this amount by the three people sharing the pizza to get a total per-person amount of 0.229 of the pizza.

5. **C.** 1 inch equals 60 miles on the map scale. You know that one inch equals 2.54 centimeters. Therefore, 2.54 centimeters equals 60 miles. Divide 6 centimeters by 2.54 centimeters and then multiply that result by 60 miles to get 141.6 miles. (6 centimeters ÷ 2.54 centimeters) × 60 miles = 2.36 × 60 miles = 141.6 miles.

6. **D.** You first have to get the total weight in ounces. 16 ounces = 1 pound, so 10,000 pounds × 16 ounces/pound = 160,000 ounces. Divide the number of ounces by the amount going into each bag (80 ounces) to get the answer. 160,000 ounces ÷ 80 ounces per bag = 2,000 bags shipped.

7. **B.** Find the total amount each group receives: $(3 \times \$675 = \$2,025)$, $(2 \times \$600 = \$1,200)$, $(4 \times \$595 = \$2,380)$. Add the total amounts to get the total amount paid out each week: $\$2,025 + \$1,200 + \$2,380 = \$5,605$. Divide that result by the nine employees to get the $622.78 average weekly pay, and divide this number by 40 hours per week to get \$15.569 or \$15.57 in average hourly pay per employee.

8. **A.** Split the total donation into units and then use the ratio to find how much goes to each recipient: $\$225,000 \div (4 + 3) = \$225,000 \div 7 = \$32,142.86$. Take this amount and multiply by 4 to get university A's amount of \$128,571.44. To double check, you can find university B's amount by multiplying \$32,142.86 by 3 to get \$96,428.58 and then add both results to ensure they equal the total donation: $\$128,571.44 + \$96,428.58 = \$225,000.02$.

9. **D.** The sum of the average of the five tests to receive an A must be 450 (90 average $\times$ 5 tests). Subtract from 450 the score of each of the four previous tests, and you have 90 left over, so that's what the student must score to average 90 and make an A in the class. You can also set the missing score as the variable x: $(88 + 84 + 92 + 96 + x) \div 5 = 90$.

10. **B.** If $a = 5b$, you can figure that $2a = 10b$, so you can substitute $2a$ for $10b$ in the second equation to get $2a = 4c$. Divide both sides by 2 to get $a = 2c$.

11. **B.** 10^6 is the same as a 1 followed by 6 zeros, or 1,000,000.

12. **C.** First, calculate the distance required until the aircraft can see each other by taking the total distance and subtracting the distance at which they can acquire one another (900 miles – 10 miles = 890 miles). Divide this distance by the combined airspeeds at which the aircraft are converging (680 miles per hour + 630 miles per hour = 1,310 miles per hour). 890 miles ÷ 1,310 miles per hour = 0.679 hours. But wait; the answer choices are in minutes! Never fear; just multiply 0.679 hours $\times$ 60 minutes to get 40.74 or 41 minutes.

13. **A.** Seven hours times the average of 61 miles per hour gives you 427 miles. Divide the total miles by the gas mileage of 27 miles per gallon. $427 \div 27 = 15.8$ gallons used.

14. **D.** First, figure out the separate rates of flow. To fill the 600-gallon tank, hose A = 600 ÷ 30 minutes = 20 gallons per minute or 1,200 gallons per hour. To empty the tank, hose B = 600 ÷ 60 minutes = 10 gallons per minute or 600 gallons per hour. If you open both, you have water coming in at the rate of 1,200 gallons per hour and leaving at 600 gallons per hour for a net filling rate of 600 gallons per hour; the tank will fill in 1 hour.

15. **B.** Use the formula $a^2 + b^2 = c^2$, or $8^2 + 12^2 = c^2$ to find the length of the hypotenuse. This setup gives you $64 + 144 = c^2$. Solving this equation gives you $208 = c^2$. Therefore, $c = \sqrt{208} = 14.42$ feet or 14 feet, 5 inches (to get the 5 inches you multiply 0.42 feet $\times$ 12 inches per foot = 5 inches). To get the triangle's perimeter, add up the three side lengths: 8 feet + 12 feet + 14 feet, 5 inches = 34 feet, 5 inches.

16. **D.** Divide 2 acres by 5 bags to get a per-acre amount of 2.5 bags of salt. Multiply this number times 6⅓ acres to get the total amount of 15.83 bags of salt.

17. **A.** Take 16 ounces $\times$ 0.4 to get 6.4 ounces of pure juice. Add 2 ounces to both the juice and the total amount. Divide the new juice amount (6.4 ounces + 2 ounces = 8.4 ounces) by the new total amount (16 ounces + 2 ounces = 18 ounces) to get 8.4 ounces. Divide that by 18 ounces = 46.7 percent, or about 47 percent.

18. **B.** 75 percent of the straws are blue, so you have a 75-percent chance, or a three out of four chance, of grabbing a blue straw.

19. **C.** You know that in a right triangle, one angle is 90 degrees, so that's the first part of the answer. You also know that the sum of the angles in a right triangle is 180 degrees. Therefore, you can subtract the known angles from that total to find the remaining angle. $180 - 90 - 25 = 65$ degrees.

20. **C.** The reciprocal of 5 is the same as $1/5 = 0.2$ or 20 percent.

21. **A.** The ladder leaning against the wall forms a right triangle, so you can use the Pythagorean theorem (the ladder is the hypotenuse): $a^2 + 16^2 = 22^2$. $a^2 + 256 = 484$. $a^2 = 484 - 256 = 228$. $a = \sqrt{228} = 15.1$ feet.

22. **B.** The total perimeter is 150 feet, which means that the total of one of the long sides plus one of the short sides equals 75 feet. You know that the short side is half the length of the long side, so one side is 25 feet and the other is 50 feet. Another way of looking at it is $x + x + 2x + 2x = 150$; $6x = 150$; $x = 25$. The short side is 25 and the long side is 2×25 or 50 feet. Now you can find the area by just multiplying the base × height: 25 feet × 50 feet = 1,250 square feet.

23. **D.** First, you must figure out the radius. Divide the diameter by 2 to get the radius of 50 centimeters. Next, convert the height of 2.5 meters to 250 centimeters so that everything uses the same scale. Use the formula for volume of a cylinder: $V = h\pi r^2$. $V = 250$ cm $\times \pi \times (50$ cm$^2) = 250$ cm $\times \pi \times 2,500$ cm$^2 = \pi \times 625,000$ cm$^3 = 1,963,495$ cm^3. (If you use 22/7 for π, you get 1,964,287 cm^3.) Now take 1,963,495 cm^3 and divide it by 3,781.4 cm^3 per gallon to get 519 gallons, Choice (D).

24. **B.** Divide the difference by the price of last year's bag to get the percentage change of this year's price from last year's price. $25.11 – $24.75 = $0.36. Divide $0.36 by $24.75 to get 0.0145 or 0.015, which equals 1.5 percent.

25. **C.** The train travels 550 miles in 6 hours or 360 minutes. Divide 550 miles by 360 minutes to get 1.53 miles per minute. Multiply this result by 22 minutes: $1.53 \times 22 = 33.61$ miles.

26. **A.** First, convert the yards to feet. 4 yards = 12 feet and 7 yards = 21 feet. To get the square footage, multiply the length times width, or 12 feet × 21 feet = 252 square feet. Multiply this amount by $3.99 per square foot to get the total price of $1,005.48.

27. **D.** On the first day, they completed $2,900 \times 1/5 = 580$ miles, and on the second they completed $2,900 \times 1/7 = 414$ miles. Subtract both of these distances from the total trip distance to get 1,906 miles left in the trip. Divide this result by the four days that they have left, and the average comes to 476.5 miles per day.

28. **B.** Multiply the available time of 2.7 hours by 8 and then divide by 5 (the number of aircraft available) to get the new amount of search time of 4.32 hours.

29. **D.** Subtract John's regular work week of 40 hours from his actual work week of 53 hours to see how much time he earns overtime for. $53 – 40 = 13$ hours. Next, multiply each amount of time by its appropriate salary. $21.50 \times 40 = $860, and $21.50 \times 1.5 \times 13$ hours = $419.25. Add the two to get $1,279.25.

30. **A.** This one is a simple chain of addition and subtraction: $360 + $50 – $27 – $250 = $133.

Subtest 2: Reading Skills Test

31. **B.**	40. **A.**	49. **C.**
32. **B.**	41. **B.**	50. **C.**
33. **C.**	42. **C.**	51. **A.**
34. **C.**	43. **D.**	52. **B.**
35. **D.**	44. **A.**	53. **D.**
36. **C.**	45. **B.**	54. **D.**
37. **B.**	46. **A.**	55. **B.**
38. **D.**	47. **D.**	56. **C.**
39. **B.**	48. **B.**	57. **A.**

Subtest 3: Mechanical Comprehension Test

58. **B.** The formula used for determining how an inclined plane reduces effort is length of ramp ÷ height of ramp = weight of object ÷ force. In this case, x ÷ 3 feet = 300 pounds ÷ 150 pounds. (The question states that the amount of force must be reduced by half, so that's why you divide 300 by 150.) x ÷ 3 = 300 ÷ 150, so x = 2 × 3 = 6 feet.

59. **C.** To carry the load evenly, you must place the load directly in the middle of the board. Because the board is 12 feet long, you must place the load at the 6-foot mark.

60. **A.** Because wheel B has a smaller circumference, it covers a shorter linear distance than wheel A when turning at the same rate. Therefore, wheel A covers a distance faster than wheel B. You can figure the circumference with the formula of πd or $2\pi r$. The circumference of wheel A is 22π = 69 feet, and the circumference of wheel B is 11π = 34.5 feet. To cover the same amount of distance, wheel B must rotate exactly twice the amount of time as wheel A at the same number of revolutions per minute.

61. **B.** A stationary single pulley allows you to change the direction of force but doesn't result in increased mechanical advantage; therefore, the correct answer is Choice (B).

62. **C.** Gear 1 will turn clockwise, and gear 2 will turn counterclockwise; because gear 2 is the same size as gear 1, both gears will turn at the same speed. Gear 3 will turn clockwise but is half the diameter of gear 2, so gear 3 will rotate at twice the speed of gears 1 and 2. Gear 4 will rotate counterclockwise and is the same size as gear 3, so it will also rotate twice as fast as gears 2 and 1.

63. **D.** The weight of A equals exactly the weight of B. An object will always remain balanced at its center of gravity by definition.

64. **B.** Gear A has 14 teeth and makes 4 revolutions, so it rotates a total of 56 teeth (4 × 14 = 56). Gear B has a total of 20 teeth, so you divide the total teeth movement of 56 by 20 to get 2.8 revolutions.

65. **A.** A *second-class lever* is a lever with force or lifting action applied to one end (handles), a fulcrum at the opposite end, and the load to be carried in the middle.

66. **C.** The number of times a rope moves through the pulley determines the mechanical advantage. In this pulley system, the advantage is 2. Therefore, by applying a 50-pound force on the end of the rope, you can lift a weight that is 100 pounds.

67. **D.** Any of these choices can promote acceleration, so Choice (D) is the best answer.

68. **B.** 2π radians equal 360 degrees. Therefore, 6.28 radians = 360 degrees. Divide both sides of that equation by 6.28 to find that 1 radian equals 57.32 degrees. Finally, take 115 degrees ÷ 57.32 = 2 radians to get the final answer.

69. **A.** *Specific gravity* is the measurement of a fluid in relation to the weight of water. The higher specific gravity of the fluid will cause the float to remain higher, so the answer is Choice (A).

70. **C.** Force equals mass (m) × acceleration (A). Therefore, because the force is equal and opposite, $m \times A = -(m_1 \times A_1)$. This setup gives you the following equation: 100 kilograms × 5 meters per second = $-(150$ kilograms $\times A)$. Simplified, you have 500 kilograms meters per second divided by 150 kilograms, or 3.33 meters per second. Because the raft is going in the opposite direction, the correct answer is –3.33 meters per second.

71. **D.** The linear distance traveled is greater on the outside but the angular distance remains constant.

72. **B.** Under the law of conservation of mass, $m_1V_1 + m_2V_2 = (m_1 + m_2) \times V$. Therefore, 5 kilograms(10 meters per second) + 10 kilograms(–5 meters per second) = (5 kilograms + 10 kilograms) × V. This math works out to 0 = (15 kilograms) × V, so V = 0.

73. **A.** Nothing will happen because in order for any movement to occur, anvil B would have to be placed more than 1.5 meters to the right of the fulcrum.

74. **A.** Pressure equals force divided by area, or $P = F \div A$; you can rearrange this equation to get $P \times A = F$. Therefore, if you plug in the numbers from the problem, 14.7 pounds per square inch × 145 square inches = 2,132 pounds.

75. **C.** The pulley function on the bottom is just to change direction, so you have a mechanical advantage of 2 on top.

76. **B.** Gear 1 rotates clockwise, and gear 2 rotates counterclockwise and turns both gear 3 and gear 5 clockwise. Gear 3 turns gear 4 counterclockwise.

77. **D.** First, you must get the total volume of the tank. Volume is length × width × height, or 5 feet × 2 feet × 3 feet = 30 cubic feet. You know that the weight per cubic foot is 62.5 pounds, so the total weight acting on the bottom of the tank is 1,875 pounds. Now you must figure out the area of only the bottom in square inches. Multiply (12 inches × 5 feet) × (12 inches × 2 feet), which equals 60 inches × 24 inches, or 1,440 square inches. Now simply divide the total weight of 1,875 pounds by 1,440 square inches to get the answer of 1.3 pounds per square inch.

78. **C.** Wheel B has a smaller circumference, so given the same number of revolutions, it will cover a smaller distance. Therefore, wheel A will reach the bottom first.

79. **A.** The formula to use is length of ramp ÷ height of ramp = weight of object ÷ effort. Using the numbers from the problem, you get 10 meters ÷ 3 meters = 100 kilograms ÷ effort. Therefore, cross-multiplying gives you 100 kilograms divided by 3.33 = 30 kilograms.

80. **B.** Because valve A is required to be open for water to flow in, you know that one must be open. Now you need to figure out how full the tank has to be to get to 75 percent. The tank holds a total of 20 inches, so take 0.75 × 20; the answer is 15 inches. If valve B is open, the water will only fill to the 2-inch mark, so that one must remain closed. If valve C is open, water will be able to fill to the 15-inch mark, so that valve must be opened. Valve D must also be open for the water to continue to flow out. The correct answer is Choice (B), valves A, C, and D.

81. **C.** Because gear 1's radius is twice that of gear 2, gear 2 will revolve twice as fast (10 revolutions) in the opposite direction of gear 1. Gear 3 will rotate opposite of gear 2 and the same as gear 1; it will rotate at 5/6 the speed of gear 2 (10 revolutions × 5/6 = 8.33 revolutions).

82. **A.** The vertical component of the momentum is 0 at this point, and the horizontal components remain unchanged.

83. **D.** The volume of water flowing past point B is the same as for points A and C. Due to the restriction of approximately half the width, the velocity approximately doubles as it passes point B. This is the law of conservation of mass, the fundamental principle that results in the Bernoulli equation.

84. **D.** Pulley D is rotating most quickly because it has the smallest circumference relative to pulley B.

85. **C.** You must figure out which brace covers the most area. Because you have a right triangle, you can use the formula $A = 1/2$ base × height. The largest area is $4 \times 4 \div 2 = 8$, which is Choice (C).

86. **B.** The shorter pendulum length B completes the swing the fastest, and the longer pendulum length A will take the longest. Interestingly, the mass of the pendulum doesn't matter!

87. **B.** The resistance in B is the sum of the two resistors and therefore twice the resistance in A and C.

Subtest 4: Spatial Apperception Test

88. **A.**	97. **C.**	106. **B.**
89. **C.**	98. **E.**	107. **C.**
90. **C.**	99. **C.**	108. **C.**
91. **E.**	100. **B.**	109. **E.**
92. **B.**	101. **D.**	110. **B.**
93. **A.**	102. **A.**	111. **B.**
94. **B.**	103. **B.**	112. **E.**
95. **D.**	104. **A.**	
96. **B.**	105. **A.**	

Subtest 5: Aviation and Nautical Information

113. **C.** 1800 is 6:00 p.m. On the 24-hour clock, you continue counting after 12 noon (1300, 1400, and so on) rather than starting over with 1:00 p.m.

114. **B.** The ailerons bank the aircraft. You must, however, use the rudder to develop a coordinated turn.

115. **B.** Again, picture the wings moving through water. When the trailing surface of one aileron goes down, it forces that wing up; the opposite wing (and it depends on the control input from the cockpit) will have the trailing edge of the aileron go up, forcing that wing to go down and creating a rolling motion.

116. **D.** Runways are aligned and numbered by their magnetic heading in most areas. Labeling a runway 36 means the runway is pointed 360 degrees, or north; the opposite runway will be pointed south, or 180 degrees, and therefore will be called runway 18.

117. **D.** When you pull the stick or yoke aft, the elevators — in unison — move their trailing edges up, rotating the nose of the aircraft up around the lateral axis of the aircraft.

118. **A.** One nautical mile equals 1.15 statute miles, and one statute mile equals 0.87 nautical miles. Therefore, 5 statute miles equals 4.35 nautical miles. *Tip:* When converting miles to nautical miles, just add 15 percent. Flip to Chapter 7 for a handy list of these and other important measurement conversions.

119. **B.** Powered boats and optional powered sailboats need running lights. Red is for the *port* (left) side, so that's your answer here. In case you were wondering, green is for the *starboard* (right) side, and any boat under 39.4 feet must have a white light at the stern and on top of the sail mast.

120. **C.** A nautical mile is 6,076 feet.

121. **A.** The *wingspan* is measured from wingtip to wingtip.

122. **D.** The tail section is known as the *empennage*.

123. **D.** A rocket engine is employed in space flight. Why can that engine work in space but not the others? Answer: The others typically get the oxygen for combustion from the atmosphere, while a rocket carries it aboard the vehicle.

124. **B.** A tailwind increases your takeoff roll. Say you need 100 knots airspeed for flight. A tailwind on 10 knots means you have to reach a ground speed of 110 knots to reach the required airspeed for takeoff. The opposite is true for headwinds; if you have a headwind of 10 knots, you have to achieve only 90 knots landspeed to reach your 100 knots takeoff speed. That's why carriers turn into the wind if at all possible.

125. **E.** The *hull* of the ship is the main protective barrier keeping the ship afloat.

126. **D.** Ah, Bernoulli's principle strikes again. If you're sailing on the correct angle, you'll get the expected ram air or *push-off speed,* but you also end up having the wind go across the curved area of the sails, creating lift. Combined with the push-off speed, that extra speed means you can sail faster than the windspeed.

127. **A.** The *windlass* is for handling the anchor chain.

128. **B.** An example of restricted airspace is the airspace over an artillery range or aerial gunnery ranges that aren't in continuous use but can pose a safety hazard to unsuspecting pilots.

129. **D.** When an airfield has no tower, nobody is around to control flight activity. In that situation, you operate by set standards and radio frequencies and keep a keen lookout for other traffic.

130. **C.** IFR stands for *Instrument Flight Rules.* Even though you may have clear skies, you operate under the rules of instrument flying, relying and navigating solely by the use of aircraft instruments.

131. **E.** Setting altimeters to 29.92 keeps flying easy and safe when everyone up there is at a known altitude. It works because everyone's altimeter matches everyone else's.

132. **A.** The *bridge* of a ship is where the ship is controlled.

133. **D.** *Soundings* determine the depth of the water.

134. **B.** Fog forms when warm air moves over a cold mass. Fog is just water droplets that have condensed from the surrounding air.

135. **C.** The *altimeter* provides you with flight information (altitude) and is a flight instrument. The other flight instruments are the airspeed, attitude (or artificial horizon), turn and bank, heading, and vertical speed indicator.

136. **A.** You must operate under IFR and be on an IFR flight plan.

137. **B.** The *tailhook* is lowered before landing at the rear of the aircraft and is designed to catch one of the arresting cables to quickly decelerate and stop the landing aircraft.

138. **A.** A *bulkhead* is a vertical surface — like a wall, but more structural.

139. **B.** Aircraft engineers design aircraft wings to attach at a slight angle, which is called the *angle of incidence.*

140. **A.** The instructions are a request that you aren't obligated to follow if you feel doing so may result in an unsafe environment. You must report to the tower whether you're going to comply; however, if you accept the instructions, you must comply unless the tower gives you permission to deviate.

141. **D.** Military airfields are identified by a green followed by two white lights on the rotating beacon. A civilian airport is one green and one white light on a rotating beacon.

142. **A.** During a high-G maneuver, you can have less blood flow to the brain, although certain actions and devices can minimize this effect. Too much loss of blood flow can result in a blackout.

Subtest 6: Aviation Supplemental Test

143. **B.** $1/2 \div 1/2 = 1$, and $\sqrt{4} = 2$. Therefore this equation is just $1 \times 2 = 2$.

144. **C.** Someone *abdicates* when he or she gives up his or her position of authority or power.

145. **D.** $(5a - 2)(2a + 2)$ gives you $10a^2 + 10a - 4a - 4$. This gives you $10a^2 + 6a - 4$.

146. **A.** First, divide the distances by the average speeds to see how much time John spent on the road each day. $343 \div 55 = 6.24$ hours; $380 \div 63 = 6.03$ hours; $224 \div 61 = 3.67$ hours. Add up the total times: $6.24 + 6.03 + 3.67 = 15.94$ hours. Add up the total mileage: $343 + 380 + 224 = 947$ miles. Divide the total number of miles by the total time: 947 miles $\div 15.94$ hours $= 59.4$ miles per hour.

147. **B.** Newton's third law states that for every action, there is an equal and opposite reaction.

148. **A.** Vitamin D is found in milk.

149. **D.** Saying something is *essential* is the same as saying it's needed.

150. **B.** Vertical angles are congruent; therefore, x can be flipped to the top of the horizontal line and placed on top between y and z. Then $y + x + z$ form a straight line, which equals 180 degrees.

151. **A.** The *quotient* is the result of a division problem. $6 \div 6 = 1$, so Choice (A) is your answer.

152. **C.** This problem is simply multiplying and cancelling as follows: $2x + 4(2x + 7) = 3(2x + 4)$. This equation simplifies to $2x + 8x + 28 = 6x + 12$. Simplifying again, you get $10x + 28 = 6x + 12$ or $10x - 6x = 12 - 28$. Almost there! A little more math gets you to $4x = -16$; $x = -16 \div 4$, or -4.

153. **B.** If gear A rotates clockwise, then gear B will rotate in the opposite direction (counterclockwise) and more quickly than gear A.

154. **D.** According to the article, a new form of life was discovered, and it was a form of bacteria.

155. **C.** A *controversial* subject is one people have strong disagreements about.

156. **C.** Dr. Hoover believes he has found fossils of bacteria from space.

157. **D.** The formula for the area of a circle is πr^2. Therefore, you multiply π by 12^2, or 3.14×144, to get 452.4 square inches. Choice (C) is incorrect because it uses the wrong units.

158. **A.** The formula for volume of a cylinder is $V = \pi r^2 h$. The diameter is 8 inches; therefore, the radius is 4 inches. The height is 2 feet, or 24 inches. $V = \pi 4^2 24 = 3.14 \times 16 \times 24 = 1,205.76$ or 1,206 cubic inches.

159. **B.** The correct answers are the forces of lift, drag, weight (or gravity), and power (or thrust).

160. **D.** Multiply 380 by 0.85 to figure the number of enlisted and then subtract that result from 380 to find out how many officers remain.

161. **B.** Aircraft 1 is 180 degrees at 160 miles per hour. Aircraft 2 is 582 miles per hour at 180 degrees. The closure speed is $582 - 160$ miles per hour, or 422 miles per hour. The distance to be closed is 200 miles. Divide 200 miles by 422 miles per hour, and you have 0.47 hours or 28 minutes.

162. **C.** Multiply length times width times height to find volume. 6 inches $\times$ 6 inches $\times$ 6 inches $= 216$ cubic inches.

163. **A.** If you turn the bolt counterclockwise or to the left, it will go up. Turning the bolt clockwise or to the right will cause it to tighten.

164. **C.** Two three-way switches. A three-way switch enables a person to turn a light fixture on or off from two different locations.

165. **B.** New Year's is the associated holiday, which you can infer from the line "The year is dying in the night."

166. **C.** Making up for wrong or injustice is what *redress* means in this poem.

167. **A.** A *feud* is an ongoing quarrel with bad feelings on both sides.

168. **D.** Pliers are an example of a first class lever.

169. **C.** First, figure out how much fuel you have on board in pounds. 360 gallons × 6.7 pounds per gallon gives you 2,412 pounds. You're burning 812 pounds per hour, and you need a 45-minute fuel reserve, so convert that reserve period to hours by taking 45 ÷ 60 to get 0.75 and then multiply that by the burning rate. 0.75 hours × 812 pounds per hour = 609 pounds for your reserve. Subtract that reserve from the available fuel, and you're left with 1,803 pounds.

     Next, figure how long you need to get to the last known contact point. It's 120 nautical miles away, and you're flying at 150 knots, so divide 120 by 150 to get 0.8 hours for a one-way trip to that point. Double that time for your round trip and multiply the total time (1.6 hours) by your fuel burn of 812 pounds per hour to get your total fuel burn for the trip: 1.6 hours × 812 pounds per hour = 1,300 pounds. Subtract this amount from what you have available: 1,803 pounds − 1,300 pounds = 503 pounds to perform your search. Divide 503 pounds by the fuel burn rate to determine that you can spend 0.7 hours, or 37 minutes searching.

170. **B.** For this problem, you simply have to figure out the area that is covered by the radar. Use the basic formula for the area of a circle, which is $A = \pi r^2$. Plug in the numbers you know: $A = \pi \times 48$ kilometers$^2 = \pi \times 2,304$ kilometers$^2 = 7,238$ square kilometers. Choice (D) is wrong because it uses the wrong units.

171. **B.** The object will be more difficult to raise because moving the fulcrum away from the object means you'll need more force to do the lifting.

172. **D.** All the answers are correct, and therefore Choice (D) is the best answer.

173. **D.** For a rectangle, the perimeter is 2 × (length + width). Plugging in the numbers for this problem, you get 2 × (200 meters + 100 meters), or 2 × 300 meters = 600 meters.

174. **B.** E = the effort needed to lift the load. $E \times 1.5 = 100$ lbs × 1. $E = 100$ lbs ÷ 1.5 = 66.7 lbs.

175. **B.** A single moveable pulley has a mechanical advantage of 2.

176. **A.** The trailing edge of the rudder moves left. This movement forces the tail of the aircraft to move to the right and the nose to move left.

Answers at a Glance

Subtest 1: Math Skills Test

1. C	7. B	13. A	19. C	25. C
2. A	8. A	14. D	20. C	26. A
3. B	9. D	15. B	21. A	27. D
4. A	10. B	16. D	22. B	28. B
5. C	11. B	17. A	23. D	29. D
6. D	12. C	18. B	24. B	30. A

Subtest 2: Reading Skills Test

31. B	37. B	43. D	49. C	55. B
32. B	38. D	44. A	50. C	56. C
33. C	39. B	45. B	51. A	57. A
34. C	40. A	46. A	52. B	
35. D	41. B	47. D	53. D	
36. C	42. C	48. B	54. D	

Subtest 3: Mechanical Comprehension Test

58. B	64. B	70. C	76. B	82. A
59. C	65. A	71. D	77. D	83. D
60. A	66. C	72. B	78. C	84. D
61. B	67. D	73. A	79. A	85. C
62. C	68. B	74. A	80. B	86. B
63. D	69. A	75. C	81. C	87. B

Subtest 4: Spatial Apperception Test

88. A	93. A	98. E	103. B	108. C
89. C	94. B	99. C	104. A	109. E
90. C	95. D	100. B	105. A	110. B
91. E	96. B	101. D	106. B	111. B
92. B	97. C	102. A	107. C	112. E

Subtest 5: Aviation and Nautical Information

113. C	119. B	125. E	131. E	137. B
114. B	120. C	126. D	132. A	138. A
115. B	121. A	127. A	133. D	139. B
116. D	122. D	128. B	134. B	140. A
117. D	123. D	129. D	135. C	141. D
118. A	124. B	130. C	136. A	142. A

Subtest 6: Aviation Supplemental Test

143. B	150. B	157. D	164. C	171. B
144. C	151. A	158. A	165. B	172. D
145. D	152. C	159. B	166. C	173. D
146. A	153. B	160. D	167. A	174. B
147. B	154. D	161. B	168. D	175. B
148. A	155. C	162. C	169. C	176. A
149. D	156. C	163. A	170. B	

Chapter 18

Army Selection Instrument for Flight Training (SIFT) Practice Test

● ●

*T*he Army Selection Instrument for Flight Training (SIFT) test replaced the Alternate Flight Aptitude Selection Test (AFAST) effective January 2013. The SIFT is made up of seven subtests totaling a minimum of 235 questions, and it takes between two and three hours to complete. (*Note:* The practice test in this chapter is a shortened version of a SIFT test. In the affected subtests, we note the time allotted and number of questions for both the full test and for this shorter test.)

The SIFT assesses your mathematical skills and aptitude, ability to extract meaning from written passages, familiarity with mechanical concepts and simple machines, ability to mentally determine an aircraft's orientation in three-dimensional space, and ability to quickly recognize patterns within objects and groups of images. The SIFT also measures your knowledge of aviation terminology, familiarity with aircraft (fixed- and rotary-wing) components and function, and grasp and knowledge of basic flight fundamentals and aerodynamic principles.

According to the Army, examinees with aviation experience typically do well on the SIFT, so consider taking pre-test flight lessons. We cover the ins and outs of this decision in Chapter 11.

You can't use a calculator on the SIFT; the math problems on the exam are designed to be completed without one. You do get a few formulas and scrap paper to help with your calculations. Keep in mind that some of the questions in this practice test are designed to explain a concept and may be difficult to solve. If you can't do the problem without a calculator, go ahead and do it with a calculator but then immediately do the calculation again by hand. This strategy will better prepare you for the actual test.

The SIFT is available only in a computer-based format. The system determines whether you pass or fail immediately, and you receive your score upon completion of the test. Possible scores range from 20 to 80, with an average of 50. The current minimum qualifying score to apply for the Army's aviation program is 40. Because the SIFT is a new test and is still being validated as of this writing, the minimum score needed to pass, as well as certain subtests, may change to correspond with the Army's aviation accessions requirements.

If you pass, you're no longer authorized to retake the SIFT, so if you barely pass and want to try again to beef up your score, you're out of luck. If you fail to attain a minimum qualifying score on your first attempt, you may retake the SIFT once, no earlier than the 181st day following the previous attempt. (So if you fail your first attempt on January 1, the earliest you can retake the test is July 1.) If you fail on your second attempt, you can't take the SIFT again.

SIFT Test Structure

The SIFT is designed to predict success in aviation training. The test comprises seven subtests and takes between two and three hours (including administrative time and an optional exam break) to complete. Here's how the subtests of the SIFT break down:

Subtest	# of items	Time
1. Simple Drawings (SD)	100	2 minutes
2. Hidden Figures (HF)	50	5 minutes
3. Army Aviation Information Test (AAIT)	40	30 minutes
4. Spatial Apperception Test (SAT)	25	10 minutes
5. Reading Comprehension Test (RCT)	20	30 minutes
6. Math Skills Test (MST)	Varies	40 minutes
7. Mechanical Comprehension Test (MCT)	Varies	15 minutes

Answer Sheet

For Subtests 1 through 6 of the exam, use the following answer sheets and fill in the answer bubble for the corresponding number, using a #2 pencil. If a subtest has fewer than 60 questions, just leave the extras blank.

Subtest 1: Simple Drawings

1. Ⓐ Ⓑ Ⓒ Ⓓ Ⓔ	6. Ⓐ Ⓑ Ⓒ Ⓓ Ⓔ	11. Ⓐ Ⓑ Ⓒ Ⓓ Ⓔ	16. Ⓐ Ⓑ Ⓒ Ⓓ Ⓔ	21. Ⓐ Ⓑ Ⓒ Ⓓ Ⓔ
2. Ⓐ Ⓑ Ⓒ Ⓓ Ⓔ	7. Ⓐ Ⓑ Ⓒ Ⓓ Ⓔ	12. Ⓐ Ⓑ Ⓒ Ⓓ Ⓔ	17. Ⓐ Ⓑ Ⓒ Ⓓ Ⓔ	22. Ⓐ Ⓑ Ⓒ Ⓓ Ⓔ
3. Ⓐ Ⓑ Ⓒ Ⓓ Ⓔ	8. Ⓐ Ⓑ Ⓒ Ⓓ Ⓔ	13. Ⓐ Ⓑ Ⓒ Ⓓ Ⓔ	18. Ⓐ Ⓑ Ⓒ Ⓓ Ⓔ	23. Ⓐ Ⓑ Ⓒ Ⓓ Ⓔ
4. Ⓐ Ⓑ Ⓒ Ⓓ Ⓔ	9. Ⓐ Ⓑ Ⓒ Ⓓ Ⓔ	14. Ⓐ Ⓑ Ⓒ Ⓓ Ⓔ	19. Ⓐ Ⓑ Ⓒ Ⓓ Ⓔ	24. Ⓐ Ⓑ Ⓒ Ⓓ Ⓔ
5. Ⓐ Ⓑ Ⓒ Ⓓ Ⓔ	10. Ⓐ Ⓑ Ⓒ Ⓓ Ⓔ	15. Ⓐ Ⓑ Ⓒ Ⓓ Ⓔ	20. Ⓐ Ⓑ Ⓒ Ⓓ Ⓔ	25. Ⓐ Ⓑ Ⓒ Ⓓ Ⓔ

Subtest 2: Hidden Figures

26. Ⓐ Ⓑ Ⓒ Ⓓ Ⓔ	31. Ⓐ Ⓑ Ⓒ Ⓓ Ⓔ	36. Ⓐ Ⓑ Ⓒ Ⓓ Ⓔ
27. Ⓐ Ⓑ Ⓒ Ⓓ Ⓔ	32. Ⓐ Ⓑ Ⓒ Ⓓ Ⓔ	37. Ⓐ Ⓑ Ⓒ Ⓓ Ⓔ
28. Ⓐ Ⓑ Ⓒ Ⓓ Ⓔ	33. Ⓐ Ⓑ Ⓒ Ⓓ Ⓔ	38. Ⓐ Ⓑ Ⓒ Ⓓ Ⓔ
29. Ⓐ Ⓑ Ⓒ Ⓓ Ⓔ	34. Ⓐ Ⓑ Ⓒ Ⓓ Ⓔ	39. Ⓐ Ⓑ Ⓒ Ⓓ Ⓔ
30. Ⓐ Ⓑ Ⓒ Ⓓ Ⓔ	35. Ⓐ Ⓑ Ⓒ Ⓓ Ⓔ	40. Ⓐ Ⓑ Ⓒ Ⓓ Ⓔ

Subtest 3: Army Aviation Information Test

41. Ⓐ Ⓑ Ⓒ Ⓓ Ⓔ	46. Ⓐ Ⓑ Ⓒ Ⓓ Ⓔ	51. Ⓐ Ⓑ Ⓒ Ⓓ Ⓔ	56. Ⓐ Ⓑ Ⓒ Ⓓ Ⓔ
42. Ⓐ Ⓑ Ⓒ Ⓓ Ⓔ	47. Ⓐ Ⓑ Ⓒ Ⓓ Ⓔ	52. Ⓐ Ⓑ Ⓒ Ⓓ Ⓔ	57. Ⓐ Ⓑ Ⓒ Ⓓ Ⓔ
43. Ⓐ Ⓑ Ⓒ Ⓓ Ⓔ	48. Ⓐ Ⓑ Ⓒ Ⓓ Ⓔ	53. Ⓐ Ⓑ Ⓒ Ⓓ Ⓔ	58. Ⓐ Ⓑ Ⓒ Ⓓ Ⓔ
44. Ⓐ Ⓑ Ⓒ Ⓓ Ⓔ	49. Ⓐ Ⓑ Ⓒ Ⓓ Ⓔ	54. Ⓐ Ⓑ Ⓒ Ⓓ Ⓔ	59. Ⓐ Ⓑ Ⓒ Ⓓ Ⓔ
45. Ⓐ Ⓑ Ⓒ Ⓓ Ⓔ	50. Ⓐ Ⓑ Ⓒ Ⓓ Ⓔ	55. Ⓐ Ⓑ Ⓒ Ⓓ Ⓔ	60. Ⓐ Ⓑ Ⓒ Ⓓ Ⓔ

Subtest 4: Spatial Apperception Test

61. Ⓐ Ⓑ Ⓒ Ⓓ Ⓔ	66. Ⓐ Ⓑ Ⓒ Ⓓ Ⓔ	71. Ⓐ Ⓑ Ⓒ Ⓓ Ⓔ	76. Ⓐ Ⓑ Ⓒ Ⓓ Ⓔ	81. Ⓐ Ⓑ Ⓒ Ⓓ Ⓔ
62. Ⓐ Ⓑ Ⓒ Ⓓ Ⓔ	67. Ⓐ Ⓑ Ⓒ Ⓓ Ⓔ	72. Ⓐ Ⓑ Ⓒ Ⓓ Ⓔ	77. Ⓐ Ⓑ Ⓒ Ⓓ Ⓔ	82. Ⓐ Ⓑ Ⓒ Ⓓ Ⓔ
63. Ⓐ Ⓑ Ⓒ Ⓓ Ⓔ	68. Ⓐ Ⓑ Ⓒ Ⓓ Ⓔ	73. Ⓐ Ⓑ Ⓒ Ⓓ Ⓔ	78. Ⓐ Ⓑ Ⓒ Ⓓ Ⓔ	83. Ⓐ Ⓑ Ⓒ Ⓓ Ⓔ
64. Ⓐ Ⓑ Ⓒ Ⓓ Ⓔ	69. Ⓐ Ⓑ Ⓒ Ⓓ Ⓔ	74. Ⓐ Ⓑ Ⓒ Ⓓ Ⓔ	79. Ⓐ Ⓑ Ⓒ Ⓓ Ⓔ	84. Ⓐ Ⓑ Ⓒ Ⓓ Ⓔ
65. Ⓐ Ⓑ Ⓒ Ⓓ Ⓔ	70. Ⓐ Ⓑ Ⓒ Ⓓ Ⓔ	75. Ⓐ Ⓑ Ⓒ Ⓓ Ⓔ	80. Ⓐ Ⓑ Ⓒ Ⓓ Ⓔ	85. Ⓐ Ⓑ Ⓒ Ⓓ Ⓔ

Subtest 5: Reading Comprehension Test

86. Ⓐ Ⓑ Ⓒ Ⓓ
87. Ⓐ Ⓑ Ⓒ Ⓓ
88. Ⓐ Ⓑ Ⓒ Ⓓ
89. Ⓐ Ⓑ Ⓒ Ⓓ
90. Ⓐ Ⓑ Ⓒ Ⓓ
91. Ⓐ Ⓑ Ⓒ Ⓓ
92. Ⓐ Ⓑ Ⓒ Ⓓ
93. Ⓐ Ⓑ Ⓒ Ⓓ

94. Ⓐ Ⓑ Ⓒ Ⓓ
95. Ⓐ Ⓑ Ⓒ Ⓓ
96. Ⓐ Ⓑ Ⓒ Ⓓ
97. Ⓐ Ⓑ Ⓒ Ⓓ
98. Ⓐ Ⓑ Ⓒ Ⓓ
99. Ⓐ Ⓑ Ⓒ Ⓓ
100. Ⓐ Ⓑ Ⓒ Ⓓ
101. Ⓐ Ⓑ Ⓒ Ⓓ

102. Ⓐ Ⓑ Ⓒ Ⓓ
103. Ⓐ Ⓑ Ⓒ Ⓓ
104. Ⓐ Ⓑ Ⓒ Ⓓ
105. Ⓐ Ⓑ Ⓒ Ⓓ

Subtest 6: Math Skills Test

106. Ⓐ Ⓑ Ⓒ Ⓓ
107. Ⓐ Ⓑ Ⓒ Ⓓ
108. Ⓐ Ⓑ Ⓒ Ⓓ
109. Ⓐ Ⓑ Ⓒ Ⓓ
110. Ⓐ Ⓑ Ⓒ Ⓓ
111. Ⓐ Ⓑ Ⓒ Ⓓ
112. Ⓐ Ⓑ Ⓒ Ⓓ
113. Ⓐ Ⓑ Ⓒ Ⓓ

114. Ⓐ Ⓑ Ⓒ Ⓓ
115. Ⓐ Ⓑ Ⓒ Ⓓ
116. Ⓐ Ⓑ Ⓒ Ⓓ
117. Ⓐ Ⓑ Ⓒ Ⓓ
118. Ⓐ Ⓑ Ⓒ Ⓓ
119. Ⓐ Ⓑ Ⓒ Ⓓ
120. Ⓐ Ⓑ Ⓒ Ⓓ
121. Ⓐ Ⓑ Ⓒ Ⓓ

122. Ⓐ Ⓑ Ⓒ Ⓓ
123. Ⓐ Ⓑ Ⓒ Ⓓ
124. Ⓐ Ⓑ Ⓒ Ⓓ
125. Ⓐ Ⓑ Ⓒ Ⓓ
126. Ⓐ Ⓑ Ⓒ Ⓓ
127. Ⓐ Ⓑ Ⓒ Ⓓ
128. Ⓐ Ⓑ Ⓒ Ⓓ
129. Ⓐ Ⓑ Ⓒ Ⓓ

130. Ⓐ Ⓑ Ⓒ Ⓓ
131. Ⓐ Ⓑ Ⓒ Ⓓ
132. Ⓐ Ⓑ Ⓒ Ⓓ
133. Ⓐ Ⓑ Ⓒ Ⓓ
134. Ⓐ Ⓑ Ⓒ Ⓓ
135. Ⓐ Ⓑ Ⓒ Ⓓ

Subtest 7: Mechanical Comprehension Test

136. Ⓐ Ⓑ Ⓒ Ⓓ
137. Ⓐ Ⓑ Ⓒ Ⓓ
138. Ⓐ Ⓑ Ⓒ Ⓓ
139. Ⓐ Ⓑ Ⓒ Ⓓ
140. Ⓐ Ⓑ Ⓒ Ⓓ
141. Ⓐ Ⓑ Ⓒ Ⓓ
142. Ⓐ Ⓑ Ⓒ Ⓓ
143. Ⓐ Ⓑ Ⓒ Ⓓ

144. Ⓐ Ⓑ Ⓒ Ⓓ
145. Ⓐ Ⓑ Ⓒ Ⓓ
146. Ⓐ Ⓑ Ⓒ Ⓓ
147. Ⓐ Ⓑ Ⓒ Ⓓ
148. Ⓐ Ⓑ Ⓒ Ⓓ
149. Ⓐ Ⓑ Ⓒ Ⓓ
150. Ⓐ Ⓑ Ⓒ Ⓓ
151. Ⓐ Ⓑ Ⓒ Ⓓ

152. Ⓐ Ⓑ Ⓒ Ⓓ
153. Ⓐ Ⓑ Ⓒ Ⓓ
154. Ⓐ Ⓑ Ⓒ Ⓓ
155. Ⓐ Ⓑ Ⓒ Ⓓ
156. Ⓐ Ⓑ Ⓒ Ⓓ
157. Ⓐ Ⓑ Ⓒ Ⓓ
158. Ⓐ Ⓑ Ⓒ Ⓓ
159. Ⓐ Ⓑ Ⓒ Ⓓ

160. Ⓐ Ⓑ Ⓒ Ⓓ
161. Ⓐ Ⓑ Ⓒ Ⓓ
162. Ⓐ Ⓑ Ⓒ Ⓓ
163. Ⓐ Ⓑ Ⓒ Ⓓ
164. Ⓐ Ⓑ Ⓒ Ⓓ
165. Ⓐ Ⓑ Ⓒ Ⓓ

Subtest 1
Simple Drawings

This subtest tests your ability to recognize which simple figure within a group of five simple figures does not belong with the others. This type of question is pretty easy, but most test-takers have a hard time completing all the questions in this subtest. Individual question completion speed is critical to your success on this subtest.

Time: 2 minutes for 100 questions. In this practice test, we give you 30 seconds for 25 questions.

Directions: With each question, you see five figures, lettered A, B, C, D, and E. Identify which simple figure does not belong with the others.

Go on to next page

6.

| A | B | C | D | E |

7.

| A | B | C | D | E |

8.

| A | B | C | D | E |

9.

| A | B | C | D | E |

10.

| A | B | C | D | E |

11.

| A | B | C | D | E |

12.

| A | B | C | D | E |

Go on to next page

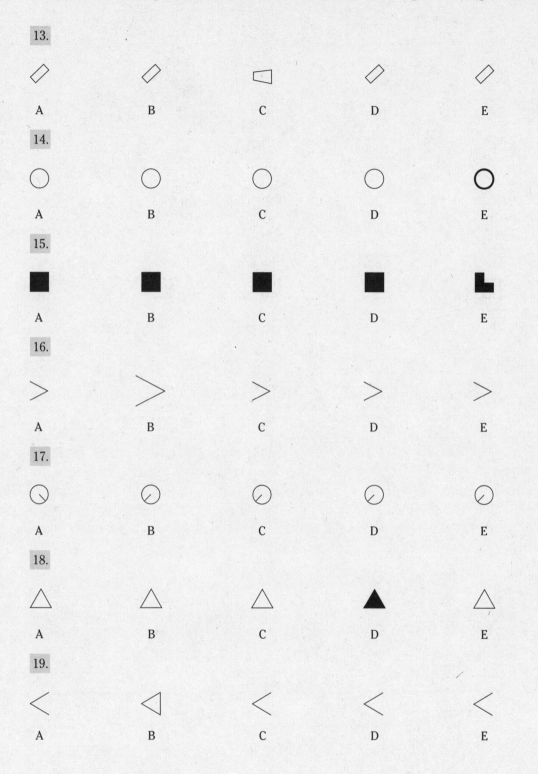

13.

A   B   C   D   E

14.

A   B   C   D   E

15.

A   B   C   D   E

16.

A   B   C   D   E

17.

A   B   C   D   E

18.

A   B   C   D   E

19.

A   B   C   D   E

Go on to next page

20.

Subtest 2

Hidden Figures

This subtest tests your ability to recognize a simple figure in a complex drawing.

Time: 5 minutes for 50 questions. In this practice test, we give you 1 minute 30 seconds for 15 questions.

Directions: Before each question, you see five figures, lettered A, B, C, D, and E. Below the figures are numbered drawings; for each drawing, identify which simple figure is in the complex drawing.

26.–30.

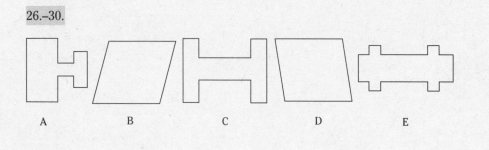

A   B   C   D   E

26.   27.

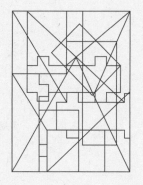   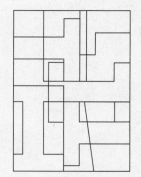

Go on to next page

28.

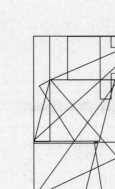

30.

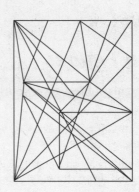

29.

Go on to next page ⟹

31.–35.

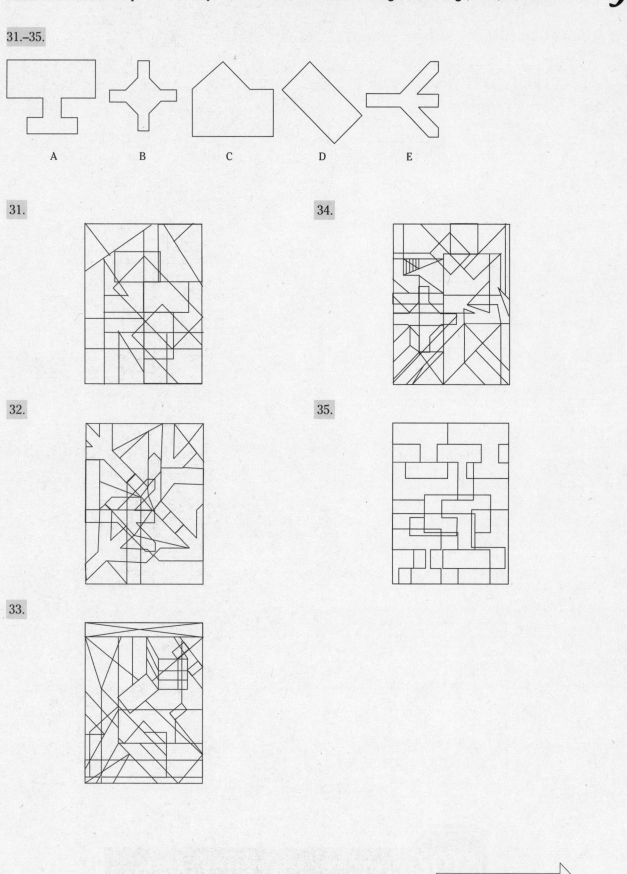

31.

32.

33.

34.

35.

Go on to next page

36.–40.

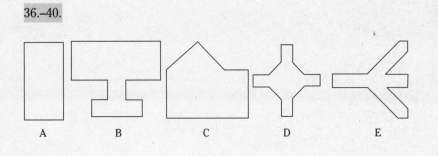

A   B   C   D   E

36.

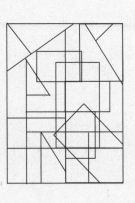

39.

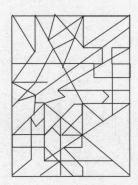

37.

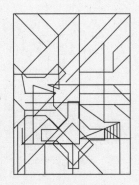

40.

40 image

38.

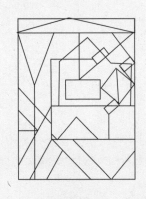

STOP DO NOT TURN THE PAGE UNTIL TOLD TO DO SO.

Subtest 3
Army Aviation Information Test

This subtest deals with your general understanding of the principles of helicopter flight.

Time: 30 minutes for 40 questions. In this practice test, we give you 15 minutes for 20 questions.

Directions: Each question contains an incomplete statement followed by five choices. Select the choice that best completes the statement.

41. During a hover, a helicopter tends to drift to the right. To compensate for this effect, some helicopters

    (A) Have the tail rotor tilted to the left

    (B) Have the tail rotor tilted to the right

    (C) Have the rotor mast rigged to the left side

    (D) Are typically loaded with an aft CG

    (E) Both Choice (A) and Choice (C)

42. The four forces that act on an aircraft in flight are

    (A) Lift, weight, thrust, and drag

    (B) Lift, mass, propulsion, and resistance

    (C) Aerodynamics, mass, propulsion, and drag

    (D) Lift magnitude, mass, thrust, and drag

    (E) Roll, pitch, yaw, and magnitude

43. A helicopter's cyclic control is a mechanical linkage used to change the pitch of the main rotor blades

    (A) All at the same time

    (B) At a selected point in its circular pathway

    (C) Proportionally to the engine's rpm

    (D) In conjunction with the desired speed

    (E) For vertical flight only

44. The lift differential that exists between the advancing main rotor blade and the retreating main rotor blade is known as

    (A) Coriolis effect

    (B) Dissymmetry of lift

    (C) Translating tendency

    (D) Translational lift

    (E) Lift vector

45. The primary purpose of the tail rotor system is to

    (A) Assist in making coordinated turns

    (B) Maintain heading during forward flight

    (C) Deflect adverse yaw

    (D) Counteract the torque effect of the main rotor

    (E) Allow coordinated flight

46. The upward bending of the rotor blades resulting from the combination of lift and centrifugal forces is known as

    (A) Translational lift

    (B) Coning

    (C) Blade flapping

    (D) Inertia

    (E) Translating tendency

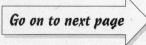
Go on to next page

47. During a hover, the helicopter tends to drift in the direction of tail rotor thrust. This movement is called

    (A) Flapping

    (B) Coriolis force

    (C) Transverse flow effect

    (D) Translating tendency

    (E) Gyroscopic precession

48. Which of the following does not affect density altitude?

    (A) Temperature

    (B) Altitude

    (C) Atmospheric pressure

    (D) Wind velocity

    (E) Humidity

49. What action should a helicopter pilot take if engine failure occurs at altitude?

    (A) Raise the collective pitch.

    (B) Aft cyclic and increase collective pitch.

    (C) Increase the throttle.

    (D) Lower the collective pitch control to maintain rotor rpm.

    (E) Reduce cyclic back pressure.

50. A helicopter center of gravity is usually located

    (A) Directly below the main fuel tank

    (B) In front of the main rotor mast

    (C) Directly above the main fuel tank

    (D) In the rear of the main rotor mast

    (E) A short distance fore and aft of the main rotor mast

51. Foot pedals in the helicopter crew member station enable the pilot to

    (A) Control torque effect

    (B) Regulate flight speed

    (C) Regulate rate of decent

    (D) Regulate rate of climb

    (E) Stabilize rotor rpm

52. Gyroscopic precision happens when

    (A) A force applied to a spinning disc has its effect 90 degrees later in the opposite direction and plane of rotation

    (B) A force applied to a spinning disc has its effect 180 degrees later in the direction and plane of rotation

    (C) A force applied to a spinning disc has its effect 90 degrees later in the direction and plane of rotation

    (D) A force applied to a spinning disc has its effect 180 degrees later in the opposite direction and plane of rotation

    (E) None of the above

53. *Translational lift* is

    (A) The lift needed to initially leave the ground

    (B) The cushioning effect encountered in a low hover

    (C) Lift developed from forward airspeed

    (D) The additional lift gained when the helicopter leaves the disturbed air from its rotor downwash

    (E) The decreased lift suffered when the helicopter leaves its downwash

54. Ground effect is most likely to result in which problem?

    (A) Inability to get airborne on a smooth surface

    (B) Settling to the surface abruptly during landing

    (C) Becoming airborne before reaching appropriate takeoff speed

    (D) The creation of wake turbulence

    (E) An increased amount of drag

Go on to next page

55. *Lift differential* (the result of one rotor losing lift because of an advancing aircraft's forward airspeed) that exists between the advancing main rotor and the retreating rotor blade is known as

    (A) Translating tendency

    (B) Transverse flow effect

    (C) Unequal lift effect

    (D) Retreating blade stall

    (E) Coriolis effect

56. The combination of factors that reduces helicopter performance the most is

    (A) High density altitude, heavy gross weight, and calm or no wind

    (B) Low density altitude, light gross weight, and moderate-to-strong wind

    (C) Low density altitude, light gross weight, and calm or no wind

    (D) Low density altitude, heavy gross weight, and moderate-to-strong wind

    (E) High density altitude, light gross weight, and moderate-to-strong wind

57. The cyclic controls the

    (A) Gyroscopic precession of the rotor blade

    (B) Torque effect

    (C) Engine rpm

    (D) Direction of the tilt of the main rotor

    (E) Pitch of the helicopter

58. The degree of movement of an aircraft around its lateral axis is known as

    (A) Yaw

    (B) Roll

    (C) Bank

    (D) Pitch

    (E) Sideslip

59. The method of control by which the pitch of all main rotor blades is varied equally and simultaneously is the

    (A) Torsion control

    (B) Collective control

    (C) Cyclic control

    (D) Tail rotor control

    (E) Throttle control

60. *Lift* is the upward force created by

    (A) Airflow as it passes around an airfoil

    (B) Blade flapping

    (C) Torque

    (D) Thrust

    (E) Airspeed

STOP DO NOT TURN THE PAGE UNTIL TOLD TO DO SO.

Subtest 4

Spatial Apperception Test

This subtest checks your ability to match external and internal views of an aircraft when you're given visual information about the aircraft's direction and orientation relative to the ground. Each question provides a view from inside the cockpit; you then have to match that diagram to one of five external views. It is assumed that when you look at the exterior view, your position is south of the aircraft looking north.

Time: 10 minutes for 25 questions

Directions: In each question, you see a pilot's view from the crew member station. Next, you see a series of five exterior, three-dimensional viewpoints of various aircraft, and you must select which aircraft best represents what's shown in the first picture.

61.

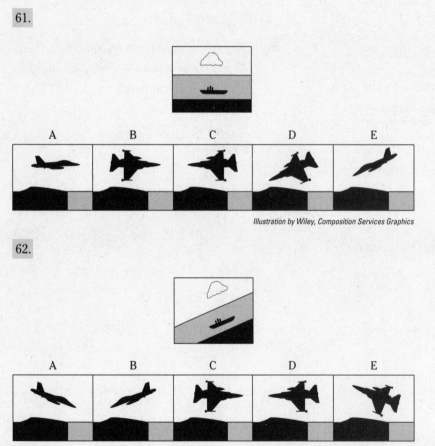

Illustration by Wiley, Composition Services Graphics

62.

Illustration by Wiley, Composition Services Graphics

Go on to next page

63.

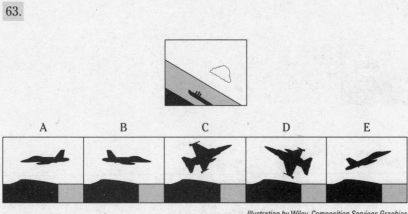

Illustration by Wiley, Composition Services Graphics

64.

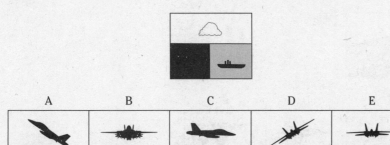

Illustration by Wiley, Composition Services Graphics

65.

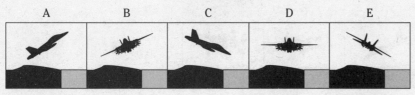

Illustration by Wiley, Composition Services Graphics

Go on to next page

66.

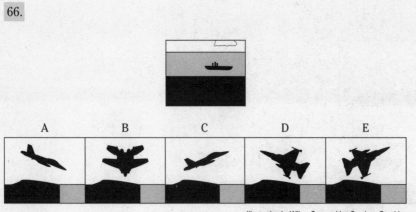

Illustration by Wiley, Composition Services Graphics

67.

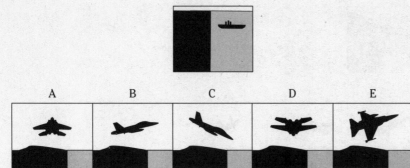

Illustration by Wiley, Composition Services Graphics

68.

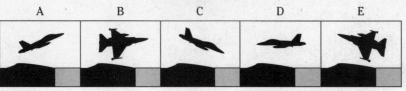

Illustration by Wiley, Composition Services Graphics

Go on to next page

69.

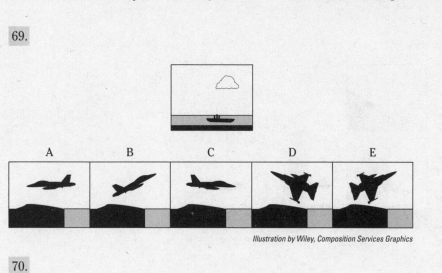

A   B   C   D   E

Illustration by Wiley, Composition Services Graphics

70.

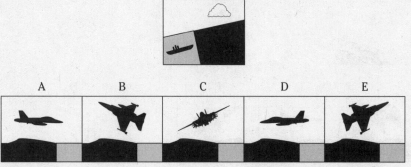

A   B   C   D   E

Illustration by Wiley, Composition Services Graphics

71.

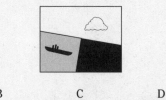

A   B   C   D   E

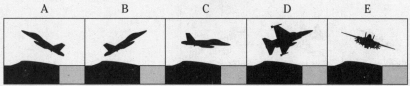

Illustration by Wiley, Composition Services Graphics

Go on to next page

72.

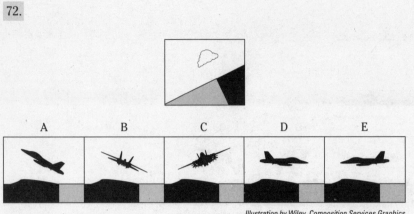

Illustration by Wiley, Composition Services Graphics

73.

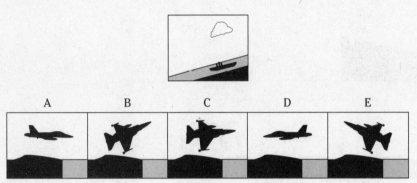

Illustration by Wiley, Composition Services Graphics

74.

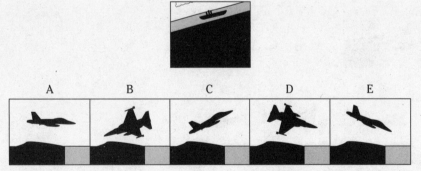

Illustration by Wiley, Composition Services Graphics

Go on to next page

75.

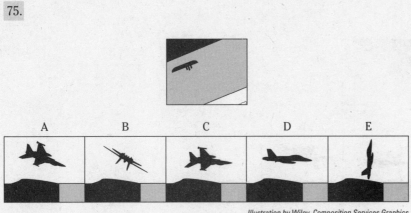

Illustration by Wiley, Composition Services Graphics

76.

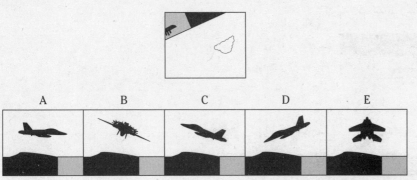

Illustration by Wiley, Composition Services Graphics

77.

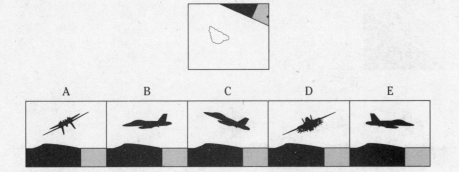

Illustration by Wiley, Composition Services Graphics

Go on to next page

78.

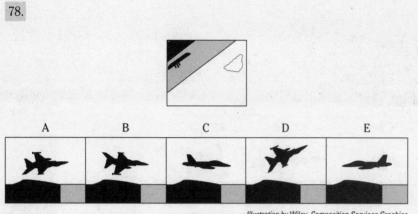

Illustration by Wiley, Composition Services Graphics

79.

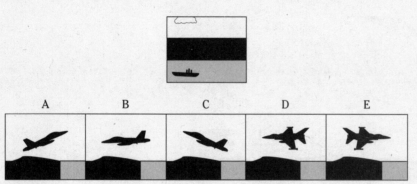

Illustration by Wiley, Composition Services Graphics

80.

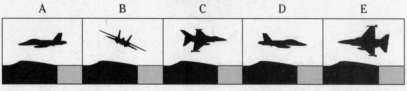

Illustration by Wiley, Composition Services Graphics

Go on to next page

81.

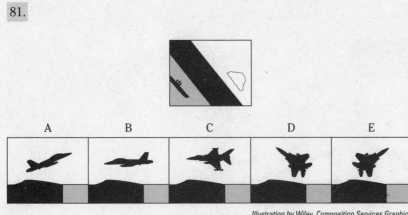

Illustration by Wiley, Composition Services Graphics

82.

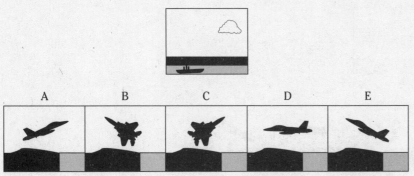

Illustration by Wiley, Composition Services Graphics

83.

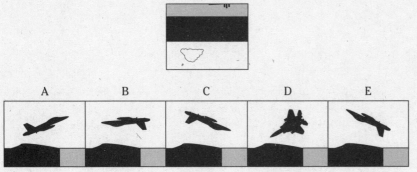

Illustration by Wiley, Composition Services Graphics

Go on to next page

84.

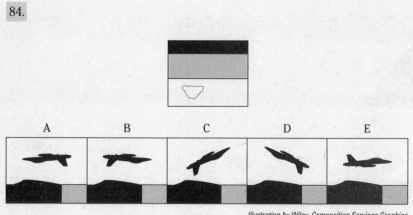

Illustration by Wiley, Composition Services Graphics

85.

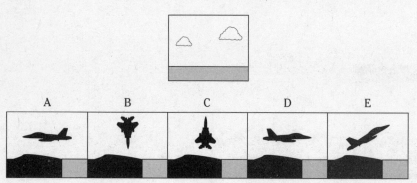

Illustration by Wiley, Composition Services Graphics

STOP DO NOT TURN THE PAGE UNTIL TOLD TO DO SO.

Subtest 5

Reading Comprehension Test

This subtest asks you to make inferences based on given text passages. Remember that more than one answer choice may look accurate; your job is to choose the one that can be derived only from the given information.

Time: 30 minutes for 20 questions

Directions: Read the short passages and pick the most-correct answers for the corresponding questions.

The state of Georgia, which has 159 counties, is located within the borders of the United States of America. Georgia is bordered by South Carolina to the east, North Carolina and Tennessee to the north, Alabama to the west, and Florida to the south. On its southeastern coast, Georgia is bordered by the Atlantic Ocean.

86. How many states share a border with Georgia?

(A) 1

(B) 5

(C) 4

(D) 2

87. What ocean borders Georgia?

(A) Pacific

(B) Atlantic

(C) Indian

(D) Gulf of Mexico

Dispensing with the traditional model of an orchestra led by a conductor, Orpheus Chamber Orchestra sets out to achieve excellence through teambuilding and collaboration. For each piece to be performed by Orpheus, an elected committee of musicians selects a concert-master, and each instrumental section chooses a representative. These chosen representatives (the *core group*) develop an overall interpretive approach to the music (including tempi, phrasing, and articulation) before the entire orchestra comes together to rehearse. The core also structures the rehearsal process for the entire orchestra. This setup provides clear leadership while ensuring that every member has a real stake in the artistic outcome of every piece the orchestra performs.

88. According to the passage,

(A) Orpheus uses the traditional model of an orchestra led by a conductor.

(B) Orpheus sells many thousands of music CDs every year.

(C) Orpheus is not led by a conductor.

(D) A conductor is essential for an orchestra to function properly.

89. According to the passage, the overall interpretive approach to the music includes

(A) Core, phrasing, and articulation

(B) Phrasing, metrics, and feeling

(C) Tempi, phrasing, and articulation

(D) Tempi, phrasing, and rehearsal

Go on to next page

Many seasoned racers consider one race to be the Mount Everest of offshore ocean racing. This competition is the 628-nautical-mile Sydney Hobart Yacht Race. Nicknamed "hell on high water" by sailors, this race offers participants a taste of both hell and high water because the racers are required to cross the eastern end of the infamous Bass Strait, which lies between the coasts of the state of Victoria, Australia, and the island of Tasmania.

90. How long is the Sydney Hobart Yacht Race?

(A) 350 miles

(B) 4,000 kilometers

(C) 600 meters

(D) 628 nautical miles

91. The Bass Strait is located between

(A) New South Wales and Tasmania

(B) Victoria, Australia and New Zealand

(C) Tasmania and Victoria, Australia

(D) Antarctica and Tasmania

The district of country known geographically as Upper California is bounded on the north by Oregon, the 42nd degree of north latitude being the boundary line between the two territories; on the east by the Rocky Mountains and the Sierra de los Mimbres, a continuation of the same range; on the south by Sonora and Old or Lower California; and on the west by the Pacific Ocean. Its extent from north to south is about 700 miles and from east to west [is] from 600 to 800 miles, with an area of about 400,000 square miles. A small portion only of this extensive territory is fertile or inhabitable by civilized man, and this portion consists chiefly in the strip of country along the Pacific Ocean, about 700 miles in length and from 100 to 150 miles in breadth, bounded on the east by the Sierra Nevada and on the west by the Pacific. In speaking of Upper California, this strip of country is what is generally referred to.

92. Upper California is bounded on the north by what territory?

(A) Washington

(B) Oregon

(C) Lower California

(D) Pacific

94. What body of water forms the western boundary of Upper California?

(A) Gulf of California

(B) Pacific Ocean

(C) Sierra de los Mimbres

(D) Salton Sea

93. The length of Upper California from north to south is approximately how many miles?

(A) 600

(B) 150

(C) 800

(D) 700

Go on to next page

The largest river of Upper California is the Colorado or Red, which has a course of about 1,000 miles and empties into the Gulf of California in latitude about 32 degrees north. But little is known of the region through which this stream flows. The report of trappers, however, is that the river is canoned between high mountains and precipices a large portion of its course, and that its banks and the country generally through which it flows are arid, sandy, and barren. Green and Grand Rivers are its principal upper tributaries, both of which rise in the Rocky Mountains, and within the territories of the United States. The Gila is its lowest and largest branch, emptying into the Colorado just above its mouth. Sevier and Virgin Rivers are also tributaries of the Colorado. Mary's River rises near latitude 42 degrees north and has a course of about 400 miles, when its waters sink in the sands of the desert. This river is not laid down on any map which I have seen. The Sacramento and San Joaquin Rivers each have a course of from 300 to 400 miles, the first flowing from the north and the last from the south, and both emptying into the Bay of St. Francisco at the same point. They water the large and fertile valley lying between the Sierra Nevada and the coast range of mountains. I subjoin a description of the valley and river San Joaquin, from the pen of a gentleman (Dr. Marsh) who has explored the river from its source to its mouth.

95. Into what body of water does the Colorado River empty?

(A) Gulf of California

(B) Green River

(C) Bay of St. Francisco

(D) Pacific Ocean

96. The largest branch of the Red River is the

(A) Virgin River

(B) Gila River

(C) Green River

(D) San Joaquin River

97. Dr. Marsh explored what body of water?

(A) Bay of St. Francisco

(B) Sierra Nevada

(C) San Joaquin River

(D) Sevier River

Go on to next page

The principal mountains west of the eastern boundary of California (the Rocky Mountains) are the Bear River, Wahsatch, Utah, the Sierra Nevada, and the Coast range. The Wahsatch Mountains form the eastern rim of the great interior basin. There are numerous ranges in this desert basin, all of which run north and south and are separated from each other by spacious and barren valleys and plains. The Sierra Nevada range is of greater elevation than the Rocky Mountains. The summits of the most elevated peaks are covered with perpetual snow. This and the Coast range run nearly parallel with the shore of the Pacific. The first is from 100 to 200 miles from the Pacific, and the last [is] from 40 to 60 miles. The valley between them is the most fertile portion of California.

98. The eastern rim of the great interior basin is comprised of the

    (A) Rocky Mountains

    (B) Sierra Nevada

    (C) Bear River

    (D) Wahsatch Mountains

99. The summits of the most elevated peaks of the Sierra Nevada range are covered with

    (A) Perpetual snow

    (B) Fertile plains

    (C) Rocks

    (D) Meadows

100. The Sierra Nevada range parallels what other range?

    (A) Rocky Mountains

    (B) Coast

    (C) Great Interior

    (D) Wahsatch

Upper California was discovered in 1548 by Cabrillo, a Spanish navigator. In 1578, the northern portion of it was visited by Sir Francis Drake, who called it New Albion. It was first colonized by the Spaniards in 1768 and formed a province of Mexico until after the revolution in that country. There have been numerous revolutions and civil wars in California within the last 20 years, but up to the conquest of the country by the United States in 1846, Mexican authority has generally been exercised over it.

101. The United States' conquest of Upper California occurred in what year?

    (A) 1846

    (B) 1548

    (C) 1768

    (D) 1492

102. Upper California was discovered by

    (A) Sir Francis Drake

    (B) New Albion

    (C) A Dutch navigator

    (D) Cabrillo

103. Upper California was first colonized by

    (A) Mexicans

    (B) Spaniards

    (C) Americans

    (D) The English

Go on to next page

The Indians reside about two hundred yards distant from the above-mentioned edifice. This place is called the rancheria. Most of the missions are made up of very reduced quarters built with mud-bricks, forming streets, while in others the Indians have been allowed to follow their customs, their dwellings being a sort of huts in a conical shape, which at the most do not exceed four yards in diameter, and the top of the cone may be elevated three yards. They are built of rough sticks, covered with bulrushes or grass in such a manner as to completely protect the inhabitants from all the inclemencies of the weather. Opposite the rancherias, and near to the mission, is to be found a small garrison, with proportionate rooms, for a corporal and five soldiers with their families. This small garrison is quite sufficient to prevent any attempt of the Indians from taking effect; there having been some examples made, which causes the Indians to respect this small force. One of these pickets in a mission has a double object; besides keeping the Indians in subjection, they run post with a monthly correspondence, or with any extraordinaries that may be necessary for government.

104. How many corporals are assigned to a garrison?

(A) Three

(B) Two

(C) One

(D) Four

105. Most Indian huts do not exceed how many yards in diameter?

(A) Two

(B) One

(C) Four

(D) Three

STOP DO NOT TURN THE PAGE UNTIL TOLD TO DO SO.

Subtest 6

Math Skills Test

This subtest checks your arithmetic and algebra skills, plus some geometry, by using equations and word problems to gauge your general understanding and ability to use mathematical relationships in problem solving. You can expect questions that require solving for variables, working with time and distance, and estimating simple probabilities.

Time: 40 minutes, test length varies

Directions: Each problem is followed by four possible answers, and you must determine which answer is most correct. Use scratch paper (provided) to do your calculations and then mark the correct answer. (*Note:* We don't provide scratch paper here, but you'll get paper at the test site.)

106. A 5-foot-tall fence post casts a 10-foot shadow. A nearby building casts a 60-foot shadow. How tall is the building?

    (A) 25 feet

    (B) 40 feet

    (C) 30 feet

    (D) 50 feet

107. A Navy Special Operations unit of six members has enough rations to last for a seven-day period. Immediately upon insertion, they capture four suspected insurgents. How long will the rations now last?

    (A) 4.2 days

    (B) 6 days

    (C) 3.5 days

    (D) 5.1 days

108. An item in a store has been marked down to 75 percent of its initial sale price. The store is running a weekend sale and has advertised that everything in the store is an additional 25 percent off. What is the final discount applied to the item in relation to the initial sales price?

    (A) 50.0 percent

    (B) 43.75 percent

    (C) 62.1 percent

    (D) 38.0 percent

109. Tom ordered a pizza, ate 5/16 of it, and then gave away the rest to three friends in his barracks. How much of the pizza did each of the three friends receive if each got an equal share?

    (A) 0.229

    (B) 0.3

    (C) 0.32

    (D) 0.25

110. The scale on a particular map is 1 inch equals 60 miles. On this map, two locations are 6 centimeters apart. What is the distance between the locations in miles?

    (A) 223.4 miles

    (B) 145.7 miles

    (C) 141.6 miles

    (D) 124.8 miles

111. A shipment of 10,000 pounds of corn meal is destined for a developing nation. The meal is packaged in 80-ounce bags. How many bags are shipped?

    (A) 1,500 bags

    (B) 4,400 bags

    (C) 2,500 bags

    (D) 2,000 bags

Go on to next page

112. At a factory, three workers earn $675 per week, two workers earn $600 per week, and four workers earn $595 per week. Assume that every employee works 40 hours per week. What is the average cost per hour the company pays its employees?

    (A) $16.50 per hour

    (B) $15.57 per hour

    (C) $14.89 per hour

    (D) $13.25 per hour

113. A man donates $225,000 to two favorite universities. The ratio of the amount that university A receives to the amount university B receives is 4:3. How much does university A receive?

    (A) $128,571.44

    (B) $129,447.27

    (C) $134,234.17

    (D) $96,428.88

114. A student receives the following test scores on four of five tests: 88, 84, 92, and 96. If the class she attends requires an average score of 90 on the five tests to receive an *A* for the course, what must her final test score be to receive an *A?*

    (A) 88

    (B) 92

    (C) 91

    (D) 90

115. If $a = 5b$ and $10b = 4c$, $a =$

    (A) $b + c$

    (B) $2c$

    (C) $4c$

    (D) $b - c$

116. 1,000,000 can be represented by

    (A) 10^3

    (B) 10^6

    (C) 10^5

    (D) 10^4

117. Two aircraft are 900 miles apart and heading toward each other. One aircraft flies at 680 miles per hour, and the other flies at 630 miles per hour. At a 10-mile separation, the pilots will be able to visually acquire each other. How long until the pilots will be able to visually acquire one another?

    (A) 38 minutes

    (B) 25 minutes

    (C) 41 minutes

    (D) 19 minutes

118. As Ensign Taylor drove 7 hours to a new duty station, her average speed was 61 miles per hour. If her gas mileage was 27 miles per gallon, how much fuel did she burn?

    (A) 15.8 gallons

    (B) 16.1 gallons

    (C) 15.4 gallons

    (D) 16.5 gallons

119. A 600-gallon tank of water can be filled with one hose in 30 minutes and drained completely with another, different-sized hose in 60 minutes. If both hoses are opened on the empty tank, how long until the tank fills?

    (A) 45 minutes

    (B) 110 minutes

    (C) 30 minutes

    (D) 60 minutes

120. What is the perimeter of a right triangle that has two base side lengths of 8 and 12 feet?

    (A) 32 feet, 1 inch

    (B) 34 feet, 5 inches

    (C) 33 feet, 8 inches

    (D) 34 feet, 1 inch

121. If you need five bags of salt crystals to de-ice a 2-acre parking lot, how many bags of salt do you need to de-ice a 6⅓ acre lot?

    (A) 17.75 bags

    (B) 16.25 bags

    (C) 19.1 bags

    (D) 18.83 bags

Go on to next page

122. You have 16 ounces of a mixture containing 40 percent juice. You add 2 ounces of pure juice to the mixture. What percentage of the mixture is juice now?

    (A) 47 percent

    (B) 46 percent

    (C) 49 percent

    (D) 53 percent

123. You have red, green, and blue straws in a bin. The red and green straws combined equal 25 percent of the total number of straws. If you blindly reach in and grab a straw, what is the probability that it will be blue?

    (A) 2 out of 4

    (B) 3 out of 4

    (C) 1 out of 3

    (D) 2 out of 5

124. One of the angles of a right triangle is 25 degrees; what are the other two angles?

    (A) 75 degrees; 105 degrees

    (B) 80 degrees; 75 degrees

    (C) 90 degrees; 65 degrees

    (D) 70 degrees; 85 degrees

125. The reciprocal of 5 is

    (A) 15 percent

    (B) 18 percent

    (C) 20 percent

    (D) 22 percent

126. A 22-foot-tall ladder is resting against the 16-foot upper wall of a building. The top of the ladder is completely even with the top of the wall. How far out from the building is the base of the ladder?

    (A) 15.1 feet

    (B) 8.9 feet

    (C) 14.5 feet

    (D) 12.0 feet

127. A rectangular enclosure's length is two times its width, and the enclosure's perimeter is 150 feet. What is the area of the enclosure?

    (A) 1,350 square feet

    (B) 1,250 square feet

    (C) 1,125 square feet

    (D) 1,500 square feet

128. A cylinder has a diameter of 100 centimeters and a height of 2.5 meters. What is the volume of the cylinder? (One gallon equals 3,781.4 cubic centimeters.)

    (A) 532 gallons

    (B) 219 gallons

    (C) 375 gallons

    (D) 519 gallons

129. Last year, fertilizer cost $24.75 per bag. This year, it costs $25.11 per bag. How much did fertilizer prices increase?

    (A) 1.6 percent

    (B) 1.5 percent

    (C) 2.1 percent

    (D) 3.1 percent

130. If a train travels 550 miles in 6 hours, how far does it travel in 22 minutes?

    (A) 25.50 miles

    (B) 18.27 miles

    (C) 33.66 miles

    (D) 41.74 miles

131. Carpet costs $3.99 per square foot. What is the cost to carpet a room that is 4 yards by 7 yards?

    (A) $1,005.48

    (B) $1,276.18

    (C) $1,345.89

    (D) $1,299.01

Go on to next page

132. A family is moving to a new duty station 2,900 miles away and has 6 days to make the trip. On the first day, the family drove 1/5 of the total distance; on the second day, it completed 1/7 of the total distance. How many miles does the family have to average each of the remaining days to arrive on time?

    (A) 521.8 miles per day

    (B) 432.2 miles per day

    (C) 502.1 miles per day

    (D) 476.5 miles per day

133. Eight helicopters can search an area of the ocean in 2.7 hours. Three of the 8 helicopters are down for maintenance. How long will the remaining helicopters need to search the same section of the ocean?

    (A) 3.14 hours

    (B) 4.32 hours

    (C) 6.7 hours

    (D) 4.15 hours

134. John makes $21.50 per hour and time and a half for any time over 40 hours per week. John worked 53 hours this week. How much did he earn before taxes?

    (A) $1,300.50

    (B) $1,289.10

    (C) $1,244.75

    (D) $1,279.25

135. Tom made $360 this week working as a handyman. He received an additional $50 tip and spent $27 on lunches. He owes a car payment this week of $250. How much does he have left over for spending?

    (A) $133

    (B) $122

    (C) $176

    (D) $144

STOP DO NOT TURN THE PAGE UNTIL TOLD TO DO SO.

Subtest 7

Mechanical Comprehension Test

This subtest asks you to apply topics common to introductory high school physics courses in various situations. Possible topics include principles related to gases and liquids and how these properties affect pressure, volume, and velocity; questions about engine components and performance; principles of electricity; gears; weight distribution; and the operation of simple machines, such as pulleys and fulcrums.

Time: 15 minutes, test length varies

Directions: You see a series of questions with given conditions. Most questions will be depicted with a graphical representation of the problem. Use the scratch paper provided to do your calculations and choose the best answer to the problem. (*Note:* We don't provide scratch paper here, but you'll get paper at the test site.)

136. A 300-pound barrel must be lifted 3 feet to the bed of a truck. An inclined plane will reduce the amount of effort required to move the barrel by half if the inclined plane is

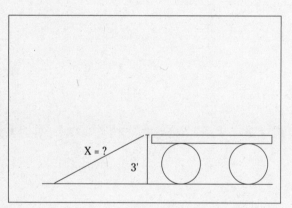

Illustration by Wiley, Composition Services Graphics

(A) 4 feet

(B) 6 feet

(C) 8 feet

(D) 10 feet

137. Two people are carrying a 200-pound crate on a 12-foot-long, 2-x-8-inch board. To distribute the load evenly between the two people, the crate should be placed

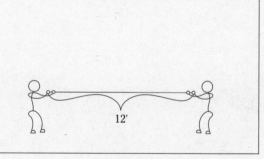

Illustration by Wiley, Composition Services Graphics

(A) 4 feet from one end of the board

(B) 5 feet from one end of the board

(C) 6 feet from one end of the board

(D) 7 feet from one end of the board

Go on to next page

138. Wheel A has a diameter of 22 feet; wheel B has a diameter of 11 feet. If both wheels revolve at the same rate, wheel B will cover a given linear distance in

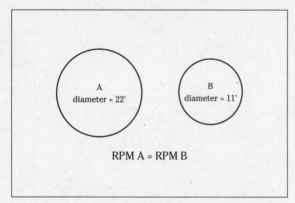

Illustration by Wiley, Composition Services Graphics

(A) Twice the amount of time that wheel A does

(B) One-half the amount of time that wheel A does

(C) The same amount of time as wheel A does

(D) Impossible to calculate

139. Not including friction, a single pulley gives a mechanical advantage of

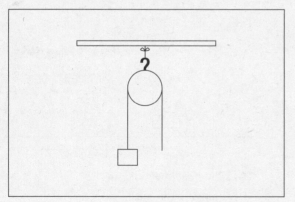

Illustration by Wiley, Composition Services Graphics

(A) 2

(B) 1

(C) 2.5

(D) 3

140. Four gears are turning in motion in a series. If gear A is turning clockwise, gear D will turn

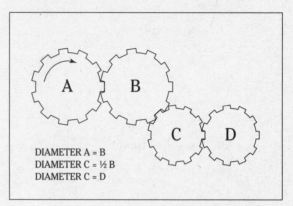

DIAMETER A = B
DIAMETER C = ½ B
DIAMETER C = D

Illustration by Wiley, Composition Services Graphics

(A) Clockwise and at the same speed as gear A

(B) Counterclockwise and more slowly than gear A

(C) Counterclockwise and more quickly than gear A

(D) Clockwise and more quickly than gear A

141. You balance a wooden beam on a fulcrum and then cut the beam exactly at the CG point into two sections A and B. Which section will be heavier?

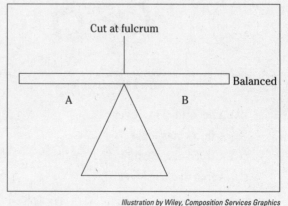

Illustration by Wiley, Composition Services Graphics

(A) A is heavier than B.

(B) B is heavier than A.

(C) Impossible to calculate.

(D) A is the same weight as B.

Go on to next page

142. If gear A, which has 14 teeth, makes four revolutions, gear B, which has 20 teeth, will make how many revolutions?

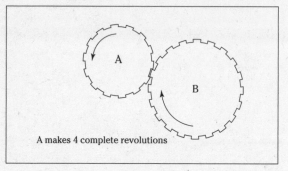

A makes 4 complete revolutions

Illustration by Wiley, Composition Services Graphics

(A) 6.1 revolutions

(B) 2.8 revolutions

(C) 7.5 revolutions

(D) 4.9 revolutions

143. The wheelbarrow is an example of

Illustration by Wiley, Composition Services Graphics

(A) A second-class lever

(B) A first-class lever

(C) A third-class lever

(D) A fourth-class lever

144. The pulley arrangement in the diagram shows a 50-pound force pulling on the rope attached to pulley A. How much weight can this pulley arrangement lift?

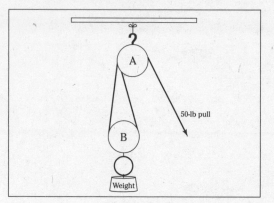

50-lb pull

Weight

Illustration by Wiley, Composition Services Graphics

(A) 50 pounds

(B) 120 pounds

(C) 100 pounds

(D) 80 pounds

145. An object can accelerate by

Illustration by Wiley, Composition Services Graphics

(A) Changing speed

(B) Changing the initial velocity

(C) Changing the direction of its velocity but not the magnitude

(D) All the above

Go on to next page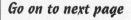

146. 115 degrees equals how many radians?

    (A) 1

    (B) 2

    (C) 3

    (D) 4

147. Floats A and B measure the specific gravity of two different samples. Which float indicates the higher specific gravity?

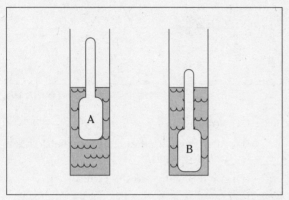

    (A) Float A.

    (B) Float B.

    (C) Neither A nor B is higher in specific gravity.

    (D) Impossible to calculate.

148. A 100-kilogram man jumps off a raft that weighs 150 kilograms. His initial velocity from jumping is 5 meters per second. Assuming that the friction resistance of the water is zero, the velocity of the raft after the man jumps will be

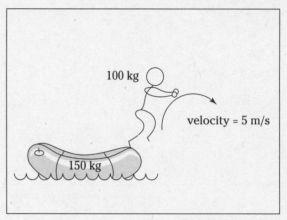

    (A) 3.33 meters per second

    (B) 2.7 meters per second

    (C) –3.33 meters per second

    (D) –2.7 meters per second

Go on to next page

149. A given wheel rotates at a constant speed. The outside of the wheel has a _____ linear speed and a(n) _____ angular speed compared to the inside of the wheel.

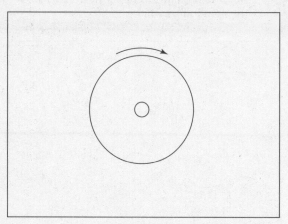

Illustration by Wiley, Composition Services Graphics

(A) Lesser; greater

(B) Lesser; equal

(C) Greater; lesser

(D) Greater; equal

150. Two objects traveling in opposite directions collide with one another. Object A weighs 5 kilograms and is traveling at 10 meters per second, and object B weighs 10 kilograms and is traveling at 5 meters per second. If the two objects remain attached following the collision, what is their combined speed?

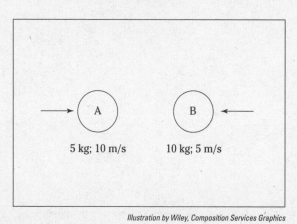

Illustration by Wiley, Composition Services Graphics

(A) 2 meters per second

(B) 0 meters per second

(C) 1 meter per second

(D) 3 meters per second

151. Given that both anvils in the diagram are the same weights, what will happen when anvil B is placed on the seesaw?

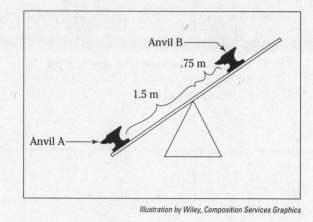

Illustration by Wiley, Composition Services Graphics

(A) Nothing.

(B) Anvil A will rise up and then settle back to the ground.

(C) Anvil B will go to the ground.

(D) Anvils A and B will reach an equilibrium at the same elevation.

152. Ambient air pressure is roughly 14.7 pounds per square inch at sea level. The total area of the top of your model airplane is 145 square inches. What is the amount of force exerted on the top of your motionless, grounded airplane at sea level?

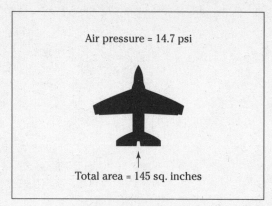

Illustration by Wiley, Composition Services Graphics

(A) 2,132 pounds

(B) 230 pounds

(C) 1,675 pounds

(D) 1,790 pounds

Go on to next page

153. What mechanical advantage does this block and tackle arrangement have?

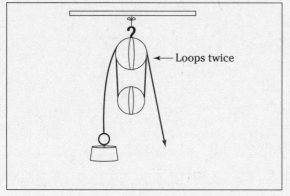

Loops twice

Illustration by Wiley, Composition Services Graphics

(A) 1

(B) 3

(C) 2

(D) 5

154. Gear 1 moves in a clockwise direction. Which other gear(s) move(s) in a clockwise direction?

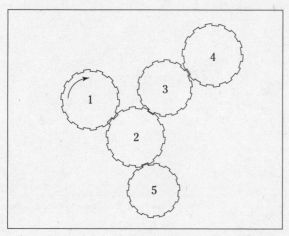

Illustration by Wiley, Composition Services Graphics

(A) 2 and 4

(B) 3 and 5

(C) 3, 4, and 5

(D) 3

155. A cubic foot of water weighs approximately 62.5 pounds. If an aquarium is 5 feet long, 3 feet deep, and 2 feet wide, what is the approximate pressure in pounds per square inch on the bottom of the tank?

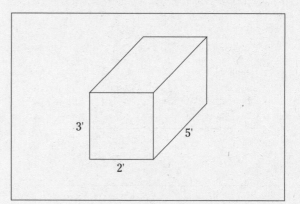

Illustration by Wiley, Composition Services Graphics

(A) 1.5 pounds per square inch

(B) 1.9 pounds per square inch

(C) 1.7 pounds per square inch

(D) 1.3 pounds per square inch

156. Wheel A and wheel B are the same distance from the bottom of the incline in the diagram. If both wheel A and wheel B revolve at the same rate, which will reach the bottom first?

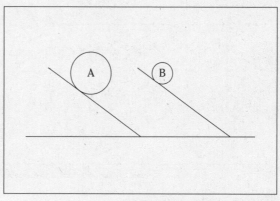

Illustration by Wiley, Composition Services Graphics

(A) Wheel B.

(B) Wheel A and B will reach the bottom at the same time.

(C) Wheel A.

(D) Impossible to calculate.

Go on to next page

157. If a ramp is 10 meters long and has a total incline height of 3 meters, an object weighing 100 kilograms requires how much effort to move on the ramp?

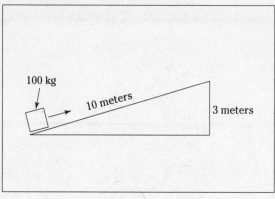

Illustration by Wiley, Composition Services Graphics

(A) 30 kilograms

(B) 40 kilograms

(C) 45 kilograms

(D) 62.5 kilograms

158. In the diagram, assume all the valves are closed. Which valves must be opened to ensure that the tank fills to and remains at approximately 3/4 volume?

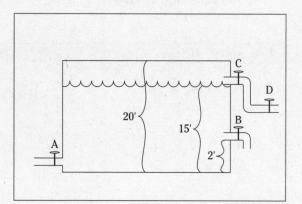

Illustration by Wiley, Composition Services Graphics

(A) A, B, and C

(B) A, C, and D

(C) B, C, and D

(D) B and C

159. If gear 1 makes five counterclockwise revolutions per minute in the diagram,

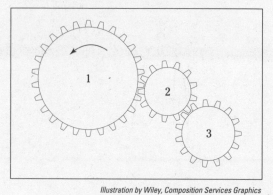

Illustration by Wiley, Composition Services Graphics

(A) Gear 3 moves clockwise 8.33 revolutions.

(B) Gear 2 moves clockwise 5 revolutions.

(C) Gear 3 moves counterclockwise 8.33 revolutions.

(D) Gear 2 moves counterclockwise 5 revolutions.

160. At which point is the baseball throw the slowest?

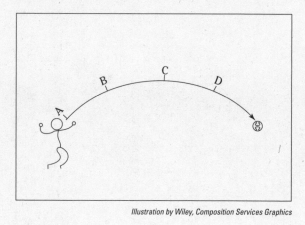

Illustration by Wiley, Composition Services Graphics

(A) A

(B) B

(C) C

(D) D

Go on to next page

161. Water is flowing through the pipe depicted in the diagram at a rate of 100 gallons per hour. The water flow starts at point A, becomes constricted to about 50 percent at point B, and then opens back up to the circumference of the entire pipe at point C. Which statement is true?

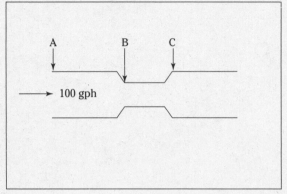

Illustration by Wiley, Composition Services Graphics

(A) The volume of water at point B is half of what it is at point A.

(B) The volume of water at point B is double what it is at point A.

(C) The velocity of the water flow is reduced at point B.

(D) The volume of water passing point B is the same as the volume of water passing points A and C.

162. Pulley B is the driver in the arrangement. The pulley that turns the fastest is

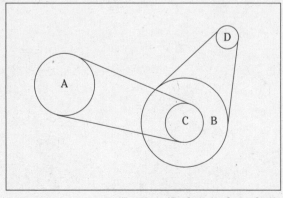

Illustration by Wiley, Composition Services Graphics

(A) A

(B) B

(C) C

(D) D

163. Which brace is more secure?

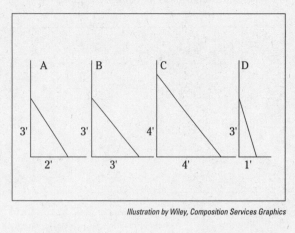

Illustration by Wiley, Composition Services Graphics

(A) A

(B) B

(C) C

(D) D

164. Which pendulum takes more time to make a complete swing?

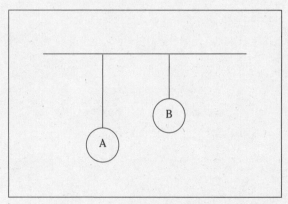

Illustration by Wiley, Composition Services Graphics

(A) Neither A or B

(B) A

(C) B

(D) Impossible to calculate

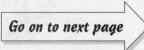

Go on to next page

165. Given the diagrams, which has the greatest resistance if all resistors are equal?

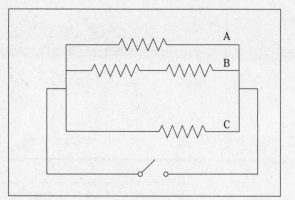

Illustration by Wiley, Composition Services Graphics

(A) A

(B) B

(C) C

(D) Impossible to calculate

STOP DO NOT TURN THE PAGE UNTIL TOLD TO DO SO.

Chapter 19

Army Selection Instrument for Flight Training (SIFT) Answers/Explanations

R eady to find out how you did on the Army Selection Instrument for Flight Training (SIFT) practice test in Chapter 18? In this chapter, we present both more-detailed explanations for the test questions and a basic answer key. We suggest checking out the explanations so that you get a better understanding of why your answer is right or wrong and get a little extra review in the process.

Subtest 1: Simple Drawings

1. **A.**	8. **C.**	15. **E.**	22. **B.**
2. **E.**	9. **E.**	16. **B.**	23. **E.**
3. **C.**	10. **D.**	17. **A.**	24. **E.**
4. **B.**	11. **A.**	18. **D.**	25. **A.**
5. **B.**	12. **B.**	19. **B.**	
6. **A.**	13. **C.**	20. **A.**	
7. **C.**	14. **E.**	21. **E.**	

Subtest 2: Hidden Figures

26. **E.**

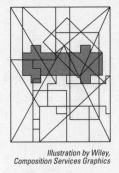

Illustration by Wiley, Composition Services Graphics

27. **C.**

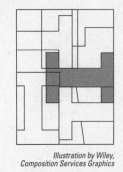

Illustration by Wiley, Composition Services Graphics

28. **D.**

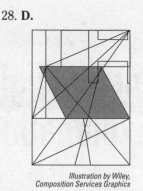

Illustration by Wiley,
Composition Services Graphics

29. **A.**

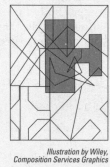

Illustration by Wiley,
Composition Services Graphics

30. **B.**

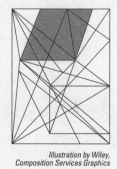

Illustration by Wiley,
Composition Services Graphics

31. **D.**

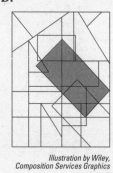

Illustration by Wiley,
Composition Services Graphics

32. **E.**

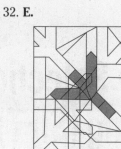

Illustration by Wiley,
Composition Services Graphics

33. **C.**

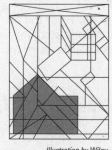

Illustration by Wiley,
Composition Services Graphics

34. **B.**

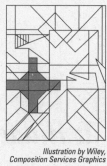

Illustration by Wiley,
Composition Services Graphics

35. **A.**

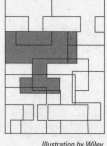

Illustration by Wiley,
Composition Services Graphics

36. **A.**

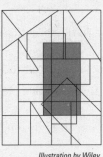

Illustration by Wiley,
Composition Services Graphics

39. **B.**

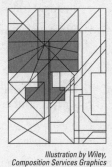

Illustration by Wiley,
Composition Services Graphics

37. **D.**

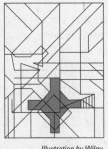

Illustration by Wiley,
Composition Services Graphics

40. **E.**

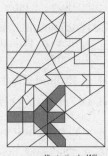

Illustration by Wiley,
Composition Services Graphics

38. **C.**

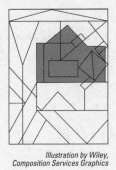

Illustration by Wiley,
Composition Services Graphics

Subtest 3: Army Aviation Information Test

41. **C.** The rotor mast is rigged to the left side.

42. **A.** The four forces that act on an aircraft are lift, weight, thrust, and drag.

43. **A.** Cyclic control changes the pitch all at the same time.

44. **B.** The velocity of air flowing over the advancing versus retreating rotor is unequal lift, called *dissymmetry of lift*.

45. **D.** The main purpose of the tail rotor is to counteract the torque effect of the main rotor blades.

46. **B.** *Coning* of the main rotor blades is the upward bending from the combination of lift and centrifugal forces.

47. **D.** When at a hover, the helicopter tends to move, or *drift,* in the direction of the tail rotor thrust; this propensity is called *translating tendency.*

48. **D.** Wind velocity is the only listed factor that doesn't affect density altitude.

49. **D.** During an engine failure, you must immediately lower the collective pitch to maintain rotor rpm and enter into an autorotative state.

50. **E.** A *weight-and-balance envelope* is a short distance fore and aft of the main rotor blade for center of gravity.

51. **A.** The foot, or anti-torque, pedals allow you to control torque effect of the main rotor blades.

52. **C.** *Gyroscopic precession* is when a force applied to a rotating disc has the effect occur 90 degrees later and in the plane of rotation.

53. **D.** When the helicopter enters into undisturbed air, additional lift, called *translational lift,* is achieved. Translational lift is the initial buffeting you feel upon takeoff and shortly before landing.

54. **C.** Ground effect can result in becoming airborne before the desired takeoff speed.

55. **D.** Retreating blade stall is where the retreating blade airspeed decreases with an increased forward aircraft speed. After you reduce the retreating rotor airspeed to a wing-stalling condition, retreating blade stall will occur (and that is bad).

56. **B.** The most favorable conditions are low density altitude, low gross weight, and moderate to strong winds.

57. **D.** The cyclic controls the tilt of the main rotor disc.

58. **D.** Pitch is the movement around the aircraft's lateral axis.

59. **B.** The collective pitch controls the pitch of all main rotor blades equally and simultaneously.

60. **A.** Bernoulli's basic principle applies here: Lift is developed when airflow passes around an airfoil (wing).

Subtest 4: Spatial Apperception Test

61. **A.**	68. **D.**	75. **A.**	82. **E.**
62. **C.**	69. **B.**	76. **B.**	83. **B.**
63. **C.**	70. **C.**	77. **A.**	84. **B.**
64. **E.**	71. **E.**	78. **A.**	85. **E.**
65. **B.**	72. **C.**	79. **B.**	
66. **A.**	73. **B.**	80. **C.**	
67. **B.**	74. **D.**	81. **C.**	

Subtest 5: Reading Comprehension Test

86. **B.**	91. **C.**	96. **B.**	101. **A.**
87. **B.**	92. **B.**	97. **C.**	102. **D.**
88. **C.**	93. **D.**	98. **D.**	103. **B.**
89. **C.**	94. **B.**	99. **A.**	104. **C.**
90. **D.**	95. **A.**	100. **B.**	105. **C.**

Subtest 6: Math Skills Test

106. **C.** (5 feet ÷ 10 feet) × 60 feet = 30 feet.

107. **A.** Seven days of rations for 6 people equals a total of 42 ration portions. Next, add the 4 insurgents to equal a total of 10 people to feed and divide the total number of rations by the number of people. 42 ÷ 10 = 4.2 days.

108. **B.** 100 percent of the initial price minus 25 percent = 75 percent. Multiply this result by 0.75 (to figure in an additional 25 percent markdown) to get a total price of 56.25 percent of the initial price. This answer means your savings is 100 percent − 56.25 percent = 43.75 percent off.

109. **A.** Subtract 5/16 from 1, and you have a total of 11/16 of the pizza leftover. Convert this result to a decimal by dividing 11 by 16 to get 0.6875, and divide this amount by the three people sharing the pizza to get a total per-person amount of 0.229 of the pizza.

110. **C.** One inch equals 60 miles on the map scale. You know that 1 inch equals 2.54 centimeters. Therefore, 2.54 centimeters equals 60 miles. Divide 6 centimeters by 2.54 centimeters and then multiply that result by 60 miles to get 141.6 miles. (6 centimeters ÷ 2.54 centimeters) × 60 miles = 2.36 × 60 miles = 141.6 miles.

111. **D.** You first have to get the total weight in ounces. 16 ounces = 1 pound, so 10,000 pounds × 16 ounces/pound = 160,000 ounces. Divide the number of ounces by the amount going into each bag (80 ounces) to get the answer. 160,000 ounces ÷ 80 ounces per bag = 2,000 bags shipped.

112. **B.** Find the total amount each group receives: (3 × $675 = $2,025), (2 × $600 = $1,200), (4 × $595 = $2,380). Add the total amounts to get the total amount paid out each week: $2,025 + $1,200 + $2,380 = $5,605. Divide that result by the nine employees to get the $622.78 average weekly pay, and divide this number by 40 hours per week to get $15.569 or $15.57 in average hourly pay per employee.

113. **A.** Split the total donation into units and then use the ratio to find how much goes to each recipient: $225,000 ÷ (4 + 3) = $225,000 ÷ 7 = $32,142.86. Take this amount and multiply by 4 to get university A's amount of $128,571.44. To double check, you can find university B's amount by multiplying $32,142.86 by 3 to get $96,428.58 and then add both results to ensure they equal the total donation: $128,571.44 + $96,428.58 = $225,000.02

114. **D.** The sum of the average of the five tests to receive an A must be 450 (90 average × 5 tests). Subtract from 450 the score of each of the four previous tests, and you have 90 left over, so that's what the student must score to average 90 and make an A in the class. You can also set the missing score as the variable x: (88 + 84 + 92 + 96 + x) ÷ 5 = 90.

115. **B.** If $a = 5b$, you can figure that $2a = 10b$, so you can substitute $2a$ for $10b$ in the second equation to get $2a = 4c$. Divide both sides by 2 to get $a = 2c$.

116. **B.** 106 is the same as a 1 followed by 6 zeros, or 1,000,000.

117. **C.** First, calculate the distance required until the aircraft can see each other by taking the total distance and subtracting the distance at which they can acquire one another (900 miles − 10 miles = 890 miles). Divide this distance by the combined airspeeds at which the aircraft are converging (680 miles per hour + 630 miles per hour = 1,310 miles per hour). 890 miles ÷ 1,310 miles per hour = .679 hours. But wait; the answer choices are in minutes! Never fear; just multiply .679 hours × 60 minutes to get 40.74 or 41 minutes.

118. **A.** Seven hours times the average of 61 miles per hour gives you 427 miles. Divide the total miles by the gas mileage of 27 miles per gallon. 427 ÷ 27 = 15.8 gallons used.

119. **D.** First, figure out the separate rates of flow. To fill the 600-gallon tank, hose A = 600 ÷ 30 minutes = 20 gallons per minute or 1,200 gallons per hour. To empty the tank, hose B = 600 ÷ 60 minutes = 10 gallons per minute or 600 gallons per hour. If you open both, you have water coming in at the rate of 1,200 gallons per hour and leaving at 600 gallons per hour for a net filling rate of 600 gallons per hour. The tank will fill in 1 hour.

120. **B.** Use the formula $a^2 + b^2 = c^2$, or $8^2 + 12^2 = c^2$ to find the length of the hypotenuse. This setup gives you $64 + 144 = c^2$. Solving this equation gives you $208 = c^2$. Therefore, $c = \sqrt{208}$, which equals 14.42 feet or 14 feet, 5 inches (to get the 5 inches you multiply 0.42 feet × 12 inches per foot = 5 inches). To get the triangle's perimeter, add up the three side lengths: 8 feet + 12 feet + 14 feet, 5 inches = 34 feet, 5 inches.

121. **D.** Divide 2 acres by 5 bags to get a per-acre amount of 2.5 bags of salt. Multiply this number times 6⅓ acres to get the total amount of 15.83 bags of salt.

122. **A.** Take 16 ounces × 0.4 to get 6.4 ounces of pure juice. Add 2 ounces to both the juice and the total amount. Divide the new juice amount (6.4 ounces + 2 ounces = 8.4 ounces) by the new total amount (16 ounces + 2 ounces = 18 ounces) to get 8.4 ounces. Divide that by 18 ounces = 46.7 percent = 47 percent

123. **B.** 75 percent of the straws are blue, so you have a 75-percent chance, or a three out of four chance, of grabbing a blue straw.

124. **C.** You know that in a right triangle, one angle is 90 degrees, so that's the first part of the answer. You also know that the sum of the angles in a right triangle is 180 degrees. Therefore, you can subtract the known angles from that total to find the remaining angle. 180 − 90 − 25 = 65 degrees.

125. **C.** The reciprocal of 5 is the same as 1/5 = 0.2 or 20 percent

126. **A.** The ladder leaning against the wall forms a right triangle, so you can use the Pythagorean theorem (the ladder is the hypotenuse): $a^2 + 16^2 = 22^2$. $a^2 + 256 = 484$. $a^2 = 484 − 256 = 228$. $a = \sqrt{228} = 15.1$ feet

127. **B.** The total perimeter is 150 feet, which means that the total of one of the long sides plus one of the short sides equals 75 feet. You know that the short side is half the length of the long side, so one side is 25 feet and the other is 50 feet. Another way of looking at it is $x + x + 2x + 2x = 150$; $6x = 150$; $x = 25$. The short side is 25 feet, and the long side is 2×25 or 50 feet. Now you can find the area by just multiplying the base × height: 25 feet × 50 feet = 1,250 square feet.

128. **D.** First, you must figure out the radius. Divide the diameter by 2 to get the radius of 50 centimeters. Next convert the height of 2.5 meters to 250 centimeters so that everything uses the same scale. Use the formula for volume of a cylinder: $V = h\pi r^2$. $V = 250$ cm × π × (50 cm^2) = 250 cm × π × 2,500 cm^2 = π × 625,000 cm^3 = 1,963,495 cm^3. (If you use 22/7 for π, you get 1,964,287 cm^3.) Now take 1,963,495 cm^3 and divide it by 3,781.4 cm^3 per gallon to get 519 gallons.

129. **B.** Divide the difference by the price of last year's bag to get the percentage change of this year's price from last year's price. $25.11 − $24.75 = $0.36. Divide $0.36 by $24.75 to get 0.0145 or 0.015, which equals 1.5 percent.

130. **C.** The train travels 550 miles in 6 hours or 360 minutes. Divide 550 miles by 360 minutes to get 1.53 miles per minute. Multiply this result by 22 minutes: 1.53 × 22 = 33.61 miles.

131. **A.** First, convert the yards to feet. 4 yards = 12 feet and 7 yards = 21 feet. To get the square footage, multiply the length times width, or 12 feet × 21 feet = 252 square feet. Multiply this amount by $3.99 per square foot to get the total price of $1,005.48.

132. **D.** On the first day, the travelers completed 2,900 × 1/5 = 580 miles, and on the second they completed 2,900 × 1/7 = 414 miles. Subtract both of these distances from the total trip distance to get 1,906 miles left in the trip. Divide this result by the four days that they have left, and the average comes to 476.5 miles per day.

133. **B.** Multiply the available time of 2.7 hours by 8 and then divide by 5 (the number of aircraft available) to get the new amount of search time of 4.32 hours.

134. **D.** Subtract John's regular work week of 40 hours from his actual work week of 53 hours to see how much time he earns overtime for. 53 – 40 = 13 hours. Next, multiply each amount of time by its appropriate salary. $21.50 × 40 = $860, and $21.50 × 1.5 × 13 hours = $419.25. Add the two to get $1,279.25.

135. **A.** This one is a simple chain of addition and subtraction: $360 + $50 – $27 – $250 = $133.

Subtest 7: Mechanical Comprehension Test

136. **B.** The formula used for determining how an inclined plane reduces effort is length of ramp ÷ height of ramp = weight of object ÷ force. In this case, x ÷ 3 feet = 300 pounds ÷ 150 pounds. (The question states that the amount of force must be reduced by half, so that's why you divide 300 by 150.) x ÷ 3 = 300 ÷ 150, so x = 2 × 3 = 6 feet.

137. **C.** To carry the load evenly, you must place the load directly in the middle of the board. Because the board is 12 feet long, you must place the load at the 6-foot mark.

138. **A.** Because wheel B has a smaller circumference, it covers a shorter linear distance than wheel A when turning at the same rate. Therefore, wheel A covers a distance faster than wheel B. You can figure the circumference with the formula of πd or $2\pi r$. The circumference of wheel A is 22π = 69 feet, and the circumference of wheel B is 11π = 34.5 feet. To cover the same amount of distance, wheel B must rotate exactly twice the amount of time as wheel A at the same number of revolutions per minute.

139. **B.** A stationary single pulley allows you to change the direction of force but doesn't result in increased mechanical advantage; therefore, the correct answer is Choice (B).

140. **C.** Gear 1 will turn clockwise, and gear 2 will turn counterclockwise; because gear 2 is the same size as gear 1, both gears will turn at the same speed. Gear 3 will turn clockwise but is half the diameter of gear 2, so gear 3 will rotate at twice the speed of gears 1 and 2. Gear 4 will rotate counterclockwise and is the same size as gear 3, so it will also rotate twice as fast as gears 2 and 1.

141. **D.** The weight of A equals exactly the weight of B. An object will always remain balanced at its center of gravity, by definition.

142. **B.** Gear A has 14 teeth and makes 4 revolutions, so it rotates a total of 56 teeth (4 × 14 = 56). Gear B has a total of 20 teeth, so you divide the total teeth movement of 56 by 20 to get 2.8 revolutions.

143. **A.** A second-class lever is a lever with force or lifting action applied to one end (handles), a fulcrum at the opposite end, and the load to be carried in the middle.

144. **C.** The number of times a rope moves through the pulley determines the mechanical advantage. In this pulley system, the advantage is 2. Therefore, by applying a 50-pound force on the end of the rope, you can lift a weight that is 100 pounds.

145. **D.** Any of these choices can promote acceleration, so Choice (D) is the best answer.

146. **B.** 2π radians equal 360 degrees. Therefore, 6.28 radians = 360 degrees. Divide both sides of that equation by 6.28 to find that 1 radian equals 57.32 degrees. Finally, take 115 degrees ÷ 57.32 = 2 radians to get the final answer.

147. **A.** Specific gravity is the measurement of a fluid in relation to the weight of water. The higher specific gravity of the fluid will cause the float to remain higher, so the answer is Choice (A).

148. **C.** Force equals mass (m) × acceleration (A). Therefore, because the force is equal and opposite, $m × A = -(m × A_1)$. This setup gives you the following equation: 100 kilograms × 5 meters per second = –(150 kilograms × A). Simplified, you have 500 kilograms meters per second divided by 150 kilograms, or 3.33 meters per second. Because the raft is going in the opposite direction, the correct answer is –3.33 meters per second.

149. **D.** The linear distance traveled is greater on the outside but the angular distance remains constant.

150. **B.** Under the law of conservation of mass, $m_1V_1 + m_2V_2 = (m_1 + m_2) \times V$. Therefore, 5 kilograms(10 meters per second) + 10 kilograms(–5 meters per second) = (5 kilograms + 10 kilograms) $\times$ V. This math works out to 0 = (15 kilograms) $\times$ V, so $V = 0$.

151. **A.** Nothing will happen because in order for any movement to occur, anvil B would have to be placed more than 1.5 meters to the right of the fulcrum.

152. **A.** Pressure equals force divided by area, or $P = F \div A$; you can rearrange this equation to get $P \times A = F$. Therefore, if you plug in the numbers from the problem, 14.7 pounds per square inch $\times$ 145 square inches = 2,132 pounds.

153. **C.** The pulley function on the bottom is just to change direction, so you have a mechanical advantage of 2 on top.

154. **B.** Gear 1 rotates clockwise, and gear 2 rotates counterclockwise and turns both gear 3 and gear 5 clockwise. Gear 3 turns gear 4 counterclockwise.

155. **D.** First, you must get the total volume of the tank. Volume is length $\times$ width $\times$ height, or 5 feet $\times$ 2 feet $\times$ 3 feet = 30 cubic feet. You know that the weight per cubic foot is 62.5 pounds, so the total weight acting on the bottom of the tank is 1,875 pounds. Now you must figure out the area of only the bottom in square inches. Multiply (12 inches $\times$ 5 feet) $\times$ (12 inches $\times$ 2 feet), which equals 60 inches $\times$ 24 inches, or 1,440 square inches. Now simply divide the total weight of 1,875 pounds by 1,440 square inches to get the answer of 1.3 pounds per square inch.

156. **C.** Wheel B has a smaller circumference, so given the same number of revolutions, it will cover a smaller distance. Therefore, wheel A will reach the bottom first.

157. **A.** The formula to use is length of ramp $\div$ height of ramp = weight of object $\div$ effort. Using the numbers from the problem, you get 10 meters $\div$ 3 meters = 100 kilograms $\div$ effort. Therefore, cross-multiplying gives you 100 kilograms divided by 3.33 = 30 kilograms.

158. **B.** Because valve A is required to be open for water to flow in, you know that one must be open. Now you need to figure out how full the tank has to be to get to 75 percent. The tank holds a total of 20 inches, so take 0.75 $\times$ 20; the answer is 15 inches. If valve B is open, the water will only fill to the 2-inch mark, so that one must remain closed. If valve C is open, water will be able to fill to the 15-inch mark, so that valve must be opened. Valve D must also be open for the water to continue to flow out. The correct answer is Choice (B), valves A, C, and D.

159. **C.** Because gear 1's radius is twice that of gear 2, the gear 2 will revolve twice as fast (10 revolutions) in the opposite direction of gear 1. Gear 3 will rotate opposite of gear 2 and the same as gear 1; it will rotate at 5/6 the speed of gear 2 (10 revolutions $\times$ 5/6 = 8.33 revolutions).

160. **A.** The vertical component of the momentum is 0 at this point, and the horizontal components remain unchanged.

161. **D.** The volume of water flowing past point B is the same as for points A and C. Due to the restriction of approximately half the width, the velocity approximately doubles as it passes point B. This is the law of conservation of mass, the fundamental principle that results in the Bernoulli equation.

162. **D.** Pulley D is rotating most quickly because it has the smallest circumference.

163. **C.** You must figure out which brace covers the most area. Because you have a right triangle, you can use the formula $A = 1/2$ base $\times$ height. The largest area is $4 \times 4 \div 2 = 8$, which is Choice (C).

164. **A.** The shorter pendulum length B completes the swing the fastest, and the longer pendulum length A will take the longest. Interestingly, the mass of the pendulum doesn't matter!

165. **B.** The resistance in B is the sum of the two resistors and therefore twice the resistance in A and C.

Answers at a Glance

Subtest 1: Simple Drawings

1. A	6. A	11. A	16. B	21. E
2. E	7. C	12. B	17. A	22. B
3. C	8. C	13. C	18. D	23. E
4. B	9. E	14. E	19. B	24. E
5. B	10. D	15. E	20. A	25. A

Subtest 2: Hidden Figures

26. E	29. A	32. E	35. A	38. C
27. C	30. B	33. C	36. A	39. B
28. D	31. D	34. B	37. D	40. E

Subtest 3: Army Aviation Information Test

41. C	45. D	49. D	53. D	57. D
42. A	46. B	50. E	54. C	58. D
43. A	47. D	51. A	55. D	59. B
44. B	48. D	52. C	56. B	60. A

Subtest 4: Spatial Apperception Test

61. A	66. A	71. E	76. B	81. C
62. C	67. B	72. C	77. A	82. E
63. C	68. D	73. B	78. A	83. B
64. E	69. B	74. D	79. B	84. B
65. B	70. C	75. A	80. C	85. E

Subtest 5: Reading Comprehension Test

86. B	90. D	94. B	98. D	102. D
87. B	91. C	95. A	99. A	103. B
88. C	92. B	96. B	100. B	104. C
89. C	93. D	97. C	101. A	105. C

Subtest 6: Math Skills Test

106. C	112. B	118. A	124. C	130. C
107. A	113. A	119. D	125. C	131. A
108. B	114. D	120. B	126. A	132. D
109. A	115. B	121. D	127. B	133. B
110. C	116. B	122. A	128. D	134. D
111. D	117. C	123. B	129. B	135. A

Subtest 7: Mechanical Comprehension Test

136. **B**	142. **B**	148. **C**	154. **B**	160. **A**
137. **C**	143. **A**	149. **D**	155. **D**	161. **D**
138. **A**	144. **C**	150. **B**	156. **C**	162. **D**
139. **B**	145. **D**	151. **A**	157. **A**	163. **C**
140. **C**	146. **B**	152. **A**	158. **B**	164. **A**
141. **D**	147. **A**	153. **C**	159. **C**	165. **B**

Part V
The Part of Tens

The 5th Wave   By Rich Tennant

"My husband named the dog. Of course, he's in
the military, and I don't have the heart to tell
the kids it's an acronym for Special Patrol
Over The Hill Tactician."

In this part . . .

In this classic *For Dummies* part, you find a couple of quick-reference chapters to improve your score on the military flight aptitude test. We cover ten things to do before you take your test and ten ways to maximize your score.

Chapter 20

Ten Things to Do Before You Take the Test

Gearing up for any endeavor involves all sorts of planning, and the military flight aptitude test is no different. In this chapter, we distill the most important activities to tackle before you sit down for the test, including prioritizing your preferred service branches, making and following a study schedule, and staying relaxed in the day or two before exam time.

Determine Which Service You Want to Fly For

Before you take a flight aptitude test, spend some time thinking seriously about what you want to fly and for whom. At the same time, be realistic about any physical or age limitations you may have. Do you wear corrective lenses? Are you too old for the Air Force program but young enough for the Army? Is your eventual goal to fly on a carrier? You must ask yourself all these questions and more to get a practical handle on which test to focus on. When coauthor Terry was young, he wanted to fly for the Navy. But he realized that his corrective lenses were a no-go in the Navy, so he set his sights (no pun intended) on the Army aviation program.

Attack Your Weak Areas

If you already fly, you know the importance of preflight planning. You'd never make a long cross-country flight without having a plan for adverse weather, fuel stops, and where the good places to eat are. The same holds true for taking your military flight aptitude test (except maybe for mapping out the food stops). You need to make a plan based on where you perceive your skills are, where they need to be, and how long you have to get them there.

The following sections help you spot the chinks in your armor and set up a solid plan to fill them in.

Identifying your weaknesses

You may be unsure where your weak areas lie (or worry that you're too weak in all areas), so the best way to assess where you are and how far you need to go is to take the practice tests in Part IV. After you score the tests, make three columns on a sheet of paper and, for each section, group the answers you got right because you knew them, the ones you got right by guessing, and the ones you got wrong. Apply half of the correct guesses to the knew-it column and half to the incorrect column and look at the distribution. On test day, you're worried only about the overall score (whether that's from guessing or remembering), but at this stage you're more concerned with how much concrete knowledge you have; we recommend dividing your correct guesses this way as a (somewhat arbitrary) method for separating your knowledge from guessing luck. Analyzing your preliminary results this way gives you a pretty clear idea of where you stand in each area of the test. (Don't worry about skewing your later results by taking the practice tests this early in the game; when you retake them after weeks of studying, you'll have either forgotten the questions or seared them into your memory, which can be a valuable weapon in your flight aptitude testing arsenal.)

Getting started

When you see what your problem subjects are, think about your history with those topics. Are your science scores low because you haven't cracked a biology or chemistry textbook since your freshman year of high school? Build your study plan to incorporate more science into your new routine. If you get stuck on vocab and reading comprehension, spend most of your time focusing your study efforts on those topics. (Flip to Parts II and III for help reviewing various test subjects.) And if your academic knowledge seems to be in order but you lack flying experience, go fly somewhere (and we don't mean take a vacation to the Keys). We discuss the benefits of pre-test flight lessons in the later section "Take Flying Lessons or Remain Current" and in Chapter 11. Resist the (all-too-human) urge to focus on the subjects you're good at.

Making plans

What gets planned gets done. The military loves plans. A small operation of only minutes at the target is the result of hours and maybe even days and weeks of actual planning. Now, we aren't saying that you should spend weeks making up a study plan, but you should set a strategy to accomplish the study goals you identify. Tailor the plan to fit your needs. We discuss study schedules in more detail in Chapter 4.

Finding the time

Finding time to study for the aptitude test is a matter of examining your priorities. If you work full time, you may have to sacrifice your social life to give proper attention to your test prep. Busy finishing up school and just don't have the extra time to study for this test on top of finals? Maybe you need to plan on taking the test a few months after school is out so you have time to devote to all your exams.

Stick to the Plan

"Stick to the plan." sounds like a simple statement, but so does "The road to hell is paved with good intentions." After you have a plan (see the preceding section), look at it as though you're on a determined diet; you have to put in the work to get the results you want. At the same time, don't beat yourself up if you stumble occasionally. Maybe your plan is to set aside two hours a day to do nothing but practice for the exam, but then you go out for a quick lunch and end up being gone all day. Don't give up completely; just start fresh the next day and get back on track. One or two missed days here or there won't hurt you; the problem starts when one or two days turn into three or four and then six, seven, or eight days.

Motivation is key. Set up a reward system and take an occasional night off. Terry spent six days a week studying; if (and only if) he made his goals in those six days, he'd go out on Friday night. Another great motivational boost is to keep a picture of the aircraft you want to fly posted near your desk. (Interestingly, the picture Terry used ended up being one of the few Army aircraft he never flew.)

Take Flying Lessons or Remain Current

The best way to maximize your score on the aerodynamics and spatial orientation sections of the test is getting some actual "stick-and-rudder" time. The best course of action is to obtain your pilot's license before you take the exam. Doing so shows the selection board that you're a dedicated and serious pilot candidate and vastly improves your flight scores (as it did for Terry). However, even a couple of hours of lessons can give you an edge. Head to Chapter 11 for more on taking flying lessons, including some sample lesson plans to maximize your instruction time.

The Air Force actually gives you a higher selection point value — up to 200 flight hours — for previous flight experience.

Boost Your Vocabulary and Read

Although we recommend studying formal language topics such as analogy relationships and reading comprehension as part of your study plan, one of the best ways to keep your language skills fresh is to read whatever you can get your hands on — light novels, old textbooks, anything. Focus on comprehending what you've read, and remember to keep a list of words that you don't know so that you can look them up later.

Study, and we mean *study,* prefixes, suffixes, and roots. If you become close friends with these subjects, the vocabulary test will be a breeze. Chapter 5 provides lists of common word parts to give you a head start on this preparation.

Refresh Your Mathematical and Science Skills

On the science front, you need to know basic biology, chemistry, and physics; important math topics include trigonometry, algebra, and geometry. Keep in mind that the tests don't focus on calculus, so don't review that. Finally, work with the mathematical order of operations (parentheses, exponents, multiplication, division, addition, subtraction) until it becomes second nature. Chapters 7 through 10 help you review and practice your math and science skills.

If time allows, consider taking refresher courses in the math and science subjects that appear on the test, or at least those you feel weak in. Terry took his first test — the Navy flight aptitude test — in August, and in preparation, he audited both Biology II and Physics I (without doing the labs) in the spring semester because he hadn't taken those subjects in four years.

Memorize Basic Mathematical and Scientific Formulas and Laws

The last thing you want to be doing during the test is fumbling for basic formulas and scientific laws. To give yourself an edge, commit to memory the main formulas you need to know, including the following. You can find many of them in the review chapters in Parts II and III.

- ✔ **Area:** Square, rectangular, circle, triangle
- ✔ **Perimeter:** Square, rectangle, circle, triangle
- ✔ **Volume:** Cube, cylinder, rectangular box
- ✔ **Distance conversion**
- ✔ **Temperature conversion**
- ✔ **Physics:** Power, force, velocity, acceleration, electrical, and wavelengths
- ✔ **Chemistry:** Acid-base relationships and common bonding

Use Training Aids

Flashcards, computer programs, word games, and other training aids can all help you perform better on the test and make your studying entertaining. Flashcards are especially good for vocabulary building; Terry found that using them first thing in the morning and last thing at night worked well for him. Chapter 5 gives you the lowdown on using vocabulary flashcards. If you don't have a lot of flying experience, consider trying a flight simulator (just don't get sucked in and spend hours and hours on it).

Take Practice Exams

As part of your preparation for the real-life test, you should sit down and take each practice exam in Part IV just like you were sitting for the actual service branch test. One exception: If you have to exceed the time requirements to complete a section, go ahead and do it; at this point, answering all the questions is more important than adhering to the strict time limit. Just realize that you're doing so and keep track of how far you go over; you'll want to work on your time management before the real deal. Complete one test at a time, and don't take the next test until you've shored up any weak spots you identify with the most recent test. Take the exams in the exact same order you plan to take the official versions. After you finish a test, check your answers and follow up on missed questions to reinforce the knowledge. Revisit missed questions the next day to see whether your review paid off.

Take your formal practice tests in an unfamiliar setting, or at least somewhere different from where you study. If you study at home, take your practice test at the library. If you study at the library, go to a different section of the library. Subconsciously, this change of scenery helps you formally process the test as a real-world event and not just another study effort.

Get Plenty of Rest Prior to the Exam

As hard as getting to sleep the night before the test may be, a restful night really does pay off on test day. Figure out what time you need to get up and start adjusting your sleep schedule around that time for at least two weeks prior to the exam. The night before the test — real or practice — do something relaxing like going out for dinner and a movie and then go to bed early. (Depressants and stimulants may hamper your sleep plan, though, so you may want to lay off the booze at dinner and the sugary candy at the theater.) Chapter 4 deals with prepping for test day in more detail.

Chapter 21

Ten Ways to Maximize Your Score

In This Chapter

▶ Setting yourself up for success

▶ Avoiding careless mistakes

The day has finally arrived! Time to put the books, study aids, and practice tests away and charge forward, confident that you'll succeed. But even the most-prepared test-taker can use a little help squeezing a few extra points out of the exam, and that's where this chapter comes in. From discussing proper nutrition to the fine art of guessing, we give you some tricks of the trade so that with any luck, you'll soon be hopping aboard a military aircraft and turning jet fuel into the sweet noise that is music to every pilot's ears.

Fuel Up Properly

You probably already know the importance of being well rested on exam day, but that's only part of the battle. To be mentally prepared for the exam, you have to nourish yourself, too. Have a slow-paced breakfast (not too big and not too heavy) focused on protein sources such as eggs, sausage, bacon, and so on. This kind of meal keeps your energy levels up throughout the morning. If you're a coffee drinker, feel free to enjoy your usual amount; just remember that bathroom breaks at the test site can be few and far between. If you're not a coffee person, don't suddenly drink eight cups that morning.

 The absolute worst thing you can do is to eat a candy bar or other sugar-laden treat right before you go into the test. Loading up on sugar can cause *hypoglycemia,* which leads to a later sugar crash; you won't have much success on the test if you're keeled over on your desk. And studies show that hypoglycemia is a leading cause of pilot error accidents, so if you're going to fly, you need to get used to eating right anyway.

You may find yourself hungry for a snack partway through the test. We recommend a healthy snack with complex carbohydrates. However, if you absolutely need a candy bar at that point in the test, you can have one; just remember the crash that will come an hour and a half or so later and plan your snack time accordingly.

Write Down Important Formulas

We hate to be the bearers of bad news, but you can't bring a cheat sheet or your own scratch paper into the exam. However, nothing prevents you from using the paper provided at the test site for largely the same purpose: keeping important formulas at your fingertips. Store those difficult formulas in your short-term memory right before you arrive for the test and then write them down on the scratch paper provided immediately after the test begins so that you don't have to worry about drawing a blank later. You have to turn in your scratch paper at the end of the test, so don't try any funny business like writing down sample questions for later practice.

Don't Watch the Clock

When you're under the gun and feeling the pressure of a timed test, not obsessing over the time can be difficult. Although occasionally glancing up to do a time check is a good idea, don't get fixated on the clock. Doing so serves only to put you in a state of anxiety and stress, which is counterproductive toward calmly performing the task at hand. Don't become so incapacitated by the fear of not finishing on time that you can't finish at all.

Read the Questions and Answer Choices Thoroughly

Make sure you have a complete comprehension of exactly what the question is asking. Don't jump the gun and assume you know what the test-makers want to know; incorrect answer choices are often based on these kinds of assumptions, so your haste may trick you into picking the wrong answer.

Similarly, look through all the answer choices before selecting one; don't just choose the first answer you come to that seems right. For example, if the question asks for the answer in cubic centimeters and you determine that the answer is 15.83, don't immediately mark Choice (A), 15.83 cubic inches, because it has the right number. If you read farther, you discover that Choice (D) gives the same number in cubic centimeters, which is the unit the question requires.

Don't Bring Outside Knowledge to Reading Passages

On the reading comprehension sections of the tests, you must be careful to not make inferences or assign meanings based on your own subjective knowledge of the subject. The test-makers aren't interested in what you know about the topic; they want to know whether you can draw conclusions based on the information given. Use only the provided information as the basis for your answer.

Know the Order of Mathematical Operations

You have to perform all mathematical operations in a certain sequence to correctly complete a math problem. In case you're a little rusty on the topic, the correct steps for mathematical operations are as follows:

1. **Calculate everything in parentheses.**

2. **Compute all exponents and roots.**

3. **Perform all multiplication and division from left to right.**

4. **Perform all addition or subtraction from left to right.**

Don't be fooled by the fact that the answer you come up with by using some other sequence is listed as one of the answer choices. Including such decoys is a common trick on the part of the test designers to see whether you're following the correct order.

Develop the Fine Art of Guessing

Guessing is really an art form, and it's one you'll have to use when you don't know the answer to a question. Through the magic of guessing, you can start with a question you feel totally clueless about and end up with a pretty decent chance of choosing the right answer. We cover educated guessing more in Chapter 4, but the basic process is to rule out answer choices you know are incorrect and then examine the remaining choices for subtle clues that eliminate them as well. If you can narrow down your four choices to two probable ones, you increase your odds of success from 25 percent to 50 percent.

Not sure about a math problem? Sometimes a faster route is to take the answers given, estimate which one you think may be the closest answer, and then plug in the numbers to solve the problem backward.

Manage Your Time by Choosing Your Battles

Some questions are harder than others, and those hard questions can tie you up if you don't manage your time well. You don't want to spend so much time untangling a tough question early on that you run out of time to answer five easy questions at the end of the section.

If you can tell a question is going to be a time-eater, skip it and answer the easier questions first. You can return to those monster questions later for a more in-depth look if you have time leftover.

Watch Your Units and Conversions

Failing to use the correct units, especially in conversions, has to be one of the single most common errors on scientific and mathematical tests worldwide. Simply put, if a test question has given factors in inches, the solution should be in inches unless otherwise stated. If you can't find the units you want in any of the answer choices, make sure you have used the correct conversion factor. As with many test sections, beware of trick answers that prey on incorrect unit usage. Two inches plus 2 inches isn't 4 centimeters; it's 4 inches (or 10.2 centimeters).

Don't Panic

We won't say that taking the military flight aptitude test is an enjoyable experience, but it doesn't have to be one big anxiety attack, either. Don't let self-doubt creep into your conscious thought process if you struggle with a couple of questions. Relax and concentrate on the task at hand.

You have studied and worked hard to prepare yourself for this moment, so the test is the time to show what you've got. Be confident in your preparation, and fear and doubt won't overwhelm you.

Index

• B •

• C •

• R •

Notes

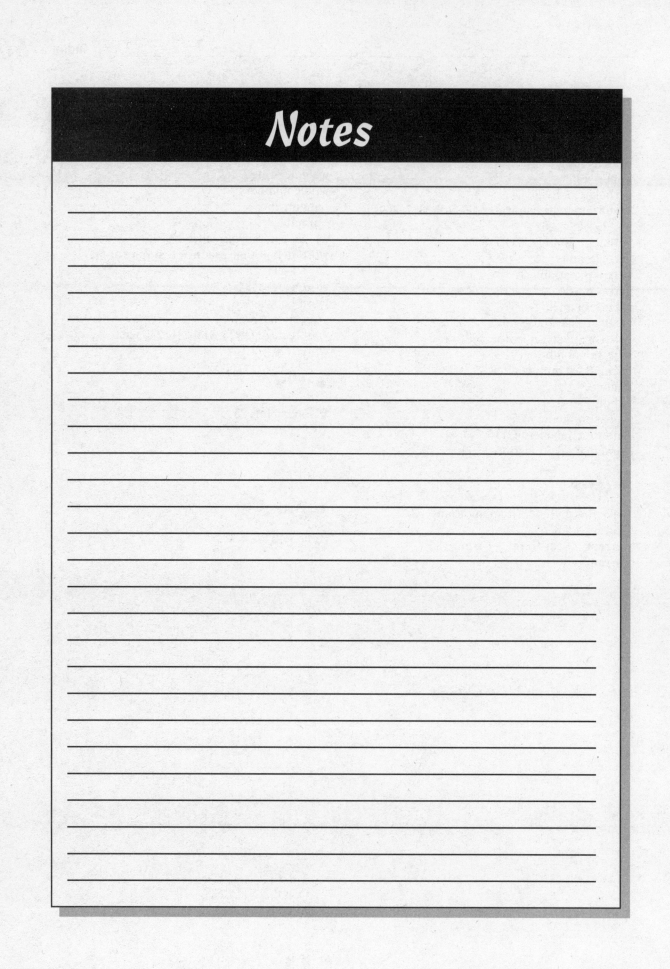

Notes

Notes

Notes

Notes

Notes

Notes

ple & Mac

d For Dummies,
Edition
3-1-118-49823-1

one 5 For Dummies,
Edition
3-1-118-35201-4

cBook For Dummies,
Edition
3-1-118-20920-2

X Mountain Lion
r Dummies
3-1-118-39418-2

ogging & Social Media

cebook For Dummies,
Edition
3-1-118-09562-1

m Blogging
r Dummies
8-1-118-03843-7

nterest For Dummies
8-1-118-32800-2

ordPress For Dummies,
Edition
8-1-118-38318-6

siness

mmodities For Dummies,
d Edition
8-1-118-01687-9

esting For Dummies,
Edition
8-0-470-90545-6

Personal Finance
For Dummies, 7th Edition
978-1-118-11785-9

QuickBooks 2013
For Dummies
978-1-118-35641-8

Small Business Marketing
Kit For Dummies,
3rd Edition
978-1-118-31183-7

Careers

Job Interviews
For Dummies, 4th Edition
978-1-118-11290-8

Job Searching with
Social Media
For Dummies
978-0-470-93072-4

Personal Branding
For Dummies
978-1-118-11792-7

Resumes For Dummies,
6th Edition
978-0-470-87361-8

Success as a Mediator
For Dummies
978-1-118-07862-4

Diet & Nutrition

Belly Fat Diet For Dummies
978-1-118-34585-6

Eating Clean For Dummies
978-1-118-00013-7

Nutrition For Dummies,
5th Edition
978-0-470-93231-5

Digital Photography

Digital Photography
For Dummies,
7th Edition
978-1-118-09203-3

Digital SLR Cameras &
Photography For Dummies,
4th Edition
978-1-118-14489-3

Photoshop Elements 11
For Dummies
978-1-118-40821-6

Gardening

Herb Gardening
For Dummies, 2nd Edition
978-0-470-61778-6

Vegetable Gardening
For Dummies, 2nd Edition
978-0-470-49870-5

Health

Anti-Inflammation Diet
For Dummies
978-1-118-02381-5

Diabetes For Dummies,
3rd Edition
978-0-470-27086-8

Living Paleo For Dummies
978-1-118-29405-5

Hobbies

Beekeeping
For Dummies
978-0-470-43065-1

eBay For Dummies,
7th Edition
978-1-118-09806-6

Raising Chickens
For Dummies
978-0-470-46544-8

Wine For Dummies,
5th Edition
978-1-118-28872-6

Writing Young Adult Fiction
For Dummies
978-0-470-94954-2

Language &
Foreign Language

500 Spanish Verbs
For Dummies
978-1-118-02382-2

English Grammar
For Dummies, 2nd Edition
978-0-470-54664-2

French All-in One
For Dummies
978-1-118-22815-9

German Essentials
For Dummies
978-1-118-18422-6

Italian For Dummies,
2nd Edition
978-1-118-00465-4

Available in print and e-book formats.

Math & Science

Algebra I For Dummies,
2nd Edition
978-0-470-55964-2

Anatomy and Physiology
For Dummies,
2nd Edition
978-0-470-92326-9

Astronomy For Dummies,
3rd Edition
978-1-118-37697-3

Biology For Dummies,
2nd Edition
978-0-470-59875-7

Chemistry For Dummies,
2nd Edition
978-1-1180-0730-3

Pre-Algebra Essentials
For Dummies
978-0-470-61838-7

Microsoft Office

Excel 2013 For Dummies
978-1-118-51012-4

Office 2013 All-in-One
For Dummies
978-1-118-51636-2

PowerPoint 2013
For Dummies
978-1-118-50253-2

Word 2013 For Dummies
978-1-118-49123-2

Music

Blues Harmonica
For Dummies
978-1-118-25269-7

Guitar For Dummies,
3rd Edition
978-1-118-11554-1

iPod & iTunes
For Dummies,
10th Edition
978-1-118-50864-0

Programming

Android Application
Development For Dummies,
2nd Edition
978-1-118-38710-8

iOS 6 Application
Development For Dummies
978-1-118-50880-0

Java For Dummies,
5th Edition
978-0-470-37173-2

Religion & Inspiration

The Bible For Dummies
978-0-7645-5296-0

Buddhism For Dummies,
2nd Edition
978-1-118-02379-2

Catholicism For Dummies,
2nd Edition
978-1-118-07778-8

Self-Help & Relationships

Bipolar Disorder
For Dummies,
2nd Edition
978-1-118-33882-7

Meditation For Dummies,
3rd Edition
978-1-118-29144-3

Seniors

Computers For Seniors
For Dummies,
3rd Edition
978-1-118-11553-4

iPad For Seniors
For Dummies,
5th Edition
978-1-118-49708-1

Social Security
For Dummies
978-1-118-20573-0

Smartphones & Tablets

Android Phones
For Dummies
978-1-118-16952-0

Kindle Fire HD
For Dummies
978-1-118-42223-6

NOOK HD For Dummies,
Portable Edition
978-1-118-39498-4

Surface For Dummies
978-1-118-49634-3

Test Prep

ACT For Dummies,
5th Edition
978-1-118-01259-8

ASVAB For Dummies,
3rd Edition
978-0-470-63760-9

GRE For Dummies,
7th Edition
978-0-470-88921-3

Officer Candidate Tests,
For Dummies
978-0-470-59876-4

Physician's Assistant Exa
For Dummies
978-1-118-11556-5

Series 7 Exam
For Dummies
978-0-470-09932-2

Windows 8

Windows 8 For Dummies
978-1-118-13461-0

Windows 8 For Dummies,
Book + DVD Bundle
978-1-118-27167-4

Windows 8 All-in-One
For Dummies
978-1-118-11920-4

Available in print and e-book formats.

Take Dummies with you everywhere you go!

Whether you're excited about e-books, want more from the web, must have your mobile apps, or swept up in social media, Dummies makes everything easier .